HEALTH, HEALING AND ILLNESS IN AFRICAN HISTORY

D0551618

HEALTH, HEALING AND ILLNESS IN AFRICAN HISTORY

Rebekah Lee

BLOOMSBURY ACADEMIC
LONDON • NEW YORK • OXFORD • NEW DELHI • SYDNEY

BLOOMSBURY ACADEMIC
Bloomsbury Publishing Plc
50 Bedford Square, London, WC1B 3DP, UK
1385 Broadway, New York, NY 10018, USA
29 Earlsfort Terrace, Dublin 2, Ireland

BLOOMSBURY, BLOOMSBURY ACADEMIC and the Diana logo are
trademarks of Bloomsbury Publishing Plc

First published in Great Britain 2021

Cover design: Terry Woodley
Cover images: From the Uganda Jubilee Report of the Mengo Medical Mission,
CMS Kampala, 1927.

A catalogue record for this book is available from the British Library.

Library of Congress Cataloging-in-Publication Data
Names: Lee, Rebekah, 1974- author.
Title: Health, Healing and Illness in African History / Rebekah Lee.
Description: London; New York: Bloomsbury Academic, 2021. |
Includes bibliographical references and index.
Identifiers: LCCN 2020038007 (print) | LCCN 2020038008 (ebook) |
ISBN 9781474254380 (hardback) | ISBN 9781474254373 (paperback) |
ISBN 9781474254397 (ebook) | ISBN 9781474254403 (epub)
Subjects: LCSH: Medicine–Africa–History. | Traditional medicine–
Africa–History. | Health–Social aspects–Africa.
Classification: LCC R651 .L44 2021 (print) | LCC R651 (ebook) | DDC 610.96–dc23
LC record available at https://lccn.loc.gov/2020038007
LC ebook record available at https://lccn.loc.gov/2020038008

ISBN: HB: 978-1-4742-5438-0
         PB: 978-1-4742-5437-3
         ePDF: 978-1-4742-5439-7
         eBook: 978-1-4742-5440-3

Typeset by Integra Software Services Pvt. Ltd.

To find out more about our authors and books visit www.bloomsbury.com
and sign up for our newsletters.

CONTENTS

FIGURES

TABLE

MAPS

PREFACE

As this book goes to press, the Covid-19 pandemic has altered the everyday lives of millions across the world. As the path of the virus spread from Asia to the Middle East, Europe and North America, to South America and Africa, states and societies have struggled with responding to the enormous health challenges this particular disease has presented – a coronavirus that is exceptionally virulent, with heightened mortality rates, unpredictable symptomology and no known cure. Hospitals have struggled to source adequate supplies of personal protective equipment (PPE) for healthcare workers, and have had to deal with the ethical and medical dilemma of triaging Covid-19 patients who were too numerous for the limited supply of ventilators at hand. Public health measures that have been instituted to varying degrees in different regional and national settings, including variations on quarantine – 'lockdown', 'self-isolation', 'sheltering-in-place' – as well as face-mask usage and personal hygiene have had some suppressive effect on mortality and morbidity curves, yet the science behind these measures' efficacy is a continual subject of debate amongst political, scientific and public health leaders and advisors, media commentators and the general public. The 'aetiology' (or disease transmission pathway) of Covid-19 is only beginning to be understood, with the only consensus among scientists being that a potential vaccine is many months or even years away.

Africa, which has experienced a later onset of the Covid-19 'wave', has not been immune to these same debates. Yet, the health challenges and risks from Covid-19 facing the continent are divergent from many of these other regions of the world. Africa's demographic characteristics, with a relatively youthful population, may provide some measure of protection against a disease whose mortality rate disproportionately features the elderly. However, there are particular vulnerabilities to consider as well: the lack of medical supplies, including diagnostic equipment and ventilators; a significant 'pre-existing' disease burden, involving significant numbers with infectious diseases such as tuberculosis and HIV/AIDS, which may make these populations uniquely susceptible to Covid-19's pathology; poor health infrastructures, exacerbated by limited numbers of medical and scientific personnel and an under-financed health services; and extreme poverty and inequality, which affect livelihoods, housing, sanitation and nutrition, all of which have been shown to influence Covid-19's differential impact on communities.

It is not yet known the extent to which these specific characteristics will determine the disease trajectory, and mortality toll, of Covid-19 in Africa. Importantly, however, they represent the twenty-first century outlines of a much longer shadow. The youthfulness of the continent's demographic profile, its disease burden and under-resourced healthcare services are not recent phenomena, but the products of particular historically contingent forces and developments. Popular responses to public health interventions – including the destruction of Covid-19 testing facilities in the Ivory Coast by protesters who believed the facility and its medical staff were covertly bringing the virus into their area, or the hashtag-propelled protests against Covid-19 vaccine trials in South Africa – are similarly reflective of a much longer history of distrust, resistance and even fear of disease prevention and eradication campaigns instituted by governments and organizations far removed from local communities and concerns. And yet, the figure of the current Director-General of the World Health Organization, Ethiopian Dr Tedros Adhanom Ghebreyesus, who is directing the global health response to Covid-19, reflects another important historical trajectory – that of the increasing agency and global influence of Africans as health mediators and providers.

The unfolding Covid-19 pandemic has accentuated that history matters, and a historical perspective is vital to understanding the health challenges of Africa's past, its present and its future. It is my hope this book contributes to that understanding.

ACKNOWLEDGEMENTS

This book began its life as a series of lectures and seminars for a module called Health, Healing and Illness in Africa that I offer to history students at Goldsmiths, University of London. When Claire Lipscomb, then-commissioning editor for history at Bloomsbury, first contacted me several years ago about writing an introductory medical history of Africa to engage students and a wider interdisciplinary audience, I could not envision the unexpected journeys, both intellectual and personal, that I would undertake in the writing of this book. I am forever grateful to Claire for that initial overture and for having faith in the scope and design of this project. I am also grateful to Bloomsbury for staying the course with this book, and for the helpful comments of the anonymous reviewers on the draft manuscript. The mistakes here are, of course, my own.

Over the many years that I have taught this module at Goldsmiths, I have had the benefit of my students' engaging and critical commentary, which have helped to frame many of the issues addressed in this study. This book would not have been the same without their input and participation. I would also like to thank the Department of History and Goldsmiths for allowing me research leave at important junctures in writing this book. To my colleagues in the department, thank you for your collegiality and good humour, and your vision for what's possible in the field of history.

I am grateful to the Swedish Collegium for Advanced Study and the Institute for Advanced Studies in the Humanities at the University of Edinburgh for providing a wonderful community of scholars and a fertile intellectual and interdisciplinary environment to write significant portions of this book.

Megan Vaughan and William Beinart have both inspired and supported me over many years, for which I am deeply thankful. I am also indebted to Megan, Walima Kalusa and Mark Lamont, my collaborators on the AHRC-funded project 'Death in Africa: A History c.1800 to Present Day'. Although this project is long ended, the issues and debates thrown up by our collective work continue to inform my understanding of African history and the everyday health concerns of African communities.

I would like to thank my PhD student, Milo Gough, for his unflagging assistance with all manner of administrative tasks in preparing the manuscript for publication, and for his helpful commentary and research assistance in the latter stages of this project's completion. I am also grateful to Milo for the image from the Sierra Leone Public Records Office used as the basis for the Source Analysis in Chapter 2.

To the women writers' group in Edinburgh, thank you for providing a useful sounding board and for reminding me that writing can be a collaborative enterprise. I am grateful especially to Mikki for her writing companionship, and for simply listening. I would like

Acknowledgements

to extend a very special thank you to Kirsty for being the ally I never knew I needed, and for providing a haven at a critical stage in the writing-up of this book.

I am grateful to my parents and siblings in the United States, and to my generous parents-in-law Ewa and Jerzy. Lastly, I offer a heartfelt thanks to my family – my husband Adam and my children Leah and Isak. Thank you for giving me the gift of time to write this, and for your unending patience, love and goodwill in supporting me to get to the end of it.

—

The author gratefully acknowledges the permission granted to reproduce the copyright material in this book. Every effort has been made to trace copyright holders and to obtain their permission for the use of copyright material.

MAPS

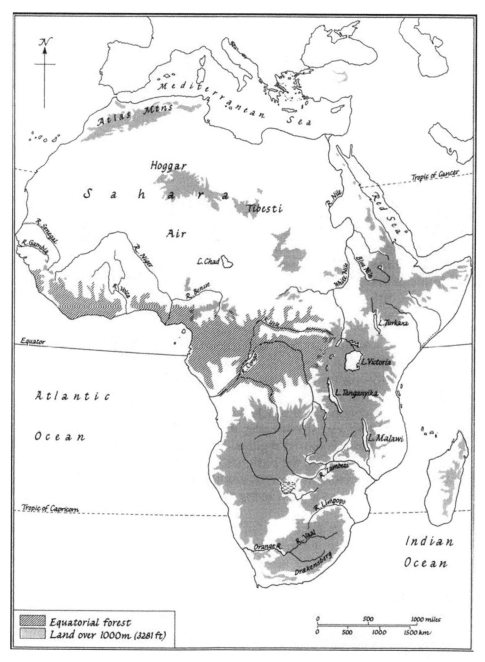

Map 1 Ecological map of Africa, from John Iliffe, *Africans: The History of a Continent*. Cambridge: Cambridge University Press. 1995, p. 2.

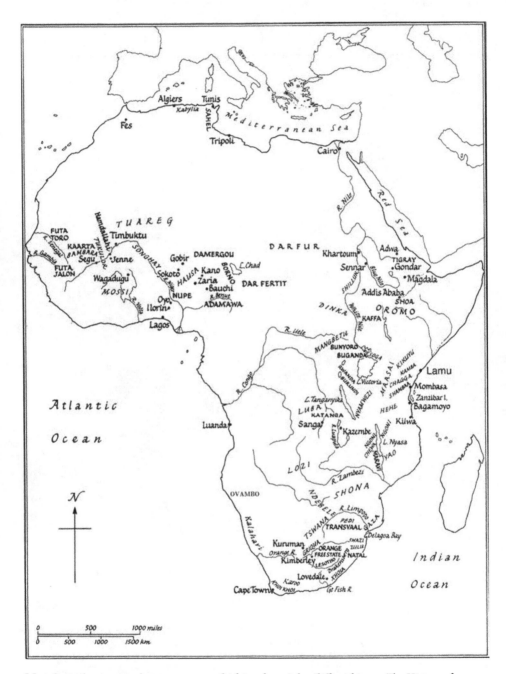

Map 2 Early nineteenth-century map of Africa, from John Iliffe, *Africans: The History of a Continent*. Cambridge Cambridge University Press, 1995, p. 160.

Map 3 Map of Africa with colonial boundaries, from John Iliffe, *Africans: The History of a Continent.* Cambridge: Cambridge University Press, 1995, p. 197.

Map 4 Map of post-independence Africa, from John Iliffe, *Africans: The History of a Continent*. Cambridge: Cambridge University Press, 1995, p. 245.

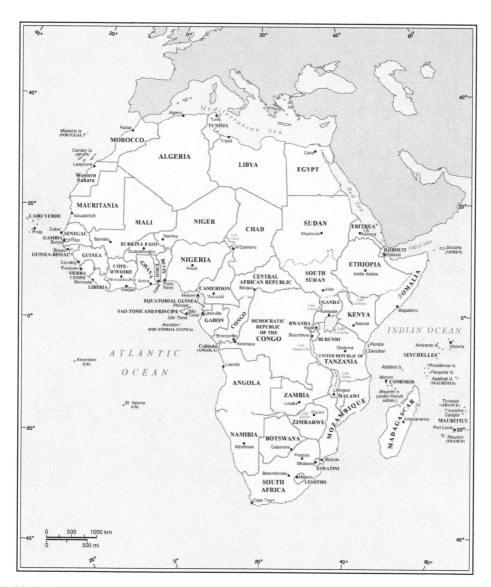

Map 5 Contemporary political map of Africa, 2018.

INTRODUCTION

Sometime in 1900, the British missionary doctor Albert Cook, who had established the first medical hospital in Uganda and would come to play an influential role in shaping colonial health interventions across East Africa, recorded the following encounter in his diary:

> Doctor: What is the matter with you?
> Patient: My name is so and so.
> Doctor: Yes, but what is your disease?
> Patient: I want medicine to drink.
> Doctor: Where do you hurt?
> Patient: I don't want medicine to swallow, but to drink.
> Doctor (sternly): WHAT IS YOUR ILLNESS?
> Patient: Oh it goes all over me it cries out 'Ka, ka.' Will you listen to the top of my head with your hearing machine (stethoscope), etc. etc.[1]

For Cook and his colonial contemporaries, this conversation was indicative of many such encounters with local Africans who seemingly did not understand the conventions of 'modern' medicine, frustrating their attempts to deliver beneficial cures. However, read in a different way, this simple dialogue can also serve to illustrate the evident gulf between Cook's and his patient's *conceptualization* of health and the healing process. The patient actively enters the frame with a clear notion of the therapy they are seeking, and asserts their identity (and humanity) at the beginning of the conversation, unprompted and undeterred by the doctor whose sole focus throughout is on identifying the patient's disease. Although much has changed since this event in the historical trajectories of biomedicine and healthcare delivery in the African context, this dialogue and the uncomfortable discursive disjunctures it throws up remain a useful reminder that the analytic framing of healing and illness was, and remains, a contested and socially and culturally mediated process.

This book's primary purpose is to offer an introduction to the wide and diverse history of health, healing and illness in sub-Saharan Africa from the 1800s to the present day. It examines the history of major diseases which have infected and affected the African populace – including syphilis, sleeping sickness, bubonic plague, malaria, tuberculosis and HIV/AIDS – their specific biological characteristics and paths of transmission, as well as the range of therapies and preventative measures developed in response. However, the focus of this book is not simply on disease but rather on how illness and health were *understood* and *managed*, and how these reveal in intricate ways the varied histories of places and peoples. Moreover, the terms 'health' and 'illness' do not simply connote a state of being. Health is constitutive of a process, a set of relations, rituals and practices, of institutions in action and interaction, with the potential for conflict, negotiation and – most importantly for historians – change. Therapeutic practices are also embedded in, and evocative of, structure – a system, or a set of systems, with hierarchies and roles. That structure can only be fully discerned through attention to wider social, political and economic contexts, and their particular historical trajectories. Finally, the study of health, healing and illness is about perception, representation and language. Illness can be a powerful marker of 'otherness'. We need only to look at present-day constructions of particular diseases as 'foreign', with a militaristic discourse deployed to describe microscopic 'invaders' as well as frame the collective response – the 'front line' of healthcare workers, the 'battle' to 'conquer' the disease, vaccination 'shots', the list goes on.

This book uses case studies drawn from sub-Saharan Africa, and an interdisciplinary perspective drawing on scholarship from history, anthropology, human geography, public health and development studies, in order to illuminate various aspects of the history of health and disease in African society. It brings to the foreground a cast of actors and institutions: African patients, their families and communities; medical practitioners, healers and healthcare workers; the state, at the local, regional and national levels; international and global health agencies; scientific institutes and medical and clinical care facilities. It introduces different modes of therapeutic and health interventions, and examines their internal dynamics as well as interactions and transformations over time. It also brings attention to changing bodies of knowledge and their circulation within and beyond healing hierarchies and African societies. These different ways of knowing can be parsed through observing how Africans have historically spoken about and framed notions of illness, health and the healing process. This book highlights the theoretical and methodological innovations which have enriched this historical study in the African context. It also introduces you to a diverse range of historical sources whose analytic potential is only beginning to be mined.

A brief tour of the historiography of African health, healing and illness

Many decades of historical and interdisciplinary scholarship helped to build the intellectual foundation on which this book now stands. Historians like to call this foundation a *historiography*, which is essentially 'the history of the history' of a given subject. A historiography is a critical catalogue of how a subject of historical interest came into being and was developed through successive scholarly enquiries. More often than not, it reveals that the historical understanding of a particular topic (or theme or event) has changed over time, through the outcome of contentious debates between scholars, new sources of data which alter previous interpretations, a different political environment that influences the research milieu within which historical enquiry takes place, or the input of new generations of thinkers who approach the topic with different analytical lenses. Examining, then, the historiography of African health and illness helps reveal the intellectual forebears of this book's particular themes, approaches and methods.

This book – and the larger, vibrant field it introduces – is the product of the convergence of several different streams of scholarship within and beyond the discipline of history in the twentieth and twenty-first centuries. I address a select few here. The initial histories of the early twentieth century charted recent advances in scientific understandings of diseases prevalent in Africa, particularly those discoveries associated with the origins and establishment of the sub-field of tropical medicine. One can argue that historians were seduced by the catalogue of successes that had led to observable reductions in European mortality from certain diseases, imposing a trajectory of progress that simplified rather than reflected the uneven process of scientific knowledge production in this period. The historian Shula Marks succinctly characterized this early phase of medical history-writing as the story of 'the triumph of science and sewers over savagery and superstition', and certainly the historical studies produced could be more aptly seen as latter-day hagiographies, highlighting the lives and glorious achievements of select scientific men such as Louis Pasteur, Robert Koch, Ronald Ross and Patrick Manson.[2] These initial studies also provided a window into the development of the medical sciences and relevant sub-disciplines, and the attendant institution-building in both colonial and metropole settings necessary to consolidate and implement emergent scientific knowledge. Importantly, this historical scholarship remained analytically separate from the contributions of colonial anthropologists who in the early decades of the twentieth century undertook fine-grained ethnographic analyses of African societies, detailing local perceptions and practices concerning prevalent diseases as well as rituals and social relations constructed around key life cycle stages of birth and death, reproduction and ageing. Thus, the early stirrings of a medical history of Africa were more concerned with the history of allopathic medicine in Africa, rather than a broader attempt to understand how African societies experienced and framed illness, or organized themselves around vital health challenges. Overcoming this analytic division would remain a key problematic for historians in latter decades.

The wave of African independence from colonial rule in the late 1950s and 1960s provided the context for a significant challenge to this historical narrative. The championing by newly independent nation-states of the recovery of local forms of knowledge production included the recognition of traditional healers, their therapeutics and knowledge of indigenous pharmacopeia. This recovery presented an alternative African genealogy of healing forms, ideas and practices that contested the hegemonic narrative and reach of allopathic medicine amongst African patients and communities. Moreover, the emergence of universities (such as the University of Ibadan in Nigeria, which became independently established in 1963) and the rise of historians as a professional class in Africa altered the power dynamics which had previously guided the production of histories about Africa. Another important challenge in this period came from Frantz Fanon, the West Indian psychiatrist and intellectual, whose clinical experience in Algerian and Tunisian mental hospitals would prove formative to the development of his searing critique of colonial psychiatry, and of colonialism itself. In his seminal text, *The Wretched of the Earth* (1961), Fanon argued that far from offering beneficial 'cures' to colonized subjects, colonialism *caused* mental illness. His framing of the 'madness' of colonialism would be taken up in subsequent decades by historians of psychiatry and mental illness in Africa, and would later feed into broader revisionist histories which emphasized the deleterious effects of the workings of 'colonial medicine' on African bodies and communities.

From the 1970s, the development of ecological and environmental approaches and their integration into historical modes of enquiry further encouraged a scholarly turn away from a narrow focus on 'microbes and men'. Historians such as Alfred Crosby, Philip Curtin and William McNeill introduced a wide-angle perspective on the spatial distribution of disease and its consequences for human history, with Africa implicated within a larger mapping of global flows of disease across migratory, military and trade routes. The 'disease exchange' model articulated in this scholarship helped to explain both the specific epidemiological characteristics of the trans-Atlantic slave trade and the enduring toll of vector-borne tropical disease on the African continent.[3] A different type of ecological and environmental orientation was advocated by John Ford in his influential work on sleeping sickness, *The Role of the Trypanosomiases in African Ecology* (1971). In it, he argued that an appreciation of the complex interactions between pathogen, humans and the wider environment needs to be central to our analysis of changing patterns of disease transmission. This work importantly acknowledged the centrality of the notion of ecological balance in indigenous techniques of disease control, and further problematized the epidemiological impact of colonial conquest and European settlement. The debates inspired by this study would form the basis of a generation of ecologically orientated histories of disease, particularly of East and southern Africa.

Post-colonialism as an intellectual project had a significant impact on imperial historiography as well as more specifically reconfiguring the writing of histories of African health and medicine in the colonial period and beyond. Post-colonial theorist Edward Said argued in *Orientalism* (1978) that the Orient was a creation of the West – through a 'system of representations,' the West was able to centre itself as paradigmatic, casting the Orient as the exotic and peripheral 'other'. Said's contribution broadened the focus of the historian beyond looking for 'facts' to examining, and interrogating, representation and image. Another prominent influence was the work of the postmodern theorist Michel Foucault, whose studies such as *The Birth of the Clinic: An Archaeology of Medical Perception* (1963) and *The History of Sexuality, Power and Knowledge* (1976) profoundly reconceptualized the relationship between state power, medical knowledge and the body. Of enduring relevance to the understanding of the multivalent meanings and mechanisms of scientific knowledge in the African context, Foucault's work has helped historians to 'see' the ways in which medicalized power could be acted *on* and *through* the body – via institutionalized tactics such as surveillance and confinement, as well as through the discursive pathologizing of patient-subjects. The potential analytic innovations opened up by these theoretical framings can be seen in the flowering of nuanced social constructionist analyses by the 1990s, particularly those which used a discursive lens to interrogate the interaction of medicine, African patient populations and the colonial state in Africa. Megan Vaughan's seminal study *Curing Their Ills: Colonial Power and African Illness* (1991) and Luise White's work on local vampire rumours circulating in colonial Uganda and Northern Rhodesia (now Zambia) are exemplary of this shift, as well as illustrative of the rich symbolic meanings and relations that could be derived from a sustained re-reading of colonial and missionary archival sources.

Revisionist studies of the development of medical science and its implementation in the colonial African context were distinctive in their emphasis on how medicalized ideas and institutions could be utilized to serve the aims of the colonial project, over and above the health needs of colonized subjects. Indeed, an early articulation by Maynard Swanson in the context of the Cape Colony's response to a bubonic plague outbreak at the turn to the twentieth century argued that the emergent medicalized language of public hygiene – what he termed the 'sanitation syndrome' – was deployed to justify increasingly coercive, and racially encoded, measures of control over African subjects.[4] Scholars of tropical medicine in Africa and in other colonial settings, such as Maryinez Lyons, Warwick Anderson and David Arnold, examined and debated the case for the *functionality* of medicine to the imperial mission, or medicine as a 'tool' of empire.

At the same time that historians of colonial medicine were re-conceptualizing the boundaries of the field, shifts within the discipline of anthropology and the emergence of the sub-field of medical anthropology encouraged a parallel turn, away from analysing local healing systems and therapeutics as 'pure' cultural expressions of a closed 'ethno-medical' unit. Instead, local healing practices and institutions were re-situated within a more dynamic constellation of interactions and relations both within and beyond the ethnically constituted group. Critically, patient decision-making was included within this expanded frame of analysis and further contributed to the productive 'blurring' of local therapeutic mappings.[5] Steven Feierman and John Janzen's volume, *The Social Basis of Health and Healing in Africa* (1992), became a definitive hallmark of this approach in the African context and remains a formative articulation of the wider field. The interdisciplinary orientation of studies in this collection further exemplified the convergence of, and dialogue between, historical and anthropological approaches focusing on processes of interaction, meaning-making, and transformation in the creation and management of a distinctive socially constituted realm of health in Africa. However, the diverse works of scholarship in Feierman and Janzen's volume were also illustrative of some of the field's conceptual limits. Studies were conducted within narrow geographic and temporal frames (wholly within the pre-colonial, colonial or post-colonial periods but not traversing across these), or were disease-specific in their analysis. Whilst this close focus allowed for rich empirical or ethnographic detail to be foreground, important connections between local and global forces or across time and space could not come into view.

To some extent, the ongoing HIV/AIDS pandemic has provided a moment of rupture that has challenged scholars of disease and medicine in Africa to further re-define these conceptual frameworks and test existing boundaries. Certainly, the tremendous human toll of HIV/AIDS over its near four decades-long span on the continent – cumulative AIDS-related mortality in sub-Saharan Africa is now well over

24 million – has instigated a profound introspective and retrospective search for new modes of explanation. The failures of the global health response to the African AIDS crisis have recalled older debates about the efficacy of colonial and international health institutions and their interventions, even as novel trans-national and trans-sectoral forms of funding and organization have changed the global health landscape into the twenty-first century. Furthermore, the HIV/AIDS pandemic has facilitated the creation of new publics and forms of patient-citizen engagement within and beyond the state, including a diverse range of health service and drug therapy providers. The emergence of first-person illness narratives, digital stories and 'body maps' of HIV+ survivors has produced a rich multi-media archive of the embodied experience of disease. These dynamics have provoked new ways of thinking about the past and its links to the present, the relationship between the local and global, mappings of the body and associated therapeutics, and the disciplinary tool-kit necessary to make sense of these complex processes.

The imprints of these developments can be seen in the burgeoning scholarship on the history of health, healing and illness in Africa since the 2000s. Didier Fassin's *When Bodies Remember: Experiences and Politics of AIDS in South Africa* (2007) and Julie Livingstone's *Debility and the Moral Imagination in Botswana: Disability, Chronic Illness and Ageing* (2005) differently exemplify the potentialities for medical anthropology to transcend disciplinary and temporal boundaries through a sustained and historically nuanced focus on the body as a repository of (sometimes violent or disabling) memory and experience. Nancy Rose Hunt's recent work, *A Nervous State: Violence, Remedies, and Reverie Colonial Congo* (2016), revisits earlier debates around the workings of colonial medicine as a form of 'biopower' but with an enhanced arsenal of methods and 'moods' to interrogate the panoply of vernacular and archival sources at her disposal, as well as an explicit strategy to destabilize historical narrative and chronology that honours the disruptive workings of violence on Congolese psyches and bodies. These three studies suggest the innovative and intimate interplay between historical and ethnographic approaches, and their strategic blurring of neat demarcations between the past and present. They also reflect the influence of the recent scholarly turn to the study of emotions, which has further enabled a consideration of the affective, psycho-social dimensions of health and illness.

Studies such as Myron Echenberg's *Africa in the Time of Cholera* (2011) and Randall Packard's and James Webb's respective global histories of malaria have stretched the conventional chronological and geographic boundaries of historical analyses of disease in Africa, their *longue durée* approaches over centuries yielding novel interpretations of African environments and responses to disease. This renewed emphasis on ecological perspectives has been expanded by the recent upsurge in environmental histories, histories of inter-species contact, conservation science, veterinary science and livestock management in Africa, including work by William Beinart, Tamara Giles-Vernick, Nancy Jacobs and Karen Brown. These studies have enhanced our understanding of environmental concerns in specific historical and regional contexts, the changing nature of human-animal-pathogen interactions, and the ways in which local knowledge and ecological approaches have addressed the problem of infectious and zoonotic disease control.

The idea of the 'state' and its relation to the history of the production and implementation of medical and scientific knowledge in Africa have been problematized in recent collected works, such as Paul Wenzel Geissler's *Para-States and Medical Science: Making African Global Health* (2015) and Anna Greenwood's *Beyond the State: The Colonial Medical Service in East Africa* (2015). Both suggest in different ways how the fractured nature of the state in colonial and post-colonial Africa yielded interstitial spaces where non-state actors and forms of organization could operate, generating novel health networks and conglomerations of medical knowledge production at the local and global level. Geissler's volume critically engages with Helen Tilley's work on the development of scientific knowledge in British colonial Africa, particularly in her emphasis on how local environments and research 'enclaves' could inform, and help mediate, global processes of knowledge exchange.

The recent contributions of African scholars such as Amina Issa and Kalala Ngalamulume have heralded new historical perspectives on urban African experiences of disease, and the interplay of religiously diverse cosmopolitan communities in shaping and understanding disease control measures. Walima Kalusa's research on mission medicine in colonial Northern Rhodesia has offered a critical, and linguistically sensitive, intervention by stressing the important and largely unacknowledged role of 'medical auxiliaries' in mediating the African patient experience, and the effects their strategic vernacular translations of biomedical terminology had on that process. Kalusa's work also adds to the growing body of historical and ethnographic research on African nurses, dispensers and other medical professionals and intermediaries in the colonial and post-colonial contexts.

What is important to gain from this brief historiographical tour is an awareness that vestiges of these previous scholarly approaches and debates continue to inform and transform our historical imagination and evocation of African health and illness. This scholarship reminds us that there is no singular narrative of African experience to capture but multiple and diverse trajectories to explore, armed with a (changing) range of historical sources, tools, and disciplinary and theoretical perspectives.

Key themes and questions

The chronological sweep and broad geographic reach of this book allow for a consideration of larger dynamics and patterns over time and space. The following key themes and questions, which have been shaped by the historiographical debates outlined above, can be utilized as anchor points as you journey through this wider history.

As the historian John Iliffe has shown, the African continent's environmentally hostile conditions – summed up as 'ancient rocks, poor soils, fickle rainfall, abundant insects' – profoundly shaped the demographic, social and political contours of its long history.[6] Africa's distinctive historical epidemiological profile (its disease transmission patterns over time) is a feature of this particular environmental inheritance. The immense human toll of malaria in Africa, for example, can be attributed to millennia-long interactions between parasite, insect and human within the specific landscape of equatorial forest regions in Central and West Africa. This extended experience of malaria endemicity also enabled the evolution of genetic adaptations in Africans in these same regions, the features of which were perceived but misunderstood by European slave traders, travellers and colonists in the eighteenth and nineteenth centuries (see Chapter 1). Another important consequence of this inheritance was that **environmental concerns and approaches** became central and not peripheral aspects of the social, spiritual and political organization of African societies. In pre-colonial African societies, hierarchies of healers were in part determined by their perceived control over scarce natural resources, and 'sacred medicine' to address a group's misfortunes was often derived through an ecologically cognizant sensibility towards restoring 'balance' across natural, human and spiritual realms. The idea of ecological equilibrium found its technical application in indigenous African methods of disease control, such as those used to suppress the spread of sleeping sickness, through the careful management of tsetse fly habitat, land use and livestock grazing (Chapter 6). These local approaches were later recognized by some colonial scientists and eventually helped form an important 'ecological critique' of narrow, 'vertical', pathogen-focused approaches to infectious disease control, which characterized much of colonial and global health disease eradication programmes in the twentieth century.

Wide-angle, ecological perspectives have also emphasized *longue durée* processes of **global flows** of people and pathogens that have profoundly shaped disease transmission patterns and African health outcomes over centuries. Slaving and trading routes across the Sahara, Atlantic and Indian Oceans enmeshed Africa within large-scale and overlapping 'disease zones'. Yet, the 'disease exchanges' which resulted from these migratory flows could be unequal, and it is evident Africa and its population bore the epidemiological brunt of highly asymmetric exchanges. A different consequence of these global mobilities was the transference across vast distance of African therapeutic models and healing traditions, as was evident in the pharmacopeia and divination practices of plantation slave societies in the Caribbean and American South (Chapter 1). Ideas crossed these permeable trans-national networks as well. Indeed, the development and establishment of tropical medicine in the early decades of the twentieth century were predicated on trans-border communication between colonial African territories, metropolitan cooperation across imperial regimes and a highly mobile cadre of scientific 'experts' whose research findings were published and disseminated to a global audience (Chapters 2, 5 and 6). International health conventions and organizations, such as the League of Nations Health Organization and the World Health Organization, were based to an extent on these earlier mobile forms of knowledge and institutional exchange. African medical professionals and researchers participated in these trans-national circulations and global processes of scientific knowledge production as well, in increasing numbers particularly from the mid-twentieth century (Chapter 3). In recent decades, a re-imagined global health paradigm has utilized new forms of cross-sector, public-private partnerships, as exemplified in responses to the HIV/AIDS epidemic as well as recent approaches to malaria treatment and prevention (Chapters 4 and 6).

Yet, these globally mediated processes of knowledge production, cooperation and exchange were never seamless. Confusion and conflict certainly characterized the early decades of tropical medicine, and medical and scientific research remains a highly diverse and contested field. Moreover, emergent medical and scientific knowledge was often unevenly implemented in the local African context, as can be seen in the wide variation in prevention and control measures applied to a host of communicable and non-communicable diseases (Chapters 2, 4, 6 and 7). Local environmental conditions and social dynamics, as well as competing interpretations of disease causation and alternative therapeutic models, posed their own significant challenges and constraints on the operation of international health or global health frameworks. Certainly, the **tension between the local and global** in the histories of colonial and international health campaigns is an illuminating thread of exploration.

Undoubtedly, the development and proliferation of a range of **medical and healing technologies**, including drug remedies and other therapies, are significant trajectories to map within the wider history addressed in this book. Advances in bacteriology, parasitology, immunology and pharmacology, amongst others, the growth of interdisciplinary sub-fields such as malariology and epidemiology, as well as the scaling up of commercial manufacturing of synthetic drugs and insecticides have at various points from the late nineteenth century onwards transformed the content and delivery of these technologies in local contexts. Indeed, African patients and communities came to understand and perceive the potentialities and weaknesses of allopathic medicine through their direct experiences with these changing medical technologies of surveillance, diagnosis and 'cure' – from lumbar punctures to cervical examinations and blood tests, mercury injections to vaccinations, mosquito nets and larvicides to DDT, antibiotics to psychotropic drugs and antiretrovirals, to name only a select few of the many evolving technologies surveyed throughout this book. Yet, the persistence of remedies in contemporary public health contexts whose historic roots lay within indigenous pharmacopeia, such as quinine and artemisinin, attests to the continuing relevance of alternative, locally derived medicinal knowledge.

The history of **African resistance** to and creative **adaptation** of these technologies is another part of this broader narrative. African adherence to biomedical surveillance and therapeutic regimes was far from universal, with wide variation, to the never-ending frustration of medical men and women involved in mission hospitals, colonial sanitary and hygiene campaigns, and global disease eradication and prevention programmes (Chapters 2, 3, 4 and 6). Seen from African patients' perspectives, however, the bodily risks of participating in painful and invasive diagnostic measures or experimental drug therapies had to be meaningfully weighed against the probabilities of genuine cure, which was itself an often ill-defined and debatable health outcome. Furthermore, it is certainly the case that the delivery of allopathic care to African communities has never been completely value-free. The histories of colonial and post-colonial infectious and sexually transmitted disease campaigns, and the history of reproductive and sexual health in Africa (Chapters 2, 3 and 4), illustrate that biomedical technologies were often accompanied, implicitly or explicitly, by what Michel Foucault has termed 'technologies of the self'.[7] These efforts to enact a prescribed bodily and moral self-transformation often interfered with, and disrupted, existing African social and spiritual relations, conceptions and practices, provoking a range of responses to allopathic institutions, therapies and health providers. The uneven success of more recent health interventions predicated on behavioural change – whether it is the 'ABC' approach to HIV-prevention or the use of insecticidal bed nets – is in part a legacy of these intrusions into local social, sexual and ritual spheres.

African healing systems and their responses to health challenges throughout history defy any neat categorizations. Early accounts suggest the healing arts in African societies were not confined to a separate sphere but could inhabit multiple and overlapping social, corporeal and spiritual realms. Therapeutic techniques, including methods for diagnosing illness, were similarly diverse and could exhibit divinatory powers, technical craft or environmental, botanical and anatomical knowledge (Chapter 1). Historical and ethnographic accounts of witchcraft and spirit possession could be read, albeit not unproblematically, as an alternative history of healing technologies (Chapters 1, 2, 3 and 5). **Medical pluralism** can be considered an enduring feature of African healing traditions, although the content and character of that pluralism were historically contingent. Even in the face of the imposition of seemingly totalizing health regimes, such as sanitary segregation campaigns or the 'lunatic' asylums of the colonial period, local healing systems continued to provide relevant therapeutic alternatives even as they opened outwards to absorb new technologies and modes of treatment (Chapters 2, 3 and 5). Indeed, the adaptability of local healing systems may be a testament to the pragmatism of African healers, as well as the relative capaciousness and malleability of cosmological and ideological frameworks, a feature evident in the broad history of the incorporation, and transformation, of both Islam and Christianity in Africa. The robustness of medical pluralism in Africa today is furthermore a testament to the autonomy and decision-making capacity of African patients as sceptical 'clients' and self-carers who adeptly operate within different publics, therapeutic regimes and conceptual registers (Chapters 2 and 3).

Finally, it is worthwhile considering how these disparate historical trajectories were manifest at the level of language and representation. From the nineteenth-century notion of Africa as the 'white man's grave' to the image of Africa as a 'diseased continent', the **symbolic representation** of disease and the diseased tended to reflect, and reinforce, larger racial, class and gendered divides separating the observer from the observed in different healthcare settings. It also reflected prevalent, and often limited, understandings of disease causation. Early European ideas of 'native immunity' among Africans, particularly with respect to malaria, meant that the immense burden of malaria morbidity and mortality in local populations, particularly among children, escaped from view. The inversion of ideas of Africans possessing 'native immunity' to Africans as inherent 'disease reservoirs' in the early twentieth century certainly provided a useful rationale for the implementation of urban sanitary segregation in some colonial territories, although this notion had little scientific basis in the nascent field of tropical medicine (Chapters 2 and 6). Until the interwar period in the gold-mining regions of South Africa, silicosis was known as the 'white death' because it appeared to afflict white mineworkers at a much higher rate than black mineworkers. This portrayal of silicosis inaccurately reflected the actual racial distribution of the disease at the time (Chapter 7). Furthermore, colonial representations of African 'madness' and African sexuality tended to reveal more about European moral and political anxieties around the colonial encounter than any objective truth about the mental or sexual health of African societies. Yet, these discursive viewpoints would powerfully shape the design and implementation of colonial medical interventions, as can be seen in the history of ethno-psychiatry and anti-syphilis campaigns (Chapters 4 and 5).

The ways in which Africans participated in these symbolic constructions are less visible in the historical record, particularly for earlier periods. They exist in episodic moments, as patches of vernacular understanding that wait to be 'sutured' into newly imagined medical histories of Africa.[8] Rumours of blood-sucking vampires employed by colonial medical authorities are perhaps one indication of the moral unease among local communities which accompanied the introduction of sleeping sickness surveillance and control measures in colonial Northern Rhodesia in the 1930s (Chapter 6). Basotho mineworkers who re-imagined mine-shafts as cannibals swallowing up miners' bodies similarly offer a critique of the insatiable extractive capacities of mining capital and its mortal health consequences (Chapter 7). The moral inversion of medical auxiliaries as principal agents of dis-ease rather than of healing can be observed in contemporary ethnographies of the local reception and perceptions of HIV/AIDS prevention and treatment campaigns (Chapter 4). The reinvention of ideas and practices around witchcraft and spirit possession in contemporary Africa attests to their enduring relevance as a responsive form of moral commentary on changing landscapes of illness and death, as well as their capacity to offer an alternative mode of therapeutics (Chapters 2, 3 and 5).

What key historical dynamics will continue to play an important role in shaping African health outcomes and experiences in the twenty-first century? This book provides tools and perspectives to help answer this pressing question. Indeed, to understand what is both 'new' *and* 'old' about global and African responses to emergent health challenges on the continent, it is necessary to examine more fully what health and illness were and meant in the past. Many new frontiers for this vibrant and complex field are waiting to be mapped.

How to read this book

The book is arranged in two parts. Part One provides a historical overview of African health and illness from the long 'pre-colonial' past through the colonial period and into the present day. The largely chronologically organized approach of Part One is designed to facilitate an understanding of broad patterns – of major disease challenges, ideas and experiences of illness, healing hierarchies and organization, therapeutic approaches, local and global health interventions – and their persistence or transformation across time. Part Two adopts a different 'case study' approach which focuses on specific health challenges – HIV/AIDS, mental illness, tropical disease and occupational disease – and their unfolding across time and space in the African historical context. These topics were chosen in part because they reflect important, and sometimes popular, preoccupations of historical study. But, as will be seen, the case study configuration offers its own type of analytic intervention. By widening the chronological frame of investigation, melding together disparate streams of study on distinct diseases, or by a sustained historicization, a useful critical synthesis can be fashioned out of an unwieldy and often interdisciplinary scholarship. Although the chapters can be read consecutively, each chapter of this book could also be studied on its own, as entryways into particular time periods or thematic areas.

Within each chapter is a selection of 'Historical Source' extracts and brief accompanying 'Source Analyses', demarcated by text boxes. Each extract is a 'primary source', which in disciplinary parlance is a textual, visual, aural or material remnant of the past that can be used subsequently to recover or reconstruct that past moment, event or idea. The source analyses provide a sense of the interpretive possibilities available, as well as an indication of the historical debates that are illuminated by the chosen primary source. In Part Two, brief medical explanations of the diseases profiled are included where necessary in each chapter – these are shown as grey boxes. Finally, the burgeoning scholarship on medical history, medical anthropology and public health in the African context means that this book can only be the starting point, and not the end, of your journey to understand the history of health, healing and illness on this continent. A brief 'Further reading' list at the end of each chapter serves as preliminary guidance towards this further study.

Further reading

Anderson, Warwick. *Colonial Pathologies: American Tropical Medicine, Race, and Hygiene in the Philippines*. Durham: Duke University Press, 2008.

Arnold, David, ed. *Imperial Medicine and Indigenous Societies*. Oxford: Oxford University Press, 1989.

Arnold, David, ed. *Warm Climates and Western Medicine: The Emergence of Tropical Medicine, 1500–1900*. Amsterdam: Rodopi, 1996.

Azevedo, Mario Joaquim. *Historical Perspectives on the State of Health and Health Systems in Africa, Volume I: The Pre-Colonial and Colonial Eras*. Cham: Palgrave Macmillan, 2017a.

Azevedo, Mario Joaquim. *Historical Perspectives on the State of Health and Health Systems in Africa. Volume II, The Modern Era*. Cham: Palgrave Macmillan, 2017b.

Beinart, William. *The Rise of Conservation in South Africa: Settlers, Livestock, and the Environment 1770–1950*. Oxford: University Press, 2003.

Beinart, William and JoAnn McGregor, eds. *Social History & African Environments*. Oxford: James Currey, 2003.

Berridge, Virginia and Philip Strong. 'AIDS and the Relevance of History'. *Social History of Medicine* 4, no. 1 (1991): 129–38.

Brown, Karen. *Mad Dogs and Meerkats: A History of Resurgent Rabies in Southern Africa*. Athens: Ohio University Press, 2011.

Crosby, Alfred W. *The Columbian Exchange: Biological and Cultural Consequences of 1492*. Westport, CT: Greenwood Press, 1972.

Curtin, Philip. 'Epidemiology and the Slave Trade'. *Political Science Quarterly* 83, no. 2 (1968): 190–216.

Curtin, Philip. *Death by Migration: Europe's Encounter with the Tropical World in the Nineteenth Century*. Cambridge: Cambridge University Press, 1989.

Curtin, Philip. 'Disease Exchange across the Tropical Atlantic'. *History and Philosophy of the Life Sciences* 15, no. 3 (1993): 329–56.

Ellis, Stephen. 'Writing Histories of Contemporary Africa'. *Journal of African History* 43 (2002): 1–26.

Fanon, Frantz. *The Wretched of the Earth*, translated by Constance Farrington. First published 1961. London: Penguin Classics, 2001.

Fassin, Didier. *When Bodies Remember: Experiences and Politics of AIDS in South Africa*, translated by Amy Jacobs and Gabrielle Varro. Berkeley: University of California Press, 2007.

Feierman, Steven and John M. Janzen, eds. *The Social Basis of Health and Healing in Africa*. Berkeley: University of California Press, 1992.

Ford, John. *Role of the Trypanosomiases in African Ecology*. Oxford: Clarendon Press, 1971.

Foucault, Michel. *Discipline and Punish: The Birth of the Prison*, translated by Alan Sheridan. First published in French in 1975. London: Allen Lane, 1977.

Foucault, Michel. *The Birth of the Clinic: An Archaeology of Medical Perception*. London: Routledge, 1989.

Geissler, Paul Wenzel, ed. *Para-States and Medical Science: Making African Global Health*. Durham: Duke University Press, 2015.

Giles-Vernick, Tamara and James Webb, eds. *Global Health in Africa: Historical Perspectives on Disease Control*. Athens: Ohio University Press, 2013.

Giles-Vernick, Tamara, Didier Gondola, Guillaume Lachenal and William H. Schneider. 'Social History, Biology, and the Emergence of HIV in Colonial Africa'. *The Journal of African History* 54, no. 1 (2013): 11–30.

Greenwood, Anna, ed. *Beyond the State: The Colonial Medical Service in British Africa*. Manchester: Manchester University Press, 2016.

Hartwig, Gerald and K. David Patterson, eds. *Disease in African History: An Introductory Survey and Case Studies*. Durham: Duke University Press, 1978.

Hunt, Nancy Rose. *Suturing New Medical Histories of Africa*. Zurich: LIT Verlag, 2007.

Hunt, Nancy Rose. *A Nervous State: Violence, Remedies, and Reverie in Colonial Congo*. Durham: Duke University Press, 2016.

Iliffe, John. *Africans: The History of a Continent*. Cambridge: Cambridge University Press, 1995.

Issa, Amina. 'Malaria and Public Health Measures in Colonial Urban Zanzibar, 1900–1956'. *Hygiea Internationalis* 10, no. 2 (2011): 35–51.

Jacobs, Nancy. *Environment, Power, and Injustice: A South African History*. Cambridge: Cambridge University Press, 2003.

Janzen, John M. *Lemba, 1650–1930: A Drum of Affliction in Africa and the New World*. New York: Garland Pub., 1981.

Kalusa, Walima T. 'Language, Medical Auxiliaries, and the Re-Interpretation of Missionary Medicine in Colonial Mwinilunga, Zambia, 1922–51'. *Journal of Eastern African Studies* 1, no. 1 (2007): 57–78.

Livingston, Julie. *Debility and the Moral Imagination in Botswana*. Bloomington: Indiana University Press, 2005.

Lyons, Maryinez. *The Colonial Disease: A Social History of Sleeping Sickness in Northern Zaire, 1900–1940*. Cambridge: Cambridge University Press, 2002.

MacLeod, Roy and Milton Lewis, eds. *Disease, Medicine, and Empire*. London: Routledge, 1988.

Malowany, Maureen. 'Unfinished Agendas: Writing the History of Medicine in Sub-Saharan Africa'. *African Affairs*, 395 (2000): 325–49.

Manton, John. 'Archives'. In *Traces of the Future: An Archaeology of Medical Science in Africa*, edited by Paul W. Geissler, Guillaume Lachenal, John Manton and Noémi Tousignant, 31–4. Bristol: Intellect, 2016.

Marks, Shula. *Divided Sisterhood: Class, Race, and Gender in the South African Nursing Profession*. Basingstoke: Palgrave Macmillan, 1994.

Marks, Shula. 'What Is Colonial about Colonial Medicine? And What Has Happened to Imperialism and Health?' *Social History of Medicine* 10, no. 2 (1997): 205–19.

Mbembe, Achille. 'The Power of the Archive and Its Limits'. In *Refiguring the Archive*, edited by Carolyn Hamilton, Verne Harris, Jane Taylor, Michele Pickover, Graeme Reid and Razia Saleh, 19–27. Dordrecht: Springer Netherlands, 2002.

McNeill, William H. *Plagues and Peoples*. Garden City, NY: Anchor Press, 1976.

Midgley, Clare. 'New Imperial Histories'. *Journal of British Studies* 35, no. 4 (1996): 547–53.

Ngalamulume, Kalala. *Colonial Pathologies, Environment, and Western Medicine in Saint-Louis-Du-Senegal, 1867–1920*. New York: Peter Lang, 2012.

Packard, Randall M. *The Making of a Tropical Disease: A Short History of Malaria*. Baltimore: Johns Hopkins University Press, 2007.

Packard, Randall M. *A History of Global Health: Interventions into the Lives of Other Peoples*. Baltimore: Johns Hopkins University Press, 2016.

Prins, Gwyn. 'But What Was the Disease? The Present State of Health and Healing in African Studies'. *Past and Present* 124 (August 1989): 159–79.

Ranger, Terence and Paul Slack, eds. *Epidemics and Ideas: Essays on the Historical Perception of Pestilence*. Past and Present Publications. Cambridge: Cambridge University Press, 1992.

Said, Edward. *Orientalism*. New York: Pantheon, 1978.

Schumaker, Lyn. 'History of Medicine in Sub-Saharan Africa'. In *The Oxford Handbook of the History of Medicine*, edited by Mark Jackson, 266–84. Oxford: Oxford University Press, 2011.

Swanson, Maynard. 'The Sanitation Syndrome: Bubonic Plague and Urban Native Policy in the Cape Colony, 1900–1909'. *The Journal of African History* 18, no. 3 (1977): 387–410.

Tilley, Helen. *Africa as a Living Laboratory: Empire, Development, and the Problem of Scientific Knowledge, 1870–1950*. Chicago: University of Chicago Press, 2011.

Vaughan, Megan. *Curing Their Ills: Colonial Power and African Illness*. Cambridge: Polity, 1991.

Vaughan, Megan. 'Healing and Curing: Issues in the Social History and Anthropology of Medicine in Africa'. *Social History of Medicine* 7, no. 2 (August 1994): 283–95.

Viterbo, Paula and Kalala Ngalamulume, eds. *Medicine and Health in Africa: Multidisciplinary Perspectives*. East Lansing: Michigan State University Press, 2011.

Webb, James L. A. *Humanity's Burden: A Global History of Malaria*. Studies in Environment and History. Cambridge: University Press, 2009.

Webb, James L. A. 'Historical Epidemiology and Infectious Disease Process in Africa'. The Journal of African History 54, no.1 (2013): 3–10.

White, Luise. 'Hodgepodge Historiography: Documents, Itineraries, and the Absence of Archives'. *History in Africa* 42 (2015): 309–18.

PART I
HISTORICAL DYNAMICS

CHAPTER 1
EARLY AFRICAN HEALING SYSTEMS, THERAPEUTIC GATEWAYS AND DISEASE EXCHANGES

Introduction

In the late eighteenth century, the Scottish explorer and surgeon Mungo Park was commissioned to 'discover' the full course of the Niger River by the Association for Promoting the Discovery of the Interior Parts of Africa, an eclectic association of aristocrats, wealthy businessmen, members of parliament, military officers and clergymen. He duly set out to explore the Niger basin in 1795 and his two-year expedition was, by all measures, a complete and utter failure. Park's voyage was beset throughout by illness, violence and lack of supplies. He was imprisoned for several months by a local Muslim chief and slave trader, and although he eventually 'found' the Niger River he was unable to follow its course eastwards to reach the fabled city of Timbuktu. A second ill-fated attempt, begun in 1805, to explore the entire course of the Niger met its tragic end when Park and the remnants of his crew perished after a riverside attack near Bussa, in what is now Nigeria. However, the written account Mungo Park left behind of his first sojourn – *Travels in the Interior Districts of Africa*, first published in 1799 – remains a fascinating glimpse into the landscapes and peoples he encountered in West-Central Africa. Given his medical background – Park qualified as a surgeon in Edinburgh, a pre-eminent medical training ground in Europe at the time – it is perhaps unsurprising that amongst the most detailed descriptions in this account was his cataloguing of common ailments and local treatments for them:

> The Mandingoes seldom attain extreme old age. At forty, most of them become grey-haired, and covered with wrinkles; and but few of them survive the age of fifty-five ... But notwithstanding that longevity is uncommon among them, it appeared to me that their diseases are but few in number. Their simple diet, and active way of life, preserve them from many of those disorders which embitter the days of luxury and idleness. Fevers and fluxes are the most common and the most fatal. For these, they generally apply saphies [charms] to different parts of the body, and perform a great many other superstitious ceremonies; some of which are, indeed, well calculated to inspire the patient with the hope of recovery, and divert his mind from brooding over his own danger. But I have sometimes observed among them a more systematic mode of treatment. On the first attack of a fever, when the patient complains of cold, he is frequently placed in a sort of vapour; this

is done by spreading branches of the *Nauclea orientalis* upon hot wood embers, and laying the patient upon them, wrapped up in a large cotton cloth. Water is then sprinkled upon the branches, which, descending to the hot embers, soon covers the patient with a cloud of vapour, in which he is allowed to remain until the embers are almost extinguished. This practice commonly produces a profuse perspiration, and wonderfully relieves the sufferer.

For the dysentery, they use the bark of different trees reduced to powder, and mixed with the patient's food; but this practice is in general very unsuccessful … On the whole, it appeared to me that the Negroes are better surgeons than physicians. I found them very successful in their management of fractures and dislocations, and their splints and bandages are simple, and easily removed. All abscesses they open with the actual cautery; and the dressings are composed of either soft leaves, Shea butter, or cow's dung, as the case seems, in their judgment, to require. Towards the coast, where a supply of European lancets can be procured, they sometimes perform phlebotomy; and in cases of local inflammation, a curious sort of cupping is practised. This operation is performed by making incisions in the part, and applying to it a bullock's horn, with a small hole in the end. The operator then takes a piece of bees-wax in his mouth, and putting his lips to the hole, extracts the air from the horn; and by a dexterous use of his tongue, stops up the hole with the wax. This method is found to answer the purpose, and in general produces a plentiful discharge.[1]

The inquisitiveness with which Park regarded Mandingo healing practices was certainly unusual among early European travelogues of Africa, his trained medical eye more keenly fixed than his contemporaries on prevalent diseases and African healers' responses to them. Park's professional disdain for the Mandingo propensity towards the use of 'superstitious ceremonies' to deal with 'fevers and fluxes' is clear. However, what is perhaps more striking is his careful scrutiny of the diverse range of therapeutic approaches that he encountered, and his measured appreciation for particular techniques and remedies.

Mungo Park fell ill with what was probably malaria soon after his arrival on the West African coast in 1795. Interestingly, it was his own experience of 'fevers' abruptly interrupting his expedition and enforcing an extended convalescence of several months which afforded Mungo Park the time and space to observe his Mandingo hosts and faithfully record his reflections. It is likely that this intense period of personal illness contributed not only to Park's professed admiration for Mandingo skills in the symptomatic relief of fever sufferers, seen in the extract above, but also to his evident sensitivity to the health concerns at stake in this region of the world.

At the time of Park's travels, the probability of death due to 'fevers and fluxes' was at the forefront of European anxieties of tropical Africa, and the high levels of European mortality there soon came to be characterized as the 'white man's grave'.[2] As Park's own account intimates, however, Africa presented a far more complex and dynamic health landscape than the European imagination of the 'white man's grave' suggested. This chapter's intention is to bring that health landscape to life, by drawing a historical portrait of African health up to the late 1800s, focusing primarily on eighteenth- and nineteenth-century dynamics and patterns. As will be seen, this portrait is far from complete, largely due to the paucity and inherent weaknesses of the historical sources at our disposal. Nevertheless, this chapter will consider what is known about both 'endemic' (meaning usually prevalent in a given population) and 'imported' diseases in sub-Saharan Africa in this period, and the broad repertoire of indigenous African healing practices that were deployed in response to these disease challenges. The chapter will also explore the ideologies, institutions and hierarchies which underpinned and gave form to these diverse African healing systems.

Finally, the history of African health in this earlier period cannot be considered in isolation. The impact of early European encounters with African societies and disease environments will be examined, in part through considering the image of the 'white man's grave' against the reality of both African and European morbidity and mortality in tropical Africa; and, more importantly, through an exploration of the demographic and health implications of slavery and the slave trade. This entails a discussion of the challenges involved in measuring the numerical extent of the slave trades (including the Saharan, Red Sea, Indian Ocean and trans-Atlantic slave trades) and in accurately capturing slave mortality, morbidity and fertility rates. Drawing on the history of slavery in Africa, the Americas and the Caribbean, the chapter also explores the mixing of therapeutic traditions in slaving societies and considers the capacity for innovation in slave healing systems. Although the historical record tends to privilege European perspectives and voices, this chapter recovers and emphasizes some important aspects of African experiences and strategies that can be derived from this record. In many respects, the inability of Europeans to manage and adapt to the disease environment in this earlier period helped to provide a more level playing field where meaningful dialogue across disparate healing systems could potentially occur, as it notably did in Mungo Park's case. The terms of that exchange would alter considerably under the context of European colonial rule, which from the late nineteenth century expanded beyond coastal enclaves and isolated territories, extending across the continent.

Tracing the imprints of the past: Sources and their challenges

How can we begin to reconstruct an early history of African experiences of illness, health and healing? This is a thorny question because of the limited sources we have at our disposal, and is part of the larger historical challenge of reconstructing African pasts in this period. Because of a relative lack of conventional written records – and by 'conventional' historians usually mean archival documentary sources – a wider net has had to be fashioned. Casting this wider net has revealed important, albeit often isolated and scattered, pockets of information.

Archeological artefacts constitute one of these valuable alternative historical sources. The cave paintings or 'rock art' of southern African hunter-gatherer societies, most famously the Kalahari San, are material records of shamanistic rituals, whose practice increased during moments of social and spiritual anxiety, and were often related to food scarcity and challenging environmental conditions such as drought. Dating and analysing these cave paintings thus give us a window into changing environmental shocks, and the ways in which ancient hunter-gatherer societies may have organized their spiritual and social lives in response.[3] In a more recent era, terracotta figures were formed in a naturalist manner by the Ife (in present-day Nigeria) from the thirteenth to the fifteenth centuries to illustrate and celebrate the human form. The characteristic deformities caused by certain diseases, such as the swelling brought on by elephantiasis (also called filariasis, a mosquito-borne parasitic disease which affects the lymphatic system), that were sculpted into these clay figurines suggest their prevalence in the region. The sculptures also hint at how the Ife understood and imagined the embodiment of these diseases.

Traces of the past can also be recovered through examining word origins and the circulation of idioms, metaphors or other verbal expressions across time and place. **Linguistic archaeology** can help ascertain whether certain observed therapeutic practices or ailments were of long-standing in a given society, estimate their geographic reach and also suggest processes of historical change. For example, there is a broad historical congruence in the general medical culture of Bantu-speaking regions of Central, Eastern and Southern Africa, because of the existence of common cognates (words of shared origins) in the 'disease lexicon' of different groups across this very wide geographical area – including vernacular terms such as for wound (*puta*), doctor (*ganga*), plant medicine (*ti*) and to bewitch (*dogo*). It can also be surmised that distinctive therapeutic approaches were introduced to a given society if there are records of 'new' terms in local usage that have no common cognates across the wider region. This was shown in seventeenth-century German missionary and traveller accounts of the Loango (in present-day Angola) which revealed its inhabitants created a new, specialized class of diviners (termed *mbana*) and associated category of sacred medicine in response to their specific experience of the slave trade.[4]

Similarly, the presence (or absence) of vernacular terms in contemporary usage can suggest whether those diseases were considered endemic to particular regions in Africa, or were introduced after European settlement. Modern-day Tswana livestock owners' lexicon includes livestock diseases which are usually referred to by their English or Afrikaans designation, with no equivalent derivation in the Tswana language. This strongly suggests those particular diseases were relatively new and introduced after sustained European settlement in the region.[5] The common usage among Malians of the proverb, 'You are as happy as lice in the hair of a leper,' signals not only the existence of the disease in Mali's distant past but also its familiarity – this sardonic expression would not have become part of local parlance had the debilitating effects of leprosy, such as losing one's fingers, not been widely understood.[6] As the example of the proverb suggests, **oral traditions** are a vital repository of public and popular memory in African societies, and their ubiquity and utility can help historians chart wide-scale processes of change. Oral traditions can reveal the effects of encounter, migration and political upheaval on vital health-related institutions and practices, including agricultural practices, nutrition and eating habits. For example, the oral chronicles of the Kwangali and Mbunza (in present-day Namibia) show how the diets of these mainly hunting-gathering societies changed profoundly after coming into contact with cattle-herding agro-pastoralists in the eighteenth century.[7]

Islam's extended presence on the continent has meant that **Arabic accounts** are a significant written source, particularly for medieval and early modern African society, politics and culture. These texts can also provide indications of disease challenges as well as local ailments and curatives. The noted Arab geographer Al Bakri wrote in the eleventh century of how severe drought in the region occasioned the Islamization of the king of Malal (in what became part of the Mali Empire), through the intercessions of a Muslim scholar in the royal court who encouraged the king to purify himself and pray to Allah, after which 'abundant rain descended upon them'.[8] Ibn Battuta, the famed Berber travel-writer, recorded his observation of the West African societies he journeyed through in the fourteenth century. Battuta describes prosaically the local curative knowledge displayed by a merchant who was bitten by a poisonous snake while travelling in a caravan between Sijilmasah and Iwalatan (in-present-day Mauritania):

> [The snake] bit the index finger of his right hand, giving him severe pain. It was cauterized, but in the evening the pain grew worse, so he cut the throat of a camel and put his hand in its stomach and left it there for the night. The flesh of his finger dropped off and he cut off his finger at the base. The Massufah told me that the snake had drunk water before biting him; if not, the bite would have killed him.[9]

In the early modern period, the workings of Islamic jurisprudence in West Africa meant that legal texts are another potential historical source to be mined. **Islamic legal records** can suggest local conceptions of, and familiarity with, certain diseases, particularly when the presence or absence of those diseases helped to determine judicial outcomes. For example, records of Islamic divorce proceedings in Mali show not only that leprosy was a familiar part of the disease landscape from as early as the sixteenth century, but also that local understandings of leprosy were sophisticated. Because leprosy was considered sufficient justification for divorce only if the severity of the debility brought on by the disease could be 'proven', the debates recorded in these legal records reveal a diverse local spectrum of categories, symptomology and bodily debility associated with leprosy.[10] However, these legal records are less revealing of extant forms of therapeutics or local healing networks utilized in response.

European missionaries and travellers left an important and potentially vibrant source of African medical practices and understandings of health and illness, as Mungo Park's account suggests. Portuguese **traveller and missionary accounts** were amongst the earliest European observations of African societies and polities, due to Portugal's early exploration and navigation of the African coast from the late fifteenth century onwards – Bartolomeu Dias 'discovered' in 1488 what he believed to be the southern tip of Africa, later named the Cape of Good Hope, linking the Atlantic and Indian Oceans, and Vasco da Gama succeeded in plotting a sea route around Africa to India in 1497 – and to its subsequent vested interests in the slave trade. The earliest written account of smallpox in sub-Saharan Africa was penned by João dos Santos, a Portuguese missionary who described a smallpox outbreak in Mozambique in 1589.[11] Portuguese missionaries in the sixteenth century reported the use of medicinal herbs and other remedies in the kingdom of Kongo (in present-day Angola) – this region has a particularly rich and extended documentary history, which continued into the seventeenth century when German travellers and missionaries made their first meticulous records of local societies and their cultural practices. However, by and large, the missionary presence in Africa until the late eighteenth century was limited to coastal enclaves and struggled for significance and continuity, largely because high rates of morbidity and mortality among missionaries discouraged their settlement. This was to change from the early nineteenth century, with mission stations occupying an increasingly significant roles in settler and colonizing societies.

Missionaries produced some of the first ethnographic accounts of Africans – like anthropologists of a later era, missionaries tended to be embedded in the communities they observed, and were attentive to the rhythms of daily life and to ritual practices, belief systems and social relations. In addition, their commitment to learning the vernacular – necessary to translate the Bible into local languages – meant that missionaries were able to, albeit imperfectly, linguistically enter into African worldviews. As the 'conversation' between the 'medical doctor' and the 'rain doctor' recorded in David Livingstone's missionary travelogue reveals (see box), this engagement with African cosmologies could prove revelatory of local ideas around illness and health, technical aspects of therapeutic approaches, as well as larger questions around the nature of the authority healers derived their healing arts from. However, the overriding missionary impulse to enact Christian conversion meant that any efforts at dialogue or exchange were limited. Although in this period the superiority of European medicine was hardly evident, that did not prevent missionaries from portraying African methods as superstitious or ineffectual, particularly in their observations of ritual realms such as witchcraft and divination.

Historical Source: David Livingstone, *Missionary Travels and Researches in South Africa* (1857)

MEDICAL DOCTOR: So you really believe that you can command the clouds? I think that can be done by God alone.

RAIN DOCTOR: We both believe the very same thing. It is God that makes the rain, but I pray to him by means of these medicines, and, the rain coming, of course it is then mine. It was I who made it for the Bakwains for many years …; through my wisdom, too, their women became fat and shining. Ask them; they will tell you the same as I do.

M.D.: But we are distinctly told in the parting words of our Saviour that we can pray to God acceptably in his name alone, and not by means of medicines.

R.D.: Truly! But God told us differently …. God has given us one little thing, which you know nothing of. He has given us the knowledge of certain medicines by which we can make rain. *We* [original italics] do not despise those things which you possess, though we are ignorant of them. We don't understand your book, yet we don't despise it. *You* ought not despise our little knowledge, though you are ignorant of it.

M.D.: I don't despise what I am ignorant of; I only think you are mistaken in saying that you have medicines which can influence the rain at all.

R.D.: That's just the way people speak when they talk on a subject of which they have no knowledge. When first we opened our eyes, we found our forefathers making rain, and we follow in their footsteps. You who send to Kuruman for corn, and irrigate your garden, may do without rain; we cannot manage in that way …

M.D.: I quite agree with you as to the value of the rain; but you can not charm the clouds by medicines. You wait till you see the clouds come, then you use your medicines, and take the credit which belongs to God only.

R.D.: I use my medicines and you employ yours; we are both doctors, and doctors are not deceivers. You give a patient medicine. Sometimes God is pleased to heal him by means of your medicine; sometimes not – he dies. When he is cured, you take the credit of what God does. I do the same. Sometimes God grants us rain, sometimes not. When he does, we take the credit of the charm. When a patient dies, you don't give up trust in your medicine, neither do I when rain fails. If you wish me to leave off my medicines, why continue your own?

Source Analysis: David Livingstone (1813–73) was a Scottish missionary, physician and explorer. He wrote Missionary Travels *after returning to Britain from a fifteen-year sojourn in southern Africa. In it, he recounts his travels from the Cape through parts of present-day Botswana, Zambia, Zimbabwe and Mozambique. Livingstone's long-standing interests in science, medicine and geology, which were cultivated alongside his early religious education in Scotland, became intrinsic to his encounters with southern African societies and intimately informed his account of the region.*

The 'conversation' was a rhetorical device frequently used in nineteenth-century mission accounts to convey a sense of the daily verbal exchanges which occurred on theological matters of importance. In this case, the issue at stake in the conversation between the 'medical doctor' (likely Livingstone himself) and the 'rain doctor' (a diviner utilized in many southern African societies to call for and predict rain) is the nature of their healing powers and the authority from which those powers are derived. The medical doctor questions the authenticity of the 'medicines' used by the rain doctor, claiming the authority to bring rain can come from the Christian God alone. The rain doctor does not dispute the existence of God but insists on the 'wisdom' conferred to rain doctors as a legitimate form of medical knowledge.

Livingstone was fluent in seTswana, so it is likely this conversation occurred in the vernacular and was an unmediated exchange between himself and the diviner, and was then recalled many years later when this account was written. This source demonstrates that medical knowledge and authority were contested terrain in mid-nineteenth-century southern Africa, and that African healers did not necessarily cede authority to European medical men. Livingstone portrays the African rain doctor as an adept debater, who both understands and critiques the ideological basis of missionary medicine. The medical doctor attempts to insert a fundamental difference between his work and the rain doctor's, while the rain doctor continually asserts their underlying similarities. It is this tension between the widening and collapsing of difference between their respective 'medicines' which makes this conversation so fascinating. This account accords a degree of African agency and voice in the encounter, as well as a vivid sense of the everyday debates which unfolded through the workings of missionary medicine in the region. As the historian Norman Etherington has suggested, the respect Livingstone showed to African healers was in part cultivated through his personal experience of debilitating illness during his travels – Livingstone's journals indicate he asked for and took medicinal treatments prepared by local specialists. Furthermore, the mutuality observed in this encounter reflects the relative autonomy of healers, and of local social and political structures, in this part of southern Africa in the mid-nineteenth century. These conditions would change markedly by the late nineteenth century as colonial rule was consolidated throughout the region.

In the eighteenth and early nineteenth centuries, European naturalists who visited Africa brought a different sort of observational sensibility to their accounts than was evident in missionary and traveller writing of the same period. Although relatively few in number, these **naturalist accounts** with their acute, empiricist observations of African flora and fauna reveal the imprint of Enlightenment-era developments in fields such as astronomy, climatology and botany, and were formative to nascent European understandings of Africa as a scientifically observable landscape. Southern Africa was a particularly appealing destination for European naturalists of the late eighteenth century, and the writings of scholars such as Peter Kolb, William Paterson and Anders Sparrman were translated and circulated widely, and reflected contemporary emphases on specimen-gathering and systematized categorization of the natural environment. It was also an early indicator of European impulses to view Africa as a 'living laboratory', ripe for scientific invention and discovery.[12] Although these naturalist accounts provided a somewhat dispassionate language and classificatory framework through which Africa could be imagined by European readers, by the mid-nineteenth century an alternative literary tradition which depicted Africa as a hostile environment 'overrun' by disease would predominate. In any case, both literary traditions tended to obscure from their fields of vision the many and multiple ways *Africans* themselves sought to shape their natural and disease environments.

Finally, a technique utilized by scholars to address the obvious and large gaps in our understanding of 'pre-colonial' African health and illness is the **retrospective application** of post-colonial- and colonial-era accounts to the more distant past. Although it may seem intuitively problematic and fundamentally *ahistorical* that later sources could be used to prove earlier realities, there is an underlying intellectual rationale to this temporal extrapolation back across decades and even centuries. Scholars across the humanities, social sciences and health sciences have recognized the resilience of African cultural practices, including expressions of 'traditional medicine', across time. Recent historical scholarship has also questioned the hegemonic power of colonialism, and latterly globalization, to fundamentally transform African health institutions and conceptual frameworks, and have argued for their limited reach. Given this rationale, then, a twentieth-century observation of a healing ritual, such as the *zar* spirit possession 'cults' in the Sudan or the use of dream interpretation amongst the Xhosa in South Africa, could be assumed to be a credible approximation of what these rituals looked like in the 'pre-colonial' past, even when there may not be corroborating evidence from the time period concerned. Similarly, early twentieth-century colonial anthropologists tended to conflate the contemporary social dynamics and configurations they observed at work in African societies, including healing regimes and therapies, with what would have existed in these same groups before the imposition of colonial rule. Viewed positively, this retrospective approach honours the survival of African cultural norms, institutions and practices. However, this tendency – surprisingly prevalent across a wide disciplinary range of scholarly studies and commentaries on African health and healing systems – creates, unwittingly perhaps, an essentialized view of African culture as static and incapable of adaptation. The present-day remnants of supposedly pre-colonial rituals are more often in reality self-consciously reinvented traditions, or are so removed from the particular socio-historical and political context in which they were originated as to render the rituals entirely new. Likewise, colonial ethnographies were more likely snapshots of societies in dynamic flux rather than freeze frames of primordial entities. Locating African 'healing pasts' within 'healing presents' is thus a problematic exercise indeed. As will be seen throughout this book, African healing institutions and agents were both malleable and resilient, but not wholly one nor the other – the routes chosen were complex and, ultimately, historically contingent.

Disease environments and health in Africa: Patterns, approaches and perspectives

Over the last half-century, ecological historians, medical historians and historical epidemiologists have developed an increasingly more detailed understanding of the ways in which large-scale dynamics involving the interaction of vast 'disease environments' have affected the historical emergence of diseases in specific moments and places.

Scholars such as Alfred Crosby and David Arnold drew from a nineteenth-century European tradition of medical geography which sought to uncover and describe the spatial distribution of particular diseases, and then widened the focal lens to consider these processes of disease transmission on a truly global scale.[13] The African disease environment became a central part of a scholarly elucidation of a 'disease exchange' model, as both a contributor to and receiver of global flows of disease via migratory, military, trade and slaving routes.[14]

Africa for much of its pre-colonial past was implicated within several overlapping 'disease zones' – at the nexus of mobile trade and slaving routes which traversed the Atlantic Ocean to the west, the Sahara to the north and the Indian Ocean to the east, connecting Africa at different points in time with the Middle East, Asia, the Americas and Europe.[15] As early as the thirteenth century, Islamic trading networks criss-crossed the Sahara, linking the Middle East with trading towns and centres of learning in West and North Africa, where slaves were bought and sold alongside valued commodities such as salt and gold. Historians of the trans-Atlantic slave trade, which spanned the sixteenth to nineteenth centuries, have established that the geographical reaches of this trade were far wider than previously understood – beyond the coastal enclaves of the Bight of Benin and the Bight of Biafra, and extending southwards to West-Central Africa around present-day Angola as well as drawing slaves from societies deep into the interior of these coastal regions, exporting to destinations including the Caribbean and the American South as well as Brazil. Spurred by the British abolition of the slave trade in 1807, alternative slaving routes to the Middle East and through Indian Ocean networks developed from the eighteenth to late nineteenth centuries, with plantation-style economies set up on the African islands of Zanzibar, Mauritius and Reunion, and the establishment of centres of slave trading in Mozambique and Tanzania. Indian Ocean maritime networks in the same period also brought to port cities and coastal islands in southern and East Africa significant populations of Indian and Malay migrants, as indentured labourers as well as political convicts. These trading routes across Atlantic Ocean, Indian Ocean and Saharan disease zones entailed a series of massive, if enforced, human migration. Disease inevitably followed on the heels of such wide-scale movements. Arguably, however, it was Africa's prolonged exposure to these global forces over several centuries which brought some measure of immunity against imported infectious diseases, such as smallpox, which exacted such a devastating toll on the 'virgin' native populations of the Americas in the sixteenth and seventeenth centuries.

Although some European ideas of disease causation in circulation in the eighteenth and early nineteenth centuries suggested that certain diseases arose out of the specific climate and environment of tropical Africa, it is now understood there is no scientific basis for the existence of specifically 'African' diseases. It is more useful to focus on understanding which diseases were endemic to sub-Saharan Africa and which were likely to have been imported. Astute contemporary observers tried to make this meaningful distinction. For example, Mungo Park's *Travels* usefully catalogues some of the diseases prevalent in the West African societies he encountered in the late eighteenth century. Alongside dysentery and guinea worm, Park noted prevalent diseases included, 'the *yaws*, the *elephantiasis*, and a *leprosy* of the very worst kind'.[16] The explorer Richard Burton wrote in his observation of Nyamwezi in the late 1850s that ivory-seeking caravans and Arab traders were thought to have brought bubonic plague to the interior of East Africa.

The origins of malaria in Africa date back 8,000–10,000 years, its distinctive epidemiological profile the result of the evolution of complex interactions of human, parasite and insect vector in the equatorial rain forest environment of West-Central Africa (see Chapter 6). Malaria was certainly an 'ancient' endemic disease and integral to the disease landscapes of tropical West, Central and East Africa but also beyond, extending as far south as northern Namibia. This historic endemicity and sustained levels of transmission influenced the evolution in West and Central Africa of unique forms of human immunity to malarial parasites, including Duffy negativity and sickle cell trait. Although the scientific basis of this inherited resistance was not fully understood until long after the formal ending of the institution of slavery in the Americas, it was the perception of 'African immunity' which was a strong epidemiological determinant in ensuring the African character of the trans-Atlantic slave trade, supplanting previous failed efforts to utilize European convict labour and Native American slave labour.[17] However, one should not necessarily overstate the theme of continuity in malaria's disease profile in Africa. Although there is scarce recorded data from the eighteenth and nineteenth centuries on the incidence of malaria among African populations, large-scale changes in agricultural practices and population movements due to slavery, warfare and labour migration in this period most probably affected malaria transmission patterns on the continent. It is generally acknowledged, for example, that the introduction of 'unseasoned' Indian indentured labourers in the nineteenth century to East and southern African coastal enclaves contributed to outbreaks of malaria and heightened rates of malarial morbidity and mortality in these areas.

Sleeping sickness was another disease with a long history on the continent – Islamic sources record that King Diata II of Mali died of what was probably the *gambiense* form of sleeping sickness in the fourteenth century – and was certainly endemic to Africa in the eighteenth and nineteenth centuries. The disease was known amongst Europeans as 'African lethargy', and trans-Atlantic slave traders in West Africa in the late eighteenth century were observed actively screening for it amongst their human cargo (see Chapter 6). Other diseases, such as leprosy, syphilis and smallpox have more complicated historical epidemiological pathways which are difficult to untangle. For example, historians tend to agree that although syphilis was endemic and familiar to societies in southern and East Africa in the eighteenth and nineteenth centuries, this was likely different from the more virulent form of syphilis introduced by Europeans, and also distinct from yaws which was an endemic communicable (but not sexually transmitted) disease whose symptoms could be confused with those of endemic syphilis (see Chapter 4). The patterns of transmission for leprosy and smallpox in sub-Saharan Africa in the eighteenth and nineteenth centuries were similarly complex, and exhibited characteristics of both endemic and imported diseases depending on regional and temporal specificities. Although leprosy was a known disease in West Africa since at least the sixteenth century, in southern Africa leprosy was most probably introduced to the Cape in the eighteenth century via Indian Ocean Dutch maritime networks linking southeast Asia to southern Africa. The same route was traversed by a virulent strain of smallpox and resulted in repeat outbreaks in the eighteenth century in the Cape, which had a significant demographic impact on 'virgin' local populations (even though smallpox had been known in parts of East Africa by this time), including slaves and Khoikhoi. A virulent form of cholera crossed the Indian Ocean disease zone from South Asia, causing repeat epidemics in mid-nineteenth-century Mauritius, Zanzibar and elsewhere along the East African coast. The Senegambia region also suffered from cholera in the mid-nineteenth century, likely brought through trading routes across the Sahara and by sea through the Mediterranean.

Although this historical disease profile of sub-Saharan Africa is far from comprehensive, the limited information at our disposal does point to certain asymmetries at work in Africa's 'disease exchange' with the wider world in this period. Africa 'received' more virulent forms of infectious diseases such as syphilis, smallpox and cholera, without a corresponding level of exchange or transfer outwards of vector-borne infectious diseases endemic to Africa such as trypanosomiasis and malaria. With regards to the global spread of malaria from its origins in Africa, malaria *vivax* is believed to have been endemic in parts of Europe for at least two millennia and that its appearance in the New World was likely a result of its transference by early European settlers rather than via the later forced migration of African slaves in the trans-Atlantic trade. It is probable, however, that malaria *falciparum*, which caused high mortality in eighteenth-century plantation societies of the American South, was brought through the importation of African slaves.[18]

Indigenous healing systems: Hierarchies, ideologies and therapeutics

How did African societies and local healing systems up to the nineteenth century respond to specific disease environments and health challenges? While it would not be possible to comprehensively catalogue the diverse range of approaches to and perspectives on the problem of ill-health across vast regions, it is pertinent to outline several important and characteristic features of local healing hierarchies, ideas of illness and modes of treatment which emerge in this period. In their seminal contribution, the volume *The Social Basis of Health and Healing in Africa* (1992), the historian Steven Feierman and anthropologist John Janzen make the case for the *inseparability* of African healing systems from their social, cultural and political contexts. Rather than viewing African healers and therapeutics as a distinct sphere or a closed 'ethnomedical' unit with African societies, they argue for the **embeddedness of health and healing** – as a set of ideas and institutions – within a much wider range of social, ritual and political realms. This embeddedness is a constituent feature, broadly speaking, of African healing systems in this early period.

It is vital to acknowledge that in societies that had long familiarity with certain diseases a well-rehearsed **repertoire of therapeutics** developed in response. As seen in Mungo Park's account, Mandingo therapies for 'fevers' ranged from a vapour treatment employing the shrub *Nauclea orientalis* which provided symptomatic relief to the use of spiritual charms held against the body. African healing could also encompass **technical solutions** based on empirical observation of the human body, such as bone-setting and some forms of surgery including amputation. The sophisticated use of local herbs and roots as well as other flora and fauna formed part of an **indigenous pharmacopeia**, a central feature of therapeutic approaches in many African societies. These herbal remedies could be ingested as purgatives or curative agents, or applied topically as ointments. Missionaries in the eastern Cape in the 1820s were shocked to observe Xhosa women ingesting herbs, including the root of the *isaquni* tree, to induce miscarriages. This was one instance of a much wider repertoire of abortifacients utilized across the nineteenth century by different ethnic groups in southern Africa, including thornbush (preferred by the Khoikhoi), the bulb of a peppery shrub called *uhlunguhlungu* (Zulu), the *siluvari* plant (Shangaan), and the bulb of a plant called *sekanama* (Sotho).[19] This diverse pharmacopeia also reflected **local environmental knowledge**, a key tool not only for sourcing curative treatments but also for designing disease prevention strategies – for example, it is recognized that some southern and East African societies in the mid-nineteenth century learned to control the spread of sleeping sickness through the careful management of the habitat of tsetse flies, including practices of transhumance and controlled bush-burning (see Chapter 6).

Alongside a diverse range of therapeutics were **diverse categories of healers**. Healing practitioners were uniform neither in kind nor in status across African societies, and were positioned in **differentiated hierarchies**. For example, in pre-colonial northeast Tanzania, healers and diviners were part of a well-developed hierarchy of control which involved chiefs and clan patriarchs, collectively exercising wide social and political power. Amongst the Tswana of southern Africa, diviners like the 'rain doctor' described in David Livingstone's account occupied a particularly powerful role above and beyond other healing practitioners, in part due to the preciousness and scarcity of that vital resource – water. The role of the diviner exemplifies how the healing arts were invested with a **sacred power** in many pre-colonial African societies. Sacred power could be derived from and expressed through the ritual control over key processes and resources such as fertility, reproduction and land, and not only informed the operation of key social and political institutions but also framed relations between the living and the dead. The act of healing, then, went far beyond the localized treatment of an ill patient. Indeed, some healing networks such as the Lemba in seventeenth-century Loango served multiple roles as a ritual healing association and trans-territorial governance structure, including priests and ritual healers but also merchants, chiefs and judges amongst their number. This particular confluence of commercial, political and spiritual agency conferred on the Lemba network an authority which was observed by contemporaries to possess 'the sacred medicine of governing'.[20]

Related to this, it is vital to acknowledge that a given society's **ideological orientation** could influence views of disease causation, determine therapeutic approaches and structure a society's healing hierarchy. A noted feature of many African societies in this period was that they were organized to maximize numbers, as a bulwark against disease and inhospitable environments. Fertility was thus a hugely important theme, both as a moral value and as a conceptual framework that helped to structure belief systems and forms of social organization. Recourse to **ritual remedies** underscored that certain illnesses could only be treated through appropriate action within a social and cosmological realm. Avoidance practices were a significant example of a ritual preventative, broadly observed amongst Bantu-speaking groups in southern and East Africa. These measures prohibited sexual or physical contact between certain individuals around specified moments of ritual 'contagion', such as menses, childbirth, lactation and death. These were ritual expressions of ideas around bodily contagion linked to the potential harmful mixing of blood and bodily fluids, and connected the realms of fertility, sexual reproduction and death with the spirit-world inhabited by the ancestors.

A key characteristic of early healing systems is that they were **receptive to change**. In areas where we have the most detailed longitudinal records – for example, in the Cape and the Loango Coast accounts spanned the seventeenth to the nineteenth centuries – it is evident that healing practices and their related ideological foundations were indeed capable of transformation. In the Loango, the Lemba 'drum of affliction' helped local communities to both demarcate growing trade and the machinations of capitalism as moral forces of illness, and offer a means of protection.[21] The Xhosa cattle-killing episode of 1856–7, in which 400,000 cattle were slaughtered by Xhosa 'believers' in response to the call of the teenage prophetess Nongqawuse, is another fascinating example. Variously interpreted as a political revolt against British encroachment or a religious movement inspired by millenarian impulses, the cattle-killing can also be seen as an internal response to a series of devastating diseases such as lung sickness, rinderpest, influenza and smallpox that had struck the Xhosa and decimated their livestock by the mid-nineteenth century. In this way, the call to slaughter can be seen as a type of 'sacred medicine' that would restore the moral order and rejuvenate Xhosa society.[22] Christianity presented another such ideological challenge, as was writ large in the history of the imposition of missionary medicine, and its uneven reception, in southern African societies over the long nineteenth century. Moreover, as the following section illustrates, the immense political, social and spiritual disruption caused by the slave trade necessitated creative responses within the realm of health.

The **mixing of therapeutic traditions** is a manifestation of the flexibility of African healing systems and their capacity to change. As Mungo Park's account briefly suggests, the Mandingo utilized 'European lancets' procured in the coastal areas to perform phlebotomies. This is but one example which illustrates that even whilst Park was trying to provide a faithful account of what he probably thought were 'indigenous' practices, there was already observable evidence of how the Mandingo had absorbed 'foreign' tools into their own healing regimes. It is important to note, however, that this mixing of therapeutic traditions was not without conflict or contestation. There is evidence that Islamic scholars debated whether the use of amulets to ward off ill-health – what Mungo Park had termed 'saphies' – could reasonably co-exist with an Islamic orientation and way of life. Some argued the production and trade of amulets were harmless, while others argued they constituted an infidel practice that should be outlawed.[23]

'Islamic medicine' as a complex itself changed greatly after its 'golden period' of the ninth to eleventh centuries, when a shared Greco-Arabic understanding of disease causation based on humoral theory and an emphasis on rational practice and observation had been the main emphasis. This transformation was related to changing political circumstances as well as an internal ideological shift away from rationality to orthodoxy. From an approach which saw medicine as a profession and distinct from the priesthood, Islamic medicine by the time it reached Hausaland (in northern Nigeria) in the fifteenth century had evolved to supernatural explanations, and ceded medical authority to the spiritual realm – observing the pronouncements of a *shaykh* became a key aspect of healing amongst Muslim followers in West Africa and the Maghreb region.[24]

Despite the immense variety and adaptation of African healing systems, the broad outlines of a few **regional 'typologies' of African healing cultures** in this period can be discerned, even if only tentatively. Environmental, demographic and epidemiological factors were critical in shaping regionally specific healing regimes. The centrality of rain divination in southern African healing systems, for example, could be attributed to the overriding socio-political problem of water scarcity in the region. West Africa's disease profile was uniquely shaped by a historical confluence of factors: the unique disease environment of its equatorial rainforest, an embedded history of pre-colonial forms of dense urban settlement, and prolonged exposure to global disease zones due to trans-Saharan and trans-Atlantic trade networks. West African death cultures, in comparison to those that emerged in southern and East Africa in this period, are another expression of these broad, regionally defined dynamics at work. The development in West Africa of a specific ritual topography of the dead in the late eighteenth and nineteenth centuries was evidenced in traditions of intramural sepulture – a mode of ritual internment of the dead in which the corpse is entombed within a domestic compound – and the performance of veneration rites at sacred shrines.[25] In contrast, the practice of corpse exposure in southern and East Africa was widely observed (and decried) by Christian missionaries in this period, and reflected regionally prevalent notions of ritual contagion. This was connected to the mandate to contain bodily pollution, which was an organizing construct across much of Bantu-speaking southern and East Africa. A final important framework broadly cognizant across Bantu-speaking groups was the notion that the experience of illness, including mental illness, itself could act as a 'sign' of one's calling to the healing profession (see Chapter 5). Certain physical or psychic debilities could serve as valued experiential prelude to the would-be healer's development of clairvoyance and other necessary healing skills. This noteworthy 'transformation of the sufferer into the healer' was a testament to the capaciousness of these groups to integrate the concept of ill-health as part of, rather than an antithesis to, the larger restoration of moral and ritual order.[26]

European health in pre-colonial Africa and the 'white man's grave'

The notion of Africa as the 'white man's grave' was a dominant trope in European imaginings of Africa up through the nineteenth century. Tropical Africa in particular appeared to reverse the terms of the 'Columbian disease exchange' as described by

Crosby – rather than native populations succumbing in large numbers to imported diseases brought by European colonizers, in the African context *Europeans* appeared the most vulnerable in the 'hostile' disease landscape. Certainly, written accounts tend to affirm the curbing effect of high morbidity and mortality rates on European expansionist designs, whether religious, economic or political. Seventeenth-century Spanish interests in Africa were beset from the outset, symbolized by the fate of Spanish Capuchin missionaries who had been dispatched to the West African kingdom of Allada [in present-day Benin] in January 1660, with five out of twelve missionaries dead from illness by that May. French Catholic missionizing to neighbouring Whydah was similarly fatally undermined by illness.[27] Mungo Park's crew which accompanied his two expeditions to explore the Niger were decimated by diseases such as malaria and dysentery. After decades of proselytizing and exploring southern and East Africa, David Livingstone succumbed to the ill-effects of malaria and dysentery in 1873 in what is now Zambia.

Alongside these qualitative sources, historians have also attempted to assess the validity of the 'white man's grave' thesis through quantitative analysis, although the evidentiary basis of calculations of European mortality in tropical Africa was not well established until at least the early nineteenth century. One historical estimate of the general European mortality rate on the west African coast in the late eighteenth century was between 300 and 700 per 1,000 per year, with deaths largely due to malaria and yellow fever. As the historian Philip Curtin has shown, statistics of military personnel stationed in West Africa make comparably robust indicators, particularly from the early nineteenth century, because European powers had a vested interest in assessing accurately the 'relocation costs' attached to sending forces to overseas units. Before the advent of international health agency frameworks and surveillance mechanisms to collect morbidity and mortality data on a global scale, these military statistics provided a comparative snapshot of potential disease 'hotspots' around the world. For example, between 1817 and 1838, European military mortality in Senegal was recorded at nearly 165 deaths per 1,000, with Sierra Leone a staggering 483 deaths per 1,000 (representing nearly 50 per cent of the standing force every year). The relocation cost in terms of increased deaths, then, for European military to be stationed in Sierra Leone was 3,057 per cent, meaning that a solider was greater than thirty times more likely to die in Sierra Leone than when stationed at 'home'.[28] European forces stationed elsewhere in the 'tropics', which included Southeast Asia and the Caribbean, also suffered high relocation costs. But in comparative terms, tropical Africa and specifically Sierra Leone appear to have exacted the deadliest toll in terms of European lives.

Although it would be tempting to treat the entire period between the seventeenth and mid-nineteenth centuries as an unbroken narrative of catastrophic European vulnerability to the particular disease environment of tropical Africa, the enduring image of the white man's grave is problematic in several respects. What large-scale data that exists from this period is far from comprehensive, and focuses on military personnel to the exclusion of other groups of Europeans present in the region such as missionaries and tradesmen. More importantly, the white man's grave thesis rested on a **flawed presumption of 'Native immunity'** to the same diseases that were decimating European populations. The idea of a complete and inherent African immunity to disease, particularly to 'fevers' such as malaria and yellow fever, persisted into the twentieth century and came to influence the design of colonial health interventions, as will be seen in the following chapter. Scientific research has now established that West and Central African populations *did* benefit from unique genetic adaptations evolved through many millennia of interaction between the malarial parasite and human hosts, conferring high levels of protection particularly against *Plasmodium vivax* and partial protection against the more deadly form *Plasmodium falciparum* (see Chapter 6). However, the partial immunity provided by the sickle cell trait against *P. falciparum* was not conferred uniformly across the population, and also did not prevent malaria incidence but reduced its potential to become fatal in an infected person. Furthermore, whilst individual resistance against malaria could be developed through surviving repeat infections at relatively stable levels of transmission, the hidden cost of this form of partial immunity was a high rate of child mortality, particularly for children under five. Thus, Africans were indeed susceptible to fevers and sometimes did die from them, but in ways that escaped Europeans' gaze.

It is also important to **contextualize changing European responses** to disease in this period, rather than assume an all-encompassing helplessness in the face of the mortal 'dangers' of the tropics. European mortality rates did shift downwards noticeably over the course of the nineteenth century, as more effective techniques of addressing the specific disease environment of tropical Africa were utilized. Quinine, the isolated compound derived from the bark of the *cinchona* tree (whose prophylactic and therapeutic qualities for treating fevers were known as early as the seventeenth century), was commercially available by the 1830s in Europe. By mid-century it had become the firm companion of European travellers, missionaries and regiments stationed in Africa, replacing therapeutic techniques such as blood-letting and the use of mercury which had only succeeded in weakening bodies. The demographic make-up of European military personnel changed significantly as well, particularly when the British recruited soldiers from slaving ships that had been captured through the naval enforcement of the 1807 ban on the slave trade. Alongside improving anti-malarial interventions, these 'West Indian' regiments in operation from the 1830s contributed to a marked decline in the British military death rate in West Africa, from 151 per 1,000 in the period 1849–75 to 32 per 1,000 in 1875–90, a nearly five-fold decrease.[29]

Historical Source: Mary Kingsley, *Travels in West Africa* (1897)

In every other direction you will see the apparently endless walls of mangrove, unvarying in colour, unvarying in form, unvarying in height, save from perspective. Beneath and between you and them lie the rotting mud waters of Bonny River, and away up and down river, miles of rotting mud waters fringed with walls of rotting mud mangrove-swamp. The only break in them – one can hardly call it a relief to the scenery – are the gaunt black ribs of the old hulks, once used as trading stations, which lie exposed at low water near the shore, protruding like the skeletons of great unclean beasts who have died because Bonny water was too strong even for them ....

While your eyes are drinking in the characteristics of Bonny scenery you notice a peculiar smell – an intensification of that smell you noticed when nearing Bonny, in the evening, out at sea. That's the breath of the malarial mud, laden with fever, and the chances are you will be down to-morrow. If it is near evening time now, you can watch it becoming incarnate, creeping and crawling and gliding out from the side creeks and between the mangrove-roots, laying itself upon the river, stretching and rolling in a kind of grim play, and finally crawling up the side of the ship to come on board and leave its cloak of moisture that grows green mildew in a few hours over all.

Source Analysis: Mary Kingsley (1862–1900) was a self-educated Victorian spinster and self-described collector of 'fish, beetles and fetish' who undertook two voyages to West Africa, in 1893 and again in 1894, visiting parts of present-day Nigeria, Gabon, Equatorial Guinea, Congo and Angola. Her vivid and humorous account of her travels was widely circulated, and she became a popular figure on Victorian lecture circuits. Kingsley returned to Africa during the Anglo-Boer War, to serve as a nurse in a prisoner-of-war camp in Cape Town, where she died of typhoid in 1900.

Kingsley's account offers us a window into late nineteenth-century popular understandings of disease causation. What is striking in this mini-portrait of the Bonny River, which feeds into the Bight of Benin, is the sinister agency accorded to both the deadly 'rotting' mangrove swamp and the 'malarial mud', which actively moved 'creeping and crawling' towards you. Kingsley's reference to the 'smell' and 'breath' of malarial mud that was 'laden with fever' shows the persistence of older European notions of disease causation, specifically the idea of miasma, translated to the specific environs of tropical West Africa. Her account also demonstrates the resilience of imaginings of tropical Africa as the 'white man's grave', an image which does not necessarily coincide with the reality of declining European mortality rates in Africa by the late nineteenth century. Kingsley's depiction of a swamp 'laden' with disease is also markedly disconnected from a very different understanding of disease causation emergent in this period – germ theory – in which microbes and not environments were the principal agents.

Finally, it is important to acknowledge the **resilience of the 'white man's grave'** as a particular frame for understanding disease and its relation to the environment of tropical Africa. The 'white man's grave' was less about the statistical reality of the disease toll on European bodies, which had its own fluctuating trajectory across the eighteenth and nineteenth centuries. It was more accurately an expression of the cultural imagination of a select cohort of observers and travellers. It was also, as can be seen in Mary Kingsley's *Travels in West Africa* (1897) (see box), a reflection of the **persistence of older European notions of disease causation** which were applied with varying interpretive effects to the specific environs encountered in tropical Africa. Humoral pathology, which can be traced back to ancient Greek understandings and was based on maintaining a bodily 'balance' of four internal fluids or 'humours' (blood, phlegm, yellow bile and black bile), was adapted and linked to climate. Climate, specifically the 'heat' of the tropics, threw the liquid balance out of order and induced disease. The idea of localism – that diseases were products of particular locations, particular soils and temperatures – enhanced the perception of tropical Africa as a uniquely threatening disease environment. Another persistent European notion of disease causation in this period centred around miasma, the poisonous atmospheric emanations from the soil which was linked in the medieval period to fears over the harmful emanations from the bodies of the deceased. Efforts to combat miasma were focused on improving ventilation or the circulation of air around people and living quarters. As will be seen in the following chapter, even as the scientific advances heralded by 'germ theory' came to supplant previous understandings of disease causation in the late nineteenth and early twentieth centuries, vestiges of these older ideas remained in circulation in the colonial African context.

Slavery and the slave trade: Demographic and health implications

Transacting in slaves was undoubtedly a defining feature of the early modern global economy. Parts of West and Central Africa were drawn into both the trans-Saharan and trans-Atlantic slave trading routes from as early as the sixteenth century. Alternative slaving routes to the Middle East and through the Indian Ocean developed from the eighteenth to late nineteenth centuries, spurred by the British abolition of the slave trade, with plantation-style economies set up in Zanzibar, Mauritius and Reunion and the establishment of 'new' centres of slave trading in Angola, Mozambique and Tanzania. Internal forms of slavery also existed in many African societies, due in part to the re-orientating of African polities towards maintaining a supply of slaves to export. The slave population in nineteenth-century Sokoto caliphate (in present-day Nigeria) is estimated to have been 2.5 million, second only at the time to the 4 million slaves in the American South.[30] By the mid-nineteenth century, on the eve of widespread European colonization, Africa as a whole had already experienced mass depopulation, internal displacement and widespread social and economic transformation due to external slave trades and internal domestic forms of slavery.

The extensive historiography of African slavery has bequeathed historians of health and medicine a set of tools and perspectives through which the health impacts of the slave trade(s) as well as the dynamics of healing systems and health decision-making at work in slave societies in Africa and beyond could be explored. These include: econometric approaches that help quantify the impact and extent of the slave trade, particularly the trans-Atlantic slave trade; an anthropological orientation towards cultural transmission within slave societies, alongside awareness of the complexity of social forms and relations between slaves and masters in both internal African and 'transplanted' African slave societies; an emphasis on ethnic and linguistic diversity within slave populations and an acknowledgement of the potential for knowledge exchange in such societies; and finally, macro-level environmental perspectives. The relative plenitude of primary source material which has enriched slave historiography, as compared to the limited archive on African societies of the same period, may well offer potential avenues through which a global history of African health and healing practices can be reconstructed.

Demographic impact of the slave trade(s)

To a certain extent, scholarly preoccupation about the demographic impact of the various slave trade(s) enmeshing Africa was a foreshadowing of present-day assessments of the human toll of the HIV/AIDS pandemic on the continent (see Chapter 4). Both are not simply intellectual calculations but reflect inherently political concerns and also deeply moral and epistemological questions about finding meaning in the context of demographic crises of unthinkable proportions. In the case of the trans-Atlantic slave trade, for example, one could ask, 'What does it mean for Africa to be emptied of 12.5 million of its inhabitants over the course of three centuries?' Scholarly debates regarding the accuracy of statistical counts continue to be fraught, even as our ability to glean and interpret the data improves, possibly because the figures themselves are suggestive about the relative centrality of slavery in African history, itself a highly contentious topic.

What do we know, then, about the demographic implications of the slave trade(s) involving Africa? The trans-national and multi-institutional academic efforts to build the Slave Voyages database, an online repository which draws on the records of more than 36,000 slaving voyages between Africa and the Americas, have provided us with more definitive numbers in terms of the total slaves exported through the trans-Atlantic slave trade in the period 1450–1900. That figure currently stands at 12.5 million, although work is continuing to identify gaps in the sources and add to the database.[31] This figure does not include other prominent slaving routes involving Africa, including the Saharan, Red Sea, Indian Ocean slave trades, which are estimated to have exported 2.2 million additional Africans between 1600 and 1800. Furthermore, these figures do not include the number of slaves in *internal* African forms of slavery, which amounted to an estimated 7 million Africans in domestic slavery cumulatively.[32]

The historian Patrick Manning, in the most recent estimation of demographic change of the African population, suggests that the various slave trades and their peak enslavement waves in the eighteenth and nineteenth centuries created 'serious negative pressure', resulting in the overall stagnation of the African population across this period.[33] The growth rate could not compensate for the loss of Africans through slavery, particularly at its most extractive form. Furthermore, the external slave trades created powerful destabilizing forces which fed political conflict and warfare throughout the same period – including the *mfecane* in southern Africa, the collapse of the Luanda state, the wars in Yorubaland and the Islamic *jihad* in West Africa. These entwined violent processes not only created a captive slave population to feed into the slave trades, but they also created conditions ripe for famine, disease and high mortality. It was not until the interwar period of the twentieth century that African population figures exhibited definitive growth and recovery from the cumulative demographic effects of these shocks. However, these population projections are problematic, not least because of the lack of reliable and comprehensive 'baseline' figures for the African population until well into the twentieth century.

Demographic historians of slavery, to an extent, have been able to disaggregate the datasets to discern the age and gender profiles of exported slaves, particularly those involved in the trans-Atlantic slave trade. Although incomplete, this statistical profile does indicate that through much of the four centuries of the trans-Atlantic trade there was a pronounced gender imbalance, with sometimes twice as many African men enslaved and shipped out as women. This in turn would have contributed to the perceived lower fertility rate in the Atlantic slave societies to which they were bound. Although the historical record shows that slaveowners in these regions articulated their concern with maintaining what is called the 'replacement rate' within slave populations, there was in practice a pronounced failure, particularly in Caribbean slave societies, to produce a self-sustaining slave population up until the mid-nineteenth century. This was possibly because of the relative cheapness of acquiring new slaves via the open market (until the enforcement of the British abolition of the slave trade in 1807 took effect) versus the perceived risks and costs of birthing and raising young slaves, and the slaveholders' own motivation for labour extraction purposes to keep a highly unbalanced gender ratio. The skewed gender profile of slaves could also reflect the ability of African matrilineal societies, from whom the majority of slaves bound for the trans-Atlantic slave trade were sourced, to hold onto its women. Polygyny is thought to have increased in many of the African societies which lost large numbers of its male members.

Yet, slave fertility was even lower than this skewed ratio would suggest, given the number of women recorded as captured and enslaved. There are several potential explanations. Slavery itself may have had a suppressive effect on reproduction. There is a wide scholarship which documents the phenomenon of 'reluctant mothers' when women live in conditions of extreme hardship, stress and violence. Enslaved women may have experienced amenorrhea or other forms of sub-fecundity, as has been documented in other historical instances of extreme enforced labour and nutritional deprivation, such as in Nazi concentration camps. Human choice was also a factor. The practice of prolonged lactation was a form of reproductive control observed in many of the same African societies from which slaves were drawn, increasing the intervals between pregnancies. Furthermore, slave women were known to source abortifacients from their local environment, as Barbara Bush has shown was common in Caribbean slave societies. Commonly used substances included manioc, frangipani and fruits such as papaya, mango and lime. Some practices recalled local knowledge of indigenous pharmacopeia. Boiling lime juice with a yellow stone was considered a Dahomian practice, and utilizing the root of cotton trees was known to be derived from the Mandingo. Tragically, infanticide among Caribbean slaves may have also contributed to the high infant mortality rate noted there.[34]

Importantly, concerns over reproduction and fertility were evident *in* Africa as well, as societies responded to the depletion of their young adult population and the slave trade's attendant forces of violence and rupture. In the lower Congo, for example, increased attention to fertility rites and the growth of sacred medicines (called *nkisi*) for pregnancy and childbirth could be attributed to the insecurity caused by the slave trade. Specialized therapeutics were developed by the nineteenth century which supported marital relations, sexual reproduction and healthy pregnancies, including the formation of women-only ritual clinics as well as herbal curatives for infertility.[35]

Mixing of therapeutic traditions

A very different consequence of the mass migration of human populations due to the slave trade was the mixing of therapeutic traditions. There are many instances in the historical record of exchanges of healing traditions occurring 'horizontally' across different enslaved or marginalized groups, as well as 'vertically' between slave communities and slaveholders. This knowledge exchange was not a historical constant, however, and depended in part on the relative socio-legal rigidity of the slaving system in question.

In eighteenth-century Île de France (now Mauritius), the common knowledge of the practice of inoculation against smallpox may have reflected the diverse origins of the island's enslaved population. The technique, also called variation and involving the deliberate exposure of an uninfected person with the remnants of smallpox scabs or pustules to induce a milder form of the disease and eventually immunity, was known amongst the resident Hindu Indian population. Evidence suggests that African slaves on Île de France were also familiar with the practice, reflecting Islamic influence filtered through East African trade networks.[36] Similarly, West African slaves brought local knowledge of the practice of variation and introduced it to America. Famously, Cotton Mather, the distinguished New England Puritan clergyman and scholar, learned about the practice from his slave, Onesimus. Mather publicized the technique and it was implemented successfully in 1721 to quell a smallpox outbreak in Boston, Massachusetts, well before Edward Jenner's development of the cowpox vaccine in 1789.

In the American South in the late eighteenth and early nineteenth centuries, the sharing of folk remedies occurred via multiple pathways across enslaved African, Native American and planter classes. This not only reflects the permeable boundaries of knowledge in slaving societies in the American South in this earlier period. It also reveals the sceptical orientation towards the medical profession and the primacy of local herbal knowledge and 'lay' health practices, characteristics which cut across class, racial and ethnic boundaries. The mixing of healing traditions across these lines became more difficult as plantation society hierarchies rigidified and increasingly strict legal codes separating slave and planter classes were enforced. By the mid-nineteenth century, local and state slave codes effectively prevented black doctors from practising on white bodies. This marginalization of folk medicine filtered into slave perceptions as well – Frederick

HEATHEN PRACTICES AT FUNERALS

Figure 1.1 'Heathen Practices at Funerals'. J.M. Phillippo. *Jamaica: Its Past and Present State* (London: J. Snow, 1843).

Historical Source: 'Heathen Practices at Funerals', in J.M. Phillippo, *Jamaica: Its Past and Present State* (1843)

Source Analysis: This is an image of 'burial divination' or the ritual interrogation of the corpse observed in mid-nineteenth-century Jamaican slave society. This practice, which has its origins in parts of West and Central Africa, should be seen as a type of ritualized post-mortem, in which questions regarding the cause of death are directly posed to the dead body. The deceased's 'response' is articulated through the physical movements of the pall-bearers, who lurch towards a person or dwelling to indicate the individual responsible for the death. The image captures a sense of the dynamism of the interrogation process – the pall-bearers are running within the circular frame created by the gathered community, the huts and the lush vegetation. A sense of anticipation as well as active involvement is conveyed through the outstretched arms of the onlookers and the child running towards the pall-bearers in the foreground.

Phillippo regarded this event as an obvious example of slaves' 'heathen' orientation, as the inscription on the print indicates. However, this image could instead be viewed as a visual testament to a resilient African healing tradition. Rosalind Shaw has shown how spiritual 'inquests' of the dead were an important form of witchfinding among the Temne in eighteenth-century Sierra Leone. The interrogation of the corpse shown in Jamaica could be similarly interpreted as a ritual response to the problem of unnatural death. This evidence of burial divination in Jamaican slaving society attests to the survival and transmission of some forms of bodily technologies across the Middle Passage. This ritual practice took on added meaning in the context of Jamaican slavery, as Vincent Brown has suggested, as a mechanism to reinforce communal values among slaves and the ideal of atonement.

Douglass, who escaped slavery in 1838 and became a prominent voice for the abolition of slavery in the United States, notably came to view slave medicine as inferior.

Slave health

The historical record on slave health tends to be more revealing of slave societies that were dominated by planter aristocracies of European extraction – this was the case in the Americas and Caribbean, as well as in some plantation economies in Africa (e.g. on Île de France). These societies had a developed legal code and thus slaves were made visible in various ways within the bureaucratic institutions and written records of the period. Furthermore, some literate slaves were able to, through the slave narrative form, create their own written testament to their experiences under slavery. Records from captured slaving vessels during the British blockade of the slave trade have been used to mine data beyond simply demographics – age and height records of captured slaves have helped provide, albeit inconclusively, a proxy of sorts for the health profile of the enslaved population.[37] In contrast, there is very little first-hand historical accounts of slave health in the less stratified slaving societies that were more common within Africa. Deaths from infectious disease probably affected African slaveholders in roughly equal measure to their slaves, on the presumption that African slaves tended to be incorporated within the residential and kin structures of their masters. It is not known whether slave diets tended to be of demonstrably less quality than that of their African owners.

In abolitionist literature, depictions of 'slave health' tended to be encapsulated by the horrors of the Middle Passage, or the singular image of the brutal whipping of plantation slaves. Whilst these whippings could leave permanent, and in some cases mortal, wounds on the bodies of both male and female slaves, the spectrum of slave health encompassed a far wider range of traumas, challenges and choices. Slave's dietary needs were by and large not sufficiently catered for, in particular in terms of nutrients from fresh fruits and vegetables, and these nutritional deficiencies made slaves more vulnerable to disease, particularly respiratory disease in the winter months. The practice of 'dirt-eating' observed in the early nineteenth century amongst slave women in the Caribbean was most likely a gendered response to extreme nutritional deficiencies in slave diets, particularly of thiamine and iron.[38] Poor sanitary conditions made communicable disease more likely to spread quickly amongst slave quarters as well. And the close and crowded confines of slave residences meant that respiratory disease could spread easily within slave dwellings. Improper footwear, if not provided, could mean frostbite during the winter, and exposure to tetanus and hookworm through lacerations on exposed feet.[39]

The health consequences of the intensive labour regime required by plantation slavery have been debated by medical and slave historians. Some have suggested, for example, that the labour demands required by the sugar regime in West Indian plantations may have led to a higher incidence of what is now termed Sudden Infant Death Syndrome, and could also partly explain the reproductive difficulties slave populations there had in reaching a replacement rate. Plantation slave 'logbooks' offer a wealth of health-related data, including births and deaths as well as records of periodic illnesses which resulted in slaves being given days off of work – vital information for slaveholders to chart productivity and record any 'losses' through slave morbidity. This detailed documentation has become far removed from its original intent as a profit-maximizing exercise – it can now be used by historians to chart, in a more precise manner, how health patterns may have correlated with labour intensity. Slave logbooks can also be utilized to provide micro-historical portraits of health in a given plantation over time. For example, the compiled logbooks of the Georgian plantation owner George Kollock constitute a unique longitudinal health record of his slaves for twenty-four years, from 1837 to 1861.[40] These logbooks, which included information on the number and timing of days off given to pregnant slave women at various stages throughout their babies' gestation period, offer intriguing glimpses into the ways in which some slave women persuasively motivated overseers for release from hard labour at crucial and early stages in their pregnancies, thus helping to ensure a better health outcome for themselves and their babies.

Historical Source: *The Interesting Narrative of the Life of Olaudoh Equiano or Gustavas Vassa, the African: Written by Himself* (1814)

Though we had no places of public worship, we had priests and magicians, or wise men. I do not remember whether they had different offices, or whether they were united in the same persons, but they were held in great reverence by the people. They calculated our time, and foretold events, as their name imported, for we called them Ah-affoe-way-cah, which signifies 'calculators or yearly men,' our year being called Ah-affoe …. These magicians were also our doctors or physicians. They practised bleeding by cupping: and were very successful in healing wounds and expelling poisons. They had likewise some extraordinary method of discovering jealousy, theft and poisoning; the success of which, no doubt, they derived from their unbounded influence over the credulity and superstition of the people. I do not remember what those methods were, except that, as to poisoning, I recollect an instance or two, which I hope it will not be deemed impertinent here to insert, as it may serve as a kind of specimen of the rest, and is still used by the negroes in the West Indies. A young woman has been poisoned, but it was not known by whom. The doctors ordered the corpse to be taken up by some persons and carried to the grave. As soon as the bearers had raised it on their shoulders, they seemed seized with some sudden impulse, and ran to and fro unable to stop themselves. At last, after having passed through a number of thorns and prickly bushes unhurt, the corpse fell from them close to a house, and defaced it in the fall; and the owner being taken up, he immediately confessed to the poisoning.

Source Analysis: Slave narratives have provided an extraordinarily rich seam of first-hand accounts that describe the experience of enslavement and slavery. The publication of slave narratives ignited fierce public debate, and they continue to be a source of contention among scholars today. Much of this debate surrounds the authenticity of these accounts and the overarching political context of abolitionism, both of which frame the question of whether slave narratives offer a 'truthful' rendition of life under slavery and the interiority of slaves themselves. Notwithstanding these challenges, slave narratives can provide important information on slave health and healing traditions. They can also be, as this extract from the first chapter of the narrative of Olaudoh Equiano reveals, a potential source for the historical recovery of African therapeutics and healing institutions.

In this account, Equiano recalls a range of 'methods' that were utilized by the 'wise men' of Eboue region, in present-day Nigeria and Equiano's natal home. He hails their ability to heal wounds and counteract poison, and attests to their overlapping roles across spiritual and medical domains – 'these magicians were also our doctors and physicians'. Interestingly, Equiano affirms the connection between the practice of corpse divination observed in the slaving societies of the West Indies and its West African origins. In his memory of this practice, the ritual post-mortem successfully reveals the identity of the poisoner who had caused the unnatural death.

A final important area of slave health to consider is the psychological toll exacted by slavery. As will be discussed in Chapter 5, statistical studies of slaves in the American South likely underestimated the extent of mental illness in slave communities, and tended to reinforce anti-emancipation sentiments that slavery was a necessary 'civilizing' institution and that freedom would disrupt the mental well-being of 'vulnerable' ex-slaves. In contrast, slave narratives themselves articulated forcefully the range of psychological harms caused by slavery, including trauma, low self-esteem and guilt. Suicide, whilst not sufficiently documented in the archive of slavery, could be seen from the slave's vantage point as the ultimate exercise of bodily agency in conditions of extreme duress and bondage.[41]

What of the psycho-social impact of the centuries-long involvement in the slave trade on communities in Africa? Although it is very difficult to quantify or describe in the absence of written source material, more recently scholars have asked how the psychological trauma of the slave trade could be passed down through communal memory expressed through other, non-literate and non-verbal forms. Amongst the Temne-speaking people of Sierra Leone, who were directly implicated in and affected by the violent machinations of the trans-Atlantic slave trade, the anthropologist Rosalind Shaw has shown how the vestiges of their experience of slavery can be read in 'practical' or ritualized form – through dwelling building practices and rites of divination which recall anxieties and vulnerabilities associated with the slave trade. Similarly, contemporary manifestations of spirit possession in former slave societies have been interpreted by scholars as societal mechanisms used to recall, and ritually cleanse, distant and difficult memories of enslavement.

Conclusion

Rather than considering African healing systems in the distant past as 'closed' entities for the historian to 'discover' or 'uncover', it would be more accurate to view them with the same complexity as they would be seen in the present – as dynamic processes that could express elements of continuity, yet also flexibly absorb external influences and adapt to prevailing disease environments as well as new health challenges. Although our understanding of the diverse range of therapeutics and healing hierarchies of pre-colonial societies is far from comprehensive, it is still possible through the limited sources at our disposal to discern the outlines of African approaches to, and understandings of, health and illness. African healing cultures that developed in the eighteenth and nineteenth centuries were products of their specific social, environmental and political contexts, with healers deriving their power and authority through not only technical prowess and the demonstration of local medicinal knowledge, but an adept traversing of spiritual and social realms. African healing systems were also susceptible to change, and pragmatism as well as eclecticism can be seen as characteristic rather than exceptional features of therapeutic approaches in this period.

In many respects, the observed malleability of slave therapeutics in eighteenth- and nineteenth-century plantation societies should not only be seen as a reaction to the specific moral and spiritual predicament of forced enslavement and its attendant mixing of different ethnic groups. It was already an observable feature of healing systems within Africa as well. Indeed, the slave trade(s) was one of the primary historical mechanisms through which African therapeutics came to have a global reach. It is hoped that this discussion of slave health, including the health outcomes and practices of diasporic African slave communities, can be included as a central element of *African* medical history and not only a feature of slave historiography.

Further reading

Abdalla, Ismail H. *Islam, Medicine, and Practitioners in Northern Nigeria.* Lewiston: Edwin Mellen, 1997.

Arnold, David. 'The Indian Ocean as a Disease Zone, 1500–1950'. *South Asia: Journal of South Asian Studies* 14, no. 2 (1991): 1–21.

Baṭṭūṭa, Ibn. *The Travels of Ibn Battuta, A.D. 1325–1354.* London: Oriental Translations Fund, 1829.

Beinart, William and Karen Brown. *African Local Knowledge & Livestock Health: Traditional, Environmental & Biomedical Approaches in South Africa.* Oxford: James Currey, 2013.

Bellagamba, Alice, Sandra Greene and Martin Klein, eds. *African Voices on Slavery and the Slave Trade. Volume 1: The Sources.* Cambridge: Cambridge University Press, 2013.

Bradford, Helen. 'Herbs, Knives and Plastic: 150 Years of Abortion in South Africa'. In *Science, Medicine and Cultural Imperialism*, edited by Teresa Meade and Mark Walker. London: Macmillan, 1991.

Bush, Barbara. *Slave Women in Caribbean Society 1650–1832.* Kingston: Heinemann, 1990.

Campbell, John. 'Work, Pregnancy, and Infant Mortality among Southern Slaves'. *The Journal of Interdisciplinary History* 14, no. 4 (1984): 793–812.

Crosby, Alfred W. *Ecological Imperialism: The Biological Expansion of Europe, 900–1900.* Cambridge: Cambridge University Press, 1986.

Curtin, Philip. '"The White Man's Grave:" Image and Reality, 1780–1850'. *Journal of British Studies* 1, no. 1 (1961): 94–110.

Curtin, Philip. 'Epidemiology and the Slave Trade'. *Political Science Quarterly* 83, no. 2 (1968): 190–216.

Curtin, Philip. *Death by Migration: Europe's Encounter with the Tropical World in the Nineteenth Century.* Cambridge: Cambridge University Press, 1989.

DeLancey, Mark W. 'Health and Disease on the Plantations of Cameroon, 1884–1939'. In *Disease in African History: An Introductory Survey and Case Studies*, edited by Gerald Hartwig and K. David Patterson. Durham: Duke University Press, 1978.

Dooling, Wayne. *Slavery, Emancipation and Colonial Rule in South Africa.* Athens: Ohio University Press, 2008.

Echenberg, Myron. *Africa in the Time of Cholera: A History of Pandemics from 1817 to the Present.* Cambridge: Cambridge University Press, 2011.

Eltis, David. 'Nutritional Trends in Africa and the Americas: Heights of Africans, 1819–1839'. *The Journal of Interdisciplinary History* 12, no. 3 (1982): 453–75.

Equiano, Olaudoh. *The Interesting Narrative of the Life of Olaudoh Equiano, or Gustavas Vassa, the African. Written By Himself.* London: Printed for and sold by the author, 1789.

Etherington, Norman. 'Missionary Doctors and African Healers in Mid-Victorian South Africa'. *South African Historical Journal* 19, no. 1 (1987): 77–91.

Fett, Sharla. *Working Cures: Healing, Health, and Power on Southern Slave Plantations*. Chapel Hill: University of North Carolina Press, 2002.

Gilroy, Paul. *The Black Atlantic: Modernity and Double Consciousness*. Cambridge: Harvard University Press, 1993.

Greene, Sandra E. *Sacred Sites and the Colonial Encounter: A History of Meaning and Memory in Ghana*. Bloomington: Indiana University Press. 2002.

Janzen, John M. *Lemba, 1650–1930: A Drum of Affliction in Africa and the New World*. New York: Garland Pub., 1981.

Janzen, John M. 'Ideologies and Institutions in Precolonial Western Equatorial African Therapeutics'. In *The Social Basis of Health and Healing in Africa*, edited by Steven Feierman and John M. Janzen. Berkeley: University of California Press, 1992.

Kingsley, Mary Henrietta. *Travels in West Africa*. London: Macmillian and Co., 1897.

Kiple, Kenneth F. *The Caribbean Slave: A Biological History*. Cambridge: Cambridge University Press, 1984.

Law, Robin. 'Religion, Trade and Politics on the "Slave Coast": Roman Catholic Missions in Allada and Whydah in the Seventeenth Century'. *Journal of Religion in Africa* 21, no. 1 (1991): 42–77.

Levtzion, Nehemia and Randall Lee Pouwels, eds. *The History of Islam in Africa*. Athens: Ohio University Press, 2000.

Lovejoy, Paul E. *Transformations in Slavery: A History of Slavery in Africa*. Cambridge: Cambridge University Press, 1983.

Manning, Patrick. *Slavery and African Life: Occidental, Oriental and African Slave Trades*. Cambridge: Cambridge University Press, 1990.

Manning, Patrick. 'African Population, 1650–2000: Comparisons and Implications of New Estimates'. In *Africa's Development in Historical Perspective*, edited by Emmanuel Akyeampong, James Robinson, Nathan Nunn and Robert H. Bates, 131–50. Cambridge: Cambridge University Press, 2014.

Morgan, Kenneth. 'Slave Women and Reproduction in Jamaica, c.1776–1834'. *History* 91, no. 302 (2006): 231–53.

Owusu-Ansah, David. 'Prayer, Amulets, and Healing'. In *The History of Islam in Africa*, edited by Nehemia Levtzion and Randall Lee Pouwels. Athens: Ohio University Press, 2000.

Packard, Randall M. *The Making of a Tropical Disease: A Short History of Malaria*. Baltimore: Johns Hopkins University Press, 2007.

Park, Mungo. *Travels in the Interior Districts of Africa: Performed in the Years 1795, 1796 & 1797*. Gullane: FrontList Books, 1799.

Parker, John. 'The Cultural Politics of Death & Burial in Early Colonial Accra'. In *Africa's Urban Past*, edited by David Anderson and Richard Rathbone. Portsmouth, NH: Heinemann, 1999.

Peires, Jeff. *The Dead Will Arise: Nongqawuse and the Great Xhosa Cattle-Killing Movement of 1856-7*. Johannesburg: Jonathan Ball, 2003.

Pratt, Mary Louise. *Imperial Eyes: Travel Writing and Transculturation*. London: Routledge, 1992.

Savitt, Todd L. *Medicine and Slavery: The Diseases and Health Care of Blacks in Antebellum Virginia*. Urbana: University of Illinois Press, 1978.

Schumaker, Lyn. 'History of Medicine in Sub-Saharan Africa'. In *The Oxford Handbook of the History of Medicine*, edited by Mark Jackson, 266–84. Oxford: Oxford University Press, 2011.

Shaw, Rosalind. *Memories of the Slave Trade: Ritual and the Historical Imagination in Sierra Leone*. Chicago: University of Chicago Press, 2002.

Silla, Eric. *'People Are Not the Same': Leprosy and Identity in Twentieth-Century Mali*. Portsmouth: Heinemann, 1998.

Vaughan, Megan. *Creating the Creole Island: Slavery in Eighteenth-Century Mauritius*. Durham: Duke University Press, 2005.

Waite, Gloria. *A History of Traditional Medicine and Health Care in Pre-Colonial East-Central Africa*. Lewiston: E. Mellen Press, 1992.

Webb, James L. A. 'Historical Epidemiology and Infectious Disease Processes in Africa.' Journal of African History 54, no. 1 (2013): 3–10.

CHAPTER 2
COLONIAL CONTROL, TROPICAL MEDICINE AND AFRICAN HEALTH

Introduction

Beginning in the late nineteenth century, revolutionary advances in several related medical and scientific fields such as immunology, bacteriology and parasitology led to profound changes in the ways in which diseases in Africa would be understood and combated. European scientists such as Louis Pasteur, Robert Koch, Charles Laveran, Ronald Ross and Patrick Manson achieved global renown for their work. 'Pasteurization', for example, has become an essential and familiar element of food and beverage processing. As will be seen, their discoveries were part of a larger transition away from earlier views of disease causation such as miasma, humoral theory and contagion, to an explanatory model predicated on a new cast of actors: microbes, vectors and hosts. Importantly, the development of 'germ theory', as this complex of discoveries came to be collectively known, occurred in parallel with tremendous shifts in global politics and economy. This was no more so than on the African continent. Much of sub-Saharan Africa was rapidly and brutally partitioned amongst several European powers in the late 1880s as a consequence of the Conference of Berlin (1884–5). This marked the beginning of a roughly seven decades-long imposition of widespread imperial governmental and administrative hegemony over African polities, the intensification of capitalist exploitation of African resources and labour, and in some areas the growth and consolidation of European settler societies. For the many Africans who during this period of wide-scale change visited a missionary-run hospital, partook in sleeping sickness expeditions or anti-syphilis campaigns, benefited from vaccinations or other medical interventions for the first time, or experienced forced relocation due to sanitary segregation measures, their experiences of both the successes and failures of an increasingly bio-medicalized approach to their health were inextricably linked to their understanding of colonial rule.

This chapter focuses on the colonial period in sub-Saharan Africa, bookended by the 'Scramble for Africa' in the 1880s and the African independence movements of the 1950s and 1960s. It briefly charts the development of medical and scientific knowledge in the late nineteenth and early twentieth century, focusing on the nascent field of 'tropical medicine' and its uneven application in the African context. It examines key shifts in demographic and health indicators in Africa in this period, including the health impact of both world wars. It characterizes colonial state interventions in the realm of

African health, considering both its reach and its limits, as well as the range of African responses to these interventions. The role of missionary doctors in the medicalization of healing in Africa will be considered, as well as the contribution of African medical auxiliaries who served as vital intermediaries between local African healing systems and the colonial medical apparatus. Continuing Chapter 1's focus on African understandings of health and disease, this chapter outlines some key developments and patterns in local therapeutics and healing regimes under the confines of colonial rule. As will be seen, although the colonial period marked a profound shift in African polities and economies throughout much of the continent, the extent of transformation wrought within the realm of African healing is rather more difficult to assess.

Historicizing health and illness in colonial Africa: Sources and approaches

There is a fascinating historiography to the study of medicine and of colonialism in the African context (see Introduction). Some historians have fused the two themes together, arguing for the emergence of a distinctive, and coercive, 'colonial medicine' or 'imperial medicine'. However, as discussed earlier, our historical understanding and imagination of the interaction between medicine and colonial rule have themselves changed over time, in surprising and significant ways. The failure of the disease eradication model espoused by the World Health Organization, the emergence of infectious diseases such as HIV/ AIDS and Ebola, and the acknowledgement that medical science has not been able to evolve drugs and pesticides to keep pace with vector and pathogenic resistance have served to remove the lustre from the scientific achievements which coincided with the colonial period. Furthermore, a broader appreciation of social, ecological and economic factors (including social stress, environmental change, migration and poverty) which profoundly affected African health outcomes has further contributed to the widening of the historical gaze beyond the narrowly defined 'successes' of biomedical science. Finally, whilst it is vital to stress the predominant structure of control which characterized many colonial health interventions in sub-Saharan Africa, the wider historiography also reminds us that oppression cannot be the overarching narrative of African health experiences in this period. As will be seen, there were also African 'traditions' of resistance, adaptation and appropriation of colonial medicine, as well as alternative and internally derived healing ideologies, that are equally significant considerations when describing African responses to the changing health landscapes of this period.

As discussed in Chapter 1, the range of historical sources – archaeological, linguistic and textual – available to reconstruct pre-colonial African health practices, experiences and concepts is limited. In contrast, the colonial period is comparably rich in source material. European colonial governments, medical officers and their administrative apparatuses left a substantial paper trail on health-related matters, including ordinances, magistrate records, maps, correspondence, memoranda and circulars. Colonial hospitals and research institutes created a further set of records, while public campaigns around particular health 'crises' generated documentation on colonial responses to specific diseases. Whilst this **colonial archive** provides a seemingly unending wealth of material, the question remains to what extent we can use these sources to accurately gauge *African* understandings and experiences of health, disease and healing. In these accounts, European conceptual and narrative frameworks predominate, often (although not uniformly) casting Africans as 'subjects' of, or 'responding to', European initiatives and ideas.

Missionary accounts – including correspondence, mission society publications, logbooks, parish registers and journals – are in many ways more richly detailed than the colonial administrative archive on the subject of local healing systems and therapeutics. Mission stations were also more assiduous than the colonial state in terms of the recording of births and deaths within Christianizing African communities, and historians have subsequently taken advantage of the rich resource provided by parish baptism and marriage registers to reconstruct patterns of demographic change in specific regions, such as Shane Doyle's study of fertility and local responses to mortality in East Africa. However, missionaries' overarching aim of conversion meant that African healing systems tended to be cast in these accounts as something to be transformed rather than a complex to be dispassionately observed. Furthermore, as will be discussed later in this chapter, Christian mission stations until the interwar years became entwined with, or in some areas fully represented, the operation of colonial health services. The successful running of mission hospitals and dispensaries in African territories relied on overseas funding, which meant missionaries' appeals to donor communities in the West tended to be couched in language that would maximize potential donations. This impetus towards fundraising coloured missionary missives, which alternately emphasized the dire 'plight' of African helplessness in the face of overwhelming disease challenges, or expressed missionaries' own frustration at what appeared to be the wilful ignorance or even intransigence of Africans who refused the 'saving graces' of Western medical therapeutics.[1]

Colonial-era ethnographies of African societies comprise another textual archive that has only begun to be fully mined by medical historians. The field of anthropology experienced a rapid growth in this period, and the expansion of imperial boundaries across non-Western societies provided a fertile field on which aspiring anthropologists could record their observations of 'primitive' societies, even as colonialism itself threatened to utterly transform them. Many anthropologists in the early decades of the twentieth century responded to the urgency to record native institutions, cultures and rituals before they were irrevocably transformed by colonial rule and the machinations of colonial capitalism. However, anthropologists were also part of imperial administrations, called upon as 'native experts' on subjects as diverse as Islamic spirit cults and witchcraft, and were utilized to help develop policies on governing colonial territories. Colonial ethnographies are valuable sources for historians in recovering native cosmologies and spiritual healing practices, and many accounts are indeed rich stores of detail regarding local pharmacopeia, divination rites, and the characteristics of healers and healing hierarchies. However, these sources are not without their analytic challenges. In their efforts to capture 'native' culture and cosmology in its supposed 'pristine' form, many colonial anthropologists (perhaps inadvertently) often reified native institutions and practices, implicitly denying the possibility that indigenous cultures could, and did, change. Ethnographies also tended to depict rural societies rather than focus on the urban epicentres which had become in the colonial period dynamic cauldrons where global and local social and cultural forces met and mixed. With respect to the history of health and illness, then, the cosmopolitan health practices and perspectives of the sizeable and burgeoning urban African population remained hidden from view.

Oral sources represent an important primary source type that historians of the colonial period have utilized to supplement and contest the written archive. Oral testimonies of those who had lived during colonial rule have been particularly helpful in recreating the lived experience of the late colonial period, from the interwar period until the independence of African states in the 1950s and 1960s (recorded oral histories from an earlier period are few in number). These accounts have helped to provide an alternative and diverse narrative of African health practices and experiences to those penned by colonial administrators, medical men and missionaries. Yet, oral historical sources are not without their own analytic challenges. Oral accounts may offer contrasting and even conflicting testimonies about the same occurrence. The memories of elderly Africans who are asked to recall their experiences under colonial rule many decades after the fact may be selective, or have gaps. More importantly, oral accounts are, like written sources, products of the contemporary perspective and context of the narrator. While they may seek to convey an 'objective' recounting of the past, oral testimonies can also be profoundly influenced by the political or social imperatives of the present. Relatedly, while the overarching narrative of subjugation under 'colonial medicine' may certainly acknowledge a general truth about the experience of colonial rule, this dominant narrative can also obscure more subtle details of ways in which health remained a locally mediated, and negotiated, domain.

Tropical medicine: Trajectories and key features

The scientific developments underpinning germ theory and the emergence at the turn to the twentieth century of a new sub-field of medicine, called tropical medicine, transformed public health institutions and practices in sub-Saharan Africa and across the colonized world. Although some of the scientific breakthroughs to be discussed have their intellectual origins in earlier periods, the latter decades of the nineteenth century until the First World War witnessed the most significant discoveries. **A note of caution:** as mentioned in the Introduction, this period has been interpreted through a triumphalist lens associated with the 'rise' of biomedicine in the West. The conventional narrative presented is of transformation from quaint folk remedies and superstitious fears to clinical and dispassionate medical science – from a world of deadly miasma and swamps to one characterized by the laboratory, the microscope and rational scientific deduction. However, it is vital to perceive the limits of this over-simplified view.

First, the characterization of this period as one of revolutionary change tends to ignore that 'science' as a field and as a deductive process (what can be called the scientific method) informed *earlier* models of disease causation and control. Edward Jenner in 1798 definitively illustrated that exposing a healthy individual to a live strain of cowpox, itself a milder form of smallpox, could eventually induce the body to provide adequate immune protection when introduced to smallpox. As we know, however, Jenner's 'discovery' of vaccination could be better viewed as the validation of the long-standing local practice of variolation that had already been in widespread use in parts of India, the Middle East and Africa, and was transferred via the Middle Passage to the Americas by African slaves (see Chapter 1). Also, careful data collection, topographical observation and the utilization of quinine as prophylaxis and treatment resulted in some measurable reduction of malaria incidence among European soldiers in tropical Africa well before the full aetiology of malaria was scientifically understood.

Second, it is vital in the study of history to be wary of overly convenient 'dualisms', in this case the neat division between an objective and scientifically informed 'modern' versus an imagined, spiritually informed 'pre-modern'. Just as it is historically inaccurate to neglect the role of science in informing pre-germ theory notions of disease, it is equally inaccurate to suggest the emergence of biomedicine in the West has wholly replaced or subsumed earlier understandings, or that biomedical science was and is somehow uniquely devoid of culturally encoded discursive dimensions. As Megan Vaughan has argued in a critical intervention on the history and anthropology of medicine in Africa, medical science is neither monolithic nor homogenous, and should be interrogated as a site of social and symbolic meaning-making.[2] If science is not merely a set of factual observations but also entails a way of speaking about and explaining the world, then this allows for an understanding of how scientific frameworks could be so differently utilized and interpreted in the colonial African context – by medical officers, magistrates, missionaries and by Africans themselves.

A final pitfall in encapsulating this history as a singular and inexorably advancing trajectory is that it transposes a theory of progress that perhaps makes sense in terms of significantly reduced mortality and morbidity rates of European settlers and soldiers, but quickly loses validity when viewed against the health outcomes of African populations in this same period. Were Africans more healthy as a result of medical advances and interventions in this period? And by whose definition of health?

As seen in the previous chapter, European notions of disease causation in the tropics until the late nineteenth century were informed by theories which, to varying levels, linked the onset of disease to an imbalance located in human constitutions (humoral theory) or to threatening and uncontained local ecological conditions or environmental emanations (localism and miasma). The fundamental and novel contribution of germ theory was to locate disease causation at the *microscopic* level. Specifically, microscopic organisms or pathogens were identified as the primary determinants responsible for specific infections and contagious diseases. The essential additional element which helped define the new sub-field of tropical medicine was the discovery of 'vectors' and 'hosts' as key to the chain of disease transmission. Vectors are the agents that physically transfer a pathogen, whereas hosts act as incubators for the pathogen and are part of the micro-organism's life cycle development. Vectors and hosts could be drawn from the animal world – including insects such as flies and mosquitoes, rodents, and humans. A brief table highlights some key milestones in this period:

Timeline of milestones

1854   Filippo Pacini observes cholera bacillus (*Vibrio cholerae*)

1860s Louis Pasteur develops vaccines for rabies and anthrax

1879   Patrick Manson discovers the mosquito *Culex fatigans* as host and vector to elephantiasis (also called filariasis). Microscopic worms or *filariae* had been observed in the 1860s and 1870s by other scientists in France, Brazil and Japan

1882   Robert Koch discovers *Mycobacterium tuberculosis* as the causative agent for tuberculosis

1884   Robert Koch isolates and identifies cholera bacillus

1880   Charles Laveran identifies the protozoan which causes malaria, *Oscillaria malariae* (now called *Plasmodium falciparum*)

1881   Carlos Finlay identifies the mosquito species (now known as *Aedes aegypti*) as the vector for yellow fever parasite

1888   Louis Pasteur founds the Pasteur Institute

1894   Bacillus causing bubonic plague (now known as *Yersinia pestis*) identified by Kitasato Shibasaburo and Alexandre Yersin

1895   David Bruce identifies trypanosome parasite (*Trypanosome brucei*) which causes sleeping sickness in cattle and identifies tsetse fly as vector

1897   Ronald Ross demonstrates *Anopheles* mosquito is host and vector to malaria

1898   Manson publishes *Tropical Diseases: A Manual of the Diseases of Warm Climates*; Liverpool School of Tropical Medicine is founded; rat connection for bubonic plague identified by Alexandre Yersin; Paul Louis-Simond identifies flea as vector for bubonic plague bacillus

1899   Patrick Manson founds London School of Tropical Medicine

1902   Joseph Dutton identifies parasite which causes human trypanosomiasis (*Trypanosome gambiense*)

1903   David Bruce identifies *Glossina* tsetse fly as vector for human trypanosome parasite and concludes sleeping sickness is caused by trypanosoma

1909   Friedrich Kleine observes the cyclical development of *Trypanosome brucei* in tsetse fly

Viewed in retrospect, this catalogue of discoveries could be read as a steady progression of pillars constructing the edifice of germ theory. However, it is important to emphasize that scientists active in this period did not necessarily envision a final 'blueprint' or outcome of their respective research agendas. Scientists focused on specialized, and sometimes isolated facets of disease, and several years could pass before the full development and transmission chain – or, its 'aetiology' – for a disease could be conclusively established. This can be seen in the timeline for trypanosomiasis, a particularly complex disease to unravel. Furthermore, some 'discoveries' were not accepted readily by the global scientific community, such as Filippo Pacini's work on the cholera bacillus which pre-dated by three decades Robert Koch's findings, and had to be re-discovered or legitimized in subsequent published research. Local knowledge could also pre-date scientific observations, or even lead to them – famously, David Livingstone suggested that testse flies were connected to animal trypanosomiasis more than four decades before David Bruce confirmed the fly as a vector; also, the rat connection to plague identified by Yersin already had been postulated as a disease 'of the rats' in local parlance in China, India and Taiwan.

An important characteristic of scientific endeavour in this period was its **global dimension**, defined by intertwined trans-national scholarly networks and aided by a relatively high speed of information flow: for example, German bacteriologist Robert Koch's second report on quinine treatment for malaria in 1899 was published by *Deutsche medizinishe Wochenschrift* for their 1 February 1900 edition. By the 10th of February, it was already translated and published in the *British Medical Journal*.[3] In the age of 'slow' media communication, this was very rapid indeed. Although many of the breakthroughs in this period highlighted European endeavour – with Italian, French, British and Dutch scientists in close interaction with each other – Asian scientists such as Kitasato from Japan were key contributors. Moreover, many European scientists conducted their lab-based research from outposts in colonial or formerly colonial territories, such as India, Vietnam, Algeria and China, and it was the disease environments in these locations that provided essential empirical data which led to the 'birth' of the field of tropical medicine. Furthermore, the continued development and establishment of tropical medicine in the early decades of the twentieth century – whether through the commissioning of cross-border scientific expeditions or through the creation of more permanent field-based research stations to investigate tropical diseases and experiment with potential interventions – relied on both inter-territorial collaboration and communication across imperial regimes (see Chapter 6).

Examining more closely the history of developing understandings on malaria can reveal some of the dynamics as well as limitations of scientific knowledge production in this period. In 1880, Charles Laveran, a French scientist stationed in a hospital in Constantine, Algeria, identified the protozoan that caused malaria. However, because of his geographical remoteness from the scientific community dominated by Pasteur and others, he was not certain of the credibility of his own discovery. The parasite *Oscillaria malariae*, now known as *Plasmodium falciparum*, presented specific difficulties with respect to verification under 'Koch's postulates', which had gained widespread currency by the 1880s. These postulates stated that in order to prove disease causation by a specific organism, one needed to first establish the presence of the organism, be able to grow that organism outside the human body, and then reproduce the disease experimentally in a healthy body. Koch's postulates worked seamlessly for bacterial infections that could be grown in artificial laboratory conditions. This was not the case for *Oscillaria malariae*. Further research needed to be done to establish the complex aetiology of this disease.

Later work that same decade by Richard, Golgi and Marchiafava built on Laveran's initial findings. Richard observed the effect the protozoan had on red corpuscles in the blood. Golgi and Marchiafava helped to describe the full life cycle of the protozoan, and linked stages of this lifecycle to the onset of clinical symptoms in the human, in particular the development of fever. Still, the problem of transmission remained – how did these organisms enter human hosts? The British scientist Patrick Manson, buoyed by his own discovery in 1879 that the mosquito was both the vector and host of elephantiasis – a physically debilitating disease caused by a worm-like parasite which results in enormous swelling of the limbs – encouraged Ronald Ross, who was then a forty-year-old British surgeon-major stationed in India, to conduct experiments on mosquitoes. Of particular relevance was Manson's observation that the parasite which caused elephantiasis underwent vital development in the stomach and chest of the mosquito. That is, the mosquito was not only the carrier of the parasite but was integral to its development. Ronald Ross was able to verify the presence of malarial parasites in the stomach of mosquitoes. He was also able to observe that specific pigmented cells developed and migrated in the stomach, moving from the stomach cavity into the wall. He saw that the pigmented cells ruptured and released spindle-shaped 'germinal rods', which were also found in a set of glands near the head of the mosquito. These glands were connected to the mosquito's proboscis that penetrated the skin, which is how the malarial parasite could enter a human body. Ross further showed that this type of pigmented cells was in only one genus of mosquito, the dapple-winged *Anopheles*.

This discovery of the aetiology of malaria showcased the global and collective endeavour of scientific research in this period and led to the prestige of a Nobel Prize in 1902 for Ronald Ross, and in 1907 for Charles Laveran. Patrick Manson was appointed as the British Colonial Office Medical Advisor in 1897, signalling a key early connection between the scientific expert community and colonial governance structures. Manson came to be known as the 'father' of the field of tropical medicine, signified by the publication of the *Manual of Tropical Diseases* in 1898. Ross and Manson soon sat at the helm of new institutions which were pioneers in their field, the Liverpool School of Tropical Medicine (founded in 1898) and the London School of Tropical Medicine (founded in 1899), which furthered their international reputations and drew in many of the brightest and most ambitious scientists into their schools' orbits. Funding for new expeditions, many based in African colonial territories, soon followed. As will be seen, tropical medicine developed beyond its initial confines as a field of scientific enquiry into a tool of health governance, and one intimately connected to Empire.

Before a consideration of the *application* of tropical medicine in the colonial African context, it is important to note a few key characteristics. The dynamic advances in the field were punctuated by significant gaps and **incomplete knowledge** of diseases and their aetiologies, which had significant consequences for the design of disease prevention and treatment initiatives. Patrick Manson, in the preface to the first edition of *Tropical Diseases: A Manual of the Diseases of Warm Climates* (1898), modestly stated his intention was to produce a 'handy size' manual which provided 'adequate information' on diseases of 'warm climates'. Manson's *Manual* was circulated widely and soon became standard issue for colonial officials and health personnel working in tropical regions. Yet, there are inconsistencies and scientific gaps evident in this seminal work. Manson distinguishes so-called tropical diseases from others by the importance of warm climates in supporting 'transmitting media' (parasites) and 'transmitting animals' (vectors) that can only survive at specific temperatures. Most of the diseases included in the first edition certainly fell into this category. However, both leprosy and

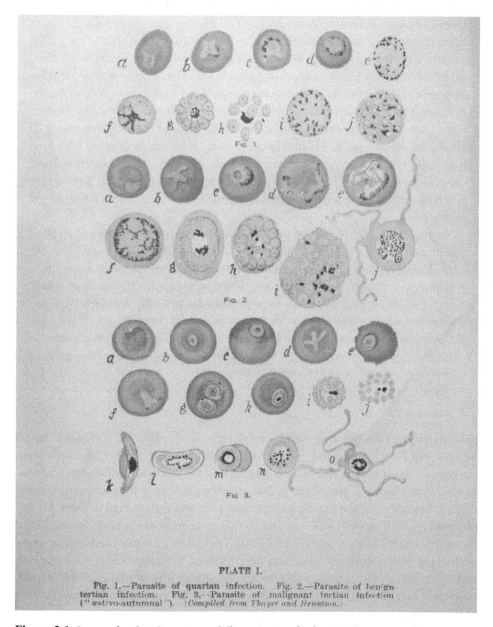

PLATE I.

Fig. 1.—Parasite of quartan infection. Fig. 2.—Parasite of benign tertian infection. Fig. 3.—Parasite of malignant tertian infection ("æstivo-autumnal"). [Compiled from Thayer and Hewetson.]

Figure 2.1 Image of malarial parasite at different stages of infection, Plate 1. Patrick Manson, *Tropical Diseases: A Manual of the Diseases of Warm Climates*, first edition (London: Cassell & Co., Ltd, 1898).

Historical Source: Image of malarial parasite, Plate 1, from
Patrick Manson, *Tropical Diseases: A Manual of the Diseases of
Warm Climates* (1898)

*Source Analysis: Although the subtitle of the Manual may have appeared to the
casual reader of the time that Manson was nodding to the persistence of humoral
theory, which considered warm temperatures an 'exciting' cause of disease, the simple
act of opening the book would reveal its very different conceptual orientation. Called
'Plate 1' and situated opposite the title page of the Manual, this was a set of other-
worldly illustrations of infection-causing parasites at various stages of their lifecycles.
Manson's set of illustrations of the microscopic world put the focus on 'germs' explicitly,
in this case the malarial parasite at different stages of development. He wrote, 'Modern
science has clearly shown that nearly all diseases, directly or indirectly, are caused by
germs. It must be confessed that although in many instances these germs have been
discovered, in other instances they are yet to find; nevertheless, their existences in the
latter may be confidently postulated.' Manson had profound faith that germ theory
was both the explanator for all currently known diseases and the cause of diseases 'yet
to find'.*

*In many ways the Manual's plate of illustrations was to have as profound an effect
on our understanding of the natural world as Carl Linnaeus's simple set of illustrations
of plant classifications in the 18th century. Its value as a historical source lies in how it
succinctly and through visual means overturned prevailing scientific understanding,
and helped to set the research agenda for decades to come. However, Manson's
illustration also revealed tropical medicine's emblematic focus on, and fascination
for, microbes. This narrow approach has been critiqued for its focus on microbes at
the expense of wider, ecological and social understandings of the interaction between
microbes, insect and animal vectors, and humans.*

bubonic plague were included even though neither fit into the 'warm climates' model
Manson put forward, and the geographical reach of both diseases historically went
far beyond the tropics. Even malaria was historically a disease which was endemic
in temperate regions of the world, despite it being considered the archetypal tropical
disease. Furthermore, the genetic adaptations to malaria that evolved in some African
populations, such as sickle cell trait and Duffy's antigen, would not be identified until
the mid-twentieth century (see Chapter 6). This meant that the nature and extent of the
underlying 'Native immunity' to fevers first observed by Europeans in the eighteenth
and nineteenth centuries were inaccurately understood for most of the colonial period,
and would have implications on the development of malaria research and the application
of control measures.

The popularity and utility of the *Manual of Tropical Diseases* were evident in the
frequent publication of new editions. By the fourth edition, in 1907, the *Manual* had

to be thoroughly revised and enlarged to keep up with the pace of discoveries. By 1921 in the preface to the seventh edition of the *Manual,* the editor was compelled to state that 'much that before was vague and hypothetical has become precise and been either confuted or confirmed'.[4]

Colonial health policies, missionary medicine and infectious disease control up to the First World War

When imperial powers assumed widespread control over the continent in the late nineteenth century, the African disease environment was both dynamic and disquieting. A series of rinderpest epidemics in the latter half of the century had devastated cattle herds in southern and East Africa, impoverishing agro-pastoralist societies and creating famine conditions in some areas. High cattle mortality was also a factor (although not understood at the time) in severe outbreaks of sleeping sickness in the 1890s and early 1900s. In East and Central Africa, sleeping sickness was a particularly deadly disease, with the decimation of local populations observed by missionaries and colonial officials. Severe drought in parts of East and southern Africa in the 1880s and 1890s led to famine which in turn exacerbated the risks of disease in vulnerable famine-stricken populations. An epidemic of smallpox in East Africa in the 1890s was likely precipitated by famine condition. The Fifth Pandemic of cholera in the 1890s affected Ethiopia and the Senegambia region, brought on via mobile trans-Mediterranean and Saharan trading routes. While some African communities came to intimately associate these disease shocks with the onset of colonial rule, colonial administrations and health officials sought to re-make African environments in response.

Sanitary segregation and urban planning

In 1900 in the midst of the Anglo-Boer War (1899–1902), the first South African cases of bubonic plague were reported in Cape Town amongst the city's Coloured and African dockworkers, eventually spreading to the other major port city in Cape Colony, Port Elizabeth. By the early 1900s, the aetiology of bubonic plague was scientifically understood – the bacterium causing bubonic plague had been identified, and the rat-flea connection underpinning its transmission had been unlocked. Moreover, preliminary statistics on plague victims showed it had infected individuals from all racial groups in the urban areas of the Colony. Yet, instead of instituting measures to destroy the rat or flea vectors, urban medical authorities enacted forced removals and destructive quarantine measures which did not map in any logical way to the actual demographic distribution of disease in affected areas. In Port Elizabeth, the houses of Africans were quarantined and their possessions burned, but white-owned shops where workers had contracted the plague were not destroyed. In Cape Town, black Africans were targeted by the municipal plague administration and forcibly removed to a hastily established

'Native location' named Ndabeni on the city's periphery, even though the Coloured population had a larger numerical incidence of the plague.

Bubonic plague occurred at a time when political insecurity, and heightened migration and urbanization were changing the social and demographic landscape of South African cities. The epidemic of plague, as epidemics are wont to do, served to catalyse these underlying tensions, and African settlement in urban areas came to be viewed by colonial authorities as a key threat to public health and associated with disease. This emerging discourse of sanitation predominated over other potentially more effective public health framings of disease challenges, and was utilized to motivate and enact increasingly racialized forms of urban segregation. In response to an outbreak of bubonic plague in Dakar in 1914, French colonial officials and municipal health officers instituted a policy of *cordon sanitaire* which in theory attempted to isolate and quarantine infected from the non-infected, but in practice operated to segregate the resident African population by relocating Africans to a newly created 'village de segregation', later renamed the Medina.[5] The 'sanitation syndrome' – as Maynard Swanson termed it – that afflicted municipal plague administrators in the Cape and in Dakar is an example of the **uneven integration** of emerging medical and scientific knowledge with colonial practice.[6] Or put in a slightly different manner, colonial responses to health dilemmas in Africa in this period were on the whole *inconsistent* with existing medical knowledge at the time.

This inconsistency was underlined by a **lack of scientific consensus** on the design of appropriate interventions to address disease transmission and treatment. Ronald Ross distinguished himself by identifying the *Anopheles* mosquito that was host and vector to malaria. Yet, even he initially did not support the screening of windows to stop mosquitoes from entering buildings, believing a moving current of air through houses would help repel mosquitoes and keep the body temperature cool, thus helping the body retain its 'natural energy'. This shows the persistence of older ideas of disease causation, which linked disease to bodily 'predisposition', even amongst the vanguard in the field of tropical medicine.

Even as the aetiology of many diseases became more commonly accepted, there was a lack of coherence around whether parasites, vectors or humans were the appropriate 'target' of control, and which prevention, containment or eradication measures should be applied. Different 'schools' of thought in the early 1900s were backed by clinical- and field-based research, and disseminated via powerful institutional networks and colonial administrative channels. Robert Ross came to favour aggressive vector eradication through the drainage of anopheline mosquito breeding pools and the use of larvicides, while Patrick Manson advocated mosquito screens and individual behavioural changes, including the regular use of bed nets and regular quinine dosage.[7] Their differing recommendations were in part responsible for the wide variation in sanitary segregation measures adopted by colonial administrations in West Africa. Robert Koch championed mass 'quininization' in German East Africa, involving widespread surveillance measures and subsequent treatment with quinine of those found with malaria – the object being to reduce the virus reservoir across a given population and thus confer preventative benefits to that group. This 'treatment as prevention' approach came to be known as

'Koch's method' and was applied to other infectious disease contexts in subsequent decades.[8]

By examining the colonial state's expanding utilization of sanitary segregation measures in the early decades of the twentieth century in response to different infectious diseases, this inconsistency can be seen at work. Urban planning measures in West Africa were particularly preoccupied with the 'problem' of malaria control, yet the 'solutions' advocated bore an uneven relation to the developing knowledge on the aetiology of malaria. In 1904 in Sierra Leone, the British established Hill Station as a European-only settlement. The location of Hill Station 750 feet above sea level was premised on an earlier colonial 'Indian model', which had utilized altitude as the primary mechanism to deter malaria. Furthermore, the striking architectural feature of Hill Station housing – capacious wooden structures built on stilts – was based on the perceived preventative benefits of promoting moving currents of air through, and under, the structure. Indeed, in 1906 in response to a British Colonial Office circular to West African governors asking what was the best housing design for European residences, screens for windows were largely seen as an impediment to the healthful ventilation of homes rather than a helpful physical barrier against mosquitoes' entry.[9] Unsurprisingly, neither the establishment of Hill Station nor the design of its homes resulted in the ending of malaria incidence amongst Europeans settled there.

Historical Source: Sanitary Report on the City of Freetown for the year 1899 by Dr William Prout, Medical Officer of Health.

I have the honour to submit for the information of His Worship the mayor, the councillors and citizens of Freetown my annual report on the Sanitary Department and the health of the city for the year ending December 1899.

I regret again to commence my report with the statement that sanitary progress has been practically at a stand still during the year and with the exception of the provision of more market accommodation by the opening of the Krootown Road Market, matters so far as sanitation is concerned remain in status quo and the long roll of deaths is undiminished. The large expenditure which would be involved in such an extensive scheme as the disposal of sewage, and the water supply, are no doubt factors which lend to delay and render it necessary that the schemes should receive careful consideration, but there are few signs that the councillors and the general public are alive to the gravity of the present sanitary condition of the city, or the dangers which will arise to all should the germs of some epidemic disease such as cholera or bubonic plague be introduced into our midst. I have no desire to pose as an alarmist, but there can be no doubt that the introduction of any such disease would be fraught with appalling results and would decimate the population. I am glad to be able to state that the suggestion which I made last year that the reports should be printed for the information and education of the general public is being carried out, and I trust that the public will then be awakened to the very insanitary condition of the city and will be prepared to have steps taken to remedy it. If we are to have health, we must make up our minds to pay for it.

Source Analysis: This 'sanitary report' on Freetown, Sierra Leone, was part of an annual reckoning by the chief medical officer of municipal public hygiene measures, and can be viewed as an assessment of the city's general health preparedness. This particular report decries the lack of awareness by both the general public and Councillors as to the 'gravity of the present sanitation condition of the city'. In unflinching terms, Prout predicts that such apathy to instituting sanitation schemes including sewage disposal and water supply would yield 'appalling results' when epidemic disease would overwhelm and 'decimate' the population. It concludes, though, on a more hopeful note by suggesting the tide of public opinion could be turned through a concerted information and education campaign.

Archival sources such as this report provide a window onto the procedural mechanisms at work in colonial and municipal health administration. It also reveals how anxieties could be voiced within this process – in this case, fears of imminent decimation from epidemic disease. Interestingly, the report mentions cholera and bubonic plague, rather than tropical diseases (such as malaria) which would come to predominate discussions of urban sanitary measures in Sierra Leone as well as other West African colonies. Furthermore, Prout's report reveals concerns over the public purse to address necessary sanitary interventions: 'If we are to have health, we must make up our minds to pay for it.' Crown colonies had to be self-supporting and did not automatically receive funds from the metropole for health and sanitation projects. The provision of appropriate financial and human resources was to be a continuing tension in the application of disease control and sanitation measures in the colonial African context into the twentieth century.

The colonial medical recommendation to form racialized 'sanitary corridors' in areas with a large number of European residents in some colonial territories of West Africa appears to be a curious amalgam of earlier contagion theory, transposed elements from the Indian colonial context, and the addition of newly emerging understandings of mosquitoes as vectors of disease. Troublingly, in this admixture Africans were implicated as 'disease carriers' even as mosquitoes' role in disease transmission was acknowledged. Indeed, this shift in the early twentieth century from perceiving Africans as possessing 'Native immunity' to being innate 'disease reservoirs' was one that was replicated in other imperial contexts, including the Philippines under American occupation.[10] These sanitary corridors were of questionable efficacy, particularly as they relied on incomplete understandings of the potential flight ranges and feeding habits of anopheline mosquitoes. For example, the Governor of the Gold Coast Matthew Nathan received considerable input from Ronald Ross and a team from the Liverpool School of Tropical

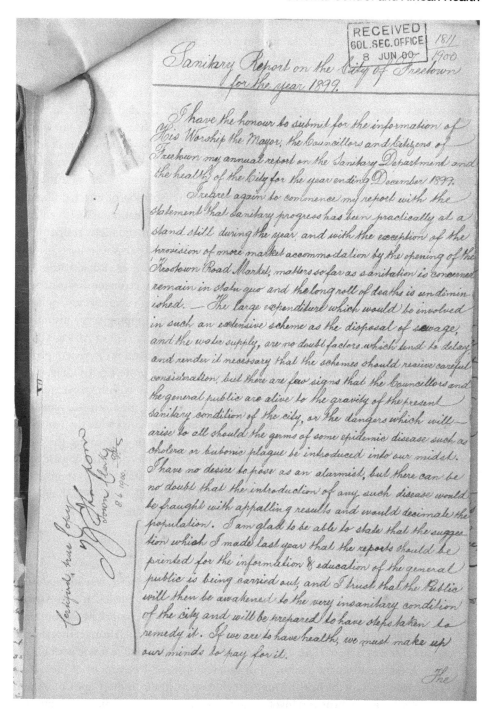

Figure 2.2 Sanitary Report on the City of Freetown for the year 1899 by Dr William Prout. Colonial Secretary's Office minute papers, Sierra Leone Public Records Office, CSO MP 1900/1811.

Medicine in 1902 on mosquito eradication measures. Yet, Nathan and his successor John Rodger imposed sweeping slum clearance measures, relocated African households, and instituted broad sanitary cordons around European residential areas.[11]

Similar contradictory processes were at work in early colonial responses to trypanosomiasis (sleeping sickness). As indicated in the timeline above, the parasite which causes one form of human trypanosomiasis was isolated in 1902, a major breakthrough in a disease with a notably complex aetiology. The evolving knowledge on sleeping sickness was unevenly applied in colonial responses to an outbreak in the Uele district in the Belgian Congo. Based on the recommendations of an expedition from the Liverpool School of Tropical Medicine, the Belgian colonial state in 1903 instituted a policy of *cordon sanitaire* which involved the isolation of infected humans into *lazarets* – essentially, isolation camps – and the close regulation and surveillance of Congolese movement. The scientific basis for these recommendations rested on an incomplete understanding of the disease's aetiology – the tsetse fly's role as vector and host to the trypanosome was only effectively established by 1909. Ronald Ross had advised isolation as a preventative measure for sleeping sickness, erroneously postulating that sleeping sickness was transmitted person-to-person through sharing close quarters at night. This policy was not only generally ineffective at stopping trypanosomiasis transmission. It had deleterious knock-on effects – up to 30 per cent of Africans given injection treatments in these *lazarets* were blinded, and the 'prison-style' system proved to be highly destabilizing and led to riots in some *lazarets* in protest.[12] Although some reform of this disastrous initial policy was instituted from 1910 with improvements in the living conditions of *lazarets* and efforts to clear tsetse bush, questions still remained as to why the Belgian state chose to focus on the isolation of humans rather than on other vector/host control strategies, for example, containing cattle or eradicating the tsetse fly. Indeed, the coercive character of colonial control strategies for sleeping sickness epidemics in the early 1900s was not limited to the Belgian state – in response to a particularly devastating epidemic around the Lake Victoria region, the British enacted forced removals of entire communities in the Uganda Protectorate.

Sexual health and venereal disease control

The control of venereal disease, or sexually transmitted disease (STD), was another early and significant preoccupation of the colonial health apparatus, particularly in African territories with a sizeable white settler population. Prostitutes comprised a prominent and visible target of these early control measures. In British-held African territories, the Contagious Diseases Acts of 1864, 1866 and 1869 created a legislative framework for the surveillance, examination and treatment of venereal disease. Derivations of these Acts followed in many parts of the British Empire, including Australia, India, Cape Colony and Kenya. Implementation measures involved the registration and periodic examination of prostitutes and others deemed vulnerable to venereal disease. If found to be infected, patients could then be held for several months in a hospital containing a locked venereal ward. In the colonial context, the Acts newly empowered police and district surgeons to round up 'syphilitics' and confine them for treatment. In the Cape this criminalization of venereal disease was reinforced by the creation of separate 'lock hospitals' alongside or within prisons, as was the case in colonial India. The crude treatment and inspection measures undertaken by doctors in lock hospitals spurred protests by detained patients, and even rioting in Cape Town. Rumours circulated about patients mysteriously dying in lock wards, which further deterred Africans from seeking treatment.[13] While not subject to a defined legislative apparatus as in British territories, in French West Africa similar mechanisms of control over STDs were enacted through a mandate by the governor-general requiring the surveillance, detainment and treatment of prostitutes.

Contagious disease policies were formulated and enforced in the late nineteenth century, when incomplete knowledge of venereal disease transmission and symptomatology made both diagnosis and treatment fraught with potential errors. Venereal syphilis was a particularly complex disease to identify in the African context – colonial health officials confused venereal syphilis with yaws and a milder endemic form of syphilis, both of which were non-sexually transmitted and were prevalent in southern and eastern Africa (see Chapter 4). Importantly, these misperceptions could result in a particular form of discursive pathologizing of Africans, not dissimilar to the trajectory observed in the shift from 'Native immunity' to Africans as innate 'disease carriers'. In South Africa in the late nineteenth century, 'pure' Africans were thought to be free from syphilis, believed instead to predominantly affect Hottentots, Bushmen and so-called half-castes. However, as Karen Jochelson has shown, from 1910 an alternative discourse emerged which suggested that Africans as a whole had become 'syphilized' to such an extent that their symptoms differed markedly from other racial groups with the same disease. This 'syphilization' thesis obscured the very real possibility that the different manifestation of symptoms was because different diseases – endemic versus venereal syphilis – had caused them.[14]

Missionary medicine and the colonial enterprise

Mission Christianity occupied a liminal space between the colonial apparatus on the one hand and ordinary African social relations and institutions on the other. This by extension meant that 'missionary medicine' in both practice and theory reflected colonial aspirations and ideologies, but in certain ways contested them as well. In order to understand the role of missionary medicine, the wider question of the place of mission Christianity in the colonial enterprise needs to be interrogated. The central question for debate in historical scholarship has been 'Were mission stations, and missionaries, "agents" of colonialism?', and relatedly 'Did Africans view and experience mission Christianity as such?'

There are several characteristics inherent to the history of mission Christianity in Africa to acknowledge when answering this central question. First, we should consider the *scale* of mission involvement. As seen in the previous chapter, the missionary imprint in Africa was evident from as early as the sixteenth century. However, from the late eighteenth century, missionary activity in Africa increased and became more pronounced and visible across the long nineteenth century, partially due to improving health outcomes of Europeans in tropical regions (see Chapter 1). By the late nineteenth century, Christian mission stations were an established presence in many African territories, particularly in rural areas where nascent colonial administrative networks did not reach. The colonial context also fundamentally altered the social and political dynamics between missionaries and local populations, which had earlier been based more on compromise and negotiation between missionaries and local political elites.

Second, the centrality of the calling to effect spiritual conversion necessitated a level of *intimacy* of missionaries' involvement in the everyday lives of Africans – missionaries tended to live in the communities they served, often for years at a time. They understood the power of language in absorbing the teachings of the Bible, and undertook, if not always successfully, to communicate with and preach in the local vernacular. Third, missionaries tended to be interested in all aspects of African social and economic lives – agriculture, fertility, rituals, marital relationships – not least because they recognized conversion as involving the fundamental re-ordering of a convert's spiritual and social universe. Fourth, although missionaries could not divorce themselves entirely from the colonial and highly racialized frameworks within which they operated, the task of conversion did allow them to focus on Africans as individuals.

Given this historical context, how can the nature of *missionary medicine* in colonial Africa be understood? It is important to consider that the model of missionaries as trained medical men, in the guise of David Livingston (see Chapter 1), was not the rule. Often, missionary 'medics' were given rudimentary training in basic medicine and equipped with a simple bag of medical supplies. In southern Africa, one estimate suggests that 'missionary medicine' as a knowledge complex consistently lagged behind the latest medical advances circulating in Europe by about twenty years, due in part to the geographical remoteness of some of the mission stations as well as the lack of medical training of missionary personnel.[15] Furthermore, from 1900 colonial medical officers began to receive training in tropical medicine from the London School of Tropical Medicine and the Liverpool School of Tropical Medicine, widening the gap in specialist medical expertise between missionary medics and their colonial counterparts.[16]

Despite this gap, colonial administrations throughout sub-Saharan Africa often relied on the dispersed network of mission stations to deliver medical care, particularly in the early decades of colonial rule. Indeed, a recognizable form of missionary medicine preceded the establishment of colonial rule, particularly in parts of East and southern Africa. As discussed earlier in this chapter, colonial state preoccupations in this period tended to coalesce around the containment and management of particular infectious diseases, such as malaria, sleeping sickness, syphilis and, to a lesser extent, bubonic plague. Colonial officials and scientists involved in sleeping sickness expeditions in Central and East Africa in the early decades of the twentieth century called upon the local knowledge of missionaries to report outbreaks as well as gather potentially infected Africans to participate in surveillance and diagnostic interventions (see Chapter 6). Also, the views of missionaries on African sexuality and sexual behaviour were integrated, although not unproblematically, into the design of colonial anti-syphilis campaigns in East and southern Africa, particularly in Uganda where the role of missionary Albert Cook and the hospital he established at Mengo Mission Station in 1897 became influential across a range of health-related matters (see Chapter 4).

Moreover, outside of these targeted 'crisis' areas which received comparably high levels of scientific, administrative and financial resources, the operation of colonial 'public health' in Africa faced chronic underfunding and staffing limitations. Mission station hospitals and dispensaries became in many territories the primary colonial space through which African health needs were observed and treated. Arguably, mission medicine in practice was a more 'horizontal' form of healthcare provisioning, as medics were embedded in the African communities they served. Certain diseases such as leprosy became the distinctive 'preserve' of missionary medicine, due to leprosy's particular pathophysiology and the extended commitment of time and personnel required for treatment.[17] 'Leper colonies' administered by mission institutions were an important feature of colonial Nigeria, Tanganyika (now Tanzania) and Nyasaland (now Malawi), although in French-controlled West African territories leprosaria were firmly part of the state's medical apparatus.[18] The separation of church and state in France in 1904 ensured the more secular character of colonial health administration in its African territories, and Christian missionaries in French-held territories were, in comparison to Anglophone and Belgian contexts, relatively peripheral to shaping healthcare provisioning and the health decision-making of colonized subjects.

Missionaries' more intimate involvement in and understanding of African social and spiritual lives may have also meant that mission medics saw each health-related encounter as an opportunity for dialogue with African patients. However, combining conversion aspirations with therapeutic ones plagued missionary attempts to distinguish their 'medicine' from African medicine.[19] Africans saw, correctly, that missionaries' framing of their medical treatments was part of a larger system of beliefs – missionaries probably did not help their cause by alluding to medical imagery in their religious preaching, or by insisting on proselytizing when offering clinical care. This in some ways undermined the scientific basis of mission medicine, which meant that in these instances Western medicine was seen by African patients as an extension of Western cultural and spiritual ideas.

This analytic slippage would help account for the flexibility with which Africans regarded and responded to mission medicine – through accepting specific 'cures' without acknowledging the overall primacy of Western medicine, or by taking the medical treatment proffered without accepting the message of Christian salvation that went with it. However, certain medical technologies were regarded by local populations in southern and East Africa as significant – and sometimes awe-inspiring – therapeutic innovations, such as the surgical removal of cataracts and tumours, and were generally well received.[20]

In British colonial territories, the influence of missionary medicine generally declined by the 1940s, as colonial medical services increased their capacity and reach, formalized medical practices and qualifications, and built new hospitals and clinics in areas previously serviced only by mission stations. There were important exceptions – for example, in Tanganyika even at the end of the colonial period mission-run hospitals and dispensaries treated over 40 per cent of the over 11 million out-patients seen in 1959.[21] However, overall, the Christian mission's lasting impact on African health was arguably less to do with their medical services to local African populations and more about their critical contributions in other realms. First, mission education provided an avenue for a small cadre of Africans to enter into health professions, whether as medical auxiliaries (discussed later in this chapter) or, increasingly into the mid-twentieth century, as doctors, nurses and midwives. As will be seen in the following chapter, the career trajectory of a generation of African medical professionals was shaped by early education in missionary institutions. Second, the mission emphasis on reforming and restructuring African sexual, gender and social relations left a lasting legacy on the form and meaning of sexual and reproductive health in the African context. Mission reforms in this intimate arena would persist into the post-colonial period, and the missionary imprint on the erasure of local forms of African sexual regulation – for example, male circumcision and 'intracrural' sexual play practices – would have a bearing on HIV transmission patterns in the twenty-first century (see Chapter 4).

War and African health in the colonial period

The South African War (1899–1902) was ostensibly a colonial war fought between the British state and the Afrikaner republics, although it should also be considered a civil war involving white Anglophone and Afrikaner settlers, as well as Africans and Coloureds as combatants and labourers. This drawn-out war was costly – by the end of the war upwards of £200 million had been spent in the British war effort, a sum so outrageous that it stoked the anger of the British taxpayer and eventually led to the withdrawal of imperial power in South Africa and the creation of the Union of South Africa in 1910. The human toll was even more significant. Communicable diseases such as typhoid, a bacterial disease transmitted in poor sanitary conditions, found a ready foothold in the barracks and military compounds of the British, resulting in a high case-mortality rate amongst British troops. Adequate hygiene measures were not enforced by military authorities, who did not understand the link between sanitation and disease prevention. In addition, Boer commandoes effectively disrupted transport lines in the country, which prevented vital food and supplies from reaching ill soldiers. Mary Kingsley, who was famously able to withstand the 'malarious air' of West Africa (see Chapter 1), died of typhoid in 1900 while volunteering to nurse captive Boer prisoners-of-war in a camp in Cape Town. Diseases also ravaged captive civilian populations in British concentration camps, where nearly 28,000 Afrikaner women and children died of dysentery, measles and other diseases. It is further estimated that 16,000 Africans who were also interned during the war died.[22] This civilian death toll was striking, and served to foment deep and lasting fissures in South African society as well as help catalyze a nascent Afrikaner nationalism fashioned in part through the rhetoric of redressing the injustices of the past.

During the First World War, sub-Saharan Africa was an important theatre of combat. Allies attacked German ports in German colonies along West, southern and East

African coasts, including territories covering present-day Togo, Cameroon, Namibia and Tanzania. Allies succeeded in taking these territories but not without a considerable struggle, particularly in East Africa. Africans were an integral part of warfare during the First World War, as soldiers but numerically more significant as porters and labourers. African labourers were by and large abysmally paid and fed, carried heavy artillery and supplies, and were easily susceptible to infectious diseases that could be transmitted as they trekked through new and unfamiliar territory. Estimates suggest that 165,000 Africans died in the war effort.[23] Although it is not known how many of these 165,000 fallen had died of diseases, since reliable statistics were not taken of non-European participants, historians hypothesize that the majority died from infectious diseases such as malaria or sleeping sickness. Thousands of Indians utilized by Allied forces in East Africa died as well – they were erroneously thought to be naturally immune to malaria but were not immune to the more virulent and deadly strain of *Plamosdium falciparum* endemic to East Africa. Indeed, although European troop mortality due to malaria declined significantly over the course of the nineteenth century, it remained a significant cause of death throughout the First World War.

The mass movement of troops across vast distances, enabled by more modern forms of transport, communication and technology, hastened processes of disease exchange. In East Africa, a significant theatre of combat, tuberculosis, malaria, bilharzia and various types of venereal diseases spread as a result of wartime mobility and social disruption.[24] The course of the devastating 'Spanish influenza' pandemic of 1918–19 certainly followed these more dynamic and far-reaching patterns of movement. There was virtually no region in the world that influenza did not touch, including the United States and Caribbean, Europe, East and Southeast Asia, Africa, Australia and New Zealand. It was a truly global pandemic. Different strains of influenza developed rapidly, which stymied efforts to develop protection and treatment measures. It is estimated that the Spanish flu killed about 25–40 million people in the span of about a year and a half. Its phenomenal and rapid movement across the globe, extraordinarily high mortality rate, and its particular demographic impact – disproportionately striking the young adult cohort aged between twenty and forty-five years – distinguished Spanish influenza from other infectious diseases, which normally hit hardest the elderly and the very young.

Historians continue to debate mortality and morbidity rates of the Spanish influenza pandemic because the lack of international coordination at the time has left a legacy of patchy data, none more so than the data on influenza's impact in sub-Saharan Africa. Recent estimates indicate that flu mortality on the continent reached a total of 2.2 million Africans, about 2.3 per cent of the approximate total population. These deaths were concentrated in a few territories – South Africa, Tanganyika, Kenya, Nyasaland, Cameroon, Gold Coast, Gambia were the most seriously affected, with mortality rates in some of these areas estimated at greater than 5 per cent.[25] The demographic impact of flu mortality on African populations is beginning to be understood, although this is still limited by a lack of firm consensus on not only flu morbidity but also population figures in colonial African territories in this period. Despite the immense global death toll of the flu pandemic, until recently the field of medical history has been relatively silent on the subject. Recent research which addresses the African experience of the flu pandemic has begun to address this silence, although these studies tend to be limited geographically in scope to specific countries or territories.

Violence can create conditions ripe for other sorts of ecological and social disasters, especially famine, by preventing Africans from planting and harvesting in season, and taking away valuable labour normally utilized for agricultural purposes. Conflict also disrupts the implementation of pre-existing indigenous techniques for protecting against drought, infestation or general poor harvests. And famine is often a precursor to infectious disease, such as smallpox, which can in tandem decimate a population. In the case of Tanganyika and Uganda in the immediate aftermath of the First World War, famine, smallpox and Spanish influenza coincided with devastating consequences. In southwest Tanganyika, the severe moral and social consequences of this demographic shock can be read in increased witchcraft accusations and the cessation of traditional burial practices by local chieftains in the 1920s and 1930s.[26]

Colonial sources indicate anxieties over a probable population decline in East and Central Africa over the early decades of the colonial period, beginning with the sleeping sickness outbreaks of the 1890s and ending with the mortality shock of the influenza pandemic at the end of First World War. The reasons for this decline up to the 1920s are varied and disputed among historians. These areas experienced a confluence of debilitating forces which may have resulted in heightened mortality and morbidity rates, as well as suppressed fertility. Coercive labour regimes associated with colonial capitalism, such as minework and the rubber regime of the Belgian Congo, exposed labourers to added health risks from accidents and illness – colonial sources estimated that the African population of the Belgian Congo during the Leopoldian era (1885–1908) was halved because of the exploitative terrors of the 'red rubber' period.[27] Labour migration and urbanization enhanced population mobility and density, which enabled new transmission pathways for infectious diseases such as malaria, sleeping sickness, syphilis and tuberculosis. Heightened incidence of venereal disease, especially venereal syphilis which was likely to have been introduced to Africa by Europeans through military and commercial routes, could lead to infertility if left untreated, although the data on syphilis incidence needs to be treated with caution (see Chapter 4). Finally, historians have also highlighted how colonial conquest eroded African capacities to control their own disease environments. New patterns of settlement, labour and land use disturbed indigenous techniques of disease control, leading to outbreaks of disease. West Africa was not generally affected by this population decline, and experienced a stable population throughout the early colonial period, likely because it was more thoroughly adapted to complex disease environments through its historical involvement in global slaving and trading routes (see previous chapter). The regionally specific population decline in Central and East Africa was followed by increased and then rapid growth from 1920s onwards across most of sub-Saharan Africa.

The interwar period: Colonial health campaigns and African medical personnel

After the First World War, the establishment of the Health Organization of the League of Nations in 1920 was important in shifting international efforts away from sanitary barriers to a broader health agenda. But it was not the first instance of nation-states coming together to discuss and decide upon important health issues. The first inter-governmental health measures arose out of the desire to contain contagious diseases, for example maritime quarantine restrictions during the Black Death of the fourteenth century. These measures were restrictive by design and used to stop the introduction of contagious disease from another country. These restrictions were regularized through a framework of International Sanitary Conferences and Conventions. Begun in Paris in 1851 and convened by the French government with diplomats and medical delegates from each of twelve nations, International Sanitary Conferences discussed cholera, plague and yellow fever, with a view to controlling transmission in relation to maritime communications. It took seven such conferences over forty years before any real agreement – the International Sanitary Convention of 1892, which laid the basis for prevention of the importation of cholera via the Suez Canal (opened in 1869) – was signed.[28] Although these conventions were important precursors to later international health efforts, they illustrated the limitations of scientific knowledge at the time – for example, conference delegates voted on whether cholera could be conveyed by water or food, and delegates were not chosen based on their medical background. These International Sanitary Conferences helped birth the idea of a permanent international health agency which was constituted in 1908 as the International d'Hygiene Publique (OIHP), with its seat in Paris. Fifty-five states were eventually on its governing body, and its initial impetus was to protect public health in Europe from 'contamination' by others. The OIHP mainly tried to administer and revise the International Sanitary Conventions. Another inter-governmental health agency was the Pan American Health Organisation, established in 1902.

Although African colonies were not included as members in these new international health structures, European imperial powers understood to an extent that the disease challenges facing African populations required a coordinated trans-national and cross-territorial response. For example, Colonial Office circulars were utilized to investigate, and regularize, disparate administrative practices in British-held territories regarding urban planning measures and sanitation practices. Moreover, as will be detailed in Chapter 6, cross-border and international cooperation (and associated funding networks) was fundamental to the work of colonial scientific expeditions and field institutes up to the Second World War, particularly with respect to research on tropical diseases such as sleeping sickness, malaria and yellow fever. By the 1940s, important 'enclaves' of scientific research had been established in sub-Saharan Africa, including the Tsetse Research Department in Tanganyika, Amani Research Station (also in Tanganyika, focusing on malaria research), the Permanent Mission to Fight against Sleeping Sickness in Cameroon at Ayos, the Yellow Fever Research Institute at Yaba, Nigeria, and the Division of Insect Borne Diseases in Kisumu, Kenya (focusing on malaria and yellow fever).[29] Some of these enclaves were to have continued significance into the post-colonial period, shaping independent African states' involvement in dynamically reconfigured global health frameworks (see Chapter 3).

Maternal health, African fertility and venereal disease control

Low birth rates, high mortality and depopulation were seen as critical problems in Central and southern Africa by the 1920s. European responses to the crisis of African reproduction during the interwar period were manifest in two predominant ways: mass syphilis prevention and treatment campaigns (detailed in Chapter 4), and maternalist programmes which promoted African fertility, maternal and child health, while transforming infant feeding and rearing practices. The participation of African women and the conceptualization of African sexuality were central to each.

The rise in STDs, such as syphilis and gonorrhea, was viewed by colonial health officers as a key determinant in depressed fertility levels. However, the target populations for venereal disease campaigns had shifted since the late nineteenth-century implementation of the Contagious Diseases Acts in southern and East Africa. In the Belgian Congo, there was recognition that European male promiscuity and practices of inter-racial concubinage were factors in the spread of venereal diseases among both the African and settler European populations. In southern and East Africa, rather than a singular focus on venereal disease in prostitutes, African women as a whole were viewed as potential 'disease reservoirs', particularly during the syphilis 'scares' of the 1920s and 1930s. Uncontrolled African female sexuality became viewed as particularly threatening, not only by colonial administrators but by African chiefs who were concerned about the crisis of social reproduction in their communities. In South Africa, as processes of urbanization and labour migration drew young men away from rural areas, controlling apparently 'syphilized' African women's mobility became an even greater imperative.[30]

In British-held African territories, maternal and infant health services became a key component of colonial medical provisioning in the interwar period, reaching a peak in the 1940s before independence. In Nigeria, antenatal and infant health clinics, education on child nutrition and food preparation as well as mobile public awareness information campaigns became visible features of this new medical network, although services were overwhelmingly concentrated in Lagos and in other urban areas.[31] In colonial Kenya, the emphasis on maternalist approaches – including the rollout of maternal and infant health services, the training of midwives and nurses, and the expansion of hospital-based care – resulted in a shift in child-birthing practices by mid-century, as Lynn Thomas has shown. For a small, middle-class and largely Christian elite, the mission or colonial hospital became the preferred space for giving birth. This process, however, was complicated by gendered and generational struggles over the meaning and practice of female initiation or excision, which became a key point of contestation between local Meru leaders and missionaries and colonial health authorities, as well as a potent source of debate within Kenya's rapidly changing and diverse African population.[32]

From the 1930s until the immediate post-world war period, the Belgian Congo was the most interventionist colonial regime in terms of African maternal and infant health. The participation of white women, as models of motherhood and moral and health educators to African women, was integral to this project. In the confined and controlled space of the mining compound in the Katanga Copperbelt, the Belgian state enacted an extraordinary and intensive experiment which came to regulate family structure, provide pre- and post-natal care, and alter infant breast-feeding and weaning patterns, in the process dismantling African post-partum abstinence practices and directly intervening in the area of African fertility.[33] The Union Minière mine was indeed successful in increasing the birth rate and decreasing infant and adult mortality. However, it is debatable whether these successes came as a result of the more moralist interventions targeting infant-rearing and post-partum practices, which it appears from African testimonies were not comprehensively eliminated, or as a result of the re-balancing of sex ratios in the mining compounds and the provision of adequate nutrition to its inhabitants.

African medical auxiliaries

Apart from a handful of exceptional cases – such as James Africanus Horton, a Sierra Leonian who received his medical degree in Edinburgh and became the Staff Assistant Surgeon of the Gold Coast in 1859 – African participation in the ranks of colonial medical institutions was narrowly defined until the interwar period.[34] Africans were initially utilized primarily as porters for medical supplies and equipment, but as the boundaries of colonial and mission health services expanded, Africans were increasingly recruited as hospital orderlies, translators, dispensers, laboratory technicians, field assistants, insect catchers and pest controllers. The full range of these auxiliaries' roles, and their particular contributions, experiences and perspectives have only begun to be mined by scholars.

A significant development during the First World War that would shape the future development of an African medical professional class was the formation of the elite African Native Medical Corps (ANMC), which drew in Africans educated in mission schools to serve as medical attendants during the war. After the war ended, the ANMC and other elite corps supplied many trained personnel to area hospitals and mission clinics. In the interwar period, although rural Africans had to rely largely on mission stations, some state-run dispensaries became increasingly available. The expanding network of rural medical services meant increased opportunities for Africans to enter into medical employment. In East Africa, dispensers and 'tribal dressers' became the first port of call in the case of unexplained death or illness, and were dispatched to work on the 'front line' of a range of infectious disease challenges in this period, including rabies, meningitis, sleeping sickness, smallpox, syphilis and leprosy. They were literate and had rudimentary training in anatomy and physiology, attended to ulcers and wounds, and were able to provide intramuscular but not intravenous injections. They also clinically assessed patients and referred to the district hospital those who were seriously ill.[35]

African laboratory and research assistants were instrumental to the advancement of scientific knowledge on several diseases, as well as performing vital clinical and diagnostic work. In the early 1900s, Africans were recruited as research and field assistants and insect catchers in large-scale expeditions to investigate malaria and sleeping sickness. As the field of tropical medicine evolved and field-based institutes became more established in some parts of Africa by the interwar period, African auxiliaries progressed to significant roles beyond technical work or research assistance. African staff played an integral role in the Tsetse Research Department, established in 1927 in Tanganyika, and some African personnel came to manage field surveys of tsetse fly distribution and lead large-scale tsetse bush clearing experiments. A notable figure at this institute was Swedi bin Abdallah, who rose through the ranks after being appointed as 'head fly boy' in 1920, eventually identifying a new species of tsetse fly. As was the case for many of this cadre of African researchers, bin Abdallah was not duly credited for his intellectual labour – the new fly species, *Glossina swynnertoni*, was named after his boss, Charles Swynnerton.[36]

African medical auxiliaries had uncertain societal positions. Because they often dealt with blood, bodily emissions and sores, they could be viewed within local communities as consorting with morally suspect forces of sorcery or witchcraft, exemplified vividly in 'fly-boys' (employed by sleeping sickness research expeditions) being implicated within local vampire rumours in northern Rhodesia (now Zambia) in the 1930s (see Chapter 6). Indigenous medical practitioners also viewed local medical auxiliaries with distrust and as potential competitors, especially with regards to rural health service provision. Medical auxiliaries also suffered from the disrespect and paternalistic attitudes of European clinical staff within hospitals, alongside persistent grievances over pay and working conditions. However, despite these severe constraints, African medical auxiliaries became important intermediaries between local patient communities and allopathic health institutions. Through their linguistic, cultural and social familiarity with patients, they were able to communicate unfamiliar medical concepts and healing technologies in ways more relatable to local cosmologies and therapeutics. In northern Rhodesia, a consequence of African auxiliaries' labour of 'translation' was that biomedicine became indigenized and adapted into existing local frameworks, a complex process that occurred in the clinical setting unbeknownst to attending colonial medical staff.[37]

The interwar period witnessed attempts at formalized medical training for Africans. One early effort was the establishment of Mengo Medical School as an adjunct to the mission hospital, opening in 1917 with seventeen students in training to be clinical assistants. Another more successful medical training scheme began in 1923 at Makerere, also in Uganda, as a technical school designed to produce 'Medical Assistants' (equivalent to Indian sub-Assistant surgeons) through training in basic sciences, medical sciences and clinical work in hospital. In 1926 it offered a five-year course which followed European medical education progression. By 1939, African Assistant Medical Officers, as graduates of the five-year programme came to be named, could head rural hospitals while lower-ranked 'medical attendants' could be posted to hospitals in subordinate roles or to rural dispensaries. Other medical education institutions which were established in the interwar period include the School of Medicine in Khartoum, opened in 1924; and in British West Africa, the medical school in Yaba, Nigeria, whose first cohort of students graduated in 1935. Medical students were generally not drawn from indigenous elites, but from mission-educated families and civil servants. Despite considerable obstacles in their educational paths, including poorly resourced learning facilities and living quarters as students, and then tremendous clinical patient loads and poor administrative support as trainee doctors, a growing group of African medical professionals by the 1940s began to assert their clinical as well as scientific independence. Internationally circulating publications authored by African doctors began to appear in this period, for example in the field of psychiatry, their work informed by their clinical research in local hospitals as well as their unique positions in the colonial social order (see Chapter 5).

Global health developments after the Second World War

Two global health developments in the immediate post-Second World War period set the stage for the impending transformation in health services and infrastructures that would be ushered in by African independence from colonial rule in the 1950s and 1960s. The first was the development of pharmaceutical drugs and chemical pesticides, including the wartime synthetic manufacture of chloroquine and the insecticide Dichlorodiphenyltrichloroethane, or DDT. As will be discussed in Chapter 6, these advances altered global health priorities in the post-war period and influenced the turn to a disease eradication agenda, which would have a significant impact on the design and implementation of prevention and control measures for infectious diseases in Africa, in particular malaria. Penicillin, originally discovered in 1928 by the Scottish scientist Alexander Fleming, was manufactured for medical purposes in the 1940s and made widely available to colonial health services a decade later. This was to have a significant and immediate impact on African health outcomes, particularly in the treatment of STDs.

The second major global development was the establishment in 1947 of the World Health Organization, the United Nations agency principally in charge of coordinating and implementing international health policies and programmes. As its founding constitution states, WHO's objective was 'the attainment by all people of the highest possible level of health'.[38] WHO's constitution also set out an expansive definition of 'health': 'Health is a state of complete physical, mental, and social well-being and not merely the absence of disease or infirmity.' WHO's first director-general, Brock Chisholm, in 1950 lauded what he called the 'revolutionary character' of this new agency, particularly for its broad-based understanding of health and its commitment to enabling the entire global community to achieve this, not just the privileged few. Chisholm's words reflected the heady optimism of the post-war global health landscape, not unlike the triumphal aura which had surrounded the development of germ theory and the inauguration of tropical medicine five decades previous: 'We know the job can be done. The means to fight and eventually eradicate most of mankind's scourges exist.'[39] 'Regionalization' was an important tenet of its international approach, so that the policies of WHO could be adopted and translated to fit the needs of a particular region. Whether this ideal would be realized in the context of Africa's dynamically changing political and health contexts would be tested in the decades to come (see following chapter).

African approaches to health and healing in the colonial period

African perceptions of and responses to ill-health in the colonial period were incredibly diverse and defy any neat categorizations. Rather than a comprehensive catalogue, the following suggests some general features of African therapeutic approaches and perspectives, stressing these characteristics must be considered historically, regionally and culturally contingent. First, it is evident that African healing systems did **respond independently to epidemic disease** during the colonial period. These health interventions could take diverse forms, even within the same society. In colonial Senegal, Sereer *saltigi* healers and villagers responded to bubonic plague outbreaks in the first half of the twentieth century in a multiplicity of ways, including ceremonial symbolic expulsion of the disease from the community, quarantine measures, prescribing medicinal solutions to drink or charms for protection, requiring the use of ritual baths called *bukut* to cleanse any Sereer who had been released from the colonial health service's *lazaretto* before being allowed back into Sereer society, and the burning of leaves and roots in ceremonial smudge pots, whose smoke warded off insect vectors. These techniques reflected both the complexity of Sereer understandings of plague causation and the wide range of its therapeutic practices.[40] More recent anthropological work on witchcraft and its relation to healing has continued a long-running thread of analysis evident in colonial ethnographies, as evidenced in the account by Monica Wilson (*née* Hunter), below. Whilst understanding the meaning of witchcraft in African society is fraught and vulnerable to misinterpretation, nonetheless ethnographic approaches have created an alternative intellectual genealogy of ill-health and potential therapeutic interventions constructed by local societies, in conversation with external and global forces of change.

Historical Source: Monica Hunter, *Reaction to Conquest: Effects of Contact with Europeans on the Pondo of South Africa* (1936)

Any slight illness (*umkhuhlane*) is regarded as being cased naturally. Informants laughed loudly when I inquired whether a cold in the head was 'sent'. 'But', they added when they had recovered themselves, 'it gives an *igqwira* (sorcerer, witch) a chance. A cold may get worse and worse, so that eventually the person dies. Then we know that it has been sent.' Always witchcraft or sorcery may be adduced as an aggravating cause.

Some regard more diseases as infectious than do others. *Impuza* (a skin disease) is generally recognized as infectious, but about smallpox and measles there is divergence of opinion, some saying they are infectious, others not. Gidli remarked of influenza, 'We see that when we go to visit some one who has it, we get it also.' Three or four men with whom I was discussing the subject said that colds in the head were infectious, they were quite sure about it, but Geza, who came from a doctor's family, had 'never heard that before'. Old women said that they had noticed that if one child in the *umzi* got whooping-cough all the children got it. Some think that epidemics just come, or are sent by God (*uThixo*), others that they are the result of an orgy of *ukuthakatha* (witchcraft and sorcery), or that they are sent by Europeans. The East Coast fever which killed so many cattle is often attributed to the machinations of Europeans. Tuberculosis is not known to be infectious, but informants remark that 'the child of a man who has it may get it; it "comes out" to them'. Leprosy also is not regarded as infectious, but it is said to run in families. 'It takes whom it likes.' 'A wife does not get it from her husband, but some of an infected man's children or grandchildren have it.' A leper was allowed to go about, attend beer drinks, and eat or drink out of the same vessels as other people. Albinism is known to run in families, but a magical reason is also adduced. It is said of a woman who bears a child who is an albino (*inkawu*, monkey), 'She has laughed at some one who was an albino.' The usual reply to an inquiry as to what caused deformed births was, 'We do not know. They were created so', or, 'They were created by God (*uThixo*).' Only one informant attributed them to witchcraft. The effect of mental worry on health is to some extent recognized. Hlupheka volunteered the remark that she was so thin because she had been accused of witchcraft. Ngote was said by neighbours to be getting thin because her husband was neglecting her.

Source Analysis: This extract from Monica Wilson's pioneering ethnography of the Xhosa-speaking Pondo reveals elements of continuity and change in Pondo cosmologies and therapeutics. In many ways, colonial anthropologists shared with Christian missionaries a complex positionality as agents within although not wholly subsumed by colonial ideologies and colonial power structures. This excerpt in a sense replicates the 'conversation' format popularized by missionaries in their accounts of African societies, seen in David Livingstone's dialogue with a rain doctor [see Chapter 1].

This historical source reveals the multivalent understandings of disease causation within Pondo society, and illustrates that indigenous knowledge was not uniformly shared and could be subject to dispute. Some diseases are attributed to a divine God, while others are the work of witchcraft or sorcery. Importantly, Europeans are implicated here as a potential active agent in the spread of epidemic diseases – 'they are sent by Europeans' – whose 'machinations' may also account for the East Coast fever which decimated cattle populations. Cattle were central to the moral and political economy in many southern African societies, and the untimely deaths of livestock figured pivotally in many collected disease narratives of African societies in this period. The direct linkage by the Pondo of cattle mortality to European intervention is its own moral commentary on the deleterious impact of colonial rule.

The history of *African* attempts to ward off STDs and regulate fertility in the early decades of colonial rule in Africa is much less documented than colonial interventions in this realm, although recent scholarship is beginning to address this gap. As Nancy Rose Hunt has shown in the Belgian Congo, the 'nervousness' of the colonial state in the face of the crisis of reproduction in the 1920s and 1930s was mirrored by the heightened anxieties over the same crisis in local communities – this disquiet about childlessness became manifest in diverse ways, including the creation of local, mobile healing networks called *Likili* to address infertility through the performative ritual purging of charms that were inhibiting reproduction.[41] In the Cape Colony, local practices of quarantining those presenting physical symptoms of endemic syphilis were established long before the medicalization of syphilis treatment and prevention through the Contagious Diseases Acts.[42] As discussed in Chapter 1, herbal abortifacients were in common circulation amongst different ethnic groups within South Africa across the eighteenth and nineteenth centuries – farmers, settlers, peasants, hunter-gatherers shared this knowledge as a way to make women's bodies 'regular'. By the late nineteenth century, white women in South Africa drew on this understanding of folk remedies and sought help from their black servants and labourers, a pattern reminiscent of an earlier period of exchange between planter and slave classes in the plantation communities of the American South. Opportunities for these exchanges declined markedly by the early twentieth century in South Africa, as segregationist policies rigidified racial divisions.[43] Finally, post-partum abstinence, male circumcision, female initiation, intracrural sexual play and levirate practices were part of the spectrum of African social and ritual practices which regulated sexual behaviour and fertility in many African societies. Yet, these were often the subject of confusion and moral condemnation by colonial and missionary observers, and were aggressively campaigned against by them over the course of the colonial period, with varying degrees of success.

A second noteworthy characteristic is that Africans pursued **pluralistic therapeutic approaches**, including but not exclusively reliant on allopathic technologies. In the cosmopolitan setting of interwar Durban, South Africa, Indian and Zulu therapeutics and medicinal knowledge overlapped and were exchanged in diverse ways – Indian spices and herbs were incorporated into local African pharmacopeia, and conversely Indians came to be registered as traders and shopowners of *muthi* [traditional medicine].[44] In the absence of quinine supplies in interwar Zanzibar, local practices of boiling *Neem* (azadirachta) leaves and bark became prominent in the treatment of malaria.[45]

Injections proved to be a particularly popular biomedical technology amongst local African populations, seen in the efficacy of yaws injection programmes in East and West Africa in the 1930s and 1940s. Vaccination programmes for smallpox and yellow fever were similarly widely taken up, with some variation, in French West Africa. As discussed earlier, simple surgical procedures demonstrated by missionary medics were generally embraced by local groups. Yet, Africans also observed the lack of success of some medical interventions, and feared certain practices were spreading rather than halting disease. Invasive and painful diagnostic procedures such as lumbar puncture (used to help diagnose sleeping sickness) and the pairing of carceral approaches with medical 'cure' – as evidenced in the treatment of syphilitics as well as the institutionalization of the mentally insane (see Chapter 5) – cast doubt within local communities of the moral intentions behind these medical interventions. The use of contaminated vaccines and the toxic and potentially fatal side effects of certain treatments further undermined local trust in allopathic approaches (see Chapter 4).

Indeed, Africans did not necessarily accede to the overarching authority of biomedicine, even when they clearly adopted particular therapies or technologies. This **resistance to the primacy of allopathic medicine** was a source of confusion and consternation for mission medics and colonial medical officers, who thought African patients had 'converted' when in reality they had merely incorporated these technologies into a larger and more diverse constellation of ideas and healing practices. It is likely, for example, that a series of seemingly successful yaws treatment campaigns run by mission clinics in south-eastern Tanganyika in the interwar period were differently conceptualized by local groups – not as submission to a superior medicine but as healing 'pilgrimages' that were legitimized within the framework of an internally derived cleansing movement.[46]

Indeed, it is important to acknowledge **local perceptions and appropriations** of colonial medical interventions and their associated social and symbolic content. In French West Equatorial Africa, a 1923 decree outlawed local practices of keeping relics, which contained the bodily remnants of the deceased, and the collection of human bones. Although this decree was seen by Europeans as necessary to stop ritual autopsies and any potential 'trafficking' of human flesh, local Africans came to view the criminalization of their ritual practices as an attempt by Europeans to hijack the spiritual 'force' from African bodies for their own nefarious purposes. The introduction of medical autopsies utilizing hospital morgues only served to confirm to local communities of European intentions to exploit the power inherent in body parts.[47] Similarly, as historical scholarship has emphasized, anti-witchcraft ordinances in place across southern and East Africa (such as the Witchcraft Suppression Act of 1895 in the Cape Colony and the Witchcraft Ordinance of 1925 in Kenya) did anything but succeed in suppressing the circulation of ideas of witchcraft. Instead, these tended to be interpreted by local groups as purposeful moral invasions into the ritual sphere by Europeans.

It is evident from the historical record that some African patients resisted full adherence to prescribed medication regimes, following their own understanding of correct dosages or blending allopathic and traditional medicines, and did not acquiesce to the authority of the dispenser, nurse or doctor. This pattern was heightened by culturally encoded lines of local authority and therapeutic consent which were divergent from Western norms. For example, the concept of a 'therapy management group' was widely part of Central and East African societies – local Tanganyika societies termed this *jamaa*. Therapy groups were typically made up of elderly kin and were responsible for giving consent for treatment of ailments. Colonial medical administrations tended not to acknowledge these diverse family arrangements, and their focus on patriarchal notions of consent meant that groups such as the *jamaa* and matrilineal descent social arrangements were ignored in medical consent and communication.[48]

As discussed earlier, the influence of both the educational and medical orientation of mission stations meant that Christianized Africans made up the majority of African medical staff in the colonial health services. African Christians also tended to be the first to receive, and accept, allopathic treatments in those areas with a strong mission presence. The District Surgeon of Glen Grey in the Cape Colony wrote in the early twentieth century that 'School' Africans (Christianized Africans) flocked to hospitals offering topical mercury treatments for syphilis, because they were impressed by the efficacy of that treatment for their skin lesions.[49] Moreover, diverse forms of *African Christianity* emerged in this period, which had implications on local conceptualizations of illness and appropriate healing technologies. For example, the Zionist movement in southern Africa had by the interwar period become a significant social and political force. Informed by global Pentecostalism, Zionist churches emphasized 'divine healing' through the inspiration of the Holy Spirit communicated through prophets. In South Africa, Zionist churches and other African Independent Churches were able to address local demands for spiritual *and* bodily healing, particularly in urbanizing areas, that could not be fulfilled by indigenous therapeutic networks that had been suppressed by formal legislation.[50]

In Senegal, local Muslim leaders of the Tijaniyya and Qadariyya brotherhoods were instrumental in encouraging local compliance to sanitation measures set up in response to outbreaks of bubonic plague in the interwar period. However, Muslim leaders in Northern Nigeria were opposed to smallpox vaccination and other colonial medical services in the early decades of the twentieth century, viewing these as unwelcome attempts to impose an alternative spiritual authority over local groups.[51]

As a general observation, the **basis of power of traditional healers was substantially eroded** in the colonial period. As seen in the previous chapter, in pre-colonial times healers could play a fundamental political and economic role in local societies, and the 'work' of healing could be intimately connected to social reproduction, material accumulation and political power. Chiefs could claim sacred powers of healing, and also worked with healers to ensure the maintenance of social reproduction through enacting initiatives such as irrigation, the burial of the dead, the placement of villages and locations for human waste, and the performance of rituals to prevent drought, famine, epidemics and damaging wars. With colonial conquest, healers were deprived to a large extent of control over these productive capacities and this direct linkage between healing and public authority was lost.

However, as this chapter has illustrated, there were **limits to the reach of colonial medicine,** partly related to the incomplete reach of the colonial state as a whole. The 'thin white line' of colonial bureaucracy evident in many African territories was certainly applicable to health administration, which focused largely on urban areas and large pools of African labour, or areas with mineral or commercial agricultural resources, to the detriment of all others.[52] Lack of resources, funding and trained personnel repeatedly strained the functioning of colonial health services in this period. Furthermore, the colonial predilection for 'vertical' campaigns targeting specific epidemic infectious diseases meant that chronic diseases, mental illness and other health concerns constitutive of what would later be called 'primary health care' remained on the whole the preserve, and responsibility, of local healing systems. Thus, the need for local healers and their therapeutics was never fully erased.

Some historians have argued that this relegation of healing to the margins afforded traditional healers a measure of a different sort of power – power over their own interpretations of health. It was precisely because of their marginal status that healers could maintain a populist base. Relegated to the private sphere and to the underground of society, healers were able to use the aura of secretiveness surrounding their techniques to their advantage to provide a distinctly African alternative to oppressive Western medical regimes. Indirect Rule was another important factor, at least in British-held African territories. Indirect Rule was devised by Frederick Lugard, Governor-General of Nigeria, and became an important form of British colonial territorial governance from the 1920s. The logic of Indirect Rule utilized local African leaders and customary practices and institutions, so that colonial governments could exercise a far more expansive control of outlying colonial populations without having to substantially widen the 'thin white line' of colonial administration. Historians have argued that Indirect Rule tended to valorize, and reify, traditional African authorities and the cultural tools used to uphold and perpetuate that authority. However, for the purposes of this discussion, it is important to note this legal protection and encouragement of African customary traditions constituted another vital element in the continuation of local African therapeutics and healing systems in this period.

A 'colonial medicine'? Was medicine a tool of colonial control?

The operation of the colonial state required mechanisms of control over a diverse and widespread African population. Medicine, and particularly the emergent field of tropical medicine, provided a conceptual framework and language which were taken up by the colonial state to enhance that control. Far from a benevolent and necessary institution, in this interpretation the provision of allopathic medical services in the colonial period could be more appropriately framed as a distinctive, and coercive, 'colonial medicine'.

As shown in Monica Wilson's dialogue with Pondo informants, it is evident that many Africans equated *disease*, and not health, with colonialism, specifically disastrous epidemic disease. This **linking of African ill-health with colonial rule** came as Africans experienced the deadly resurgence of 'old' diseases such as smallpox and sleeping sickness in the colonial period and the introduction of 'new' ones such as venereal syphilis. To some extent, then, it is no surprise that Africans sometimes treated colonial medicine with caution, particularly if accompanied by intrusive and socially disruptive measures (as they often were), including surveillance, *lazarettes* and *cordon sanitaire*, the burning of villages and clothing and possessions, mass fumigation campaigns, and the restriction of funeral practices. For many Africans, their formative experiences of colonial public health were through specific disease intervention campaigns, whose militaristic and carceral features were difficult to ignore, whatever the intention of colonial authorities.

However, more complex dynamics were at work than a simply coercive 'colonial medicine'. There are several important mitigating factors to consider. Regional variation and the concentration of labour and resources were strong determinants in shaping medical initiatives and institutions. As a general rule, the more urban a population, the greater the level of state intervention through medical means. The same applied for areas with a greater concentration of natural resources and exploitable labour. Indeed, the most aggressive sanitary segregation programmes were centred around important hubs of wealth creation for the various European regimes. Furthermore, it is generally agreed that missionary medicine, which was an important conduit through which Africans received medical treatment particularly outside of major urban centres, was more concerned with local health outcomes, at least before the 1930s when missionary medicine became incorporated much more fully into colonial medical structures. This concern with the health of local populations derived, in part, from the call to conversion as well as the embeddedness of missionaries in local communities.

African agency needs to be foreground in this debate. Often the strength of African opposition determined the extent of imposition of medical technologies and therapeutic regimes onto local populations. And even in areas where colonial medical interventions went unchecked, smaller less visible instances of resistance and rebellion were evident. Moreover, the apparent resilience and adaptability of indigenous understandings of health and healing caution against any totalizing narrative of 'colonial medicine'. African medical auxiliaries and the emergent cadre of medical professionals from the interwar period onwards were a significant force in translating and re-fashioning the terms through which medical care was provided to and imagined by local communities.

Certainly, it would be rash to assume a homogeneity in both practice and design across and within different colonial regimes. British, French, German, Belgian, Portuguese regimes possessed different institutional hierarchies and trajectories in relation to their imperial projects, which tended to affect the ways in which medical knowledge was passed through these structures and the design of appropriate health interventions in their colonial territories. There is little denial that the Belgian state's violent, extractive and militaristic approach to colonial rule was reflected in the 'terrors' associated with its medical interventions. The influential role of Christian missionaries and mission hospitals was most pronounced in British colonial health services, while in French-held territories public health interventions had a pronounced secular orientation and favoured mobile, mass treatments. In addition, the role of individual doctors, colonial medical and sanitation officers, and colonial administrators could determine the shape and implementation of medical interventions and regulations in particular territorial and municipal contexts, as well as the extent to which certain 'solutions' such as segregation were implemented.

The application of allopathic therapies could be viewed as beneficial to African health outcomes, rather than primarily concerned with consolidating mechanisms of control. Koch's call for mass quininization was taken up in East Africa by the German colonial state and continued to influence anti-malarial programmes in the region after the First World War. The widespread rollout of vaccinations for smallpox and yellow fever across French colonial African territories is another example. And, finally, colonial health policies could themselves transform, as exemplified in the expansion in the 1930s and 1940s of medical hospitals and medical training for Africans in British colonial territories, and the 'turn' to a maternalist policy in Belgian and British approaches to sexual and reproductive health.

Conclusion: A final assessment

Arguably, there was a marked 'medicalization of power' at work through colonial health interventions concerned with the regulation of African movement, African bodies and bodily practices. Germ theory became uniquely translated through the racial asymmetries of power at work in the colonial context, shifting colonial perceptions of Africans from being endowed with 'native immunity' to being innate 'disease carriers', whose threat needed to be checked through urban segregation, enforced quarantine and behavioural change. Colonial health interventions enacted in many African territories, particularly in the early decades of colonial rule, were designed not to ameliorate the problem of infectious disease afflicting African bodies but to formulate diseased African bodies as *the* problem that needed to be isolated, examined and, ultimately, managed.

And yet, as this chapter has highlighted, 'colonial medicine' was hardly the solid edifice it sought to be – implementation was uneven and marked by variation across the rural-urban divide, and across different regions and imperial contexts. Arguably, the single-most important factor shaping, and limiting, the reach of European medical institutions and medical men was the resilience of local healing systems and perspectives on health. It is evident that Africans did not necessarily adopt biomedicine as an overarching framework, even when they adopted particular medical remedies. Africans made their own judgements about the efficacy of Western medicine and created their own hierarchies and pathways of treatment. Furthermore, African societies entered the colonial period with sometimes elaborate understandings and practices which regulated well-being and responded to disease challenges. These local healing systems adapted to, and in some cases incorporated, fundamental features of allopathic therapies and technologies. But they also developed and responded to internal dynamics of their own, and should not solely be viewed through the paradigm of subjugation or resistance to a Western model.

A final assessment of whether medicine in the colonial period amounted to a type of 'colonial medicine' could be considered through asking, simply, were Africans more healthy? Certainly, the onset and consolidation of colonial rule coincided with an extraordinary period of the emergence and resurgence of deadly diseases which contributed to a demographic shock observed in Central and East Africa in the 1920s and 1930s. It is unlikely that African health outcomes were markedly improved by any of the vertical medical interventions which sought to address aspects of this dynamic disease landscape. Furthermore, from an African standpoint, the collateral damage of measures such as forced relocation and quarantine only served to further undermine health by disrupting livelihoods and communal ties. Indeed, medical campaigns such as sanitary segregation should be viewed as part and parcel of the same institutionalized footprint imposed by colonial regimes (hut taxes, migrant labour, appropriation of land) that resulted in the widespread impoverishment of large segments of African societies and the suppression of local controls over disease transmission. It is likely that these larger social and political forces were ultimately more responsible for local populations' increased vulnerabilities to disease in this period, and contributed to the demographic decline observed with anxiety by Africans and European interlocutors in affected regions. Equally, the sustained growth in the African population from the 1920s, which accelerated at mid-century, needs to be contextualized. The pro-natalist policies implemented in colonial health services from the 1930s may be a contributory force in increased fertility and child survival rates. However, the data from the diverse range of these maternalist interventions as well as other important advances – such as the introduction of penicillin – has yet to be comprehensively assessed. Determining the overall health impacts on African societies of medicine during the colonial period, then, remains a still-relevant question for future scholarship.

Further reading

Anderson, Warwick. 'Immunities of Empire: Race, Disease, and the New Tropical Medicine, 1900–1920'. *Bulletin of the History of Medicine* 70, no. 1 (1996): 94–118.

Anderson, Warwick. *Colonial Pathologies: American Tropical Medicine, Race, and Hygiene in the Philippines*. Durham: Duke University Press, 2008.

Arnold, David, ed. *Imperial Medicine and Indigenous Societies*. Oxford: Oxford University Press, 1989.

Arnold, David, ed. *Warm Climates and Western Medicine: The Emergence of Tropical Medicine, 1500–1900*. Amsterdam: Rodopi, 1996.

Azevedo, Mario Joaquim. *Historical Perspectives on the State of Health and Health Systems in Africa, Volume I: The Pre-Colonial and Colonial Eras*. New York: Nature America Incorporated, 2017.

Bell, Heather. *Frontiers of Medicine in the Anglo-Egyptian Sudan, 1899–1940*. Oxford: Oxford University Press, 1999.

Bradford, Helen. 'Herbs, Knives and Plastic: 150 Years of Abortion in South Africa'. In *Science, Medicine and Cultural Imperialism*, edited by Teresa Meade and M. Walker. London: Macmillan, 1991.

Cabrita, Joel. *The People's Zion: Southern Africa, the United States, and a Transatlantic Faith-Healing Movement*. Cambridge, MA: Harvard University Press, 2018.

Charumbira, Ruramisai. 'Administering Medicine without a License: Missionary Women in Rhodesia's Nursing History, 1890–1901'. *Historian* 68, no. 2 (2006): 241–66.

Crozier, Anna. *Practising Colonial Medicine: The Colonial Medical Service in British East Africa*. London: I.B. Tauris, 2007.

Curtin, Philip D. 'Medical Knowledge and Urban Planning in Tropical Africa'. *The American Historical Review* 90, no. 3 (1985): 594–613.

Dumett, Raymond. 'The Campaign against Malaria and the Expansion of Scientific Medical and Sanitary Services in British West Africa, 1898–1910'. *African Historical Studies* 1, no. 2 (1968): 153–97.

Echenberg, Myron. *Black Death, White Medicine: Bubonic Plague and the Politics of Public Health in Colonial Senegal, 1914-1945.* Oxford: James Currey, 2002.

Elison, James. "'A Fierce Hunger': Tracing Impacts of the 1918-19 Influenza Epidemic in Southwest Tanzania'. In *The Spanish Influenza Pandemic of 1918-19: New Perspectives,* edited by Howard Phillips and David Killingray. London: Routledge, 2003.

Flint, Karen. *Healing Traditions: African Medicine, Cultural Exchange, and Competition in South Africa, 1820-1948.* Athens: Ohio University Press, 2008.

Greenwood, Anna, ed. *Beyond the State: The Colonial Medical Service in British Africa.* Manchester: Manchester University Press, 2016.

Hardage, Jeanette. 'Not Just Malaria: Mary Slessor (1848-1915) and Other Victorian Missionaries in West Africa'. *Journal of Medical Biography* 14, no. 4 (November 2006): 230-5.

Hartwig, Gerald and K. David Patterson eds. *Disease in African History: An Introductory Survey and Case Studies.* Durham: Duke University Press, 1978.

Hobbins, Peter. 'The Whole Country Is Poisoned: Fratning Disease Mortality in the Historiography of the South African War'. *War & Society* 28, no. 1 (1 May 2009): 29-60.

Hunt, Nancy Rose. *A Colonial Lexicon of Birth Ritual, Medicalization, and Mobility in the Congo.* Durham: Duke University Press, 1999.

Hunt, Nancy Rose. *A Nervous State: Violence, Remedies, and Reverie in Colonial Congo.* Durham: Duke University Press, 2016.

Hunter, Monica. *Reaction to Conquest: Effects of Contact with Europeans on the Pondo of South Africa.* London: Oxford University Press, 1936.

Iliffe, John. *East African Doctors: A History of the Modern Profession.* Cambridge: Cambridge University Press, 1998.

Jochelson, Karen. *The Colour of Disease: Syphilis and Racism in South Africa, 1880-1950.* London: Palgrave Macmillan, 2001.

Kalusa, Walima T. 'Language, Medical Auxiliaries, and the Re-Interpretation of Missionary Medicine in Colonial Mwinilunga, Zambia, 1922-51'. *Journal of Eastern African Studies* 1, no. 1 (2007): 57-78.

Kalusa, Walima T. 'Missionaries, African Patients, and Negotiating Missionary Medicine at Kalene Hospital, Zambia, 1906-1935'. *Journal of Southern African Studies* 40, no. 2 (2014): 283-94.

Lachenal, Guillaume. 'A Genealogy of Treatment as Prevention (TasP): Prevention, Therapy, and the Tensions of Public Health in African History'. In *Global Health in Africa: Historical Perspectives on Disease Control,* edited by Tamara Giles-Vernick and James Webb. Athens: Ohio University Press, 2013.

Lyons, Maryinez. *The Colonial Disease: A Social History of Sleeping Sickness in Northern Zaire, 1900-1940.* Cambridge: Cambridge University Press, 2002.

MacLeod, Roy and Milton Lewis, eds. *Disease, Medicine, and Empire.* London: Routledge, 1988.

Manton, John. 'Making Modernity with Medicine: Mission, State and Community in Leprosy Control, Ogoja, Nigeria, 1945-50'. In *The Development of Modern Medicine in Non-Western Countries,* edited by Hormoz Ebrahimnejad. London: Routledge, 2008.

Marks, Shula. 'What Is Colonial about Colonial Medicine? And What Has Happened to Imperialism and Health?' *Social History of Medicine* 10, no. 2 (August 1997): 205-19.

Neill, Deborah Joy. *Networks in Tropical Medicine: Internationalism, Colonialism, and the Rise of a Medical Specialty, 1890-1930.* Stanford: Stanford University Press, 2012.

Ngalamulume, Kalala. *Colonial Pathologies, Environment, and Western Medicine in Saint-Louis-Du-Senegal, 1867-1920.* New York: Peter Lang, 2012.

Patterson, K. David. *Health in Colonial Ghana: Disease, Medicine, and Socio-Economic Change, 1900-1955.* Waltham: Crossroads Press, 1981.

Phillips, Howard. *In a Time of Plague: Memories of the 'Spanish' Flu Epidemic of 1918 in South Africa*. Cape Town: Van Riebeeck Society, 2018.

Phillips, Howard and David Killingray, eds. *The Spanish Influenza Pandemic of 1918–19: New Perspectives*. London: Routledge, 2003.

Ranger, Terence. 'Godly Medicine: The Ambiguities of Medical Mission in Southeast Tanzania, 1900–1945'. *Social Science & Medicine. Part B: Medical Anthropology* 15, no. 3 (1981): 261–77.

Ranger, Terence and Paul Slack, eds. *Epidemics and Ideas: Essays on the Historical Perception of Pestilence*. Cambridge: Cambridge University Press, 1992.

Sadowsky, Jonathan. 'The Long Shadow of Colonialism: Why We Study Medicine in Africa'. In *Medicine and Health in Africa: Multidisciplinary Perspectives*, edited by Paula Viterbo and Kalala Ngalamulume. East Lansing: Michigan State University Press, 2011.

Silla, Eric. *People Are Not the Same: Leprosy and Identity in Twentieth-Century Mali*. Oxford: James Currey, 1998.

Swanson, Maynard W. 'The Sanitation Syndrome: Bubonic Plague and Urban Native Policy in the Cape Colony, 1900-1909'. *The Journal of African History* 18, no. 3 (1977): 387–410.

Thomas, Lynn. *Politics of the Womb: Women, Reproduction, and the State in Kenya*. Berkeley: University of California Press, 2003.

Tilley, Helen. *Africa as a Living Laboratory: Empire, Development, and the Problem of Scientific Knowledge, 1870–1950*. Chicago: University of Chicago Press, 2011.

van Heyningen, Elizabeth B. 'The Social Evil in the Cape Colony 1868–1902: Prostitution and the Contagious Diseases Acts'. *Journal of Southern African Studies* 10, no. 2 (1984): 170–97.

Vaughan, Megan. *Curing Their Ills: Colonial Power and African Illness*. Cambridge: Polity, 1991.

Vaughan, Megan. 'Healing and Curing: Issues in the Social History and Anthropology of Medicine in Africa'. *Social History of Medicine: The Journal of the Society for the Social History of Medicine* 7, no. 2 (1994): 283–95.

Warwick, Peter. *Black People and the South African War 1899-1902*. Cambridge: Cambridge University Press, 2004.

White, Luise. *The Comforts of Home: Prostitution in Colonial Nairobi*. Chicago: University of Chicago Press, 1990.

White, Luise. 'Tsetse Visions: Narratives of Blood and Bugs in Colonial Northern Rhodesia, 1931–9'. *The Journal of African History* 36, no. 2 (1995): 219–45.

Worboys, Michael. 'Manson, Ross and Colonial Medical Policy: Tropical Medicine in London and Liverpool, 1899-1914'. In *Disease, Medicine, and Empire*, edited by Roy MacLeod and Milton Lewis. London: Routledge, 1988.

CHAPTER 3
CHANGING LANDSCAPES OF HEALTH AND
ILLNESS IN CONTEMPORARY AFRICA

Introduction

Thomas Adeoye Lambo, born in 1923, was raised in south-western Nigeria. After a Christian mission school education in his hometown Abeokuta, he attended the University of Birmingham, completing his medical studies in 1948. He continued his studies at the Maudsley Hospital in London, obtaining a psychiatric specialism in 1952 and thereby becoming the first Nigerian psychiatrist to be trained in Europe. In 1954 he became the first medical superintendent of Aro Mental Hospital, established the year previous and located near Abeokuta. Lambo quickly distinguished himself as a pioneer in the fledgling field of transcultural psychiatry, through his innovative clinical care approach and research at Aro. The 'Aro Village system' became a hallmark of transcultural psychiatry, and a model of the ways in which local healers could be meaningfully incorporated into biomedical therapies and institutions. His published studies forcefully critiqued the racialized gaze of ethno-psychiatry, which had previously dominated psychiatric discourse on mental illness among Africans in colonial territories (see Chapter 5). Lambo's book *African Traditional Beliefs: Concepts of Health and Medical Practice* (1963) remains an important statement of the ways in which local cultural perspectives could be meaningfully integrated into clinical care.

Lambo became the founding chair of the Department of Psychiatry of the University of Ibadan in 1963 and engaged in research with international collaborators, most notably on the Cornell (University)-Aro Mental Health Research Project, which developed an epidemiology of psychic distress among the Yoruba, employing novel cross-cultural approaches. He also was instrumental in developing the World Health Organization's (WHO) work on psychiatric epidemiology, and eventually became Deputy Director-General of WHO, a position he served from 1973 to 1988.[1] Writ large within Thomas Adeoye Lambo's extraordinary professional trajectory are dynamics that would come to define the health horizons of a politically transformed continent – differently conceived pathways of learning, knowledge exchange and therapeutic care, played out in a re-imagined global health landscape.

This chapter discusses the emergence and development of public health institutions and actors in post-colonial Africa, alongside a broad historical overview of changing health and disease patterns in Africa from the mid-twentieth century to the present day. The effects of the uneven development of public health infrastructures on the continent in the wake of independence from colonial rule in the 1950s and 1960s, as well as the rise of an African medical professional class, will be explored. The ideological innovations introduced by African nationalism and their impact on the 'Africanization' of biomedical practices and institutions are discussed. Concurrent transformations within and across indigenous healers' organizations and networks, and their incorporation into state health structures are also considered and historically contextualized alongside WHO's own changing stance on what it broadly termed 'traditional medicine'. The chapter continues the debate on the resilience and innovative capacity of local healing systems and ideas of well-being and disease. The chapter also seeks to historicize international interventions in African health across the post-colonial period, particularly with respect to disease eradication campaigns, and asks to what extent these have reproduced or altered earlier colonial dynamics. The recent emergence of 'global health' as an intellectual as well as political paradigm, and its influence on African health patterns and health agendas will be considered.

Understanding health and illness in the African postcolony: Concepts, approaches and sources

It is important to clarify at the outset some of the dynamic processes that have characterized health and healing since the widespread ending of colonial rule in Africa in the mid-twentieth century. A prominent dynamic is the Africanization of health services, in which the role of Africans as healers and healthcare providers as well as the complex decision-making of African patients has become more foreground. The movement back into the public sphere of local health practitioners and indigenous therapeutics, which was hidden from view or marginalized by colonial health structures, was one aspect of this process. 'Traditional medicine', as WHO would come to phrase it, experienced a resurgence and a reinvention in the post-colonial period. In the early decades of independence, some African states looked to older indigenous forms of healing much the same way they looked back to older forms of knowledge production, such as through oral historical sources, as a way to reclaim an African past and to define their independence from colonial frameworks and institutions. As will be seen later in this chapter, WHO contributed to the recognition and legitimation of traditional healers and their methods, and argued for their incorporation into a 'primary healthcare' model of public health in the developing world context.

Another facet to the Africanization of health services is the dramatic transformation in the staffing and administration of allopathic health institutions. Medical and scientific training provided by colonial health services, mission hospitals and internationally recognized research institutes (see Chapters 2 and 6) had by the interwar period created a nascent class of medical auxiliaries and a small elite corps of African medics and research scientists. This process was accelerated in the post-independence period. Medical training was progressively rolled out and expanded to Africans, and working in public hospitals, dispensaries and clinics became a recognizable and desired profession within the civil service. Nursing and midwifery became important career routes particularly for African women, and helped women achieve some measure of newfound agency within health structures as well as afforded them opportunities for economic and geographical mobility. With the growth and consolidation of a biomedically trained class of healthcare providers, the colonial-era distinction between biomedicine (as Western) and local healing systems (as African) could no longer hold, although it is arguable that this dichotomy was ever clear-cut, as has been explored in previous chapters. Africans became champions, and in many cases gatekeepers, of biomedical knowledge and were to play prominent roles in defending medically driven prevention and treatment programmes in the face of prominent disease challenges during this period, such as HIV/AIDS. Also, as will be discussed, the increasing role in the turn to the twenty-first century of locally based health volunteers and advocates, working in tandem with large-scale global health initiatives such as those set up in response to HIV/AIDS and Ebola, has meant lay individuals have become familiarized with areas of biomedical knowledge and discursive frameworks.

Another aspect in the Africanization of health is the progressive **medicalization of African healing** institutions, therapeutics and agents. An example of this is the utilization of scientific research to isolate and test the chemical properties in African traditional therapies, to derive and synthetically reproduce their healing effects. The modernization of traditional herbal medical practices also involved technological advances in storage and preparation processes for remedies. Similarly, some African states' attempts to register and regulate traditional healers and their treatments in the post-colonial period point to the application of standards and formal regulatory rubrics previously only associated with allopathic healthcare systems.

The **indigenization of biomedicine** was a process that occurred in parallel to the medicalization of African healing networks and practices. Just as local forms of healing were being incorporated into a biomedical institutionalized framework, other products and agents of that same infrastructure were being co-opted to further alternative therapeutic modes of healing. As will be seen, pharmaceutical drugs and medical care service providers came to be incorporated into 'folk' healing traditions and social networks. Similarly, in the case of HIV and Ebola, biomedical explanations for disease causation preferred by globally funded and framed intervention efforts were integrated into established local aetiologies of disease, suffusing older notions of contamination and contagion with new meanings and moral imaginaries.

The outcome of these processes of medicalization and indigenization is the overlapping of multiple therapeutic traditions and conceptual frameworks of disease – **medical pluralism** in action, although this generic term can mask what are in fact more specific and complex processes. Medical pluralism is not simply the co-existence in parallel of autonomous healing systems that exert no influence on each other. Pluralism can be expressed through the mixing of therapeutic traditions by a given healer, or by the agency of a patient who consciously chooses a range of potential therapies from multiple sources. Medical pluralism is due in part to the continuing resilience and reinvention of indigenous health institutions and therapies as well as the compatibility of African ideologies, which includes 'indigenized' Christianity and Islam, to healing frameworks.

In comparison to earlier periods (see Chapters 1 and 2), the volume of recorded statistical health data on Africans has increased exponentially in the post-colonial period. The range of sources available to us to historically reconstruct African health patterns and experiences has also diversified, particularly with respect to understanding the individual perspectives of African patients and healthcare workers. Although the increased diversity of sources, as well as their temporal proximity to the present-day, may create an enhanced aura of authenticity, it remains vital for scholars of history to maintain analytical distance to source material and to subject them to critique in the same manner as for older historical records on African health and illness. Furthermore, as Achille Mbembe and Luise White point out, the documentary archive in and of the African 'postcolony' needs to be seen as fractured, 'multi-sited', full of 'fragments of lives' as well as 'debris'.[2] How to recover the recent past through working with, and not against, these silences and fissures is a key analytic and methodological challenge for the historian.

A significant new source of **health data** on the African population was generated by newly **independent African states** that had a vested interest in accurate data collection both as a state-of-the-nation assessment mechanism and as a globally visible testament that African governments were capable of modernizing their own institutions of statecraft and surveillance. These data collection exercises produced a significant new body of raw demographic and health data, for example, census records, as well as state-sponsored surveys – at national, regional and local levels – of health indicators, including maternal and child health, mortality and death rates, and life expectancy. Fine-grained clinical research in hospitals has contributed to this body of information, through institutional-level data on the prevalence of communicable and non-communicable diseases (NCDs) as well as nutritional deficiencies, among others. The use of **clinical data from hospital records** and their publication in scientific journals can be traced back to the colonial period – for example, in the assiduous yet problematic collection of statistics on the presentation of 'mental derangements' in the few psychiatric hospitals in colonial African territories (see Chapter 5). However, arguably the scale and research context of these clinical studies have shifted in recent decades. These, alongside locally based administrative sources, have helped to produce rich **institutional histories** of influential hospitals in contemporary Africa, a genre particularly well represented in the southern African context, exemplified by the histories of Groote Schuur Hospital in the Western Cape by Anne Digby and Howard Philips, and Chris Hani Baragwanath Hospital in Soweto Township by Simonne Horwitz. Histories of scientific research institutes in Africa which have bilateral and international origins have additionally contributed to a changing history of scientific knowledge production in Africa at critical junctures, as can be seen in responses to malaria, sleeping sickness and HIV/AIDS (see Chapters 4 and 6).

In addition to these state and institutional records, there is a large corpus of **health data collected by international health agencies** which have become a significant force in responding to health challenges in Africa in the post-colonial period. WHO has made country-level and regional-level data collection a central part of their remit, and such detailed data has become integral to shaping their global health policies and agendas. Increasingly this data has been digitized, such as in the case of HIV/AIDS (see Chapter 4), so that the general public can at the click of a mouse procure fine-grained detail on disease prevalence, its demographic distribution as well as longitudinal patterns. Furthermore, WHO has its own documentary repository in Geneva and this archive has been utilized by historians of medicine to chart the organizational history of this unique institution as well as the history of international health as a political and ideological construct. It has also been used to catalogue and interrogate WHO's evolving health policies with respect to the Africa region, such as their changing position with regards to malaria disease eradication (see Chapter 6 and accompanying Source Analysis of a WHO 1960 report).

Whilst certainly these sources represent a significant advance on the limited and uneven data collection endeavours of the colonial state, large gaps of understanding remain. Data gathering and diagnostic and surveillance measures are themselves resource-intensive exercises, sometimes requiring skilled technicians and health professionals. Gaps emerge in the data where such human and technical resources are themselves spread thinly, or because of other less acknowledged factors. For example, the recording of AIDS-related deaths remains a haphazard affair (see Chapter 4), due to wide discrepancies amongst pathologists and medical professionals in the reporting of AIDS as a secondary cause of death, as well as the desire to avoid disclosing the HIV-status of the deceased to the family. This means that AIDS-related complications may remain under-reported in mortality statistics. Furthermore, as will be discussed in this chapter, the lack of 'baseline data' on many basic health and demographic indicators means it becomes difficult to verify and accurately describe large-scale theories of 'transition' – including the 'demographic transition' and the 'epidemiological transition' – which have been applied in recent decades to the African health context.

The growth of medical anthropology as an important sub-field of anthropology from the 1980s onwards has resulted in the publication of a number of **medical ethnographies** of African therapeutics and healing systems. Although on the one hand these are considered 'secondary sources' in the same way as other scholarly accounts, historians can utilize these more recent ethnographies in the same way that historians have utilized colonial ethnographies of African societies – as snapshots in time of contemporary practices and perceptions. These ethnographies are valuable for their specificity in describing local therapeutic practices as well as their attention to the social relations and spiritual paradigms underpinning African management of health and illness. Some medical anthropological approaches, however, do not have a sustained connection to historical patterns and dynamics, which limit their capacity to perceive and accurately historicize areas of widespread change or adaptation in forms of healing and local knowledge.

Oral testimonies are a significant source type utilized by historians of the post-colonial period. Oral sources could include testimonies of patient experience, but also oral histories of medical professionals, medical auxiliaries and local healers which may provide enriching detail on employment pathways within healing professions as well as unique perspectives on therapeutic interventions and decision-making. Although documented 'conversations' play a role in some colonial-era accounts including colonial ethnographies, and oral histories of elderly Africans have been utilized by historians to depict experiences of medical interventions in the 'twilight' of colonial rule, these are relatively few in number, far from comprehensive and temporally constrained. In contrast, oral sources are much more voluminous as well as more centrally integrated into historical accounts of post-colonial African experiences of health, particularly those accounts situated in the very recent past. They have helped, alongside hospital-based archives, to create a rich genre of **collective biographies** of African medical professionals, including those of doctors and nurses – seen in historical studies by John Iliffe of East African doctors and Shula Marks of South African nurses – in different African national contexts.

Finally, as will be discussed in Chapter 4, the HIV/AIDS pandemic has spurred the proliferation of other types of **first-person accounts**, utilizing a **multi-media** range of tools, including digital and internet-based technologies, visual media, and arts and crafts techniques. These accounts often express a very personal 'illness narrative', and provide poignant and potentially analytically powerful portrayals of an individual's experience of illness, as well as their own embodied understanding of the particular disease's impact. Although these first-person accounts have opened up new potentialities with respect to understanding the experiential dimension of illness, they are like other historical sources never wholly 'truthful' or unproblematic. The production of these accounts, as with oral testimonies, is affected by the power dynamics inherent in the settings in which they were created.

African independence and the re-shaping of health infrastructures, 1950s–70s

In the 1950s as independence movements were proliferating across colonial territories, the health prospects of Africans hung in the balance. As seen in the previous chapter, the immediate post-Second World War period witnessed several significant advances in the manufacture of chemotherapies and insecticides that emboldened calls for malaria eradication. Penicillin, first manufactured in the 1940s, was made more widely available in Africa by the 1950s, which enabled significant reductions in venereal syphilis. Other infectious diseases such as smallpox, bubonic plague, yaws and leprosy were effectively contained and were no longer experienced in devastating epidemic form as was the case earlier in the colonial period. Outbreaks of sleeping sickness, which had caused widespread mortality from the late nineteenth century and added to colonial anxieties over population decline in East, Central and southern Africa, had been suppressed dramatically by mid-century (see Chapter 6). However, malaria remained endemic and reached huge numbers, in some cases spreading into previously unaffected areas, while infectious diseases such as bilharzia and measles posed new and important health challenges.

Although by the 1950s colonial governments in Africa were responding to the crisis in rural healthcare by promoting the growth of 'health centres' and district hospitals, as was evident in East Africa, the legacy of uneven and under-resourced provision of colonial health services loomed large. Local healers remained an important therapeutic option throughout the colonial period in many areas. Indirect Rule may have enhanced the reach and cultural authority of traditional healers, as a viable alternative to the vertical model of healthcare employed in colonial medical interventions, particularly infectious disease campaigns. Furthermore, apart from a select few institutions such as in Uganda, Nigeria and South Africa, tertiary medical training for Africans was virtually non-existent. Very few trained medical personnel existed, then, to take up clinical positions as they opened up in the immediate post-colonial period. Available statistics from this time period are telling: in 1962 in Tanzania, there were only 12 registered African doctors and 5 interns in the government service; in Uganda, out of 102 nurses, only 24 were Ugandan; and in Kenya at its independence in 1963, medical doctors numbered approximately 750, but of these only 49 were African.[3]

The Africanization of health services: Early indications

With the formation of African nation-states, beginning with Ghana which achieved independence in 1957 and continuing in quick succession in other European-held territories throughout the 1960s, colonial governmental control over existing health infrastructures was at once removed. This had a profound effect at many different levels of healthcare delivery. The Africanization of health services in the immediate post-independence period can be understood in several different ways. First, simply, African states upon independence took over the medical administrative apparatus set up by the colonial powers. This included not only hospitals and medical training institutions but also the network of regional and rural clinics and dispensaries that existed. A key obstacle to the effective takeover of colonial health infrastructures was the colonial legacy of limited advanced medical training in African territories. Establishing new medical training institutions was key to addressing this pressing need, and several training centres were created, such as in Nairobi in 1967 with Kenyatta National Hospital as its primary teaching hospital, and a medical school attached to Muhimbili Hospital in Tanzania in 1963 whose primary aim was to produce future District Medical Officers to practise community medicine in rural areas. Cheikh Anta Diop University in Dakar was an important site of tertiary education in the 1960s and 1970s for Senegalese pharmacists, who became the 'first generation' of medical professionals as well as civil servants for the country's newly reconfigured public health system.[4]

By the late 1970s, the existing web of hospitals, clinics and dispensaries in many African nations came to be staffed primarily by Africans, and administered at the local, regional and national level by newly constituted state structures. The racialized distinctions in colonial hospital settings amongst and between staff and patients were effectively removed through this process. This was of course markedly different from the dynamics at work at the same time in South African hospitals, as apartheid policies mandating racial segregation were made manifest through the separate provision of 'European' and 'non-European' wards, and through mundane details such as racially divided entrances and colour-coded crockery and hospital bedding.[5] Research institutes also went through a process of Africanization with changes of personnel at every level and an emphasis on African authorship of research publications, as can be seen at Amani Hill Research Station (established in 1919 in colonial Tanganyika) whose first African director, Kenyan Philip Wegesa, took up his post in 1971 after working his way up the institute as a junior laboratory assistant and earning a diploma in applied parasitology and entomology at the London School of Hygiene and Tropical Medicine.[6] However, it is important to note that many qualified doctors left medical practice in the transitional and immediate post-independence period to serve in government, whether as newly elected representatives or as appointed ministers (such as covering the health portfolio) or other prominent public postings. Some of these doctors, like T. Adeoye Lambo, had been educated in overseas universities and medical schools in Europe and the United States. The presence of doctors in all the key health ministerial positions in newly independent Kenya and Uganda would have an important influence in national health policies over the subsequent two decades. Other trained medical personnel in fledgling African states took on roles in international agencies – many senior doctors worked with WHO or with the United Nations. Finally, the process of 'Africanization' changed the composition of professional associations binding medical practitioners together, although these newly constituted 'boards' did not necessarily afford medical doctors more professional security or influence in a rapidly changing public health landscape.

Second, the Africanization of health services was evidenced through the more public embrace of indigenous healing. In many African countries, the pivoting towards an Africa-centred as opposed to Western medical tradition was part and parcel of the larger cultural project espoused by African nationalism to re-orientate knowledge production. In the same way that many African nations looked to the 'recovery' of local oral forms of history-telling in order to re-assert an African framing of their pasts, African pharmacopeia and healing regimes were put centre-stage as exemplars of a renewed African link with its indigenous roots. In Tanzania, indigenous therapeutics were given equal footing as 'modern' medicine as part of the ruling party's socialist prioritization of rural health services over urban hospital-based care. One way in which indigenous healing was promoted in these new nation-states was to formalize and recognize associations of traditional healers. For example, Kwame Nkrumah, the first president of Ghana, encouraged the formation of a traditional healing association, the first of which was formed in 1963. Many other countries followed suit. Regional and national traditional healers' associations became evident and active in Ghana, Zambia, Tanzania, Botswana and Nigeria, among others. This growing level of organization amongst traditional healers was not wholly a new phenomenon – networks of healers existed in some form in the pre-colonial period – but acquired a new air of legitimacy within medical and scientific spheres. These associations established guidelines, promoted training and acted as referral centres.

Concurrently, efforts were begun in this period to better understand the scientific basis of African herbal remedies. Research units were set up to categorize the chemical, pharmacological and clinical benefits of certain medicinal plants. In 1974, the University of Dar es Salaam in Tanzania established the Traditional Medicine Research unit which to this day continues to carry out such research. African herbalists took their own routes to standardize the production of their remedies, with some entrepreneurial herbalists setting up shop in towns and cities and selling their products much like drugs in modern-day dispensaries. Patients were able to purchase these cures and self-medicate in the convenience of their homes.

A parallel development to this was the emergence as early as the 1950s of quasi-medical practitioners – widely known as 'needle-men' in East Africa – who administered allopathic drugs outside of a conventional hospital or clinic setting. The increased availability of chemotherapy as well as the relatively low level of skill involved in administering certain allopathic curatives meant that drug therapy was decoupled from clinical regimens. From the point of view of the patient, this was a positive development because it increased the range of curative choices available, particularly for those living distant from regional or district hospitals or a specialist clinic. In the decades to come, this shifting of the distribution of pharmaceuticals to folk or lay health practitioners would become a significant expression of the indigenization of biomedicine.[7]

The shift from colonial medicine to international health in Africa

This phase of the Africanization of health services coincided with a period of intense activity in the arena of international health, led by WHO. Africa was to play a large role not only as a key testing ground for new, bold collaborative approaches to international health, but also in forcing fundamental transformations to those approaches. The story of the challenges, successes and failures of these health interventions on African soil is also a story of the changing nature of WHO itself, its goals and capabilities.

In the early 1950s, WHO entered into what has been called the 'global disease eradication' phase of its history, lasting until the Alma Ata Conference of 1978 when a distinct shift to primary healthcare occurred. The global disease eradication agenda was characterized by its vertical approach and its operationalization of large cadres of medical personnel charged with surveillance and recording disease incidence. The focus was less on disease management or the health of individuals. Disease eradication was spurred not only by mid-twentieth-century advances in chemotherapy and insecticidal chemicals, but also by the urgency of knowing the impending development of vector and pathogenic resistance that would render those same chemicals powerless. Rather than focusing on building systems and structures to deal with disease control, which was seen as ultimately more costly, the goal was to swiftly overwhelm and then eradicate the disease.

Certainly, the crowning achievement of this first phase was the successful global eradication of smallpox, which was declared 8 May 1980. This was from a situation where, in the early 1950s, WHO had reported an estimated 50 million cases per year, with 60 per cent of the world's population at risk. No effective treatment, other than immediate post-exposure vaccine, was known for those with smallpox. WHO's programme to eradicate smallpox was based on three broad principles, in some ways drawing from lessons learned from the failures of the malaria eradication programme, which had been operating for several years up until this point: the participation of all countries; flexibility; and, ongoing research in the lab and field. The development of a freeze-dried vaccine which could be deployed to mobile vaccination points, bringing vaccines within close proximity of every household, was instrumental. Surveillance systems were effective and encouraged the prompt reporting of outbreaks. Smallpox itself was relatively easily identifiable, and research showed that it spread more slowly than previously believed, meaning that it could ultimately be contained. These factors contributed to the programme's eventual success, despite shortage of vaccines and other resources. Importantly, as has been pointed out by historians cognizant of colonial dynamics, widespread and regular smallpox vaccination programmes from the early twentieth century in colonial African territories and particularly throughout French West and Equatorial Africa laid the infrastructural and procedural groundwork for that success. Smallpox outbreaks had been contained and reduced by mid-century in colonial Africa, through the same sorts of systematic monitoring and isolation procedures and cross-border cooperation which later characterized WHO-led eradication efforts.[8]

The weaknesses of the disease eradication model can be seen clearly when looking at attempts to address African incidence of malaria (discussed at length in Chapter 6) and yellow fever, a viral infectious disease transmitted by the *Aedes* mosquito with monkeys as an animal reservoir for the virus. In the interwar period, deadly outbreaks of yellow fever occurred in Nigeria and Sudan, and in the 1960s further outbreaks in Ethiopia and Senegal were observed. Well before WHO's efforts in the late colonial period, an effective vaccine had been developed and trans-national cooperation was in place with regards to yellow fever prevention – in French-held West African territories, an estimated 25 million were immunized every four years in a highly successful programme. Although WHO developed a more comprehensive system for prevention and emergency treatment for yellow fever, involving surveillance, immunization and mosquito control, the implementation of this complex system was difficult and required thorough-going cooperation from local authorities and clinics. Constant testing was necessary because of yellow fever's tricky pathophysiology, which could be mistaken with viral hepatitis or malaria in its early stages.

WHO underestimated how disruptive these measures would be on communities, and how much surveillance and control would put immense strain on local resources and institutions. By the 1960s, many countries in Africa had switched from routine immunization to post-outbreak emergency immunization, a shift WHO was partly responsible for in its desire for disease eradication over preventative measures. The end result was that there was a resurgence of yellow fever outbreaks in 1980s in Africa, such as in Nigeria and Ethiopia. It was only in the 1990s that WHO's Expanded Immunization Programme returned to the earlier emphasis on disease prevention, advocating for the delivery of yellow fever vaccines alongside measles vaccinations.

WHO's orientation during this roughly three-decade period from the 1950s to 1970s has strong echoes of the vertical approach which had marked some aspects of colonial health policies in Africa of the preceding decades, particularly those concerning infectious disease containment and control (see Chapters 2 and 6). Indeed, it is fair to suggest, as some scholars have done, that WHO's emphasis demonstrated a *continuation* of colonial health policies in its focus on combatting infectious disease over a more broad-based approach to preventative and community-based healthcare. Recent research has disrupted this narrative of WHO's narrow emphasis on disease eradication in Africa this period, suggesting instead that WHO was well aware of the need for health services and infrastructures to be developed in newly independent nation-states, and elaborated a planning apparatus to drive that development forward beginning in West Africa – in Gabon, Mali, Liberia, Sierra Leone and Niger. However, these plans to enhance health services capacity in these nations were themselves largely created in a top-down fashion with little input provided by local agencies and health authorities, and ultimately were not adopted by the countries concerned.[9]

Furthermore, it is important to reflect on the consequences of this vertical approach at the precise time when many newly independent African states were seeking to shed colonial legacies and implement a more de-centred, inclusive and 'horizontal' system of healthcare. WHO's work prior to 1979 can be seen as a type of 'medical paternalism', because it was largely driven by a commitment to Western biomedicine as its main health systems model.[10] It was not until the post-Alma Ata era that alternative pathways of therapeutic care were more fully recognized by international health actors and institutions. This mismatch of domestic to international health priorities had manifold consequences.

From Alma Ata to the emergence of HIV/AIDS: Primary healthcare and its limits

Primary healthcare and traditional medicine

In 1978, WHO in concert with the United Nations International Children's Emergency Fund (UNICEF) developed a definition of primary healthcare at the Alma Ata Conference which was to have implications on the evolution of a more inclusive framework of healthcare in developing countries. Alma Ata represented a key shift in the international health agenda away from a focus on mass disease eradication campaigns to return to the lines of WHO's foundational statement. This shift was to some extent the result of the sobering realization of a lack of consistent funding for international health initiatives by donor nations, as well as the severe lack of resources (human and financial) in the developing countries which were the object of these interventions. It was also the result of disillusionment with the vertical eradication model that was championed in earlier decades. Despite the singular success of smallpox eradication, the recurrence of yellow fever outbreaks and the persistence of malaria were two key examples which illustrated the failings of the disease eradication approach.

The emphasis shifted to holistic treatment and preventative care rather than post-outbreak intervention. Particularly, research on vaccine development and routine immunization for children became a key focus. WHO's Expanded Immunization Programme in the 1990s can be seen as the culmination of this two decades-long approach. Furthermore, WHO shifted its view of traditional medicine, and advocated working with indigenous healers and institutions. In the context of WHO's shift to 'community health', which included a framework of health delivery that emphasized community participation and also the values of autonomy and patient choice, traditional healers were identified as critical players.

The models presented by the system of socialized healthcare in China and the Soviet Union in this period were influential in challenging the hegemony of a biomedical model premised on the ideological superiority of the West, and the Soviet Union in particular advocated strongly for a global turn to the primary healthcare approach as well as rethinking the direction of disease eradication approaches. Community-based health surveillance methods were one innovation. Indeed, during a time of Cold War politics, the Soviet Union saw health as a potential arena where 'soft diplomacy' could be levied on a global level. The Soviet Union trained a cadre of African doctors as well as collaborated on medical and scientific research projects with African institutes. Amani Research Station, a key research institute for malaria and vector-borne diseases in Tanzania, utilized a Soviet method of establishing the physiological age of a female mosquito, called the 'Polovodova method', which was taught by Tatjana Sergeevna Detinova on a WHO-commissioned journey in 1962 to various field stations in Africa. Dating mosquitoes accurately was considered critical in assessing the efficacy of DDT-spraying campaigns.[11] The New Nyanza General Hospital in Kisumu, Kenya, was gifted by the Soviet Union in 1969. Soviet expertise contributed to the hospital design, and the hospital was established fully equipped with X-ray facilities, laboratories, an operating theatre and a pharmacy. Locals to this day refer to the provincial hospital as, simply, 'Russia'.[12]

The African economic and political context is a vital consideration in this changing orientation. The 1970s and 1980s have generally been considered by historians to be a time of growing pessimism about the potential of independent African states to realize widespread freedoms as well as economic development. The democratic governments of African states after independence had been replaced, in some cases, by military rule (such as in Ghana and Nigeria) or despotic regimes (such as in Zaire, now the Democratic Republic of the Congo). Several African states entered into a period of crippling debt and economic decline, including painful structural adjustment policies which were imposed as a condition for the disbursement of large loans provided by the International Monetary Fund and World Bank. The conditions of repayment meant that precious few national resources could be devoted to maintaining already overburdened health infrastructures, leading to the decline of public healthcare provisioning. Zambia's experience of structural adjustment imposed by the International Monetary Fund and the World Bank in the 1980s and its relation to healthcare provisioning is a case in point, as the historian Randall Packard has shown. The impact of structural adjustment was felt across the manufacturing, agriculture and mining sectors, decreasing employment and suppressing wages whilst increasing per capita debt, the latter having a direct impact on per capita government expenditure on health, which declined precipitously through the 1990s. At the same time, stagnating wages meant that many trained healthcare workers, in particular nurses, left Zambia to work in South Africa or further afield. The imposition of user fees by the Zambian government in 1993 made basic healthcare even less accessible to Zambian households, in particular rural households. These growing inequities, coupled with drug shortages as well as changing settlement patterns, resulted in resurgence of infectious diseases such as malaria and tuberculosis in Zambia in the 1990s and early 2000s.[13] The out-migration of health professionals as well as the privatization of healthcare services, including drug dispensing, was a consistent theme in other African states by the 1990s.

In this context, traditional medicine played a vital role in fulfilling WHO's and UNICEF's vision of effective and fully participatory healthcare, and was seen as a necessary partner to fill the breach left by deteriorating allopathic health systems. Attempts were made to integrate traditional healing and therapeutic knowledge more functionally into the provision of healthcare on the ground. African traditional healers were recognized for their enduring role within communities as healthcare providers, particularly in rural areas where medical clinics and hospitals were too distant to access. Traditional healing came to be recognized in this period for its user-appeal, its affordability and accessibility, and low healer-to-patient ratio compared to the distribution of healers in the allopathic medical system. As an indication, in Ghana the doctor-to-patient ratio was estimated at 1:10,000 in 1980, and in Zambia at 1:9,000 in the mid-1980s.[14] By 1995, it was estimated that over 75 per cent of the rural population in Africa sought healthcare among traditional healers.

In many parts of Africa, WHO's envisioned incorporation of indigenous medicine into primary and public healthcare structures was not completely seamless. Paternalistic attitudes still pervaded many supposed 'collaborative' schemes involving traditional healers. Some local healers themselves resisted integration into biomedical institutional frameworks – they were reluctant to divulge their curatives and healing techniques, concerned that their authority could be undermined if this knowledge was widely shared. This was particularly the case for those for whom divination rather than herbal knowledge was the basis of their healing technology. Tellingly, in a 1990s survey of Maasai 'medicine-men', 84 per cent stated that there should not be cooperative relationships between them and health personnel in primary healthcare delivery, and 98 per cent of those surveyed dismissed the need for any training in modern healthcarre.[15] Such views reflected an unwillingness to be answerable to dictates from an allopathic framework which was largely constructed, in their view, in opposition to their own.

The Traditional Medicine research project (TRAMED) was launched in South Africa in 1997 as a research project involving the University of Cape Town and the nation's Medical Research Council to create a database of traditional medicines used in southern and East Africa, and to conduct lab-based testing for traditional cures for certain diseases, such as malaria and tuberculosis. The newly democratic South African state found it difficult to regulate traditional medicine, despite the passing of the South African Medicines and Medical Devices Regulatory Authority Act in 1998. This included traditional medicine as a 'complementary medicine' in its remit and required all *muthi* [traditional medicine] to be formally registered with the Medicines Control Council. The regulation and registration of traditional healers were later formalized, as was the production of guidance on the training and qualifications required to become a traditional healer. However, *muthi* regulations were not enforced strictly, and traditional healers in South Africa resisted attempts to standardize their profession and resented being positioned in a largely subordinate role as peripheral to biomedical institutions and mainly as referral agents to hospitals or doctors.

Notwithstanding these challenges, there have been successes. In Kenya, the Karati Rural Service Centre used local herbal techniques to treat diseases such as hypertension, asthma, diabetes, arthritis, diarrhoea. The modernization of herbal remedies was effected through technological and manufacturing innovations, from simple distillation and canning to technically difficult hygienic drying, grinding, mixing, packaging and storing.[16] The Kenyan Ministry of Health advocated for the training of herbalists in patient care at the Kenyatta National Hospital. The relationship was reciprocal, and during the HIV/AIDS pandemic the Ministry called on herbalists to join them in search of treatments. More recently, plants that were long part of indigenous pharmacopeia have become recognized for their chemical and healing properties, with local groups profiting from their commercialization. The active ingredient of the plant *Hoodia gordonii*, used historically by the Kalahari San to stave off hunger during long hunts, was licensed to a pharmaceutical company which then sold the rights to the manufacturer Pfizer and marketed *Hoodia* as an organic diet pill. The San won a landmark deal in 2003 ensuring they would be paid royalties from the sales.

The declining resources within public health services, the weakening of the state and the need to adapt healthcare delivery to local conditions, which the turn to traditional healing was meant to address, had another perhaps unintended consequence – the indigenization of biomedical practices and products. This can be most clearly seen in the ways in which biomedical technologies, especially pharmaceutical drugs, by the 1990s had become firmly integrated into local healing regimes. This was not simply the *co-existence* of multiple therapeutic ideas and practices, but rather an illustration of the *permeability* of boundaries between allopathic and local knowledge practices and systems. Indigenization in this context, as the anthropologist Susan Reynolds Whyte illustrated with respect to Uganda, involved the administration of drugs and the application of diagnostic techno-practices (involving stethoscopes, blood pressure meters, blood sugar readers) by folk health practitioners. These practitioners were themselves not wholly 'outside' of the system of allopathic care – they could be employed in clinic, dispensary or hospital settings, positions which often helped gain access to drugs and diagnostic tools, even though their therapies were conducted outside of these biomedical institutions. The archetypal East African 'needle-men' continued to remain visible and offer relevant therapeutic options to local communities, although it was clear that by the 1990s the tools of their craft – the needle and syringe – as well as the drugs customers would pay to have injected came from a widening array of sources and webs of relations that reflected the changing health landscape of the time. These relations could be formed via local trade networks, through direct or indirect links with a clinic, dispensary or hospital, or through participation in international health initiatives, the latter often offering basic medical training to lay individuals that could be re-purposed to further livelihoods long after the health intervention programme itself ended. The indigenization of these biotechnologies, then, did not fundamentally alter the meanings and therapeutic relations and principles within which local healing tended to operate. Rather, the healing remedies diversified to include allopathic treatments.

The turn to primary healthcare in the late 1970s and 1980s was meant to address the failings of the eradicationist agenda and help pivot African health provisioning towards a more inclusive, therapeutically diverse and community-orientated approach. Although there were some welcome developments in this regard particularly with more formal recognition for herbalists and plant-based traditional remedies, the larger structural social and economic forces which underpinned domestic health service capacity and delivery failed to be addressed by WHO's primary healthcare model. As African nation-states entered into the 1990s, political instability and painful structural adjustment policies added further downward pressures on vulnerable healthcare infrastructures, exacerbating the medical 'brain drain', reducing health sector wages and public health financing, and spurring the privatization of drug procurement and medical care. These processes would be put to the test during the ensuing HIV/AIDs pandemic.

HIV/AIDS and global health paradigms

The more virulent form of Human Immunodeficiency Virus, HIV-1, first emerged in western equatorial Africa in the mid-1970s, its particular epidemiology confirmed a decade later. As the historian John Iliffe has shown, HIV-1 (the strain most common in sub-Saharan Africa) spread first to East Africa in the late 1970s, then southwards and finally into West Africa by the 1980s, where the less pathogenic HIV-2 had already become established. HIV's long incubation period in humans as well as the extended duration between infection and the development of symptoms and full-blown AIDS meant that the virus moved through African communities silently for much of the 1980s. Even when HIV/AIDS was recognized as spreading in epidemic form and constituting a serious health issue, African states and health infrastructures were slow to respond to the epidemic in its first decade and a half (see Chapter 4 for a detailed analysis of HIV/AIDS and history).

The consequences of this delayed response were manifold. By the time African nations were ready to intervene, not only had HIV transmission rates already reached intolerable levels, but the scope had narrowed dramatically for developing a locally tailored approach to prevention and treatment. The 'script' for 'successful' HIV/AIDS intervention programmes had already been set by global health authorities, honed in the specific cultural and political milieu of homosexual populations in Western countries most affected by HIV, and largely predicated on the assumption of patients' autonomy over their own sexual decision-making as well as inalienable principles of 'patient rights' including voluntary testing and drug-taking regimes.[17] This script proved to be ill-fitted to address the vastly different political and cultural contexts of a largely heterosexual HIV+ population whose life choices were profoundly constrained by asymmetrical economic, sexual and power dynamics.

In the first years of the new millennium, scientific advances in the pharmaceutical industry allied to a growing sense of urgency amongst African nation-states and the philanthropic might of privately funded donor organizations such as the Bill and Melinda Gates Foundation helped to usher in a pivotal milestone in the history of the AIDS pandemic – the development and widespread rollout of generic antiretroviral (ARV) drugs. This made large-scale HIV treatment fiscally and administratively possible in many parts of the continent. Botswana, for example, which has one of the highest national prevalence rates in the world – averaging around 25 per cent adult prevalence rate in the 2000s – went into a multi-year partnership in 2000 with the Bill and Melinda Gates Foundation to distribute ARVs, build HIV-testing and treatment clinics, and embed prevention programmes in local communities. In other countries, the transition to wide-scale rollout was a contentious process, as in South Africa in 2002 when the government was successfully challenged in the Constitutional Court by the Treatment Action Campaign, an AIDS-advocacy group, and compelled to distribute ARVS more widely.

The rates of new cases of HIV as well as AIDS-related mortality in sub-Saharan Africa peaked in the early 2010s, and levels of HIV transmission have shown progressive decline in some areas. Combination ARV therapy has been a life-saving treatment for many HIV+ survivors. These developments, when combined with the promise of immuno-therapy interventions to 're-set' the body's immune system as well as the development of pre-exposure prophylaxis (or PrEP), appear to have augured a 'new era' in the continent's front-line battle against HIV/AIDS. WHO has confidently set a new goal of eradicating HIV by 2030. Taken as a whole, public health approaches of African nation-states towards HIV/AIDS have moved from a 'crisis' model towards 'management' and long-term sustainability – this coincided with the ending of major internationally funded initiatives such as the Gates Foundation partnership programme in Botswana (in 2007) and the Médicins sans Frontières intervention in Lusikisiki, South Africa (in 2006). Similarly, HIV+ survivors in many parts of the continent with adequate access to low-cost ARV medication are increasingly able to view their disease as a chronic condition to be managed rather than a death sentence. Volunteer-led peer-support groups and the rise of local HIV+ health advocates have encouraged greater levels of testing amongst community members, as well as helped HIV+ participants adhere to their drug-taking regimens.

However, it is worthwhile to caution against any view of wholesale transformation or 'triumph'. There is no inevitable trajectory, or 'teleology' as historians like to call it, towards inevitable mastery over the disease. There are currently 25.6 million HIV+ survivors in sub-Saharan Africa.[18] As will be seen in Chapter 4, the experiences of survivors reveal how uncertain the health outcomes have been for many millions with a positive diagnosis, and the tremendous toll of that uncertainty on bodies, families and societies. Furthermore, the mutation of the HI virus may yet yield strains that are resistant to the cocktail of ARV medication currently standard in treatment regimens throughout the continent. The pharmaceutical development of so-called third-line drugs that would protect against these resistant strains is in its infancy, despite insistent calls by African AIDS advocacy groups to accelerate this research.

The interventions of the Gates Foundation in African HIV/AIDS treatment and prevention are emblematic of a broader shift in funding landscapes and global health partnerships that emerged at the turn to the new millennium. These new alliances were to some extent born of necessity, a consequence of decades of under-investment in African health infrastructures and in medical training which had left African states under-equipped and under-mobilized to deal with an epidemic of this magnitude. Alongside philanthropic funding bodies such as the Gates Foundation, other public-private and cross-sectoral alliances came into being. Chief amongst these was the establishment in 2001 of the Global Fund to Fight AIDS, Tuberculosis and Malaria. The Global Fund is in essence an international health financing institute. It works with, but is autonomous from, the United Nations and WHO, as well as with governments, civil society and the private sector. Crucially, the Global Fund does not implement health programmes but gives grants to others organizations and agencies to run them in local settings. In 2006, the Gates Foundation made a $500 million contribution to the Global Fund, illustrating the linkages across these funding institutions. Bilateral health organizations, such as the President's Emergency Plan for AIDS (PEPFAR) created by United States President George W. Bush in 2003, is another key player in the new global health landscape. Crucially, PEPFAR's funding for HIV/AIDS interventions was orientated towards faith-based non-governmental organizations (NGOs) which ran local HIV prevention programmes that had an explicit promotion of abstinence. The Product Red campaign, famously launched by the musician Bono in 2006, heralded a new fundraising strategy which appealed to the public's consumerist instincts as a means to increase awareness of global health challenges (proceeds from a purchase with the Product Red logo would go directly to the Global Fund) as well as popularize the fund's appeal to younger audiences.

The proliferation of these new funding bodies and alliances signalled a shift not only to novel cross-sectoral global health partnerships but also to a performance-based funding model. This global health paradigm would be re-deployed, with variations, to address other health crises, such as malaria and Ebola. As Randall Packard has shown in his history of global health, this approach has favoured clearly defined and finite interventions with demonstrable outcomes over and above longer term, and thus harder to assess, investments in personnel and health infrastructures. This orientation thus reproduces some of the classic weaknesses of WHO's disease eradication model.

Although the notion of a top-down global health paradigm imposed uniformly on local settings is persuasive, the everyday operation of global health is more variegated and complex, as Paul Wenzel Geissler has argued, and works through multiple and criss-crossing local, national and supra-national agents, organizations and institutions –

what he has termed the 'para-state'. The para-state framework offers an alternative perspective on global health dynamics, one that recognizes the critical contributions of local actors and research 'enclaves', some of which have origins dating back to the colonial period. Entire cities could become zones of the para-state, as Geissler and Ruth Prince have shown for Kisumu, Kenya, which had been a major internationally funded hub for malaria research and then became reactivated as an enclave geared towards HIV/AIDS research. Kisumu is now an archetypal 'global health boomtown' because of its saturation of international scientific research and intervention units.[19] Many African countries where NGOs are particularly active experience this saturation, and local communities have become well acquainted with the phenomena of 'research fatigue' through being co-opted into a plethora of health and development studies and surveys.

African researchers and medical professionals contributed valuable epidemiological and clinical research in the early decades of the HIV epidemic. Cameroonian researchers from the mid-1980s carried out epidemiological investigations on HIV/AIDS, utilizing the existing research enclaves of the Pasteur Centre of Cameroon (CPC) and the Organization for the Control and Fight against Great Epidemics in Central Africa (OCECA), both established in Cameroon the mid-twentieth century. One influential Cameroonian scientist was Professor Lazare Kaptue, a French-trained serologist who became the director of the National Programme for the Fight against AIDS in the late 1980s, and was known as 'Mr. AIDS'.[20] East African doctors were also a formative force in researching HIV in its early years, in particular establishing its epidemiology through heterosexual transmission (what would become the predominant form of HIV transmission globally), despite the considerable constraints of poor laboratory equipment and lack of specialist training. South Africa was another important globally connected enclave of HIV/AIDS research, producing studies from the 1980s that were published in the *South African Medical Journal* on both homosexual and heterosexual HIV transmission, which reflected the particular clinical environment and HIV patient cohorts in this country.[21]

Finally, Africans cannot be viewed as merely passive bystanders who received global health interventions unproblematically. They may also prove adept at traversing local and global settings. Many of the local NGOs utilized as conduits for global health interventions had cut their teeth on earlier community health or social issues. In South Africa, the vibrant civil society engendered by the anti-apartheid movement provided a well-networked set of local organizations as well as seasoned activists who were adept at using local, national and international media channels. The trajectory of the Treatment Action Campaign, and its main figurehead Zachie Achmat, is an archetypal example of how older channels and strategies of political activism could be re-purposed for AIDS advocacy. Furthermore, HIV+ survivors themselves became a vocal group, utilizing their own personal narratives of illness to embrace a more globally orientated and empowered notion of 'biological citizenship', which helped produce a sustained political challenge to African governments to provide affordable access to HIV medication and treatment (see Chapter 4).[22]

Religion, faith-healing and medical pluralism

Religious and spiritual beliefs intersected with the HIV/AIDS epidemic in multiple ways. As will be seen in the following chapter, Christian moral proscriptions embedded in some HIV prevention programmes – for example, in the call for abstinence as opposed to the promotion of condom use – had colonial antecedents in missionary attempts to regulate African sexual behaviour. Furthermore, Christian imagery framed the experiential trajectory of HIV+ survivors, through their public participation in new 'confessional technologies' which expressed the power of the transformation from 'near death' to 'new life' wrought through the taking of ARVs. For the minority Muslim community in Kisumu, Kenya, the conventions of Islamic religious education presented a forum through which to engage in moral as well as medical debates about HIV prevention and transmission, and its relative prevalence in Muslim versus non-Muslim communities in Africa. Whilst positing a view of a dominant Islamic sexual ethics, these discussions also yielded the opportunity to frame Islam in Kisumu as ultimately a modern, engaged and relevant religion.[23] In the Bushbuckridge region of South Africa, as Isak Niehaus has shown, the failure of biomedical 'cures' and interventions in an area of high HIV prevalence created the analytic space within which communities could re-fashion AIDS through local moral discourses of death, and utilize still-relevant therapeutic tools of dream interpretation to fully comprehend the bodily effects of taking ARVs.[24]

Christian churches differently responded to the crisis of mortality hastened by the AIDS epidemic. In Tooro, western Uganda, a revivalist charismatic movement within the Roman Catholic Church enabled it to actively engage with, rather than suppress, local discourses of witchcraft and cannibalism associated with the rise in AIDS-related deaths. As a consequence, previously dormant groups within the auspices of the Church became re-activated to ritually cleanse and purge the area of suspected 'pagans'.[25] Christian churches could also be spaces of comfort and spiritual healing for AIDS-ravaged communities. As Frederick Klaits has shown through his ethnography of an Apostolic Church in Botswana, the 'intersubjectivity' of care practised by church members – through singing, prayer and funerary rites – could re-inscribe AIDS-related deaths within a newly imagined moral community, one in which sentiments such as love could constitute a central therapeutic device.[26]

To some extent, the HIV/AIDS epidemic catalysed religious and spiritual dynamics that were already in flux in the post-colonial period. Scholars have pointed to the declining capacity of the state in many parts of Africa in the 1970s and 1980s, and how that created a space in which religion could take on a more 'public' role.[27] Worsening public health infrastructures, constrained access to allopathic therapies and drugs, and the limited success and reach of global health interventions in this same period reinforced that the search for efficacious healing could not be guaranteed within a biomedical framework. Local healers and their remedies, as well as forms of faith-healing and spirit-healing within charismatic and African Independent Churches, found new purchase within this context:

Historical Source: *Madumo: A Man Bewitched*, by Adam Ashforth (2000)

'Hhayi! Man,' he said. 'When that [Zionist Christian Church (ZCC)] prophet hit me in the chest – did you see that? – then all of a sudden I became sick. I mean, I'm sick, Adam. Seriously sick. I could feel this thing moving up and down inside. But I didn't know this thing was going to give me such a serious fight. The whole night I've been fighting it. But now I have a problem .... ' He slumped back onto his pillow.

Madumo's problem was that he was already undergoing treatment with *muthi* [medicine] provided by the *inyanga*, Mr. Zondi. It was Mr. Zondi's duty to heal him in all regards. If the ZCC prophet was speaking the truth, and Mr. Zondi had not spotted the *isidliso* [poison], then Madumo should follow the prescriptions of the prophet and drink the FG coffee. He was supposed to boil the whole half-pound packet in a saucepan of water – 'boil it to the amen,' he said – and then drink it down while it cooled. Then vomit. But this entailed a major risk. For the medicine of the ZCC might clash with the medicine of the traditional healer, the *inyanga*. The spirits of the church (which empower the coffee) are totally opposed to the spirits of the *inyangas*. 'It can kill me,' Madumo said, his face bearing the strain of his terror. 'Do you see that?' 'This thing is going to give me a hell of a problem. Because it's man-made. And the one who created it is quite aware that I'm fighting this thing off. And he's going to put more effort, or she, whatever it is, is going to put more effort in, just to make this thing kill me.'

Source Analysis: From the chapter entitled, 'Isidliso Nights', this evocative extract is noteworthy for several reasons, not least for its direct and vivid imagery, and the utilization by the anthropologist Adam Ashforth of a rhetorical device – the dialogue between an 'afflicted' African and a Western observer – that can be traced back to nineteenth-century missionary 'conversations' and colonial ethnographies [see Chapters 1 and 2]. In this case, Madumo, the central protagonist and subject of Ashforth's account, is struggling to balance the prescriptive treatments of two different healing regimes – one proferred by the Zionist Christian Church, of which he is a long-time, though lapsed, member and the inyanga, *who had prescribed* muthi *for Madumo to take.*

This extract illustrates medical pluralism at work, one healing tradition involving an African Independent Church and the other invoking traditional Zulu therapeutics, although Ashforth stresses in his account that by the end of the twentieth century, even inyangas *had to adapt their 'traditional' methods to accommodate the rapidly changing socio-economic and political environment of the post-apartheid city. In one sense, this encounter depicts African patient-clients as autonomous individuals who do not necessarily accept the authority of a single healing system and pursue alternative, co-existing therapeutic strategies. However, the extract also reveals that the search for the correct diagnosis and cure could be accompanied by anxiety over which therapeutic approach was authentic, and whether the remedies prescribed could be mixed at all. This account also reveals the 'terror' Madumo experienced in trying to determine the source of witchcraft, whose potentially lethal poison (isidliso) was, in his view, definitively 'man-made'.*

Transition theories, African realities and 'new' disease frontiers

Scholars have tried to discern broad trends and patterns of change in African health outcomes across the twentieth and twenty-first centuries. Two such important 'transition theories' which describe the arc of those changes are the *demographic transition* and the *epidemiological transition*. Because of the lack of baseline data in African historical health contexts, it is difficult to verify the starting point from which these theories of transition and change are constructed, and determine the shape of the resultant curve. Some scholars working with transition theory argue that the exceptions and variations to the rule are equally as critical to our understanding as describing the general curve. Others argue that the exceptions reveal the hollowness and inaccuracies of the model.

Demographic transition? Fertility and reproductive decision-making

Why are demographics important to the historical study of Africa? Demographic change is one way to measure the severity (i.e. the cost in human lives) of an event or health crisis, as seen in the contentious debates around the demographic impact of the slave trade (Chapter 1) and in the wake of the HIV/AIDS pandemic (Chapter 4). But demographic change is indicative of larger socio-economic and political shifts as well – population studies are not only about counting people but also about the social and cultural context of population changes. For example, fertility is not just a biological trait made up of fecundity (which measures female reproductive potential, for instance through the number of eggs in one's ovaries). It is about reproductive *choice* as well, and in that decision-making lies a whole host of contingent issues – gender relations, access to education, resources, existent knowledge. As seen in Chapter 2, fertility and reproductive concerns were of interest to the colonial state. Population growth was not merely about numbers – it was about structures, modes of surveillance and control that could penetrate very deeply into the most intimate spaces and regimens of one's lives. And ideas regarding African fertility were never far divorced from perceptions about African sexuality, which framed and complicated colonial responses to sexually transmitted disease. So, the history of population change and the changing history of reproductive strategies can give us another window into the broader social history of Africa.

Census data, unlike in the West which undertook census-taking in the late eighteenth and early nineteenth centuries, did not become a reality for most African countries until well into the 1970s, as newly independent African states needed time to develop proper infrastructures to conduct full-scale censuses of their populations. These new census-recording infrastructures had to be developed from the ground up – most colonial regimes in Africa had not bothered with comprehensive census data of their territories. Missionary-held birth and death records, while a very useful longitudinal record of certain parishes or districts in Africa, were woefully short of being comprehensive. An exceptions to this general pattern were those African polities that were ruled by white minority regimes, which were more invested in both longitudinal and comprehensive population counting exercises as a manifestation of anxieties around African population growth. However, even these states produced problematic census figures – for example in South Africa, which arguably had one of the most well-developed local, provincial and national infrastructures producing a regular series of population figures according to race across the twentieth century, the data was still flawed. The miscounting or undercounting of urban African populations was a consistent theme, exacerbated by apartheid legislation which resolutely saw Africans as permanently rural, particularly in its early decades, and the determination of Africans to evade surveillance mechanisms. Even in the waning years of apartheid, the state used aerial snapshots of black townships as viable estimates of the black population, although faulty assumptions of what a 'typical' black household size could be complicated their calculations, illustrating its unwillingness to devote the manpower necessary to conduct door-to-door census gathering of these areas. When South Africa finally became a democratic state, its first census in 1994 showed that the black African population was significantly smaller than had been projected and assumed (TFR, defined as the number of children a woman would have during her reproductive life-span if the current age-specific levels of fertility remained constant).[28]

As discussed in Chapter 2, there is a consensus that there was a demographic decline in East and Central Africa in the early colonial period between 1880 and 1920, culminating with high mortality caused by the influenza pandemic at the end of First World War. West Africa, in contrast, had a relatively stable population throughout this period. It is also generally acknowledged that from the 1920s onwards most of sub-Saharan Africa experienced significant and rapid population growth. The latest estimates suggest that the African population increased from approximately 145 million in 1890 to 220 million in 1950, reaching 807 million by 2000, with net annual growth rates between 1950 and 2000 at more than 2.5 per cent.[29]

This rapid population growth, underpinned by decreasing mortality rates and what appeared to be declining fertility rates in the second half of the twentieth century, led many commentators in the 1980s and 1990s to suggest that the African continent was undergoing a 'demographic transition'. This is a transition theory which describes the underlying changes in the rates of increase in a given population as a sort of dome-shaped curve, moving from conditions of high mortality coupled with high fertility to low birth and low mortality rates. It is generally agreed that the West experienced a gradual demographic transition from the late eighteenth through the nineteenth centuries, associated with industrialization, control over epidemics, increased infant survival, and migration out of Europe which relieved Malthusian population pressures and eased resource scarcity. By the late twentieth century, some European countries began to experience below-replacement levels of fertility and the ageing of the population. Scholars have suggested that developing countries in the non-Western world have experienced a different sort of demographic transition. First, it starts later – rather than in the eighteenth century, its beginning point is in the twentieth century. Also, the transition is over a much shorter period of time, with a higher fertility rate at the start of the transition combined with rapid decreases in mortality, creating a steeper and narrower curve with a higher peak rate of increase. Countries in Africa are already experiencing steep drops in fertility rates, which have meant annual rates of increase have declined rapidly as well.

Although the demographic transition theory is appealing, Africanist scholars have criticized it for being based largely on Western models. They argue that fertility is an elusive strategy to capture adequately, whether through models or in broad surveys. For example, in the 1980s in southern Africa fertility rate was seen to be declining dramatically. However, the declining TFR in this region cannot simply be understood as a by-product of increasing income and industrialization, which are typical of explanations for such a trend in the West. In southern Africa, the observed decline in TFR was not accompanied by an increase in income – it was rather a response to the *decrease* in real incomes in many countries in the 1980s, when much of southern Africa was experiencing painful structural adjustment and depressed economies. A decreased TFR should thus be seen more appropriately as a response to the need to concentrate family resources on existing children. Another important factor to consider is increasing education levels for girls – even a primary school education shows strong correlation with decreased fertility rates as young women have improved bargaining power over reproductive choices, differently imagined futures, and may learn about contraception through informal peer networks that may encourage their covert use.

Furthermore, fertility control in the form of family planning needs to be taken into account as part of this larger story of transition. The United Nations' Decade for Women (1976–85) provided an important backdrop, as the international public health agenda put reproductive health and also maternal rights at the forefront of their global agenda. Interestingly, Lesotho had very low fertility rates in the 1970s, but has only recently been involved in family planning initiatives. The strong presence of the Catholic Church in the country prevented contraceptive use, so the explanation for low fertility rates would need to be found elsewhere. The infamous 1974 'Family Planning Programme' instituted in South Africa was decried at the time as a blatantly racist manifestation of an apartheid regime determined to stem the growth of non-whites in the country even as it pursued simultaneously an aggressive white immigration policy. As seen in earlier attempts to regulate reproduction in African communities, these were met with suspicion. However, seemingly contradictory processes were at work. Through this programme, South African women were amongst the first in the continent to be given control over family planning, and the evidence is that African women utilized these contraceptive services even if reluctantly – African women in South Africa showed higher rates of contraceptive use in the region, 44 per cent of African women used some form of contraception by 1991, and South Africa was one of the first countries in sub-Saharan Africa to experience a really significant and overall fertility decline, with a TFR of about three children per woman.[30] South Africa provided free birth control through the myriad network of family planning clinics available in even the most remote areas where no other healthcare was provided – one estimate is that by 1992 family-planning clinics numbered over 65,000 in the country.[31]

Undoubtedly, reproductive decision-making has been transformed as a result of the HIV/AIDS pandemic, but the complexity of these diverse shifts across different regions and groups has made a comprehensive mapping of changing trajectories very difficult. The most illuminating studies are qualitative and locally based, and survey perceptions as well as practices regarding contraception use and the negotiation of sexual relationships. For example, an illuminating focus group-based study in Zimbabwe in 2001 showed an overall decline in fertility among respondents, and that this was regardless of socio-economic status or whether they lived in rural or urban areas. Importantly, high AIDS mortality in the region did not result in families pursuing an 'insurance strategy' of increased child-bearing. Instead, AIDS mortality caused limited child-bearing because HIV/AIDS was associated both with child death and heightened risk of adult mortality, with pregnancy being viewed as contributing to bodily vulnerability to the virus. The study also found that parents used the health of their youngest children as a sign of parental HIV status – that is, if a child was found to survive to five years, then that meant the parents did not have HIV and could base their reproductive decisions on that health status. Although this was based on an erroneous assumption about mother-to-child transmission of the HI virus (that it was 100 per cent in all cases), the stigma around HIV testing in these communities meant such a gradual diagnosis was preferable.[32]

The history of abortion in the second half of the twentieth century in Africa, like the history of fertility control and contraceptive use, is yet to be fully mapped. At mid-century, medical techniques and the development of powerful antibiotics had advanced far enough to ensure a reasonably safe medical procedure. In places with developed hospital infrastructures, abortions were thus procedurally possible. However, throughout this period by in large, medically induced abortions were not an available option to African women. This reality was underpinned by abortion laws which were in a sense continuations of colonial policies that criminalized abortion and only allowed it under highly exceptional circumstances. In South Africa in the 1960s and 1970s, the harmful consequences of botched or incomplete abortions procured outside the medical sector were made worryingly clear – in one isolated study of one hospital (Groote Schuur Hospital in Cape Town) between 1965 and 1972, 13,681 patients were admitted with sepsis as a result of an incomplete and illegal abortion. Over the same period, a third of women of child-bearing age admitted for tetanus was due to the same cause.[33] South Africa's 1975 Abortion and Sterilisation Act enshrined state surveillance mechanisms and reduced the scope for illegal abortions, although those with the financial resources and freedom of mobility could obtain abortions by travelling to London or Amsterdam as 'health tourists', which white women reportedly did in large numbers from the 1970s. Interestingly, the narrowing scope for legal abortions in the Abortion and Sterilisation Act was at odds with the increased access to contraceptives generally provided to African women in the same period.

South Africa is now distinctive in that due to the 1996 Choice Act, one of the signal pieces of legislation of the newly democratic government, it has one of the most liberal abortion policies in sub-Saharan Africa, although this legislation has not necessarily protected women from experiencing social stigmatization from medical personnel or obstacles to access for abortion procedures. In contrast, most of sub-Saharan Africa has restrictive abortion policies – with few exceptions (mostly in southern African countries), abortion is illegal except in case of a threat to maternal life or health. As a whole and distinct from Western nations, sub-Saharan Africa has a conservative and restrictive approach to the legal provision of abortion.

Epidemiological transition? Chronic illness and the 'rise' of non-communicable diseases

As the outlines of the 'post-AIDS' health landscape of the twenty-first century come into focus, and HIV/AIDS itself becomes a more manageable condition in sub-Saharan Africa, there is an increased awareness of chronic illness as one of the 'new' public health challenge on the continent. Scholars have focused on the increased incidence of conditions such as diabetes, hypertension and cancer and argue the rise of such non-communicable diseases is indicative of a type of 'epidemiological transition' occurring in some parts of the continent. The epidemiological transition describes, like the demographic transition, an overall trajectory of change, in this case from a society where morbidity and mortality patterns are predominantly defined by infectious diseases to one where NCDs are more influential. The theory is predicated not only on a changing disease profile, but also on so-called lifestyle factors – nutrition and exercise, for example – which are premised, for the most part, on wealth and income. It is widely agreed that in the West, this epidemiological transition occurred over the last two centuries, as the disease burden shifted to one where heart disease and cancer rather than infectious disease became the leading causes of deaths.

When surveying twenty-first-century African states' changing health priorities, it is clear that NCDs have become more important, as measured in the proliferation of new clinics focusing on cancer, diabetes and hypertension. In Uganda, the vernacular terms which are used to denote NCDs to some extent confirm their 'newness' in Ugandan society, as the terms are closely adapted variations from the English terminology rather than existing in an indigenous lexicon: *plesa* (meaning high blood pressure), *sukari* (high sugar, meaning diabetes), *kansa* (cancer) and *asama* (asthma).[34] Amongst cancer patients in Botswana, where cancer care and treatment are located in Princess Marina Hospital in the capital Gabarone, there is a striking incidence of 'viral associated' cancers (such as Karposi's sarcoma and genital cancer) in HIV+ patients that is linked to their history of immunosuppression. 'Co-infection' between HIV and cancer is difficult to treat because ARV therapy may interfere with cancer treatment, and vice versa. However, breast and prostate cancer diagnoses are also on the rise, though the reasons for this rise are diverse – better screening facilities, patient awareness, and changing health indicators such as rising levels of obesity.[35]

The epidemiological transition model is both imprecise and misleading when applied to the African context. First, as mentioned earlier, is the problem of the 'baseline'. There is insufficient data to determine the extent to which conditions such as diabetes or illnesses such as cancer were part of the health profiles of Africans in earlier periods. Colonial health interventions, and thus data collection efforts, tended to focus on infectious disease. So, the narrative of the 'discovery' of NCDs in the late twentieth and twenty-first century is not wholly accurate, since this merely indicates when those diseases began to be recorded and not when they began to be prevalent. Moreover, as Megan Vaughan has argued, the implicit assumption that NCDs are lifestyle diseases may not wholly represent the forces at play underpinning the rise of so-called metabolic disorders in parts of Africa.[36] The concept of lifestyle disease does not wholly recognize that for many Africans, diet, for example, is closely correlated to income, and the poorest households have very little access to fresh fruit and vegetables which could reduce sugar levels. It also strongly suggests that the prevention of chronic illness is, simply, a matter of self-discipline, rather than the product of a much wider set of dynamics external to the person.

In addition, infectious disease continues to be an important element of the overall disease burden facing African communities. HIV/AIDS itself, although acknowledged as exhibiting some characteristics of 'chronic' illness, cannot wholly be considered a NCD, even with patients' faithful adherence to ARV medication. Other, resurgent, infectious diseases such as malaria, tuberculosis, cholera and sleeping sickness continue to demand considerable resources from state and para-state agents and health institutions. Critically, the transition theory paints a picture of NCDs replacing communicable diseases, when there is a growing body of research that shows how in Africa infectious disease and chronic illness can be mutually reinforcing. For example, Julie Livingstone has shown in her ethnography of the only cancer ward in Botswana, a country where HIV adult prevalence was estimated to be 25 per cent during the 2000s, that HIV-immuno suppressed bodies could be particularly vulnerable to viral-associated cancers, like those linked to human papilloma virus. Other co-indications are relevant for this discussion. For example, infection and inflammation can be seen as a risk factor in cardio-vascular disease – this links back to HIV, in that inflammation associated with immune-depressed bodies may heighten risk of cardio-vascular disease. Other southern African-based scholarship has also shown that the relationship between tuberculosis and HIV is mutually contributory. Whilst these linkages are not entirely direct or clear-cut, the importance of co-infection and co-indications that cross the communicable and non-communicable disease boundaries is very important to consider. The reality is more complex – beyond the 'double' burden of communicable and non-communicable disease, there is increased recognition that many Africans' health realities encompass 'multiple-morbidities', experienced as 'syndemic suffering', as Emily Mendenhall has shown.[37] These multiple morbidities include infectious disease, chronic illness and psychological stress and distress. Syndemic suffering is a way to acknowledge the intersectional nature of patient experience, as well as a way for patients to express, categorize and compare the different illnesses they confront. What is clear is that NCDs will continue to shape the disease landscape of Africa for decades to come. However, the long shadow of HIV is not far from these dynamics, and is part of understanding the role of co-morbidity and multiple-morbidities of disease. How African patients understand and navigate these pathways is integral to consider in future research.

'Old' and 'new' infectious diseases

In recent decades there have been resurgences of infectious diseases which have a long history in the African context. These outbreaks are linked to structural factors such as increased violence and economic insecurity, as well as changing ecological conditions, migration patterns and declining healthcare provisioning. Cholera resurgence has posed a conundrum in that it is a relatively easily treatable bacterial disease – through inexpensive oral rehydration treatments – yet it has become endemic in many African countries. Lake Chad has freestanding cholera which means outbreaks can be activated and spread to bordering countries, potentially exposing millions. A deadly outbreak of cholera in 1994 was, predictably, centred around a refugee camp in Goma in the aftermath of the Rwandan genocide, due to poor hygiene and limited access to treated water and sufficient nutrition. An epidemic of cholera in Zimbabwe in 2008–9, which reached 100,000 cases and claimed nearly 5,000 lives, was in large part attributed to the repressive policies and social breakdown engendered by then-President Robert Mugabe. In 2006, cholera cases in Africa accounted for 99 per cent of the global total.[38] This is similar to the overwhelming African character of the global malaria disease burden, although the sheer numbers of malaria morbidity are distinctive – 213 million Africans were infected with malaria in 2018 alone. Sleeping sickness has re-emerged in Africa, particularly in areas of ecological change that have been disrupted by migration, changing settlement patterns or violent conflict, after a brief period in the mid-twentieth century when disease transmission had been effectively suppressed. Both sleeping sickness and malaria have in recent decades been the focus of multi-sector collaborations and global health initiatives – the Roll Back Malaria campaign (launched in 1998), the campaign to designate sleeping sickness a Neglected Tropical Disease (achieved in 2012), and most recently the first phase of the rollout to three African countries of the Malaria Vaccine Implementation Programme in 2019. The historical trajectories of malaria and sleeping sickness in Africa, as well as a critical history of these and other international health interventions, are explored in detail in Chapter 6.

The Ebola epidemic of 2014–15 in West Africa revealed to global public health bodies the infectious disease landscape in Africa was ever-evolving and complacency could have devastating consequences. Ebola is a rare but frequently fatal viral haemorrhagic disease which spreads between humans through direct contact with an infected person's bodily fluids. The outbreak was focused primarily within only three countries – Sierra Leone, Liberia and Guinea – and the total number of cases did not reach 30,000. However, its high case-mortality rate – the 2014–15 epidemic had a near 40 per cent case-mortality rate – compared to other prevalent infectious diseases as well as its distressing symptomatology (particularly the uncontrollable haemorrhaging) meant that in its short time span Ebola eclipsed all other health crises in the public imaginary, even HIV/AIDS. Huge resources were deployed by WHO and mobilized within the global research community, eventually leading to expedited human clinical trials and distribution in 2016 of an Ebola vaccine. International charities which operate in an explicit 'crisis-response' mode such as Médecins sans frontières dispatched teams to affected areas to work on surveillance, control and treatment measures. This global mobilization was accompanied by often sensationalist media coverage, which reproduced problematic historical associations of Africa as the 'diseased' continent and the West as its 'saviours'. At the local level, Ebola stretched already poorly resourced health services in these three countries. It also claimed the lives of many front-line local healthcare staff, amongst the first to die before Ebola was properly diagnosed and containments strategies begun.

Although media coverage treated Ebola as a wholly 'new' disease with unparalleled destructive potential (although it had been first documented in the 1970s in Zaire, now the DRC), there are ways to see local African responses to Ebola as echoing earlier historical dynamics. For example, similarities have been drawn between the communal violence against health workers and Ebola clinics that erupted in the face of quarantine restrictions and proscriptions on mobility with the violence that accompanied cholera outbreaks in Eastern and Western Europe and North America in the nineteenth and twentieth centuries.[39] Clinics became places of death in the local imaginary so people avoided them, which inadvertently increased the risk of further transmission. In the context of African medical history, there is also a striking similarity in terms of the centrality of burial and funerary rites in terms of both the spread of the disease and also consequently its containment. Clusters of cases of Ebola were linked to funerals, large social occasions where members travelled from far distances to attend and then scattered back, widening at once the geographical reach of this disease. Both local and global health authorities attempted to restrict funerary rites and burial procedures as part of quarantine and mobility control measures. As discussed in Chapter 2, colonial health interventions sometimes involved the disruption of local African burial practices, as seen in the case of medical responses to bubonic plague in French West Africa. These measures often brought resistance, both overt and covert, with Africans choosing to bury in secret and defy restrictions rather than risk the wrath of the dead or the ancestors or provoke communal disruption. In a similar vein, the imposition of 'safe burials' by public health officials overseeing Ebola containment was seen by local communities as clear violations of sacred customs. Secret internments again became part of the repertoire of communal responses to public health interventions. These helped to worsen the risk of infection as corpses, unless disposed of under a rigid protocol, could still carry the live virus. The 2014 Liberian government's declaration

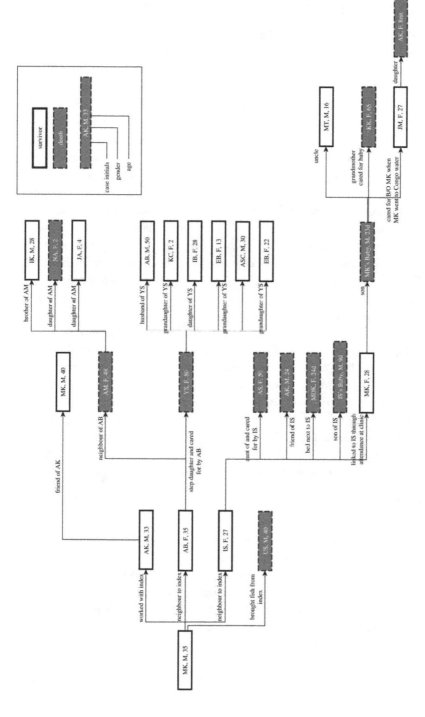

Figure 3.1 Ebola Virus Disease (EVD) transmission chain, Western Area of Sierra Leone, July–August 2015. Senga et al., 'Contract Tracing Performance during the Ebola Virus Disease Outbreak in Kenema District, Sierra Leone', *Philosophical Transactions Royal Society B*, 372 (2017).

Historical Source: Ebola Virus Disease (EVD) transmission chain, Western Area of Sierra Leone, July–August 2015

Source Analysis: *This transmission chain shows how a cluster of infections of EVD was spread through person-to-person contact. It is a highly detailed mapping that lists the health outcomes of those infected (i.e. whether they died or survived Ebola infection), ages and also, where possible, the associational link between the infected (whether through kinship relations or other happenstance, such as the example of 'linked through attendance at clinic'). Transmission maps such as this were vital in controlling Ebola transmission, because they enabled health monitors to trace how an infectious virus spread through a given social network. It is widely acknowledged that the more detailed and effective the 'contact tracing performance' of a given area, the greater chances that Ebola could be successfully contained. It is important to note the immense manpower resources that are necessary for creating a chart of this level of detail – local assistants were hired as they had familiarity with local languages and everyday practices, such as the mobility habits and patterns of the target population. However, the effectiveness of contact tracing measures was constrained by levels of distrust from local populations, differing literacy levels and technological deficiencies (e.g. a lack of electrical power, lack of computers for data entry purposes, lack of a workable mobile option for inputting this type of data).*

This chart may represent a 'new' type of primary source, albeit for a very recent history of a specific disease. This fine-grained record is novel as it precisely illustrates the ways in which Ebola took hold and spread in communities at the level of the individual, from one person to a web of others. It is also, like many of the most illuminating types of historical sources, illustrative of more than simply a biomedical reality – this is not simply a 'transmission chain' but also a social mapping of this particular region of Sierra Leone. We are given a small window into the kinship and associational links which connect people, as well as a sense of their mobility across space and time (e.g. 'brought fish from' or 'cared for MK when MK went to Congo', etc).

that Ebola victims be cremated further frayed the bonds of trust necessary for local compliance with state health authority measures.

Towards the end of the epidemic, in a marked innovation, WHO and other health bodies and NGOs began to employ anthropologists familiar with local languages, customs, social networks and disease cosmologies, and this began to reap rewards in terms of community communication and compliance with tracking, isolation and containment measures. One of the more striking visual 'aide-mémoires' produced by this interdisciplinary and cross-sectoral collaboration was the intricate charting of Ebola virus disease 'transmission chains' that mapped in painstaking detail how Ebola spread out from a single person through their dense association of social and familial contacts.

Not only could this be a tool for future generations to understand the micro-level detail through which a virus like Ebola could spread – it also is a source to understand the density and complexity, and mobility, of social and kin networks in those regions of West Africa. Whether this integrated strategy involving anthropologists and public health authorities, and linking local scales to globally mediated approaches, is a harbinger of new alliances for future health interventions remains to be seen.

Conclusion

It is evident that in the post-colonial period the indigenization of medicine and the Africanization of health were incomplete processes, fraught with messy contradictions and blurred boundaries. The contributions of Africans like Thomas Adeoye Lambo, no longer bound by the strictures of colonial rule, were key to both processes. The ways in which Africans entered into the medical profession and into biomedically mediated environments expanded and multiplied, and they have shaped both healthcare delivery and medical and scientific knowledge production in significant ways. The disquieting legacies of the vertical, disease-focused approach evident in colonial applications of tropical medicine were reproduced to an extent in WHO's embrace of a disease eradication programme agenda in the 1950s and 1960s, and continue to linger in global health approaches applied to contemporary Africa. African healing systems responded to these changing health landscapes in imaginative and resolute ways, engaging in the modernization of their therapies as well as finding new and more public forms of expression, and competition, in an increasingly diverse and multivalent therapeutic market.

The HIV/AIDS pandemic straddled the end of one millennium and the beginning of another. It represented a pivotal moment in the health landscape of Africa, and the health prospects of its people, in many respects. The demographic impact of AIDS mortality has yet to be fully realized, but it is evident that in many parts of Africa the mean life expectancy has precipitously declined. It is also recognized that HIV/AIDS has profoundly altered reproductive decision-making, although in ways that are not yet fully understood. Both these dynamics have affected the course of the demographic transition. The crisis of AIDS mortality has re-shaped local moral imaginaries, and provoked debate about the potentialities, and limits, of spiritual and religious therapeutic approaches. The AIDS pandemic also ushered in collaborative alliances – public-private, local-global, state-non-state – that whilst not entirely new were certainly more varied and pronounced in form. Whilst HIV/AIDS stripped many communities of their most able-bodied members, it also created a powerfully articulate (if not fully empowered politically) bio-citizenry, whose successes are testament to their ability to straddle multiple publics, multiple registers and multiple subjectivities in an African 'para-state'. The health dynamics in the twenty-first century in Africa have been irreparably shaped by HIV/AIDS and continue to resonate, even as the epidemiological landscape has shifted.

Further reading

Ashforth, Adam. *Madumo: A Man Bewitched*. Chicago: University of Chicago Press, 2005.

Azevedo, Mario. *Historical Perspectives on the State of Health and Health Systems in Africa. Volume II, the Modern Era*. African Histories and Modernities. Cham, Switzerland: Palgrave Macmillan, 2017.

Becker, Felicitas and Wenzel Geissler, eds. *AIDS and Religious Practice in Africa*. Leiden: Brill, 2009.

Behrend, Heike and Ute Luig, eds. *Spirit Possession: Modernity and Power in Africa*. Oxford: James Currey, 1999.

Chigudu, Simukai. *The Political Life of an Epidemic: Cholera, Crisis and Citizenship in Zimbabwe*. New York: Cambridge University Press, 2020.

Comaroff, Jean and John L. Comaroff. *Modernity and Its Malcontents: Ritual and Power in Postcolonial Africa*. Chicago: University of Chicago Press, 1993.

Cooper, Frederick. *Africa since 1940: The Past of the Present*. New York: Cambridge University Press, 2002.

Cross, Jamie and Hayley Macgregor. 'Knowledge, Legitimacy and Economic Practice in Informal Markets for Medicine: A Critical Review of Research'. *Social Science & Medicine* (1982) 71 (2010): 1593–600.

Digby, Anne and Howard Philips. *At the Heart of Healing: Groote Schuur Hospital, 1938–2008*. Auckland Park: Jacana, 2008.

Dionne, Kim Yi. *Doomed Interventions the Failure of Global Responses to AIDS in Africa*. Cambridge: Cambridge University Press, 2018.

Geissler, Paul Wenzel, ed. *Para-States and Medical Science: Making African Global Health*. Durham: Duke University Press, 2015.

Geissler, Paul Wenzel, Guillaume Lachenal, John Manton and Noémi Tousignant, eds. *Traces of the Future: An Archaeology of Medical Science in Africa*. Bristol: Intellect, 2016.

Geschiere, Peter. *The Modernity of Witchcraft: Politics and the Occult in Postcolonial Africa*. Charlottesville: University of Virginia Press, 1997.

Gifford, Paul. *African Christianity: Its Public Role*. Bloomington: Indiana University Press, 1998.

Giles-Vernick, Tamara and James Webb, eds. *Global Health in Africa: Historical Perspectives on Disease Control*. Athens: Ohio University Press, 2013.

Hodes, Rebecca. 'The Medical History of Abortion in South Africa, c.1970–2000'. *Journal of Southern African Studies* 39, no. 3 (2013): 527–42.

Horwitz, Simonne Janine. *Baragwanath Hospital, Soweto: A History of Medical Care 1941–1990*. Johannesburg: Wits University Press, 2013.

Iliffe, John. *East African Doctors: A History of the Modern Profession*. Cambridge: Cambridge University Press, 1998.

Iliffe, John. *The African AIDS Epidemic: A History*. Oxford: James Currey, 2006.

Klaits, Frederick. *Death in a Church of Life: Moral Passion during Botswana's Time of AIDS*. Berkeley: University of California Press, 2010.

Last, Murray and G. L. Chavunduka, eds. *The Professionalisation of African Medicine*. Manchester: Manchester University Press, 1988.

Lee, Sung. 'WHO and the Developing World: The Contest for Ideology'. In *Western Medicine as Contested Knowledge*, edited by Andrew Cunningham and Bridie Andrews. New York: Manchester University Press, 1997.

Livingston, Julie. *Improvising Medicine: An African Oncology Ward in an Emerging Cancer Epidemic*. Durham: Duke University Press, 2012.

Manning, Patrick. 'African Population, 1650–2000: Comparisons and Implications of New Estimates'. In *Africa's Development in Historical Perspective*, edited by Emmanuel Akyeampong, James Robinson, Nathan Nunn and Robert. H. Bates, 131–50. Cambridge: Cambridge University Press, 2014.

Manton, John and Martin Gorsky. 'Health Planning in 1960s Africa: International Health Organisations and the Post-Colonial State'. *Medical History* 62, no. 4 (2018): 425–48.

Marks, Shula. *Divided Sisterhood: Class, Race, and Gender in the South African Nursing Profession*. Basingstoke: Palgrave Macmillan, 1994.

Mbembe, Achille. *On the Postcolony*. Berkeley: University of California Press, 2001.

Mbembe, Achille. 'The Power of the Archive and Its Limits'. In *Refiguring the Archive*, edited by Carolyn Hamilton, Verne Harris, Jane Taylor, Michele Pickover, Graeme Reid and Razia Saleh. Dordrecht: Springer Netherlands, 2002.

Mendenhall, Emily. *Syndemic Suffering: Social Distress, Depression, and Diabetes among Mexican Immigrant Women*. California: Left Coast Press, 2012.

Moore, Henrietta and Megan Vaughan. *Cutting down Trees: Gender, Nutrition and Agricultural Change in the Northern Province of Zambia, 1890–1990*. London: J. Currey, 1994.

Niehaus, Isak. *AIDS in the Shadow of Biomedicine*. London: Zed Books, 2018.

Packard, Randall M. *The Making of a Tropical Disease: A Short History of Malaria*. Baltimore: Johns Hopkins University Press, 2007.

Packard, Randall M. *A History of Global Health: Interventions into the Lives of Other Peoples*. Baltimore: Johns Hopkins University Press, 2016.

Potts, Deborah and Shula Marks. 'Fertility in Southern Africa: The Quiet Revolution'. *Journal of Southern African Studies* 27, no. 2 (2001): 189–205.

Robins, Steven. '"Long Live Zackie, Long Live": AIDS Activism, Science and Citizenship after Apartheid'. *Journal of Southern African Studies* 30, no. 3 (2004): 651–72.

Schneider, William. 'The Long History of Smallpox Eradication: Lessons for Global Health in Africa'. In *Global Health in Africa: Historical Perspectives on Disease Control*, edited by Tamara Giles-Vernick and James Webb. Athens: Ohio University Press, 2013.

Sindiga, Isaac, Chacha Nyaigotti Chacha and Mary Peter Kanunah, eds. *Traditional Medicine in Africa*. Nairobi: East African Educational Publishers, 1995.

Tilley, Helen and Robert J. Gordon, eds. *Ordering Africa: Anthropology, European Imperialism and the Politics of Knowledge*. Manchester: Manchester University Press, 2007.

Tousignant, Noémi. *Edges of Exposure: Toxicology and the Problem of Capacity in Postcolonial Senegal*. Durham: Duke University Press, 2018.

Vaughan, Megan. *The Story of an African Famine: Gender and Famine in Twentieth-Century Malawi*. Cambridge: Cambridge University Press, 1987.

Vaughan, Megan. 'Conceptualising Metabolic Disorder in Southern Africa: Biology, History and Global Health'. *BioSocieties* 14, no. 1 (2019): 123–42.

Viterbo, Paula and Kalala Ngalamulume, eds. *Medicine and Health in Africa: Multidisciplinary Perspectives*. East Lansing: Michigan State University Press, 2011.

White, Luise. 'Hodgepodge Historiography: Documents, Itineraries, and the Absence of Archives'. *History in Africa* 42 (2015): 309–18.

Whyte, Susan Reynolds. 'Pharmaceuticals as Folk Medicine: Transformations in the Social Relations of Health Care in Uganda'. *Culture, Medicine and Psychiatry* 16, no. 2 (1992): 163–86.

Whyte, Susan Reynolds, Sung-Joon Park, George Odong, Moris Ojara and Alice Lamwaka. 'The Visibility of Non-Communicable Diseases in Northern Uganda'. *African Health Sciences* 15, no. 1 (2015): 82–9.

Wylie, Diana. *Starving on a Full Stomach: Hunger and the Triumph of Cultural Racism in Modern South Africa*. Charlottesville: University Press of Virginia, 2001.

PART TWO
CASE STUDIES OVER TIME AND SPACE

CHAPTER 4
HIV/AIDS IN HISTORICAL PERSPECTIVE(S)

Introduction

Sub-Saharan Africa is at the epicentre of the global AIDS pandemic. A recent international census of HIV/AIDS incidence by UNAIDS (the United Nations agency entasked with collecting data and coordinating resources to respond to the AIDS crisis) revealed that in 2018 nearly 68 per cent of the global HIV+ population resided in Africa, amounting to 25.6 million Africans. Of this number, 14.8 million adult females were HIV+, illustrating that the HIV pandemic disproportionately affects females. In South Africa, which has the largest national HIV+ population in the world, 7.7 million people were living with HIV in 2018, a figure representing over 13 per cent of its total population. The rate of prevalence in the cohort of adults aged fifteen to forty-nine years in the country was a staggering 20.4 per cent, meaning one in five young adults had HIV. A quick scan of the interactive global map on the UNAIDS website would easily reveal that this high prevalence rate was by no means an anomaly in the wider southern African region – Botswana's adult prevalence rate was similarly hovering at 20.3 per cent, whilst Lesotho recorded an even higher 23.6 per cent, and Swaziland still higher at 27.3 per cent.

HIV/AIDS: The basics

Human immuno-deficiency virus, or HIV, is transmitted through bodily fluids – blood, semen or breastmilk. Sexual intercourse, blood transfusions, sharing intravenous drug needles, pregnancy and childbirth, and breast feeding are the most common means through which HIV can be passed from human to human. In the African context, the dominant mode of transmission by far has been through heterosexual intercourse, and secondarily through pregnancy and childbirth. The HI virus attacks T-helper cells, also called CD4 cells, which are an integral part of the body's immune system. As the virus invades these cells it replicates itself, lowering the CD4 count and thereby reducing the capacity of the infected person to effectively respond to external pathogens. The CD4 count and measuring the 'viral load' in one's blood are the primary ways in which HIV's progress is monitored.

The point at which a person is declared to have Acquired Immuno-deficiency Syndrome, or AIDS, varies from country to country, but generally it is when an individual's immune system is so weakened by the HI virus and the CD4 count becomes so low that a serious illness results. It is important to remember that AIDS is in itself not a disease. It is a syndrome – it does not kill directly but allows opportunistic infections to debilitate the human body with little resistance. Importantly, in a healthy and adequately fed person, the progress from HIV+ status to what is known as full-blown AIDS may take as long as ten years. This relatively slow progression of the HI virus to the more debilitating manifestation of AIDS is a defining characteristic of this disease – that a HIV+ person may be infectious for many years before showing any obvious symptoms is considered a key reason for its largely unimpeded global spread.

HIV's characteristic as a 'retrovirus' means it remains essentially invisible to the body's normal immune defences, and it has a demonstrated capacity to evolve drug resistance. Advanced clinical trials in southern Africa for a HIV vaccine, based on a version of a vaccine that was found to be moderately successful in preventing the strain of HIV more common in southeast Asia, have recently concluded in failure – the vaccine was found to offer no significant protection against HIV compared to a placebo. Scientific research has confirmed that male circumcision confers some level of protection against acquiring HIV, and the World Health Organization is advocating for increased rates of medically supervised male circumcision in HIV-affected regions. Pre-exposure prophylaxis, or PrEP, can be taken prior to sexual intercourse and has been shown to confer high levels of protection against acquiring HIV, although PrEP needs to be taken regularly in the required dosages to maintain its efficacy. Nevirapine is a type of antiretroviral (ARV) – a drug that blocks the virus from replicating – which helps prevent mother-to-child transmission (MTCT) of HIV during pregnancy and childbirth. Whilst scientific advances in blocking viral transmission at the microbial level are developing apace, utilizing physical barriers remains a relatively low cost and effective preventative strategy, for example through using condoms during sexual intercourse, offering clean needles to intravenous drug users, and preventing breastfeeding of babies if the mother is HIV+.

There is currently no accepted cure for HIV. In terms of post-infection treatment, the current medical protocol is to provide combination antiretroviral therapy, referred to as Highly Active Antiretroviral Therapy (HAART), thought to be most effective in terms of preventing the virus from developing drug resistance. For many HIV+ and AIDS sufferers, HAART has proven to be a life-saving treatment, raising CD4 levels. Two recent and highly publicized cases of HIV+ individuals (the 'London patient' and the 'Berlin patient') who underwent bone marrow transplants for cancer and became HI virus-free offer some hope for an eventual gene therapy or immuno-therapy cure, but this is in the distant horizon and is currently prohibitively expensive.

Until the early years of the 2000s, when low-cost generic ARVs (the primary drug-based intervention for HIV) were able to be rolled out throughout the continent, for most Africans contracting HIV was tantamount to a death sentence. This is reflected in mortality figures. Annual AIDS-related deaths on the continent amounted to 470,000 in 2018, but at its peak in 2004 annual deaths in sub-Saharan Africa had reached 1.43 million. Cumulative AIDS-related deaths figures over the span of the pandemic are equally instructive. UNAIDS estimates that from 1990 (when it began more comprehensive data collection on HIV/AIDS) to 2014, 24.8 million Africans died from AIDS-related illness. In South Africa, the cumulative national figure for AIDS-related deaths over the same period was 4.4 million – this represented approximately 8.3 per cent of the national population of the time.

It would be worthwhile to reflect on these sobering statistics. What does it mean – socially, economically, politically and existentially – for a continent to have lost 24.8 million inhabitants over the relatively short course of two and a half decades? What does it mean to a nation such as South Africa to lose over 8 per cent of its population? This chapter's main purpose is to provide a historical and gendered perspective on the current HIV/AIDS pandemic – that is, to make some sense of these staggering numbers by filtering them through useful analytical lenses. As will be seen, although HIV/AIDS is entering into its fourth decade on the African continent, academic and media analyses of the epidemic continue to be conducted largely in the present tense. This chapter provides a corrective to this 'presentist' mindset by exploring the manifold ways in which the pandemic can be understood *as* **history** and *through* **history**. It situates HIV/AIDS in a broader history of sexually transmitted diseases (STDs) in Africa and draws connections with earlier sexual health crises such as the syphilis 'epidemic' during the colonial period in southern and East-Central Africa. The chapter discusses how anxieties around African sexuality and its regulation, within colonial as well as subsequent post-colonial African polities, contributed to powerfully gendered perceptions of and approaches to these diseases. It considers the impact of psycho-social responses to STDs in African communities, including shame and stigma, and highlights the extent to which these mechanisms have been reproduced in the present day. Throughout the chapter, a key question posed is how to recover the experiences of Africans, and in particular of African women. To this end, we examine and critique some of the key historical sources which inform this intimate history, from missionary accounts to contemporary video diaries and 'body maps' produced by HIV+ survivors. The chapter also considers the widespread mortality wrought by HIV/AIDS (and new cultures of death which AIDS mortality has engendered) and situates this particular epidemic in the context of other demographic catastrophes – including the slave trade and the influenza pandemic – that have deeply influenced the course of African history.

Thinking through HIV/AIDS in Africa *historically*

'Let us not equivocate: a tragedy of unprecedented proportions is unfolding in Africa.' Nelson Mandela, International AIDS Conference, Durban (July 2000)

'... no parallel in history for AIDS.' Professor J.H. Coovadia, AIDS in Context Conference, Johannesburg (April 2001)

'Never before have resources from so many HIV/AIDS-related programmes and
services been assembled in one place.' Festus Mogae, World AIDS Day, Botswana
(December 2002)

These statements, delivered at a time when the immense scale of the pandemic was
beginning to be grasped, depict Africa's experience of HIV/AIDS as wholly exceptional,
'unprecedented' and 'without historical parallel'. More than a decade later in 2015, a
UNAIDS overview report on 'fifteen lessons' learned from its response to the pandemic
similarly cast AIDS as a meta-transformation of incomparable significance: 'AIDS
CHANGED EVERYTHING' the cover page shouted, emblazoned in oversized capital
letters. In the course of my own research on the history of death in Africa, a project
that was in part motivated by a desire to understand the impact of widespread AIDS
mortality on ideas and practices around death and dying, my collaborators and I were
confronted with the overwhelming presentist focus of pronouncements (scholarly,
political and media-based) on HIV/AIDS.[1] We remarked that it seemed that history
itself began with the AIDS epidemic! Those trying to think of AIDS in Africa *historically*
were far fewer by comparison.

It is perhaps not surprising that a sort of ahistorical exceptionalism has been until
very recently the dominant discursive framing of the HIV/AIDS pandemic. Activists,
governments, leaders, health organizations and scholars were in their own ways complicit
in shaping and promoting this presentist narrative, born out of the necessity to galvanize
the global community to action in the face of political intransigence and, in some cases,
outright AIDS denialism. It was only by casting this health crisis as unprecedented, the
logic went, that large-scale change could be effected at local, national and international
levels. The quotes cited above can be interpreted in this light. However, in recent years
there has been an important shift from 'crisis' to 'management' in the global reckoning
of HIV/AIDS due to several converging factors (as discussed in Chapter 3), including
the widespread rollout of relatively cheap generic antiretrovirals (ARVs), declining HIV
infection rates, the influential role of global funding bodies such as the Bill and Melinda
Gates Foundation and the Global Fund, and the growth of politicized survivor-driven
communities engaged in drug activism and promoting HIV awareness on the ground. A
positive diagnosis no longer equals a death sentence, as it did for the majority of HIV+
Africans in the early decades of the pandemic. Increasingly in sub-Saharan Africa there
is a shift to seeing HIV/AIDS as a chronic disease that could be managed through faithful
adherence to prescribed medication. Because of this shift away from crisis, there is more
analytical space to reflect back, perhaps somewhat more dispassionately, on the nearly
four decades in which AIDS has been a feature of the African continent. Exploring that
analytical space to historically think through Africa's singular experience of HIV/AIDS
is the central purpose of this chapter.

There are three disparate but interlinked ways we should think about the vital
relationship between *history* and HIV/AIDS. The first is to consider the HIV/AIDS
pandemic *as history* – that is, to look at the four decades of the AIDS epidemic in Africa as
a subject of history in and of itself. This would entail mapping the history of the advance

of the HIV virus across the sub-Saharan African continent, its varying spread across different regions and nation-states, as well as the uneven trajectories of responses to the HIV/AIDS crisis of African governments, global health organizations, AIDS advocacy groups and HIV+ survivor communities. The second manifestation of AIDS and history can be seen in the development of a corpus of first-person narratives on the experience of being infected or affected by the virus – in other words, to look at *histories of* HIV/AIDS, with the emphasis of 'histories' on the plurality of individual accounts. The third perspective is to view the HIV/AIDS pandemic *in history*, that is, within the context of a larger history, be it a demographic, socio-political, cultural, medical or regional history. What can be learned if we insert HIV/AIDS into these broader trajectories? How does our grasp of the experience of HIV/AIDS change in amidst these wider reference points?

HIV/AIDS *as* history

John Iliffe's seminal and comprehensive history of AIDS in Africa, *The African AIDS Epidemic: A History* (2006), is exemplary of the recent 'historical turn' in scholarly writing on HIV/AIDS. It is not the task of this chapter to reproduce Iliffe's definitive account but rather to highlight the contours of the themes, debates and issues that his work and other new historical studies of the African AIDS pandemic have brought into sharp relief. Although this scholarship is disparate in focus, what unites their approaches is the understanding that the AIDS pandemic in Africa has not remained static and has evolved and transformed over time. Subject to historical forces, then, it is indeed a worthy subject of the historian's gaze.

As emphasized throughout this book, the veracity and scope of any historical study are dependent on the relevant sources at the historian's disposal. And like any other subject, the sources that can be used to construct a history of HIV/AIDS in Africa have their own particular strengths and weaknesses. One of the features of the HIV/AIDS pandemic that distinguishes it from earlier episodes of epidemic or infectious disease is the abundance of **data** we have at our disposal, particularly from the 1990s onwards when HIV intruded onto the mental and moral maps of Western superpowers and the global health community. You can now go to the UNAIDS information website and collect longitudinal data on a multitude of specific indicators of HIV infection by gender, area and age cohort, and also chart HIV prevalence, AIDS-related mortality and the number of AIDS orphans by country, by region or globally.[2] The abundance of medical and social science research on HIV/AIDS in sub-Saharan Africa has generated even more finely grained detail on HIV transmission, uptake of ARVs, reproductive decision-making, life expectancy and so on.

However, the plenitude of data should not mask its fallibility. For example, seroprevalence, or the percentage of a given population that is HIV+, is generally calculated using the rate of HIV infections of pregnant women who attend ante-natal clinics in a given area, and then extrapolating that percentage to determine a local, provincial or national figure. This is the globally accepted method of obtaining HIV infection rates.

This method was deemed the most accurate available due to the very high participation of pregnant women in local ante-natal clinics. That is, if a clinic exists, the likelihood of a pregnant woman from the local community regularly attending is extremely high, even where no other health infrastructure exists. Also, in areas with resource-poor health systems, regular testing in a dedicated HIV/AIDS clinic would not be feasible. Critics have argued that urban women (and thus urban female infection rates) are disproportionately represented, and some have expressed doubt that male rates of infection, the elderly and rurally based cohorts can be accurately assessed through this method.

Another potential statistical blind spot is AIDS-related mortality figures. An individual does not die of AIDS per se, but of opportunistic diseases which take advantage of immuno-suppressed AIDS bodies. This means that AIDS-related mortality may not be accurately recorded. A patient who has AIDS could die of complications from tuberculosis, for example, and the attending clinician or health official may not record the death as AIDS-related. As a case in point, death certificates in South Africa include categories for 'primary' and 'secondary' causes of death, the latter category being optional. In areas where there is a low level of disclosure of HIV-status amongst family members and a high level of social stigma attached to a positive diagnosis, local medical professionals may feel compelled to avoid revealing the deceased's HIV+ status to unknowing close kin or others (such as local funeral directors) who are able to view the death certificate – I have observed this avoidance of disclosure in my own research, even in cases where AIDS was clearly a precipitating factor. The potential statistical undercounting of AIDS-related mortality may be further influenced by the reluctance of some African countries to actively investigate, and acknowledge, the full extent of the epidemic for political or economic reasons. Thus, any attempts to derive an accurate and long-range empirical depiction of HIV/AIDS in Africa must take into consideration some of the inherent weaknesses in these complex data sets.

Media accounts of the AIDS pandemic, including newspaper and tabloid press, investigative reports, online and broadcast news, are another important primary source type which could be mined to produce a history of AIDS in Africa. Media depictions of HIV/AIDS in Africa have been criticized for either silencing the magnitude of the crisis or, conversely, over-sensationalizing and simplifying the life challenges faced by the wider HIV+ community – the wide variation in coverage of the pandemic in global and African media outlets can be partly explained by the relative political and economic capacity of HIV+ survivor communities to thrust their plight into the media spotlight and shape its depiction. A genre of long-form journalistic accounts has also emerged out of the pandemic – some prominent examples including Jonny Steinberg's *Three Letter Plague* (also published as *Sizwe's Test*, 2006), Liz McGregor's *Khabzela!* (2006) and Uzondinma Iweala's *Our Kind of People* (2012) – these are semi-autobiographical narratives of 'return' in which individuals who are not HIV+ explore anew their personal and political relations to their home countries through the prism of the pandemic. Their witnessing of others' HIV-journeys, the internal reflections this witnessing prompts and the traversing of an insider-outsider divide by the authors (whether lines of belonging are determined by HIV status, race, gender or class) drive the principle narrative dynamic in the story-telling. A related and significant media source for historians is the growing body of local, media-driven health interventions and public health awareness campaigns. These could include radio spots or television programmes specifically targeting vulnerable populations, such as youth. Popular media sources could be utilized to develop a chronology of change in public health approaches to the HIV/AIDS pandemic as well as chart AIDS activists' nascent appropriation of media technologies, as Rebecca Hodes has shown through a history of the South African television series *Beat It!* Documentary films and photographs produced by activists and artists have further contributed to the corpus of visual media sources available on the pandemic, and its particular trajectories amongst HIV+ groups and individuals.

Published **scholarly works on HIV/AIDS** and **scientific institute records**, taken as a corpus, constitute another relatively untapped historical source type. This archive is of significant value, for example, in the historical reconstruction of changing theoretical and scientific understanding of HIV/AIDS – that is, the creation of an intellectual genealogy of AIDS knowledge. Guillaume Lachenal utilized the archive of the Pasteur Centre of Cameroon to reconstruct a history of research into HIV/AIDS in Cameroon, and in the process highlighted the crucial role of Cameroonian researchers in epidemiological investigations who operated within the competitive global scientific milieu of the early years of the pandemic in Africa.[3] Relatedly, historians have also begun to mine these sources to trace the history of contentious and problematic ideas on HIV/AIDS circulating in and around the scientific community. Far from being neutral scientific terrain, medical research particularly in the early years of the pandemic in Africa employed discursive frameworks that could propagate racialized assumptions of Africans (and Haitians in earlier discredited theories) as innate 'disease carriers', as Carla Tsampiras has traced in published studies in the *South African Medical Journal* from 1980 to 1995.[4]

The final and in many ways the most significant historical source type that has emerged from the pandemic is the proliferation of **narrative accounts from HIV+ persons**. These individual testimonies are unique sources in several respects and present for the historian of AIDS in Africa distinct challenges and opportunities, which will be explored in detail in the next section.

Given the limitations of and potentialities in the primary sources at our disposal, what are the central themes that emerge from a history of AIDS in Africa? Much of the historical debate has been shaped by the overriding question of why a disease that is so *preventable*, and a disease over which most of the Western world had earlier and relatively rapidly reached a level of control, has become a demographic catastrophe in sub-Saharan Africa. Examining the critical differences between the historical trajectory of HIV transmission in the West versus that in sub-Saharan Africa is one facet of this still relevant and pressing question. Another important avenue of historical enquiry has been influenced by the assessment of the social, economic, political, demographic and spiritual toll of the pandemic. A third seam of debate concerns the 'origins' of HIV/AIDS, which most scientists now agree began in western equatorial Africa as a virus in primates which then crossed the animal-human divide through accidental blood-to-blood contact. Although the earliest confirmed tissue sample testing positive for HIV dates to 1959 (to a case in Kinshasa), scientists now suggest that HIV crossed to human populations in West and Central Africa several decades earlier.[5] A recent call for historians of Africa to critically engage with the disciplines of virology, primatology and evolutionary biology, amongst others, to examine the HI virus's historical 'emergence' in Africa is a case in point. History's orientation towards capturing wide-scale social, cultural and environmental processes could potentially further scientific research by illuminating key dynamics – such as human-animal interactions, urbanization and mobility patterns – related to HIV's particular pattern of emergence, transmission and spread in Africa and globally.[6]

Crucially, a historical overview of the pandemic suggests that many of the root causes of the virus's pervasive spread across the continent as well as regional particularities have not been fully acknowledged nor addressed. Without this, HIV/AIDS will continue to remain entrenched even as transmission rates show some levels of decline. For example, the gendered dimensions of the pandemic suggest that unless widely asymmetrical gendered power and sexual relations are fundamentally redressed, African women will continue to bear a disproportionate load of new HIV cases. Science has shown that women have a biological vulnerability to acquiring the HI virus – the probability of male-to-female transmission is thought to be around three to four times that of female-to-male transmission.[7] This is due to the greater exposed area for viral transmission of female sexual organs, the higher concentrations of HIV in semen than in vaginal fluid, the longer duration in which semen is in present within the vaginal tract, and that vaginal membranes are more penetrable than those of the penis. Furthermore, HIV transmission has been shown to increase with the presence of other STDs, and since STDs in women are harder to detect, they may be at increased risk of acquiring the virus during sexual intercourse. Finally, extensive research has established the multiple ways that the social and economic vulnerability of women undermine their ability to negotiate sexual decision-making. In many social and familial scenarios, African women are unable to successfully implement 'safe-sex' measures. Studies, such as Carolyn Bailey and Janet Bujra's collaborative work on the gendered dimensions of HIV/AIDS in Tanzania and Zambia, have shown that even within the close confines of long-term and marital relationships, women feel they cannot demand that their partners 'condomize', for fear of being accused of being unfaithful.[8] Generational asymmetries also play a significant role in perpetuating gendered patterns of HIV transmission, with young women particularly vulnerable. Also, men and women may engage in transactional sexual relations, which involve monetary or financial exchange but are not solely defined by it, and do not neatly fit into the rubric of prostitution. This more ambiguous area of sexual decision-making, and the moral and political economy underpinning these relationships, is under-explored by both scholars and health practitioners, with Mark Hunter's study *Love in the Time of AIDS* (2010) a critical exception.

A historical vantage point is also useful in explaining the root causes for the pronounced level of *regional* variation in HIV/AIDS morbidity and mortality rates. The southern African region has borne the brunt of the disease burden of HIV/AIDS. East and Central Africa follow, with West Africa experiencing relatively low prevalence rates of HIV, although the absolute number of HIV+ individuals in Nigeria in 2018, for example, was 1.9 million – behind only South Africa and Mozambique. Without over-simplifying what are in fact overlapping and multiple causal pathways, one of the most important historical factors which has shaped the southern African region's particular experience of HIV/AIDS is the migrant labour system. This specific and massive movement of migrant labourers, which dates back to the initial mineral discoveries of the late nineteenth century in South Africa and, more latterly, to the copper discoveries of southern and northern Rhodesia (now Zimbabwe and Zambia, respectively), was characterized by the cyclical migration of young male labourers from rural areas throughout southern Africa to the urban domains where mining industries predominated. This regional circulation involved several colonial territories, in particular from Nyasaland (now Malawi) and Basotholand (now Lesotho), and was a profoundly powerful force that re-ordered generational, gendered and kinship relations across African communities in both rural and urban areas. The migrant labour system was also a powerful disease conduit, as will be discussed in Chapter 7 with respect to tuberculosis. In southern Africa, HIV followed labour migration routes, like with tuberculosis, into rural areas where transmission levels soared and health infrastructures were often poorly resourced. Pointedly, tuberculosis is synergistic with HIV, which means that those testing positive for tuberculosis are more vulnerable to acquiring the HI virus. Moreover, tuberculosis is a primary cause of AIDS-related death.

Another prominent aspect of the historical scholarship on HIV/AIDS, and the southern African region's particularities, is the critique of the vacuum of political leadership. Much of the focus is on the controversial stand and HIV/AIDS policy of former South African President Thabo Mbeki (whose presidency was from 1999 to 2008). Famously, at the International Conference on AIDS in Durban in 2000, while Mandela was emphasizing to conference attendees the necessity to galvanize the global community in Africa's fight against AIDS, Mbeki controversially asserted that AIDS was caused by poverty. In his speech, he argued that the solution to reducing AIDS was to step back from the disease itself and look at other socio-economic factors: poverty, violence, crime and inequality. This was interpreted by contemporary observers as a manifestation of 'AIDS denialism', as it appeared to put into question the causal connection of HIV with AIDS. Later in the course of his presidency, he became known for his strident critique of ARVs, arguing against their efficacy and also framing their introduction by global health authorities as a thinly veiled attempt by Western pharmaceutical companies to make profits by exploiting Africans as experimental guinea pigs for potentially toxic treatments that would not pass stringent testing protocols in America or Europe. Through the mounting backlash from international and domestic media, and the direct challenge to his policies by local activist groups such as the Treatment Action Campaign, Mbeki stepped back from the most controversial of these views in 2002 and no longer actively tried to intervene in scientific debates about the nature of AIDS causation and the efficacy of drug therapies.

Mbeki's harshest critics have pointed to his becoming the darling of a global network of AIDS dissidents, and how his ambiguous and seemingly denialist stance prevented the South African public from engaging in a frank dialogue about HIV transmission and prevention, and stalled international efforts to provide cheap and safe ARV therapy to hundreds of thousands of HIV+ South Africans. First-hand testimonies from HIV+ individuals who lived through the uncertainty of his leadership certainly attest that this delay in access to treatment cost lives. However, given the aetiology of HIV and the pattern of transmission in South Africa, it is likely that Mbeki's questionable decision-making was not solely responsible for South Africa becoming the HIV 'capital of the world'.[9] Several scholars such as Didier Fassin have produced more nuanced assessments of Mbeki's complex positioning around the multiple scientific, political and media discourses generated by the global AIDS pandemic. Furthermore, as considered in Part One of this book, the historical legacy of colonial and white settler health regimes has intruded in multi-faceted and surprising ways onto post-colonial African health decision-making. Seen in this way, many of Mbeki's most strident views on HIV/AIDS tapped into, rather than necessarily fed, local and popular discourses widely in circulation. These narratives could be understood as re-articulations of an older distrust of Western medical interventions, including failed experimental drug therapies, as well as an expression of historical resistance to encroachments onto the realm of African sexual health (as will be seen later in this chapter).

Histories of HIV/AIDS

Bongiwe is a South African female HIV+ survivor whose body map offers a different entry point into thinking about the relation between HIV/AIDS and history. As the source analysis suggests (see box), Bongiwe's body map is more than a snapshot of her current self-representation – it captures a distinctly *historical* journey of social and bodily well-being. Body maps and other first-person illness narratives created during the HIV/AIDS pandemic are thus *inherently* historical sources. Within them is described, and inscribed, a trajectory of change. It is important to acknowledge both the multiplicity and the coexisting inter-relationship, or entwinement, of the temporal arcs revealed in these narratives – for example, Bongiwe's journey towards self-understanding as a HIV+ survivor cannot be neatly divorced from her earlier experience of sexual violence and the emotional and bodily scars that event left.

Furthermore, first-hand testimonies of living with the HI virus like those embedded in body maps are not merely experiential accounts. They are confessional in character. The confessional has emerged as a dominant expressive paradigm within AIDS advocacy circles, as anthropologists Vinh-Kim Nguyen and Steven Robins have shown in their respective studies of AIDS ARV activism in Burkina Faso and Côte d'Ivoire, and South Africa. The script of the confessional follows a particular narrative arc in which the

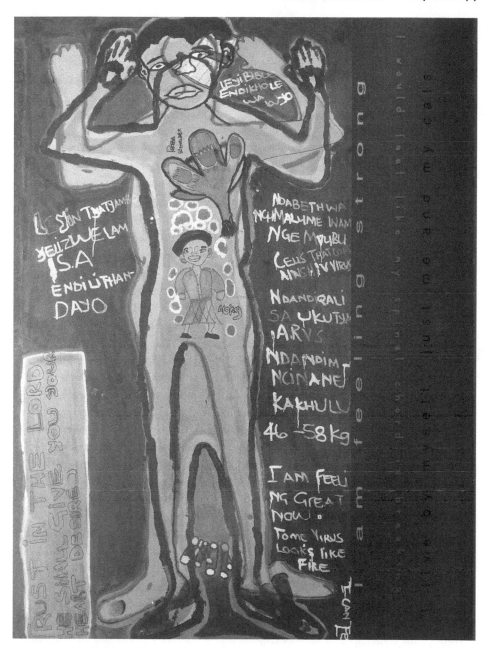

Figure 4.1 Body map of Bongiwe. Courtesy of Bongiwe Mba.

Historical Source: Body map of Bongiwe

Source Analysis: Bongiwe's visual representation as a HIV+ survivor through this body map is striking in many respects. It is at once an evocative snapshot of how she imagines the virus working within her physical self, as well as a visual testament to a longer process of self-formation that incorporates, but not exclusively, her particular illness journey. HIV is visually rendered by the logs aflame placed between her feet, with the explanator that, 'to me virus looks like fire', and further illustrated by the bright red cells moving through her central body cavity. The figure placed in her belly is the image of a 'mini' Bongiwe – a miniature replica of herself drawn inside the larger outline of her body, with the tag '46kg' placed next to it. This is a clear reference to the Bongiwe that 'was', that is, her AIDS-compromised body before she began taking antiretrovirals. In the margins of her body map, Bongiwe includes the inscription '46–58kg', an unassuming statistic at first glance, but when combined with the 'mini' Bongiwe image reveals itself much more powerfully to connote the 'before' and 'after' versions of herself. Taken together, these visual and textual cues show the visceral transformation her body underwent first through the workings of the virus and then through antiretroviral treatment.

However, HIV is not the singular narrative in this story. Bongiwe's strong Christian identity is indicated in the placement of an image of the Bible inside her as well as the biblical injunction to 'Trust in the Lord' placed alongside her body. The protea, the national flower of South Africa, drawn by her heart points to her emotional allegiance to the country of her birth. Other more painful associations are alluded to in this body map – for example, on her bent arm near the elbow, there is a slash mark rendered bright red. The accompanying textual narrative, found in the Long Life book in which this body map was first published, reveals that this scar marks a violent incident a few years previous to her HIV diagnosis, when she was abducted and gang-raped in her local neighbourhood. Indeed, there are multiple temporal arcs expressed in Bongiwe's body map – a past experience of sexual violence which pre-dates her diagnosis as well as her personal journey from ill-health towards wellness after contracting HIV.

Body maps such as Bongiwe's are the visual tool for, as well as poignant end-product of, a particular kind of therapeutic intervention for HIV+ survivors which emerged in the early 2000s in South Africa, when access to ARVs was not widely available, societal stigma and fears of disclosure of a positive diagnosis were high, yet new forms of advocacy and activism were being galvanized by the HIV/AIDS crisis. Body maps in this context became a potent visual symbol of 'positive living', enacted through the conscious and public declaration of one's HIV+ status and the entering into a new community of HIV+ survivors and advocates. The format of the body map workshop was in a sense designed to facilitate this transformation into positive living – usually through a workshop format, small groups of HIV+ participants alongside trained facilitators engaged in participatory exercises which encouraged the sharing of illness narratives and personal struggles through artistic expression. To an extent, the creative agency of these body maps may have been circumscribed by the *overriding therapeutic and institutional contexts in which they were created. Scholars such as Annie Coombes, Hayley MacGregor and Heather Mills have interrogated the therapeutic settings within which body maps have been produced and the oftentimes unequal relations of power which have shaped the wider circulation of these body maps in South Africa and beyond. Ultimately, despite these limitations, body maps offer striking and intimate visual narratives of individual experiences of illness which have shaped the global public's imagination of the personal and bodily toll of the HIV/ AIDS pandemic.*

HIV+ 'victim' experiences 'near death' through disempowerment and ill-health, finding redemption and a newfound personal agency by publicly acknowledging their HIV status and committing to a 'new life' characterized by faithful adherence to ARV medication within a community of fellow HIV+ survivors and advocates.[10] However, many of these confessionals are produced in the context of grossly unequal power structures, where performance of this script is seen as obligatory in order to access globally financed drug and treatment regimens as well as communal networks of support. Despite these limitations, it is important to acknowledge that confessionals are, like body maps, inherently historical formulations. They describe an internally realized trajectory of change.

Another striking characteristic of these new testimonies is their creative, multi-media dimension. As seen in the example of body maps, much of the emergent visual and digital archive of HIV+ survivors has been produced via art-based therapeutic interventions initiated by local and international HIV/AIDS organizations. The awe-inspiring tapestry created by women from rural Keiskamma in the Eastern Cape in South Africa, an area decimated by HIV/AIDS, is another example. The process of designing, weaving and stitching the tapestry allowed women in the community to express an irreparable sense of loss, described as a 'slow eating away at the whole fabric of a community. Each day another thread is lost, and suddenly an entire generation has disappeared. It has seemed that as we stitched in panic and in sorrow against this disintegration, more holes have appeared and gaps that could not be mended.'[11]

Importantly, these therapeutic interventions have encouraged HIV+ survivors to become, in effect, curators of their own life histories. 'Memory boxes', for example, were designed so that HIV+ survivors could choose items to place in their boxes that have personal significance to pass down to their children and loved ones – these could include photographs and other mementos from different stages of their lives, including post-diagnosis.[12] Recording digital stories that can be shared easily online is another popular manifestation of the act of self-witnessing – these video accounts often combine personal testimonies of HIV+ survivors with photographs and visual montages of their neighbourhoods and families. Although evoking a strong narrative voice, many of these multi-media sources are highly managed and curated by the organization or institution which has helped to produce them, and survivors may have little control over the dissemination of their own accounts, nor can they necessarily shape public consumption or interpretation of their stories.

Despite their limitations, these first-person accounts represent the first time in African history that such a large corpus of the personal and experiential dimensions of a particular disease has been recorded for posterity, presenting a powerful corrective to what had been the 'Achilles heel' in the historiography of health and illness in Africa – the lack of first-hand testimonies. These individual histories also begin to redress a deep gendered imbalance in the historical record – women's voices and experiences are foreground in the majority of these sources. As Bongiwe's body map shows us, the gendered and historical contours of the HIV/AIDS pandemic, and the emotional and embodied linkages made by HIV+ survivors to larger concerns regarding sexual violence, stigma and insecurity are but some of the analytical landscapes that can be more clearly discerned through this new source material. They may also constitute the empirical basis of future histories of AIDS activism as well as collective biographies of HIV+ survivors.

HIV/AIDS *in* history

The third major way to think through the relationship between AIDS and history is to situate the AIDS pandemic *in* history. As an entry point into this framework, consider HIV/AIDS in Africa in the context of other diseases and 'mortality shocks' faced by the continent via the simple table below:

Table 4.1 Comparative African mortality and morbidity: HIV/AIDS, Ebola, malaria, Spanish influenza and trans-Atlantic slave trade

Disease/mortality shock	Deaths	Cases	Case-mortality rate	Disease-mortality rate (per 100,000 population per year)
HIV/AIDS, 2014	730,000	27,000,000	2.7 per cent	75
Ebola, 2014–16	11,300	28,600	39.5 per cent	25
Malaria, 2015	394,200	188,320,000	0.2 per cent	40
Spanish flu pandemic, 1918–19	2,200,000 (estimated)	—	—	900
Slave trade 1500–1900	1,820,000	12,520,000	14.5 per cent	—

Sources: UNAIDS, https://aidsinfo.unaids.org; Centre for Disease Control and Prevention, '2014–2016 Ebola Outbreak in West Africa'; World Health Organization, *World Malaria Report 2015*; Niall Johnson and Juergen Mueller. 'Updating the Accounts: Global Mortality of the 1918–1920 "Spanish" Influenza Pandemic'. *Bulletin of the History of Medicine* 76 (2002): 105–15; Slave Voyages Database, https://slavevoyages.org; World Bank population data for Sub-Saharan Africa, https://data.worldbank.org/indicator/SP.POP.TOTL?locations=ZG; Patrick Manning, 'African Population, 1650–2000: Comparisons and Implications of New Estimates'. In *Africa's Development in Historical Perspective*, edited by Emmanuel Akyeampong, James Robinson, Nathan Nunn and Robert H. Bates. Cambridge: Cambridge University Press, 2014, 131–50.

It is evident that in comparison to HIV morbidity in 2014, the contemporaneous Ebola epidemic in West Africa had a much lower total caseload. That said, Ebola's exceptionally high case-mortality rate at 39.5 per cent over the course of the outbreak is one of the defining characteristics of that particular disease. Malaria, by contrast, in 2015 had a far lower case-mortality rate (at 0.2 per cent) compared to HIV/AIDS and Ebola. However, total malaria morbidity certainly dwarfed both – sub-Saharan Africa has close to 90 per cent of global malaria incidence (see Chapter 6) and the roughly 154 million African cases of malaria outnumber exponentially the 27 million HIV cases in Africa over the same period. The total number of deaths from Spanish influenza for the continent was much lower than cumulative deaths of Africans over the course of the AIDS pandemic – 24.8 million estimated dead from 1990–2014, as mentioned earlier in this chapter. However, the Spanish flu's extraordinarily high disease-mortality rate (as distinct from case-mortality rate) is worth noting, although this figure should be taken with caution as it is based on estimates of both flu incidence and the size of the African population. Historians suggest that the territories worst affected by the Spanish flu – South Africa, Tanganyika (now Tanzania), Kenya, Nyasaland, Cameroon, Gold Coast, Gambia – had estimated mortality rates of greater than 5 per cent of their populations, which would be comparable to the mortality rates of the worst AIDS-affected countries.[13] Another striking feature of the flu pandemic of the First World War was that it disproportionately affected the young adult population. The Spanish flu's asymmetrical impact, which went against typical patterns of demographic vulnerability to infectious disease (striking usually either the very young or the very old), is shared by the HIV/AIDS pandemic. Finally, it is worth pointing out that – in terms of the sheer demographic impact, and the effects on political structures, kinship and social networks as well as on moral and spiritual imaginaries – perhaps the most apt comparison for the HIV/AIDS pandemic is not to a disease at all but to Africa's involvement in the slave trade. The figures above indicate the estimated numbers of slaves taken out of the continent through the trans-Atlantic slave trade, but do not include the number of slaves who perished within Africa or were enslaved and exported via other slave trading routes.

A significant way to examine HIV/AIDS *in* history is to insert it into a larger history of sexually transmitted diseases, which is the predominant expression of HIV in the sub-Saharan African context. Why is including HIV/AIDS as part of a history of STDs important? First, there is a proven epidemiological link between HIV and other STDs, in that having a STD makes you more biologically vulnerable to HIV infection – for example, having syphilis means you are at an estimated two to five times more likely of acquiring HIV at time of exposure.[14] Second, transmission patterns indicate the HI virus in many regions of high prevalence in sub-Saharan African traversed strikingly similar transport and mobility routes – between rural and urban areas within countries and also trans-nationally – which more than five decades preceding had facilitated the spread of previous outbreaks of STDs. Both of these factors justify a more historical understanding of STDs which pre-dated, and helped define, HIV's transmission and spread. Furthermore, a historical approach which centres African responses and approaches to earlier episodes of STDs and sexual health initiatives could provide important insights into why many latter-day HIV/AIDS treatment and prevention campaigns have failed to significantly alter transmission patterns and mortality rates. It is vital to acknowledge that, in Africa and worldwide, STDS have proven to be particularly susceptible to social constructions, more so than other disease types.[15] The conceptualization of STDs uniquely touches on issues of both power and intimacy through their impact on sexual relations, sexual behaviour and fertility. Historically in Africa this social construction has occurred in the context of often vastly unequal power relations which structured the behaviour and expectations of African patients, health practitioners, and colonial and state agents. These factors ultimately influenced both Africans' perception of STDs and their reception of health campaigns targeting STDs in local communities. Finally, certain STDs such as syphilis historically commanded comparably high levels of colonial resources and attention. STDs were thus more visible in the colonial archival record compared to other disease types such as occupational disease (see Chapter 7). This, combined with the wealth of contemporary evidence generated by the HIV/AIDS pandemic, means that a relatively sustained historical comparison can be achieved, something that is difficult to do in other disease contexts in Africa.

Syphilis in the colonial period

One critical point of comparison to the current HIV/AIDS pandemic can be found in the history of syphilis in Africa from the late nineteenth to the mid-twentieth centuries, a period punctuated by syphilis 'epidemics' in interwar East-Central and southern Africa. The territories concerned include Nyasaland, Uganda, Cape Colony and the Transvaal (later South Africa), and Northern and Southern Rhodesia, and Senegal (in West Africa). In terms of source material, there is a large body of **colonial medical reports** and **correspondence** as well as **mission hospital records** and **missionary medics' accounts** of syphilis treatment and prevention campaigns. The development of anthropology as a discipline in the early decades of the twentieth century ushered in writings on sexual and gender relations as part of larger **ethnographies** of African societies. Whilst colonial anthropological literature is not directly concerned with STDs, this corpus of writing helps to inform our understanding of the social organization of sexual and conjugal relations and behaviours, which had a bearing on how Africans socially constructed STDs and may have interpreted anti-STD campaigns.

There is considerable historical debate on whether the incidence of syphilis in Africa, even in the worst affected areas of the interwar period, amounted to an epidemic. Certainly, contemporary estimates in some regions of the above colonial territories pointed to an 'epidemic' of crisis proportions, and the colonial record reflects that level of alarm. As early as 1908, medical journals such as *The Lancet* and the *British Medical Journal* broadcast concern over reported figures of an 'outbreak' of syphilis in the Uganda Protectorate which had infected an estimated 80 per cent of the Buganda population. Although that figure was decades later revised down to 65 per cent, the relative enormity

Syphilis: The basics

Syphilis is a bacterial infection caused by close bodily contact with someone who has an infected sore. It is normally transmitted through anal, oral or vaginal sexual intercourse. Pregnant women with syphilis can also transmit it to their unborn baby, which can result in miscarriage, stillbirth or the birth of a congenitally syphilitic baby. The appearance of syphilitic sores, called chancres, are the tell-tale symptom of primary-stage syphilis. Secondary stage symptoms include rashes, fever, hair loss, joint and muscle pain, and swollen lymph glands. If left untreated – latent syphilis can exist in the body for many years – syphilis can cause severe debility, including blindness, dementia and organ dysfunction, and can be fatal. Syphilis can be effectively treated through a course of antibiotics. Transmission can be prevented through the use of female and male condoms during sex. Testing for syphilis is now done through a blood test and the swabbing of sores.

Syphilis was a known disease as early as the 15th century. Although its origins are debated, it is generally agreed that it was a disease endemic to the Americas and was brought to Europe from the New World. Mercury, in both ingested and topical form, was used as a treatment in Europe since the 16th century. Despite being lethal if taken in high dosages, mercury remained a popular treatment until 1910, when an arsenic based compound called Salvarsan was manufactured. This, in combination with the development in 1906 of an antibody test for syphilis called the Wasserman reaction, was a significant milestone. However, Salvarsan also had toxic side effects and the use of arsenic-based drugs in combination with small amounts of mercury or bismuth continued as the standard treatment until the introduction of penicillin in 1943 ended the use of all metal-based forms of chemotherapy.

of the 'crisis' of syphilis in Uganda remained a prominent trope amongst colonial and medical missionary circles until the 1930s.[16] South African press reports in the 1920s, similarly, suggested from 50 per cent up to as high as 80 to 90 per cent of the African population had syphilis, although these estimates were not accepted by the national Department of Public Health.[17] In Senegal, medical reports in the 1920s suggested doctors believed that upwards of 80 per cent of the population of Dakar had syphilis, and that certain ethnic groups – the Fulani and Tukulor – had nearly their entire population infected.[18]

An important caveat for the more extreme figures is that the correct diagnosis of venereal syphilis for much of this time period was complicated by the presence of yaws and another form of non-venereal syphilis thought to have been endemic in Africa. Both of these diseases were transmitted by skin-to-skin contact in the context of poor sanitation and hygiene measures, rather than through sexual intercourse. Endemic syphilis and yaws present similar symptoms to venereal syphilis, and even a test that was hailed at the time to definitively diagnose syphilis – called the Wasserman test, used from 1906 – would show positive for *both* endemic and venereal syphilis. It is now acknowledged that these earlier figures probably grossly exaggerated the extent of syphilis in these regions. Despite this, historians have acknowledged that a decline in the population of Central and East Africa likely did occur in the 1920s and 1930s, and so the larger demographic crisis underpinning colonial anxieties with regards to syphilis should not be discounted. As discussed in Chapter 2, the reasons for population decline in the interwar period may have had more to do with mortality from other infectious diseases and the violent effects of oppressive colonial policies involving land and labour, which removed indigenous controls over the environment and extracted a heavy toll on African bodies.

Colonial medical responses to syphilis evolved throughout this period. It was far from static and changed dependent on prevailing political ideologies and available resources as well as medical developments in the understanding of STDs and their treatments, particularly through scientific advances in the field of bacteriology. The following brief timeline provides a sense of some of the broad patterns of change in the period under consideration – a further review of these policies in the larger context of colonial health administration is provided in Chapter 2. The Contagious Diseases Act was a succession of acts in the latter half of the nineteenth century imposed in British colonial territories in Asia as well as Africa. These were an extension of similar legislation enacted in the London metropole, premised on the tight surveillance of 'target' populations – usually prostitutes – and the use of lock hospitals to enforce treatment and monitoring of those confirmed with a STD. Broadly across the British Empire, these lockdown hospitals ended in the early twentieth century due to their expense as well as the political backlash against them evident both in the metropole and amongst settler populations. In French West Africa, although there was an absence of a formal decree comparable to the Contagious Diseases Act, the governor-general mandated at the turn to the twentieth century a series of surveillance, detention and treatment measures of prostitutes across all its municipalities which closely followed the British lock hospital model.

In the early decades of the twentieth century, there was an evident shift away from the forcible separation and seclusion of a 'target' female population to a more outwardly facing 'public health'-style intervention. Francophone approaches applied to West Africa were heavily influenced by European hygienist concerns, which linked syphilis with other perceived diseases of industrialization such as tuberculosis and alcoholism. In the British territories, colonial campaigns against venereal disease tended to be closely associated with the work of mission hospitals, and this linkage was evident in the moralistic propaganda that was produced in this period and accompanied medical treatment. In keeping with the mission emphasis to work in the vernacular, anti-venereal disease campaigns were translated into local languages to reach as broad a base as possible.

From the 1930s, another shift was discernible, moving away from a focus on STDs to a more concerted effort to tackle the observed alarming decline in fertility in the two decades previous. This involved a turn to maternalist policies and a concern with child welfare and nutrition, including breastfeeding, and tackling high infant mortality rates. The maternalist policies enacted within the mining compounds of the Belgian Congo

Copperbelt are an example of this shift in focus, although similar interventions could also be broadly seen in French West Africa and British-held territories, including Uganda, Nigeria, Tanganyika and Kenya. Penicillin became available in the late 1940s as a treatment for syphilis, and its availability was largely responsible for the decline in syphilis cases and helped enable the shift towards maternalist policies. Previous medical treatments, such as mercury-based treatments common until the 1910s and 1920s and then arsenic-based therapies of the 1920s and 1930s, were uneven in their effectiveness and potentially toxic – and in the case of mercury treatments, had proven deadly on occasion.

A useful perspective through which to view the complex social construction of STDs during the colonial period is to consider the wide disparity in contemporary views of African sexuality. Put more simply, there was a pronounced gulf in this period between *European* views of African sexuality and *African* views of African sexuality, and this gap goes a long way towards explaining the poor fit of colonial medical interventions to the problems posed by STDs, and their uneven reception among African communities.

Embedded in European discourses framing colonial responses to STDs were competing notions of African sexuality, as Megan Vaughan has shown in the context of syphilis control in colonial East and Central Africa. In some quarters, African sexuality was viewed as essentially 'primitive' and uncontrolled, and disease was the inevitable result of or punishment for unchecked predatory sexual behaviour. Missionaries contributed to this view through their persistent focus on re-shaping African conjugal and sexual relations, in particular their drive to stamp out what they viewed to be particularly morally reprehensible practices, including polygyny, levirate practices in which a widow could be required to have sexual relations with a member of her dead husband's kin group, and male initiation rites involving circumcision. In colonies with significant settler societies like in southern Rhodesia, African men were constructed as a 'black peril', a particular violent sexual threat to European women. But in other colonial contexts, African women could be viewed as the predator. The second prominent European view of African sexuality was that Africans were 'innocents' in need of protection. In this vein of thinking, STDs were the result of the breakdown of traditional controls over sexual behaviour due to the combined deleterious effects of Christianity, colonialism, urbanization. Civilization and modernization were in effect proving detrimental to African sexual and social reproduction, and a return or reinforcement of 'tradition' was seen as the most appropriate antidote.[19]

The perceptions of Africans as 'predator' or 'innocent' could be profoundly influenced by Africans themselves. For example, African chiefly authorities in many parts of southern, East and Central Africa supported and contributed to the social construction of a dangerous, predatory African female sexuality in the colonial period, particularly as chiefs sought to re-assert control over women's bodies as a way of maintaining social and ritual authority in the context of land loss to colonizers, Christianization and labour migration. In colonial Kenya and in the urbanizing areas of South Africa, entrepreneurial migrant women from certain ethnic groups – for example, the Ganda in Kenya and Basotho in the gold mining area of the Witwatersrand – developed a particular reputation amongst colonizers as well as other Africans for being dangerously 'other'. The perception that these women engaged in sexually deviant behaviour informed their outsider status, a status reinforced by their mobility and relative economic independence in the urban setting. Basotho women, for example, engaged in beer-brewing, an informal economy which was linked to promiscuous sexual activity and forms of prostitution.

Needless to say, neither the African as 'predatory' nor the African as 'innocent' does justice to the complex positioning and meaning of sex within colonial African societies. Piecing together African views of African sexuality through contemporary accounts is difficult as the historical record is extremely limited in this respect. Very few first-person accounts written by Africans exist on this subject, and this may reflect cultural proscriptions in African societies that guarded the discussion of matters relating to sexual behaviour as well as the general dearth of African voices in the colonial archive (see Chapter 2). Instead, the historical record is shaped by European observations of local African cosmologies and ritual behaviour, and these need to be read through the filter of the European observer's perspective.

These contemporary accounts suggest the regulation of sexual behaviour in African societies should be seen as part of the management of a larger moral and spiritual sphere. For example, missionary and traveller accounts on the funerary and mortuary practices of southern African societies reveal that a key preoccupation was the importance African societies placed on containing 'contagion' or the ritual pollution of the dead. These concepts of deathly contagion were closely linked to other embodied notions of ritual impurity at key stages in the life cycle or at moments of potential contamination, which included sexual activity, lactation or menses. Ludwig Alberti, a German-speaking officer and then administrator within what was then the Dutch-held Cape Colony, was an enthusiastic proto-ethnographer of the Cape's Xhosa population. In his account of the Xhosa published in 1807, he provided a lengthy list of those the Xhosa considered ritually 'impure': children, women during menstruation and during the first month after confinement, an unmarried woman who has lived with a man, a widower, a mother whose child has died, all men returning from battle. He further specifies, 'persons who are afflicted with impurity may not, during that time, wash or colour themselves, drink milk or make love'.[20] Sexual intercourse with those who were ritually impure would invite moral pollution, disease and potentially death. In this context, then, sexual activity was neither inherently wrong nor right, but depended on its timing and its confluence, or mixing, with other factors and fluids such as semen, blood and milk.

The concept of ritual contagion and the discourse of pollution within which proscriptions against sex were justified were broadly present, although not uniformly, in southern and Central and East African societies throughout the nineteenth and early twentieth centuries. Amongst the Tswana in southern Africa, sexual intercourse was prohibited with a widow or widower soon after the death of their spouse. This was because the blood of the widowed spouse became 'hot' as a result of their death. However, as the anthropologist Isaac Schapera recorded in his conversation with a Tswana diviner named Rapedi in 1942, if a married couple was childless and one partner died, the surviving spouse would not have to follow the proscriptions against sexual intercourse because their blood had not become 'hot'. 'They have nothing to be sorry for,' Rapedi was said to have informed Schapera. In this case, it is reproduction which confirms the bodily link between wife and husband, which is then rendered 'hot' when one of them dies.[21] Thus, broadly speaking, a striking feature of African approaches to the regulation of sexual behaviour in the colonial period was that these mechanisms of control were developed to manage the larger problem of ritual pollution, which included the sphere of sexual activity but was not its exclusive moral focus.

Moral versus technical approaches

One could characterize the range of responses to syphilis from colonial health administrations through the useful analytic tension between 'moral' and 'technical' approaches.[22] Throughout British-held southern and East Africa, a combination of moral and technical approaches prevailed throughout this period. This amalgamation is evident in late nineteenth-century lock hospitals which provided treatment but in effect incarcerated the sick and labelled women's very movements as criminal, and in interwar anti-venereal disease campaigns which tended to combine mass injections of syphilitics with public propaganda that encouraged 'appropriate' sexual behaviour. The promotion of a sense of shame among Africans to highlight the health risks inherent in polygyny and other 'irregular' sexual relations could be discerned in anti-STD initiatives even into the 1940s, although shame's effectiveness as a public health tool was debated amongst colonial medical advisors.[23] This dualist approach in British African territories was reinforced by the colonial state's tendency to utilize mission hospitals and medical missionaries as an extension of the colonial medical apparatus, due to the limitations of colonial finances and manpower resources.

Interestingly, in colonial Senegal as in much of French West Africa, the pervasive role of Islam meant Christian missionaries had far less impact on matters of sexual health and on the regulation of gender and sexual relations more generally. Also, the separation of the church and state in France in 1904 meant its colonial health administration adopted an avowedly secular and less socio-moralizing tone as seen in other colonial African contexts. Instead, STDs became incorporated into a broader focus on surveillance and control of infectious disease, utilizing a combination of community clinics and mobile health units, called from 1944 the General Mobile Hygiene and Preventive Service. These mobile units, employing trained African staff, were at the forefront of successful mass campaigns to treat yaws and syphilis in the 1950s. Furthermore, in the postwar period the licencing and medical inspection of sex workers in Senegal was accompanied by readily available access to treatments such as antibiotic injections, which were generally welcomed by patient populations. These initiatives helped to establish an institutional and infrastructural network of surveillance and treatment around STDs, as well as a level of compliance in terms of drug regimes, that would bear fruit decades later in the early years of the HIV/AIDS pandemic.[24]

Some interventions did focus on addressing the larger political economy underpinning sexual relations rather than attempting to regulate sexual behaviour per se, and these had a degree of beneficial impact in containing STD transmission. For example, on the mines of the Northern Rhodesian Copperbelt, mining officials were relatively successful in keeping rates of STDs low among miners in the 1930s and 1940s. This was facilitated by a mine industry-sanctioned approach to labour stabilization similar to that at work in the Belgian Congo Copperbelt, a policy which allowed mining men to live with their wives instead of in single-sex compounds, and effectively limited interactions with single women in town who had been stigmatized by both European observers and traditional authorities as morally problematic and 'disease reservoirs'.[25] Mining officials' advocacy of enforced surveillance of symptoms of STDs, whilst draconian in some respects, served to longitudinally track the health of miners and deliver treatment when necessary.

By the 1950s, a general shift to wholly technical approaches could be seen throughout colonial Africa, especially as the widespread effectiveness of penicillin came to be understood. That said, the larger discursive paradigm of 'dangerous' sexuality, particularly that of single and mobile African women, continued to be evoked in other state spheres, for example in the development of pass laws by the apartheid state in South Africa. This evocation of 'loose women' was used to justify the regulation and limitation of movement of unaccompanied African women into urban areas.[26]

Broadly speaking, as we saw in African responses to medical missionaries in Chapter 2, African communities tended to respond more positively to the *technical* aspects of colonial medical interventions in the realm of sexual health while evading their *moral* implications. Part of the enthusiasm towards technical solutions should be seen in the light of the relative lack of local African treatments for venereal syphilis, compared to the use of segregation and seclusion which was an established tool to address endemic syphilis. This disparity could be a reflection of the relative 'newness' of venereal syphilis in many African regions, something that was also expressed linguistically. For example, the foreign origins of venereal syphilis can be discerned in Zulu terminology for the disease, which entered into the local lexicon in the early twentieth century: *isifo sabelungu* ('disease of the white man') or *isifo sedolopi* ('disease of the town').[27] However, this does not mean African communities were unable to internally respond to the threat of STDs. Novel mechanisms of control were developed. In the male-only compounds on the gold mines of the Witwatersrand in South Africa, STD morbidity rates among mineworkers were very low from the mid-1930s to 1940s – 0.6 per cent for syphilis and 0.2 per cent for gonorrhoea – far lower than comparable rates outwith the mines in rural and urban areas of South Africa.[28] At a time when syphilis was reaching supposedly 'epidemic' proportions elsewhere in southern, Central and East Africa, miners on the Rand had developed internal mechanisms of control to prevent risky sexual liaisons with 'town women', including abstinence and homosexual relations with other miners.

To some extent vernacular expressions of venereal syphilis such as *isifo sabelungu* capture another aspect of African understandings of STDs – that colonial occupation could be implicated within the onset and spread of STDs in Africa. A telling early example of this linkage could be found in the 1909 venereal disease treatment campaign in Kampala, Uganda. The intervention was severely hampered by local African fears of mercury poisonings, which had been the direct cause of a number of deaths. But the campaign was also dogged by local rumours circulating that the treatments' so-called injections of fire were removing blood and causing miscarriages.[29] The irony of these rumours could not be more powerful – in the eyes of ordinary Kampalans, colonial rule became associated with the *introduction* of STDS and declines in fertility, and not with the solution to these problems. This moral and discursive inversion would re-surface many decades later in discussions around the responsibility, and culpability, of Western and global health interventions with respect to the African AIDS crisis.

HIV/AIDS and syphilis – connections and divergences

There are some important continuities to consider in the history of both of these STDs in the African context, despite the enormous transformations in the political, economic and health landscapes of Africa in the intervening period. The *tension* between moral and technical approaches seen in responses to syphilis is certainly indicative of the vast panoply of HIV/AIDS treatment and prevention interventions. The lack of a definitive cure or vaccine for HIV throughout this period within a context of poorly resourced post-colonial African health systems has meant that, similar to colonial medical responses to syphilis, technical approaches have tended to be combined with moralistic ones, particularly in HIV preventative campaigns. One only needs to look at the widely utilized and criticized 'ABC'-approach to see this tension at work. 'Abstain, Be faithful, Condomize' – the first two tenets are moral approaches with only the third considered technical, although the issue of condom usage became in the early years of HIV prevention a contentious flashpoint for Catholic as well as Muslim African clerics, religious congregations and faith-based NGOs.

Certainly, one of the factors cited by scholars for the high prevalence of HIV in southern Africa is the legacy of previous moral interventions by Christian missionaries, which diminished existing indigenous controls regulating sexual behaviour. It is widely accepted that circumcision reduces biological vulnerability to HIV infection, which means areas where male circumcision was effectively abolished through missionary intervention were adversely affected – for example, in Zululand in the eighteenth century and amongst the Tswana in the early twentieth century. These areas have amongst the highest HIV prevalence rates in sub-Saharan Africa. Other examples of missionary interventions which had potential negative consequences for African sexual health include the discouragement of sexual play such as intracrural sex (a form of non-penetrative sexual activity) and the abolition of male and female initiation groups which had traditionally provided a place for frank discussion of, and guidance on, sexual activity and sexual behaviour.

Conversely, when health interventions have been decoupled from prescriptions for 'proper' sexual behaviour, such as when the Western Cape provincial government broke away from national policy in 1999 by offering nevirapine to pregnant HIV+ mothers to help prevent mother-to-child transmission (a full three years before the South African government was compelled by the Constitutional Court to rollout the programme to

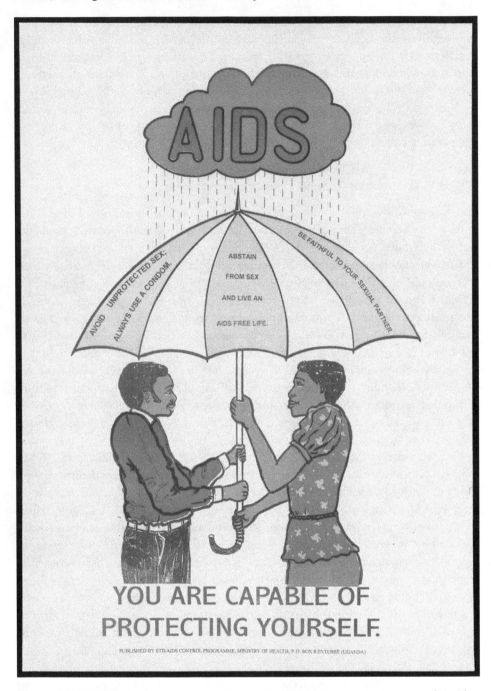

Figure 4.2 HIV/AIDS prevention poster, STD/AIDS Control Programme, Ministry of Health, Uganda, undated.

Historical Source: HIV/AIDS prevention poster, Ministry of Health, Uganda

Source Analysis: This poster is an elegant visual iteration of the 'ABC'-approach (Abstain, Be faithful, Condomize) to HIV/AIDS prevention campaigns that was adopted across many African states. The couple stand beneath the protection of a giant ABC umbrella, with the cheery colours and the couple's smiling faces conveying assurance they will be safe from the storms caused by AIDS as long as they choose to shelter underneath. The bold message underneath the couple, 'You are capable of protecting yourself', further emphasizes that all three tenets of the ABCs are individual choices that can be made, and that protection is contingent on adherence to those choices.

As a historical source, this poster is a record of the Ugandan health ministry's attempt to convey a simple yet powerful message through an accessible visual format. Posters such as these were placed in prominent and visible public spaces, such as health clinics, busy road intersections, taxi and bus depots and train stations. Public outreach through visual media was an important tool for a variety of health initiatives, and became even more critical as the HIV/AIDS epidemic unfolded, particularly as a means to reach youthful audiences.

Although the poster's message appears straightforward, there are ambiguities which complicate its effectiveness as a public health intervention. First, the ABC-approach, like many HIV prevention initiatives, assumes that behavioural change could be and should be the main driver to halt HIV transmission. Individuals, and particularly women, may not have equal capacity to negotiate safe sexual encounters. The intimation that 'you are capable of protecting yourself' does not take into account, for example, instances of violent sexual assault where consent is not a factor, or situations in which sexual partners refuse to use condoms. An emphasis on behavioural change places agency, as well as blame, on the individual's choices, rather than focusing on a broader array of social, economic and political factors which shape sexual relations and decision-making. Second, scholars have shown that each element of the ABCs was not equally promoted by health authorities and organizations in HIV prevention campaigns. Faith-based groups and organizations, for example, tended to focus on abstinence and fidelity in their outreach efforts at the expense of condom-distribution. In Uganda, the Catholic Church resisted the promotion of condom usage in the critical early years of the transmission of HIV and this was a view shared by ordinary Ugandans as well as, initially, President Yoweri Museveni (1986–present). By the time Ugandan views on condom usage had shifted in the late 1990s, peak HIV transmission levels had already been reached (with adult prevalence at between 10 per cent and 10.4 per cent from 1990 to 1994).[30]

the entire country), these were readily taken up by patient communities. In Senegal, its secularist approach to sexual health helped to prevent the social stigmatization of HIV+ individuals, and encouraged testing as well as the uptake of allopathic remedies. Furthermore, widespread male circumcision amongst its predominantly Muslim population added to the 'epidemiological advantage' Senegal possessed, like other West African countries, through facing the less virulent HIV-2 strain of the virus in the early years of the pandemic.[31] Senegal's HIV prevalence rate is currently 0.4 per cent.[32]

Echoes of colonial debates on the nature of African sexuality are present in more recent scholarship on the HIV/AIDS pandemic, albeit expressed in different forms. The controversial views of demographers John and Pat Caldwell have attributed the HIV/AIDS epidemic in Africa to a particular model of African sexuality. They have argued that African sexual systems evolved around lineage organization with an emphasis on reproduction and descent, which resulted in an emphasis in African societies on polygyny, weak conjugal bonds and a lack of shame around sex, extra-marital or otherwise. In their view, sexual activity became transactable because of the historical embeddedness of this system.[33] Like colonial views on a 'predatory' African sexuality, this has been criticized as an over-simplification. Certainly, there is no one model of African sexuality, nor can it be fixed primordially in time. Furthermore, scholars such as Suzette Heald have shown that the Caldwells' perspective fails to engage with how African societies may consider the regulation of sexuality as part of a larger moral and spiritual sphere. Situating sexual behaviour in the context of a broader struggle over ritual contagion has its own long history in southern and East African contexts, as discussed earlier in this chapter. With respect to HIV/AIDS, the lack of understanding of the complexity of African ideas around pollution and sexuality can mark even the most well-intended and resourced interventions out for failure. Amongst the Venda in South Africa in the early 2000s, local female HIV peer educators became targeted by members of the community as *vectors* of the disease in part due to their inability to maintain the necessary 'degrees of separation' from the rumoured causes of unnatural death, of which HIV was one of many unspoken forces. Instead, female volunteers' public and forthright speaking about HIV transmission was perceived to be a flagrant violation of ritual proscriptions around unnatural death which required their silence. Because of these dangerous associations, female peer educators' liberal distribution of condoms became perceived as the vehicle for *causing* AIDS rather than *preventing* it.[34]

Suspicion of condoms may also be traced back to attempts by the colonial state to regulate and control African sexual activity and fertility. In the 1970s and 1980s in Zimbabwe and South Africa, African populations were actively, and sometimes coercively, encouraged by minority white regimes to decrease their fertility rate. This went alongside efforts, which were also ultimately unsuccessful, to encourage white populations in these same countries to increase their fertility rates to ensure they maintained or even increased their percentage of the overall population. The dark legacy of these 'family planning' initiatives may be seen in suspicions over the true motives behind the promotion of condom use in HIV prevention campaigns. It is telling, for example, that in the early years of the pandemic black South Africans appropriated a different interpretation of the AIDS acronym – 'Afrikaner Invention to Deprive us of Sex' – signifying underlying fears as well as mocking efforts to intervene in the intimate sphere of sexual relations. Interestingly, young Francophone Africans expressed similar sentiments on this unwelcome intrusion, deriding SIDA (the French acronym for AIDS) as 'Syndrome imaginaire pour décourager les amoureux [trans. an imaginary syndrome to discourage lovers]', which suggests that the shadow of distrust cast over sexual health interventions was both wide and long.[35]

Conclusion

This chapter has been concerned with how a broader historical perspective can illuminate Africa's time of AIDS. Although in many respects the immense demographic, social and economic toll of the HIV/AIDS pandemic on the continent is yet to be fully realized, I have argued that the discipline of history can provide powerful analytical routes to understand this still-unfolding story. Through a historical lens, HIV/AIDS becomes more than a present-tense crisis but an object of study subject to the historians' gaze and to their particular tools and critical frameworks. Rather than solely considering HIV/AIDS as a continuing demographic tragedy of unspeakable proportions, which of course has its own irrefutable moral truth value, history requires us to think about HIV/AIDS through a framework of trajectories, wider contexts, earlier reference points, changing experiences and, ultimately, ideas of and in transformation.

Historical analysis also necessitates a focus on primary sources, the 'stuff' of history. Particularly in the humanities and the social sciences, the intervention of HIV+ survivors and the proliferation of first-person accounts in textual, visual, aural and digital forms have been critical in engendering a 'historical turn' in scholarship on the AIDS pandemic in Africa. Through these individual accounts, HIV+ survivors have focused attention on the experiential aspects of their illness narratives, in all their embodied and historical complexities. This archive is yet to be fully mined by historians, and the potential remains for these sources to transform our historical understanding not only of the HIV/AIDS pandemic but of the experience of health and illness in Africa.

Finally, a historical perspective may offer insight into the more recent successes and failures of HIV/AIDS intervention programmes in Africa. In looking at how syphilis 'epidemics' were both constructed and addressed by colonial health authorities, we can appreciate how wide the gulf was between European views of African sexuality and Africans' own perspectives, which were rooted in a broader moral and conceptual plane. This can serve as a powerful reminder that African perceptions and cosmologies should be considered in the design and implementation of effective HIV treatment and prevention measures. Furthermore, the history of syphilis control as well as a broader history of sexual and reproductive health provides a window onto patterns of African resistance – resistance to intrusions into the realm of sexual behaviour as well as resistance to medicalized forms of surveillance, treatment and control – which may have persisted or become re-articulated in the HIV/AIDS context.

Further reading

Baylies, Carolyn and Janet M. Bujra, eds. *AIDS, Sexuality and Gender in Africa: Collective Strategies and Struggles in Tanzania and Zambia*. London: Routledge, 2000.

Becker, Felicitas and Wenzel Geissler, eds. *AIDS and Religious Practice in Africa*. Leiden: Brill, 2009.

Caldwell, John C., Pat Caldwell and Pat Quiggin. 'The Social Context of AIDS in Sub-Saharan Africa'. *Population and Development Review* 15, no. 2 (1989): 185–234.

Campbell, Catherine. *'Letting Them Die': Why HIV/AIDS Prevention Programmes Fail*. Oxford: James Currey, 2003.

Coombes, Annie E. 'Positive Living: Visual Activism and Art in HIV/AIDS Rights Campaigns'. *Journal of Southern African Studies* 45, no. 1 (2019): 143–74.

Cross, Sholto and Alan Whiteside, eds. *Facing Up to AIDS: The Socio-Economic Impact in Southern Africa*. Basingstoke: Macmillan, 1993.

Denis, Philippe and Charles Becker, eds. *The HIV/AIDS Epidemic in Sub-Saharan Africa in Historical Perspective*. Online edition. Louvaine la-Neuve and Paris: Published by Academia-Bruylant and Karthala, 2006. https://www.dphu.org/uploads/attachements/books/books_1448_0.pdf, accessed 5 June 2020.

de Waal, Alex. *AIDS and Power: Why There Is No Political Crisis – Yet*. London: Zed Books, 2006.

Dickinson, David. *A Different Kind of AIDS: Alternative Explanations of HIV/AIDS in South African Townships*. Johannesburg: Jacana Media, 2014.

Dionne, Kim Yi. *Doomed Interventions: The Failure of Global Responses to AIDS in Africa*. Cambridge: Cambridge University Press, 2018.

Doyle, Shane. *Before HIV: Sexuality, Fertility and Mortality in East Africa, 1900–1980*. Oxford: Oxford University Press, 2013.

Fassin, Didier. *When Bodies Remember: Experiences and Politics of AIDS in South Africa*, translated by Amy Jacobs and Gabrielle Varro. Berkeley: University of California Press, 2007.

Giles-Vernick, Tamara, Ch. Didier Gondola, Guillaume Lachenal and William H. Schneider. 'JAH Forum: Social History, Biology, and the Emergence of HIV in Colonial Africa'. *Journal of African History* 54 (2013): 11–30.

Golomski, Casey. *AIDS, Work and Cultural Change in an African Kingdom*. Bloomington: Indiana University Press, 2018.

Heald, Suzette. 'The Power of Sex: Some Reflections on the Caldwells' "African Sexuality" Thesis'. *Africa: Journal of the International African Institute* 65, no. 4 (1995): 489–505.

Hodes, Rebecca. *Broadcasting the Pandemic: A History of HIV on South African Television*. Cape Town: HSRC Press, 2014.

Hunter, Mark. *Love in the Time of AIDS: Inequality, Gender, and Rights in South Africa*. Bloomington: Indiana University Press, 2010.

Iliffe, John. *The African AIDS Epidemic: A History*. Oxford: James Currey, 2006.

Iweala, Uzodinma. *Our Kind of People: A Continent's Challenge, a Country's Hope*. New York: HarperCollins, 2012.

Jochelson, Karen. *The Colour of Disease: Syphilis and Racism in South Africa, 1880–1950*. Basingstoke: Palgrave Macmillan, 2001.

Klaits, Frederick. *Death in a Church of Life: Moral Passion during Botswana's Time of AIDS*. Berkeley: University of California Press, 2010.

MacGregor, Hayley. 'Mapping the Body: Tracing the Personal and the Political Dimensions of HIV/AIDS in Khayelitsha, South Africa'. *Anthropology and Medicine* 16, no. 1 (2009): 85–95.

McGregor, Liz. *Khabzela: The Life and Times of a South African*. Johannesburg: Jacana Media, 2005.

Mcneill, Fraser G. *AIDS, Politics and Music in South Africa*. Cambridge: Cambridge University Press, 2011.

Mills, Heather. 'Art, Vulnerability and HIV in Post-Apartheid South Africa'. *Journal of Southern African Studies* 45, no. 1 (2019): 175–95.

Morgan, Jonathan and Kylie Thomas and the Banbanani Women's Group. *Long Life: Positive HIV Stories*. Cape Town: Double Storey, 2003.

Nattrass, Nicoli. *The Moral Economy of AIDS in South Africa*. Cambridge: Cambridge University Press, 2004.

Nguyen, Vinh-Kim. *The Republic of Therapy: Triage and Sovereignty in West Africa's Time of AIDS*. Durham, NC: Duke University Press, 2010.

Niehaus, Isak. *AIDS in the Shadow of Biomedicine*. London: Zed Books, 2018.

Rasebotsa, Meg Samuelson and Kylie Thomas, eds. *Nobody Ever Said AIDS: Stories and Poems from Southern Africa*. Cape Town: Kwela Books, 2004.

Robins, Steven. *From Revolution to Rights in South Africa: Social Movements, NGOs & Popular Politics after Apartheid*. James Currey: Woodbridge, 2008.

Setel, Philip, Milton James Lewis and Maryinez Lyons, eds. *Histories of Sexually Transmitted Diseases and HIV/AIDS in Sub-Saharan Africa*. Westport: Greenwood Press, 1999.

Steinberg, Jonny. *Three-Letter Plague: A Young Man's Journey through a Great Epidemic*. Johannesburg: Jonathan Ball Publishers, 2008.

Tsampiras, Carla. 'From "Dark Country" to "Dark Continent": AIDS, "Race," and Medical Research in the South African Medical Journal, 1980–1995'. *Journal of Southern African Studies* 41, no. 4 (2015): 773–96.

Vaughan, Megan. *Curing Their Ills: Colonial Power and African Illness*. Cambridge: Polity, 1991.

Webb, Douglas. *HIV and AIDS in Africa*. London: Pluto Press, 1997.

White, Luise. *The Comforts of Home: Prostitution in Colonial Nairobi*. Chicago: University of Chicago Press, 1990.

CHAPTER 5
MENTAL ILLNESS AND THE 'AFRICAN MIND'

Introduction

The history of mental illness in Africa is, much like the history of mental illness in the West, only beginning to be written. The hiddenness of mental disorder and the difficulties in categorizing, diagnosing and treating a complex spectrum of pathologies have contributed to our lack of understanding of the nature and extent of mental illness in present-day African society, let alone societies of the past. In this sense, the African case is emblematic of a larger global gap in both medical and historical scholarship. However, as will be seen, the ways in which mental illness has been both hidden and 'discovered' in the African context also illustrate a particular and contingent history.[1] It is to tracing the contours and fault lines of this difficult history that this chapter now turns.

As a general observation, historical scholarship on mental illness in Africa has tended to conglomerate around where written sources are either plentiful or potent with meaning, such as the institutional records produced through the operation of so-called lunatic asylums in colonial territories – including in Nigeria, the Gold Coast Colony (Ghana), Algeria, Nyasaland (Malawi), Southern Rhodesia (Zimbabwe), Kenya, Natal and Cape Colony (South Africa). The often highly racialized and pseudo-scientific pronouncements embedded in asylum case notes, as well as in contemporary published studies of a few prominent colonial psychiatrists, have tended to attract most intensely the historians' gaze. Analysing the discursive power of these sources, and the changing intellectual and institutional milieu that underpinned their production, has resulted in a rich seam of historical scholarship. However, this preoccupation has also left large gaps. The history of the incarcerated insane represents only a small proportion of the total caseload of mental illness in Africa, and we do not have sufficient historical data to even approximate the numbers of non-institutionalized mentally ill. Also, certain types of mental disorder – for example, depression – left a much less visible imprint in colonial legislative and medical records. Similarly, this archive is profoundly silent on the extent of mental illness among rural populations and women. Furthermore, this concentration on a virulent racialized and largely penal form of colonial psychiatry leaves unanswered a consideration of pre-colonial features, particularly of African approaches to and understandings of mental illness. It also tends to obscure important *continuities* in mental healthcare across time, between pre-colonial, colonial and post-colonial periods. As this chapter will show, the nascent expressions of an 'Africanized' psychiatry in newly independent African states did not completely remove the power asymmetries and cultural divides between the 'observer' and the 'observed' once associated with the colonial asylum. In addition, local forms of identifying and addressing mental disorder, some with antecedents dating back to the pre-colonial past, have found renewed expression and meaning in the post-colonial context.

This chapter re-situates the relatively brief period of colonial psychiatry in a longer history of attempts to understand and treat mental illness. It draws out connections and divergences across this history, and examines post-colonial dynamics in light of earlier patterns. As will be seen, much of what constitutes a history of mental healthcare in Africa could more appropriately be viewed as attempts to peer into and understand the 'African mind'.[2] As such, this chapter considers alongside this history the parallel, and manifestly flawed, attempts in the early twentieth century to measure African 'intelligence'. Like the long shadow cast by colonial psychiatry's workings on the African continent, these attempts to gauge African mental capacities have resonance in the present.

The visible and invisible: Conceptualizing and tracing mental illness in African history

There are several key conceptual challenges to the historical study of mental illness in Africa: the **invisibility of mental disease**; the difficulty evident in contemporary accounts of **establishing the baseline** from which to measure significant deviations from mental well-being; the reliance on **subjective observation** (on the part of the health professional, colonial official or healer) for diagnosis; and the **problem of communication** between the mental healthcare provider and the ill patient, particularly if that communication occurred across largely intractable cultural, linguistic and political divides.

Because mental disorders are not necessarily accompanied by overt physical symptoms, they are more difficult to diagnose and categorize. This inherent invisibility of mental illness was in the African historical context powerfully shaped by the perception of many early European observers that African societies were, somehow, impervious to mental disorder. The myth of the 'happy African', which gained intellectual and cultural traction in early twentieth-century European discourse, drew in part on Jungian psycho-analytic conceptions of Africans as primeval 'innocents' free of inner psychic turmoil.[3] This perception was also politically expedient and, similar to earlier pro-slavery discourses of the 'happy slave' which had emerged in the American South in the mid-nineteenth century, helped to justify attempts in some colonial quarters to restrict African exposure to progressive forces such as freedom and education, in the guise of protecting their psychic health.[4]

The colonial state and its psychiatric apparatus in a sense operationalized this hiddenness by choosing to deal with African cases of mental illness largely when, and where, it most threatened the colonial order – in instances of psychoses which led to criminal or violent behaviour, and primarily located in urban areas. So the contours of mental illness in rural contexts and the experiences of Africans with mental disorders that did not result in socially threatening behaviour were much less documented by colonial courts and psychiatric institutions. The experience of African women is even more obscured from view, as the vast majority of confined (and thus recorded) cases of mentally ill Africans were male. If mental illness did exist within the inner reaches of African society, the colonial state expected (and indeed preferred) that Africans treat their own. It is arguable that the very effectiveness of indigenous African social and spiritual institutions to locate, confront and control many forms of mental illness meant that it appeared, to the external observer at least, that disorders such as depression did not exist. It was this capacity of African societies to integrate, rather than isolate, their mentally ill that helped contribute to the very hiddenness of mental illness in the historical record.

Mental illness, more so than other realms of 'dis-ease', enlists the subjective perspective of the learned observer to discern and define its presence in an ill patient. The power of determining African 'madness' was very much vested in the eye of the beholder. For Frantz Fanon, whose work as a psychiatrist in a colonial asylum in Algeria and later in newly independent Tunisia proved formative to his theorizations on race and the psychological impact of colonialism, this gaze was absolute: 'In the psychological field the abnormal is he who demands, appeals, and begs.'[5] Historians of colonial psychiatry in Africa such as Richard Keller, Megan Vaughan and Julie Parle have vividly illustrated that European perceptions of mental illness were indeed profoundly complicated by power asymmetries, as well as the cultural disjunctures provoked by the colonial encounter with African societies and cosmologies. For many European observers, the entire complex of African rites, beliefs and worldviews represented the 'abnormal'. How then, as Vaughan has asked, could a reliable yardstick be established to delineate 'abnormal Africans' from the 'normally abnormal'?[6] Cultural and linguistic divides, which most Western clinicians were unable or unwilling to bridge, further operated as effective communicative barriers to understanding where and how those boundaries could apply within each individual patient's case history. Colonial psychiatrists and medical officers largely failed to address this slippery conceptual terrain in their diagnoses, rendering these records ineffectual as historical indicators of the incidence of mental illness among African patient populations, although this paper trail did lay the groundwork for a later generation of historians of the colonial period to understand *European* ideas and anxieties around cultural difference and the deleterious effects of colonial rule. Finally, because of continuing developments in the psychological, neurological and biological mapping of mental illness which have resulted in an ever-evolving 'nosology' (or classification system) of psychiatric disorders, present-day historians need to be wary in their attempts to retrospectively examine past diagnoses.

It is important not to over-privilege these largely Western-mediated efforts. The ways in which *Africans* perceived and responded to the problem of mental illness within their own communities over the *longue durée* need to be placed in historical dialogue with how 'African madness' was constructed by and through the colonial gaze. In reality, African societies had long struggled with and recognized the debilitating power of mental disturbances, and had by the time of their earliest encounters with Europeans developed their own methods of diagnosis and cure. As we shall see, mental illness within an African context was far from invisible and merited a direct, and considered, response.

The written record of mental illness in Africa shares the same problematics as that of the West – whilst the fewer and more visible instances of psychically 'disturbed' individuals were captured through the lens of criminality, violent behaviour and incarceration in asylums, the vast number of the mentally unwell who did not fit into those limited categories tended to be much more obscured from view. The overwhelming focus of the historiography has been on the discursively potent archive of psychiatric and psychologically suspect cases of 'mad Africans' during the colonial period. This textual archive takes two major forms – one produced by the workings of the colonial judicial system, the other by the institutionalization of psychiatric care in select regions. The records of **magisterial cases** are an important judiciary source. These tended to be accounts of court proceedings in colonial territories where some form of relevant legislation existed, such as Lunacy Ordinances (in place in some form as early as 1838 in French colonial territories, in Natal from 1868, in Nigeria from 1906, in Southern Rhodesia from 1908 and Nyasaland from 1913) and Witchcraft Ordinances (such as the Witchcraft Suppression Acts of 1895 in the Cape Colony and of 1899 in Southern Rhodesia, and the Witchcraft Ordinances of 1911 in Nyasaland and of 1925 in Kenya). Cases tried under Lunacy Ordinances tended to be *de facto* diagnostic exercises enquiring into the state of mind of suspected 'lunatics' who posed a threat to the colonial social order. Witchcraft Ordinances, on the other hand, operated under different presumptions of rational behaviour and agency and were created primarily to suppress the practice of witchcraft accusations, which colonial officials felt undermined their authority and destabilized social and economic cohesion in African communities. Alongside the legal documentation generated by the operation of colonial ordinances, there are also records of colonial **inquests** into cases of unnatural deaths. These can provide rare glimpses into African articulations of their mental state, as is evident in 'suicide notes' lodged within the records of suicide inquest proceedings in colonial Nyasaland.[7]

In the handful of asylums that operated in colonial Africa, the **case notes** of patients generated through its day-to-day running have proven to be a critically important historical source, particularly with regards to creating institutional-based histories of psychiatric care in Africa. Beginning with Megan Vaughan's seminal micro-study of Zomba Lunatic Asylum in 1983, this burgeoning genre of historical studies of specific asylums and their patient populations includes work by Lynette Jackson, Harriet Deacon, Leland Bell, Jonathan Sadowsky and Sally Swartz. Case notes recorded observations of patient symptoms and behaviour, and their change over time, as well as clinical diagnoses and treatments. Some historians have argued that case notes erased the identity, and humanity, of African patients, particularly those subjected to the highly racialized and restrictive environs of the colonial asylum in the early twentieth century. Others have countered that tersely worded case notes could not reflect the totality of care and treatment which psychiatric patients may have been given. Both views are mutually tenable. Even the case notes of the infamous colonial ethno-psychiatrist and Head of Muthari Mental Hospital (Kenya) J.C. Carothers contain glimpses of the voices of African patients and their families. Despite their formal structure and often racialized language, case notes may provide a window, however fleeting, into how Africans viewed their own mental condition. **Recorded testimonies of asylum staff** as part of numerous colonial commissions or committees of enquiry provide further site-specific information on the conditions and operating procedures of these mental health institutions, as well as an indication of the extent to which evolving psychiatric explanatory frameworks were implemented by medical staff, as Jock McCulloch has illustrated in his study of colonial psychiatric science in Africa.

The published papers of international meetings and in **scientific journals** constitute another important historical source, particularly with respect to twentieth-century developments. The proceedings of congresses in the early twentieth century – for example, the *Congrès des médecins aliénistes et neurologists de France et des pays de langue française*, a global gathering of Francophone psychiatrists and neurologists – provided the latest state-of-the-art research in the rapidly evolving and contested fields of neurology, psychiatry, psychoanalysis and psychology. These regularly recurring international conferences were a formative dissemination platform for globally circulating psychiatrists of empire, allowing them to stay connected with developments in metropolitan centres as well as compare findings across colonial settings and to other trans-national contexts, particularly the United States. Similarly, many psychiatrists based in colonial asylums who conducted clinical research in these institutions published in a wide array of scientific journals such as the *New York Medical Journal, American Journal of Psychiatry, British Journal of Psychology, Journal of Mental Science, East African Medical Journal* and the *Annales Medico-Psychologiques*, which allowed their research to reach a global audience. A journal which both symbolized and effected the transition towards transcultural psychiatry in the post-colonial period is *Psychopathologie Africaine*, established in 1965 out of the Dakar-based 'Fann School' of psychiatry.[8] Many of these journals continue to publish scholarship today. As historical sources they are potentially the most useful as barometers of change in how scientists and clinicians framed and understood mental pathologies of Africans across the colonial and post-colonial period, rather than as factual evidence of the extent of, and explanations for, those pathologies.

Scholars need to cast a wider net for sources beyond those produced by the colonial and medical establishment to fill in the sizeable gaps evident in the history of mental illness in Africa. As seen in Chapter 1, archaeological and linguistic artefacts have complemented a limited literate source base to help reconstruct pre-colonial African patterns of health and illness – object remains such as the Ife statuary provide a fleeting sense of how Africans may have imagined the physical embodiments of certain diseases. Mental pathologies, however, leave less visible traces in the material record. Instead, **missionary sources** and **travellers accounts** offer ways to approximate, albeit unevenly, how African societies may have approached the 'problem' of mental illness in the eighteenth and nineteenth centuries, and organized their healing systems in response. Similarly, in-depth **anthropological studies** of African societies from the early twentieth century onwards could be used selectively to derive changing African understandings of, and ways of speaking about, various manifestations of mental disorder. Although largely conveyed through the problematic prism of European and Christian ideological frameworks and idioms, these more ethnographic accounts suggest that African societies did not necessarily consider mental disorders in isolation as a discreet category of illness with specialized therapeutics and associated healers. Rather, as we shall see through a preliminary reading of this archive, instances of mental disorder and heightened or disturbed mental states tended to be described as constituent features of the ritual realm, including but not limited to witchcraft, spirit possession and divination. It was also the case that mental *well-being* in many African healing systems was seen as both a necessary accompaniment to curative measures (irrespective of whether the initial illness was located in the psyche) and a valuable health outcome in its own right. Thus, one could argue that the history of African *mental health* rather than the more narrow history of mental illness can be discerned more visibly in these accounts if using this wider lens, alongside other dimensions of African healing practices.

Mental illness within African healing systems and cosmologies – notes from southern Africa

In 1854, Henry Callaway first journeyed to southern Africa to serve as an Anglican missionary. In subsequent years, he made it his life's work to scrupulously observe and record Zulu religious beliefs and customs. Written in a striking dual-language Zulu and English format, *The Religious System of the Amazulu* (1870) was the culmination of his efforts, and in it he provided an extraordinarily detailed account of the 'initiation' of an *inyanga*, a diviner-healer (see Figure and Historical Source).

Historical Source: 'The Initiation of a Diviner' in Henry Callaway *The Religious System of the Amazulu* (1870).

The condition of a man who is about to be an *inyanga* is this: At first he is apparently robust; but in process of time he begins to be delicate, not having any real disease, but being very delicate. He begins to be particular about food, and abstains from some kinds, and requests his friends not to give him that food, because it makes him ill … he is continually complaining of pains in different parts of his body. And he tells them that he has dreamt that he was being carried away by a river. He dreams of many things, and his body is muddled and he becomes a house of dreams … At last the man is very ill, and they go to the diviners to enquire. The diviners do not at once see that he is about to have a soft head. It is difficult for them to see the truth; they continually talk nonsense, and make false statements, until all the man's cattle are devoured at their command, they saying that the spirit of his people demands cattle, that it may eat food …. At length an *inyanga* comes and says that all the others are wrong. He says, '… The disease does not require to be treated with blood … I tell you you will kill him by using medicines. Just leave him alone, and look to the end to which the disease points. He will not die of the sickness for he will have what is good given to him.' ... People wonder at the progress of the disease. But his head begins to give signs of what is about to happen. He shows that he is about to be a diviner by yawning again and again, and by sneezing again and again ... After that he is ill; he has slight convulsions, and has water poured on him, and they cease for a time. He habitually sheds tears, at first slight, and at last he weeps aloud, and in the middle of the night, when the people are asleep, he is heard making a noise, and wakes the people by singing; he has composed a song, and men and women awake and go to sing in concert with him. In this state of things they daily expect his death; he is now but skin and bones, and they think that to-morrow's sun will not leave him alive ... whilst he is undergoing this initiation the people of the village are troubled by want of sleep; for a man who is beginning to be an *inyanga* causes great trouble, for he does not sleep, but works constantly with his brain; his sleep is merely by snatches, and he wakes up singing many songs ... And then he leaps about the house like a frog; and the house becomes too small for him, and he goes out, leaping and singing, and shaking like a reed in the water, and dripping with perspiration. At that time many cattle are eaten. The people encourage his becoming an *inyanga*; they employ means for making the *Itongo* [the spirits] white, that it may make his divination very clear. At length another ancient *inyanga* of celebrity is pointed out to him. At night whilst asleep he is commanded by the *Itongo*, who says to him, 'Go to So-and-so; go to him, and he will churn for you emetic-*ubalawo*, that you may be an *inyanga* altogether.' Then he is quiet for a few days, having gone to the *inyanga* to have *ubalawo* churned for him; and he comes back quite another man, being now cleansed and an *inyanga* indeed.

Source Analysis: This passage is fascinating for its behind-the-scenes relating of the lengthy and arduous initiation process undertaken by an inyanga, *and its vivid evocation of the initiate's liminal state through descriptions of physical and psychic distress and heightened mental states. Callaway's use of the present-tense heightens the suspense of this narrative. The uncertainty of the appropriate cure for the stricken initiate is striking, with the initiate at the mercy of false diagnoses offered by charlatans who cannot 'see the truth' and 'continually talk nonsense', whilst ordering his cattle to be 'devoured at their command'.*

According to The Religious System of the Amazulu, *the diviner-healer figure was one of four integral elements of the Zulu belief system, alongside ancestors, magical forces and the self-originating deity uNkulunkulu (which Callaway pointed out had been erroneously interpreted by earlier missionaries as a Creator God figure). In some respects, Callaway's preoccupation with the spiritual world of the Zulu could be seen as a necessary corollary of his heeding of the Christian call to proselytize. However, Callaway's careful attention to Zulu turns of expression and imagery as well as his extended and detailed descriptions of Zulu beliefs and ritual practices marks this study out against other missionary accounts of southern African cosmology. Furthermore, his intense focus on exploring an inner universe created and inhabited by the Zulu makes it possible to re-read Callaway's account as more than a vestige of the Christian encounter, but as part of an alternative mapping of Zulu healing approaches, of which the diviner-initiate's journeying beyond mere 'madness' to diagnosis and cure could be seen as a key experiential component.*

IZINYANGA ZOKUBULA;

OR,

DIVINERS.

The Initiation of a Diviner.

UKUMA kwomuntu o za 'kuba inyanga i loku, ukuba kukqala u nga umuntu o kqinileyo emzimbeni; kepa ekuhambeni kwesikati a kqale ngokutetema, e nga guli umzimba wake, u tetema kakulu. A kqale ngokuketa ukudhla, a zile okunye ukudhla, a ti, "Ukudhla okutile ni nga ngi pi kona; ku ya ngi bulala umzimba uma ngi ku dhlile." A zinge e puma ekudhleni, e keta ukudhla a ku tandayo, nako a nga ku kqiuisi; a zinge e zibikabika. Futi e tsho nokuti, "Ngi pupe ngi muka namanzi." E pupa izinto eziuingi, umzimba u

THE condition of a man who is about to be an inyanga[1] is this: At first he is apparently robust; but in process of time he begins to be delicate, not having any real disease, but being very delicate. He begins to be particular about food, and abstains from some kinds, and requests his friends not to give him that food, because it makes him ill. He habitually avoids certain kinds of food, choosing what he likes, and he does not eat much of that; and he is continually complaining of pains in different parts of his body. And he tells them that he has dreamt that he was being carried away by a river. He dreams of many things, and his body is muddled[2]

---

[1] See note 6, p. 131.

[2] *Dungeka.—Ukudunga* is to stir up mud in water, so as to make the water turbid, or muddy; and is hence applied by metaphor to

Figure 5.1 A page from Henry Callaway's *The Religious System of the Amazulu* (1870), showing its original dual-language format

In Callaway's vivid re-telling, a precarious descent into illness was a necessary prelude for the initiate to eventually realize his 'calling' as a diviner-healer. Importantly, the liminality of the initiate is marked not only by his progressive physical deterioration but also by a sort of psychic awakening described in all its poignant vulnerability – he 'becomes a house of dreams' and has a 'soft head'. This enhanced psychic activity – he 'works constantly with his brain' – is not without its costs. The initiate experiences bouts of emotional instability ('he habitually sheds tears'), insomnia ('his sleep is merely by snatches') and the loss of bodily control ('he leaps about the house like a frog'). He also hears voices, which we are told are the spirits of the dead speaking to him, the *Itongo*.

In this liminal period, the initiate's community expresses doubts as to the authenticity of his calling even as it seeks out the counsel of other diviners to return the initiate to full health. Could he be 'merely mad', the villagers ask, and with that question Callaway invites us as readers to consider that possibility as well. It would be tempting to read this account as an early expression of 'madness' in Zulu society, or more prosaically psychopathology manifest as manic-depression and schizophrenia. However, what is perhaps more intrinsic to the significance of this account apart from this retrospective diagnosis is that it reveals that for the Zulu mental disorder was not necessarily seen as a debilitating condition to be cured, but a state of being through which the initiate could gain an appropriate frame of mind and sensitivity to the spirit world. As the experienced *inyanga* counselled, the villagers ought not to dwell on the initiate's present struggles but to 'look to the end to which the disease points', predicting that through this encounter with illness the initiate 'will have what is good given to him'. In Zulu cosmology a heightened dreamscape signified the attempts of ancestral spirits to communicate directly with the living individual, and dream interpretation was an important diagnostic tool for Zulu diviner-healers, as was the case among other southern African groups. Thus, the experience of physical debility and psychic vulnerability was seen to lay the groundwork for the development of clairvoyance and related interpretive skills to be fully realized in the would-be diviner.

An account of a neighbouring ethnic group a full four decades on from Callaway's incisive study of the Zulu offers the opportunity to consider these issues in comparative perspective. Henri Junod was a Swiss Protestant missionary to southern Africa in the late nineteenth century. Like Callaway before him, Junod recorded his observations of the environment and the region's inhabitants while engaging in missionary work. His careful two-volume study of the Tsonga people *The Life of a South African Tribe* (1912 and 1913) is considered one of the first comprehensive ethnographies of its type – a singular, in-depth study of the social and cultural organization of a specific ethnic group in one locale, based on long-term close-hand observation. In the second volume of this work, subtitled 'Mental Life', Junod turns his attention to different aspects of the mental and spiritual life of the Tsonga – folklore, music, ideas of 'man and nature', religion and 'magic'.

Junod observed that Tsonga conceptions of illness were derived from the dual domains of religion (composed of a 'well-defined' theology and moral-ritual sphere) and magic (the realm of harmful and protective spirits), with each domain 'adulterated' by the other. In addition was the domain of the 'scientific', including those Tsonga ideas and ritual practices 'inspired by a true observation of facts', but which Junod saw could be 'invaded' by magical conceptions. This dynamic Junod observed of 'adulteration' and 'invasion' across these conceptual and experiential realms of religion, magic and the scientific provides an important perspective on Tsonga approaches to mental illness. It explains how what Junod termed the 'curious psychic phenomenon' of spirit possession, understood by the Tsonga to be the 'madness of the gods (*bubabyi bya psikwembu*)', could be simultaneously a 'disease' deriving out of a religious explanatory framework (in this case ancestral worship) but needing the attention of 'recognized magicians' to apply the necessary curative rites. Similarly, in Junod's description of 'nervous diseases' along with their putative treatments, we see the ways in which Tsonga scientific and magical domains overlapped:

> *Nervous diseases* are peculiarly feared by Natives. *Melancholia* is believed to be caused by those spirits of possession ... Delirium (*mihahamo*) is cured by *Mbulula khutla*. The patient must enter the hole from which clay is taken for smearing the huts, and is washed with a decoction of the drug when in this hole. Moreover a stick of the same tree is cut and kept in the roof of the hut, and the person who sleeps with the patient will take it every night and place it near his head. 'Thus we kill delirium.' (Mankhelu). – Another form of insanity is called *rihuhe*, 'the disease which comes from far away with the winds' – '*rip fa timhehwen*' (Mankhelu). A drug is prepared with the *shiromo* root, mixed with the lung of a sheep and the blood found inside its heart. All these things are burnt in a broken pot, and made into a medicinal powder. The patient is brought to the broken pot; a cut is made in his head, so that it bleeds abundantly until the pot is filled with blood; the blood boils in the pot, it solidifies and is burnt. The ñanga takes it and buries it in an ant's nest according to the *timula* rite described below. The wound of the patient is filled with the medicine; he eats the meat, he sleeps: – 'if you have been equal to the occasion, he will be cured; you have given him lots of sleep. – You have killed the *rihuhe*' (Mankhelu).[9]

The ascribing of separate vernacular terms to specific mental disorders and the existence of elaborate therapeutic regimens suggest the Tsonga had a historical familiarity with these conditions. Interestingly, Junod's ability to 'translate' some, although not all, of the various illnesses recounted by the Tsonga into named psychoses such as melancholia and delirium owed much to the developing importance by the early twentieth century of the fields of neurology, psychology and psychiatry, and the widespread public circulation of associated terminology, a lexicon unavailable to his fellow missionary Callaway four decades earlier. It may also reflect the institutionalization of psychiatric care that had by this time established a firm hold in Natal and the Cape Colony, including several asylums in Cape Town as well as in Pietermaritzburg, Grahamstown and Port Alfred. However, equally important is that Tsonga healing systems derived ideas of causation and cure in ways that were markedly distinct from Western psychiatric conventions prevalent contemporaneously in colonial settler and urban contexts. Furthermore, as is evident in Junod's subsequent description of his encounter with a man afflicted by spirit possession who later became a skilled exorcist, the Tsonga shared with the Zulu the propensity to view certain experiences of psychopathology as *enabling* rather than disabling, conferring unique healing powers on the sufferer.

Although both accounts point to the resilience and marked capacity of southern African healing systems to conceptually absorb and therapeutically address a spectrum of psychic and 'nervous' disorders, it is crucial to acknowledge that local approaches to mental dis-ease were neither uniformly effective nor impervious to change. Indeed, the Tsonga naming of *rihuhe* as 'the disease which comes from far away with the winds' suggests an awareness of the potential risks brought by contact with external forces, whether environmental, social or political. Tellingly, in the same period Junod was recording his observations, an 'epidemic' of *indiki* spirit possessions was sweeping Zululand, afflicting mainly young, unmarried women and posing probing questions for both Zulu chiefly authorities and the colonial government. Contemporary sources indicate *indiki* possession was considered a wholly new disease by the Zulu, who could not draw on their existing therapeutic repertoire to respond.[10] In a sense, the particular gendered and generational dimensions of *indiki* spirit possession was reflective of a larger moral crisis facing Zulu society, itself transformed – through land loss, the imposition of colonial rule, and the out-migration of young men to the urban areas and gold mines of the Rand – in the intervening years since Callaway's defining study.

Colonial psychiatry, racialized science and intelligence testing – late nineteenth- to mid-twentieth-century developments

The establishment of asylums in colonial territories by the early twentieth century – including Yaba Lunatic Asylum (Nigeria, established in 1906), Ingutsheni Mental Hospital (Southern Rhodesia, 1908), Zomba Lunatic Asylum (Nyasaland, 1910), Mathari Mental Hospital (Kenya, 1910) and Valkenberg Asylum (South Africa, established in 1891 with its first African patients in 1916) – was a defining shift in the provision of psychiatric care to Africans. Most of these asylums became notorious for their poor conditions and even poorer health outcomes and were, at least in their earlier decades of operation, synonymous with forms of detention – of incarceration rather than cure. Hôpital Psychiatrique de Blida, established in 1938 in Algeria, provided one of the clinical backdrops for Frantz Fanon's blistering critique of the psychological trauma and alienation caused by colonialism. For a time these institutions certainly appeared to epitomize the workings of a coercive 'colonial medicine' (see Chapter 2). However, the intellectual development of colonial psychiatry and its institutionalization within the African context were less straightforward in their trajectories than these asylums' eventual hostile clinical environments would suggest.

Early precursors: 'Moral management' in the Cape and 'primitivism'

There were important antecedents to the colonial African asylum of the early twentieth century – some became 'blueprints' for, while others represented an 'alternative future' to, the rigid racialized system of psychiatric care in both Anglophone and Francophone psychiatric contexts. Alternative pathways of diagnosis, treatment and care for mental illness were already entrenched and at work in African societies by the late nineteenth century, as seen among the Zulu and neighbouring groups, although these largely escaped the gaze of colonial administrators and the nascent psychiatric profession.

The grounds of Cape Colony's Robben Island (more famously known for its maximum security prison facility where Nelson Mandela was incarcerated for eighteen years) housed a lunatic asylum from 1846, alongside a leper colony and an infirmary for the chronically ill. In its first few decades, Robben Island's asylum attempted to operationalize a form of 'moral management' in its care for resident lunatics. This shift from detention towards a more humane form of treatment was in response to the local outcry of liberals and humanitarians in the Cape over the asylum's poor conditions, as well as a product of the 'moral treatment' movement in metropolitan psychiatric and psychological circles. Although the asylum was not immune to racial and classist bias, the Cape liberal ethos – that everyone possessed the innate potential to become 'civilized' – allied with moral management ideas, and allowed a degree of erasure of notions of difference between patients from disparate backgrounds, and between doctor and patient. The focus was on treatment without restraints and a high staff-to-patient ratio, as well as urging that the standard of care for the insane should be the same in Robben Island as it would be in Britain. This version of an enlightened 'scientific humanitarianism' was short-lived, as the management of the asylum and its multi-racial patient population succumbed to the same segregationist impulses and racialist discourses which were sweeping the mainland, and indeed colonial territories further afield.[11] By the 1890s, the experiment was effectively over and racial segregation with its attendant structured hierarchies of resources, treatment and care was firmly in place at Robben Island's asylum, as it was in other psychiatric institutions in the Cape. Kissy Lunatic Asylum in Freetown, Sierra Leone, appears to have experienced a similarly short-lived foray into moral treatment in the mid- to late nineteenth century, when 'kindness' was the guiding principle of care and therapies included leisure activities and voluntary casual labour. In the twentieth century, treatment at Kissy reverted back to, although never completely, its custodial and carceral origins, in part due to extreme limitations in funding and staff resources.[12]

A type of comparative psychiatry emerging out of France's troubled engagement with and occupation of Algeria (from 1830 to 1962) was an equally important antecedent to the racialized psychiatry at work in both Francophone and Anglophone colonial African contexts in the twentieth century. Until the establishment of Blida psychiatric hospital in 1938, those Algerians deemed lunatics and thus mandated to be interned by existing French legislation (in place since 1838) had no local mental institution to house them. This anomaly spurred the creation in the late nineteenth century of a policy of transporting lunatic Algerians to asylums located in southern France, and was replicated in parts of French West Africa. This trans-Mediterranean reverse flow of Algerians to the metropole did not result in better health outcomes for patients who were undoubtedly exposed to social and cultural dislocation and isolation in these new environments, with the annual mortality rate for Muslim patients in one such asylum reportedly at 49 per cent in 1872 (compared to 13–14 per cent for Europeans).[13]

An important comparative racialized discourse – juxtaposing the 'Oriental mentality' against the 'Occidental mentality' – developed out of the observation and treatment of Algerian insane in the late nineteenth century and up to the First World War. It not only was the intellectual product of a nascent Francophone colonial psychiatric establishment but was also shaped by European travellers, scholars and other social commentators in the region. This discursive framing highlighted the specific cultural and behavioural traits of these two very broad yet ill-defined ethnic groupings, and provided an explanatory rationale for their contrasting predispositions to mental disorder. Algerians (and particularly Muslims) were considered lacking in initiative compared to the more 'modern' and 'civilized' Occidental, but within this framing the absence of drive conferred to the Oriental a protective 'screen' from insanity. Muslim women's seclusion from the modernizing influences of education was viewed as another such screen from madness. This rationale, while not uncontested, laid the groundwork for the so-called Algiers School of ethno-psychiatry which later emerged in the interwar period and meshed with developments in Anglophone African psychiatric contexts.

This 'discovery' of an Oriental mentality was but one expression of the broader trans-national ideological current of 'primitivism' circulating in the mid-nineteenth century. Although primitivism in this period was a flexible and multi-faceted range of ideas and modes of expression, it possessed a specific utility for those theorizing about the root causes of insanity and its links to cultural difference and the impact of wide-scale social change. 'Primitive' peoples were considered in this rubric to be inherently immune from mental illness, with insanity described as the unfortunate by-product of 'civilization' and the enhanced mental capacities of a more developed mind. For those observing the incidence of mental illness among African-American slaves as well as colonial African subjects in this period, the notion of primitivism helped to frame attempts at civilizing 'Native minds' as a potentially harmful act. Pro-slavery advocates in the antebellum American South, for example, argued that emancipation would produce a deleterious mental effect on freed slaves. Similarly, the Medical Superintendent of Grahamstown Asylum in the Cape published clinical research in the mid-1890s in the *American Journal of Insanity* and the *Journal of Mental Science* which 'proved' the harmful effects of close contact with civilization by comparing relative rates of mental illness in Khoikhoi versus Bantu African peoples. This research purported to show the Khoikhoi, who were considered more Christianized and assimilated into Western culture, had higher rates of insanity than the Xhosa or Mfengu, groups which had historically shown resistance to not only cultural penetration from settler societies but British military rule as well.[14]

Certainly, primitivism as an explanatory framework for understanding differential and historical patterns of mental illness among ethnically 'Othered' populations has been thoroughly discredited. The manifold assumptions underpinning primitivist theories have been exposed as fundamentally flawed – that non-Western groups were fundamentally impervious to mental illness, that mental illness was never a feature of earlier Western society, that modernization was equivalent to civilization, that modernity was inevitably accompanied by developing mental capacities and that expanded mental capacities necessarily linked to heightened rates of mental illness. However, the expression of primitivism in the latter half of the nineteenth century, and its yoking to debates around freedom and the consequences of cultural change, was foundational to the development of a distinctive colonial ethno-psychiatry which flourished in subsequent decades.

The 'deculturation' thesis and ethno-psychiatry

The interwar period marked a seminal moment in the relationship between psychiatry and empire. The establishment of a network of asylums in colonial territories in Africa beyond the handful that had been operating since the nineteenth century – including those in the specific settler environs of Natal and Cape Colony as well as Kissy Lunatic Asylum, which was founded in the 1820s in Freetown – was symbolic of the institutionalization of this relationship. However, it was the continuation of ideological debates around the causes of African 'madness', and its relation to notions of innate racial or cultural difference and to the wide-scale transformation wrought by the colonial encounter which would have the greater impact.

What has now come to be known as the 'deculturation' thesis owed much to earlier nineteenth-century expressions of primitivism and comparative psychiatry, as was articulated in the American South and in the Algerian and Cape colonial contexts.[15] As with primitivism, the focus of anxiety was on the deleterious, and ultimately psychopathological, effects of modernity on the Native mind. Within this view the supposedly progressive forces of modernity (such as education, Christianity, urbanization) had rendered the decultured Native psychically vulnerable, unmoored from familiar belief systems, practices and communities. The 'mad African' was, thus, not the tribalized Native who countenanced witchcraft or ancestor worship, but someone dangerously aspirational and suspiciously Westernized in outlook – for example, in the 1930s at Zomba Lunatic Asylum, patients classified as suffering from schizophrenic delusions of a 'European' type were said to harbour beliefs they were European, of European royal lineage and could be involved in inter-racial liaisons.[16]

For all its echoes of earlier primitivist articulations, ideas of deculturation were decisively shaped by the scientific, intellectual and political developments of the interwar years, which gave this theory its particular expression, rationale and form. For example, colonial asylums in this period functioned as a trans-territorial laboratory of sorts which provided a fresh corpus of clinical data on the extent and presentation of psychopathologies in African patient populations, and patterns of incidence across different ethnic groups. Questions of cultural variation and ethnic difference were also the domain of the young academic discipline of anthropology, and its ethnographic lens in this era became trained on some of the same dynamics of change which concerned colonial authorities, such as the apparent breakdown of 'tribal' African societies. Furthermore, the growth in the field of evolutionary biology and its (mis-)application to understandings of human difference (this mis-application most tragically fed eugenicist ideas circulating in the same period) brought a language of biological determinism to deculturationist frameworks.

The so-called Algiers School was an early and influential articulator of ethno-psychiatry, with an explicit comparative element and racialized ordering at its core. The Algiers School is most strongly associated with the work of Antoine Porot, a French professor of neuropsychiatry based at the Faculty of Medicine in Algiers from 1916. Porot and his students absorbed the earlier preoccupations of French comparative psychiatry with describing an Oriental mentality against the Occidental and pushed out the boundaries of this framework in troubling ways. A type of sliding scale of comparative non-European mentalities was postulated, for example, averring that Central Africans were not as evolved as Algerians, with presumably Europeans at the 'developed' end of the scale. The Algiers School extended the disquieting typology of the 'normally abnormal Native' to its extreme, arguing that 'normal' Algerians were *essentially* pathological, and even criminal.[17] Moreover, Algerian Muslims were considered particularly prone to fatalism and lethargy, features ascribed to the influence of Islam.

The early decades of the twentieth century witnessed an increasingly global dialogue about these issues. The idea that insanity could be a disease of civilization was shared by colonial and metropolitan medical psychiatrists, as well as those across the Atlantic concerned by the apparent rise of mental illness amongst African Americans post-emancipation.[18] A 1926 article in the *American Journal of Psychiatry* argued that emancipation was more mentally traumatic than slavery itself, because the freed slave's mind was not sufficiently biologically developed to cope with the psychic challenges of freedom. This was a trans-Atlantic expression of the deculturation thesis, melded as it was with older ideas of the inherent civilizing institution of slavery. The knowledge exchange traversed in both directions. Studies of African-American patient populations cited earlier research in the colonial southern African setting, such as the work conducted in Grahamstown Asylum in the 1890s apparently proving Khoikhoi proximity to Europeans made them more susceptible to insanity than their Bantu neighbours, to support their clinical findings.[19] Conversely, as will be seen, colonial psychiatrists utilized data on mental illness rates among African Americans to confirm the observations drawn from their work in African asylums. The global circulation of scientific and medical journals, as well as the mobility of medical officers and psychiatrists who frequently traversed these colonial-metropolitan and trans-Atlantic pathways, ensured these ideas travelled far beyond the institutional and local confines in which they were first tested.

The 'East African School', and the work of its most noted proponent J.C. Carothers, exemplified deculturation theory's diverse ideological and scientific origins, and its trans-Atlantic orientation. Despite a rather rudimentary training in psychology and a background in tropical medicine, Carothers was appointed in 1938 head of Mathari Mental Hospital in Nairobi. Carothers used this clinical base over the next twelve years to cement his authority in the field of ethno-psychiatry, producing a large corpus of published studies on patterns of, and explanations for, the mental morbidities he observed amongst Mathari's Kenyan patient population. This work culminated in his published treatise *The African Mind in Health and Disease: A Study in Ethno-psychiatry* (1953) and his British government-commissioned report *The Psychology of the Mau Mau* (1954), both of which were written after his twelve-year tenure as head of Mathari had come to an end. The more controversial of his research findings argued African brains demonstrated 'primitive' brain activity and bore similarities to the lobotomized brains of Europeans.[20] However, his contribution to articulating a distinctive theory of African 'mental derangement' and its linkage to processes of cultural and political change were perhaps more complex than this crudely biologically determinist argument would suggest, as can be seen in his study published in 1947 in the *Journal of Mental Science* (see box).

Historical Source: J.C. Carothers, 'A Study of Mental Derangement in Africans, and an Attempt to Explain Its Peculiarities, More Especially in Relation to the African Attitude to Life', *Journal of Mental Science* (1947)

All these facts point in the same direction, namely that so long as an African remains at home he is very unlikely to be certified insane, but as soon as he leaves his home his chances of being so certified are much increased. Now the primitive African has a very definite culture and attitude to life, as will be seen in Part 6 – the old idea of the happy-go-lucky uncultured savage has been recognized as false long since. Unlike the Bushman and certain other primitive races, the East African native has however an immense admiration for European institutions and manner of life, so that contact with this alien culture is rapidly destroying his own. The conflicts and difficulties engendered by this tendency might well be expected to be a potent source of mental breakdown, and it is with this aspect of the problem that this section of our article is concerned ... The tribes, irrespective of race, that are most detribalized are those with the highest certification rate ....

The facts have now been described, and from these facts the following appear to emerge as the most significant peculiarities:

a) The incidence of insanity among Africans living in their natural environment is probably very low.
b) The incidence of insanity among Africans working away from home is probably considerably higher than that of those living at home, but is still low.
c) General paralysis is rare in the indigenous population.
d) Arteriosclerosis is rare.
e) The relation of paranoia to certain modes of living.
f) The relation of mania to responsibility and the absence of depression (manic-depressive type).
g) The absence of ideas of guilt in involutional melancholia.

h)   The common occurrence of 'frenzied anxiety' and the apparent absence of most of the types of anxiety state seen in Europeans.

i)   The absence of obsessional neuroses.

Most of these peculiarities can be addressed in relation to the African's attitude to life, arising out of his peculiar culture and thinking.

Source Analysis: It is difficult to ignore Carothers' charged references to 'primitive Africans' and their 'peculiarities' in the text. This deeply problematic language was accepted (although not uncontested) in psychiatric and mental science publications of the time, and exemplifies the resilience of primitivism as an organizing construct even into the mid-twentieth century. Carothers' use of language may have also reflected his specific position within the minority white settler community of colonial Kenya, although it is interesting how Carothers attempts here to distance himself from what he regards as outmoded depictions of Africans, such as the 'happy-go-lucky uncultured savage'. His adoption of the social scientific framing of 'tribe' rather than the narrower settler framing of 'race' is another example of this analytic distancing.

This study is valuable as a historical record of prevailing psychiatric classifications, or nosology, of mental disorders (such as mania, depression, paranoia, involutional melancholia, obsessional neuroses) utilized in the colonial asylum context. More importantly, this study is illustrative of how a deculturationist framework could be deployed in scientific writing – that is, how observed clinical patterns of 'mental derangement' in asylum patients could become the basis for a broader theorization of the causes of that derangement. In this excerpt, Carothers posits an explicit correlation between the incidence of insanity among Africans and their levels of contact with 'alien culture' as well as the relative distance from their 'natural environment'. As historians of psychiatry have observed, Carothers' explanatory framework is based on faulty assumptions that 'alien' and 'African' cultures were both distinctive and 'natural' entities, rather than inherently heterogenous and fluid social constructions. For Carothers and other deculturationists, this 'primordial' understanding of culture lended itself to explanations for mental disorder, in that perceived deviations from one's 'natural environment' (measured through relative levels of migration and education and other proxies for cultural change) could then be linked to differentiated patterns of mental illness among ethnically divided population groups.

The remarked 'absence' of depression among Mathari's patient population is noteworthy, although Carothers acknowledges elsewhere in the study that those with depression may have 'fail[ed] to reach the mental hospital' because their illness was not recognized, or because they had committed suicide before diagnosis. The notion that Africans were less prone to suffer from depression and other 'neurasthenic' syndromes (such as nervousness and fatigue) was widely held amongst colonial psychiatrists. However, the theoretical and empirical bases of this view have come into question – scholars have shown the invisibility of depression in clinical records from this period had more to do with the capacity of local healing systems to absorb and address cases of depression, as well as the propensity of colonial psychiatric systems to prioritize the diagnosis and treatment of patients with more socially 'threatening' forms of psychoses, such as schizophrenia and mania.

This lengthy article, based on five years of clinical research at Mathari, was more than an account of the incidence and typology of mental disorders of admitted patients, although much of its detailed statistics are painstakingly marshalled towards this task. It was an attempt to illustrate, through these statistics and typologies, *why* particular groups of East Africans suffered from particular forms of mental illness. It is instructive that his study begins with sections outlining the 'Historical Background' and 'The Racial and Anthropological Background' of 'Kenyan Africans', because his focus on processes of social and cultural change was integral to his argument.

Specifically, it was Kenyan Africans' degree of exposure to the forces of 'detribalization' that determined their susceptibility to 'mental breakdown'. As the study concludes succinctly, 'The tribes, irrespective of race, that are most detribalized are those with the highest certification rate.' Carothers' study is also noteworthy for its frequent referencing of contemporaneous rates of mental hospital admissions (along with extrapolated rates of illness in the general population) of African-Americans for a range of pathologies. This explicit trans-Atlantic comparative framework functioned to highlight key commonalities – such as the high percentage of admissions within both groups for 'organic psychoses' and 'schizophrenia', as compared to other types of mental disorder. Furthermore, Carothers' invocation of the consistently higher rates of 'mental derangement' of the general African-American population across all categories, as compared to estimated rates for Kenyan Africans, conveniently served to illustrate his central tenet that increased contact with an 'alien culture', if left unchecked, would result in a higher propensity towards mental illness.

By mid-century, counter-narratives contesting some of the underlying assumptions and problematic discursive frameworks of deculturation theory could be discerned. Arabic-speaking psychiatrists in North Africa as well as a young Frantz Fanon produced studies which both acknowledged the existence of and treatment for mental illness in indigenous societies and challenged the Algiers School's overtly racialized hierarchies. In the United States, an alternative stream of social scientific and psychiatric research, including studies by African-American academics, rejected notions of innate racialized differences in mental capacities, and argued instead for sustained analyses of the socio-economic impact of racism on the black psyche. Furthermore, colonial scientists – and even ethno-psychiatrists such as Carothers – acknowledged the potential link between infectious diseases such as syphilis and trypanosomiasis and the altered mental states of patients. Importantly, a growing cadre of trained African medical professionals, including psychiatric clinical caseworkers, contributed to these efforts to produce alternative aetiologies of mental disorder. For example, Eria Muwazi had qualified as an African Assistant Medical Officer at Makerere (in Uganda) and successfully co-authored a paper on liver disease before taking up a post at Mulago Mental Hospital. In 1944, Muwazi and H.C. Trowell co-published a paper on the classification of neurological cases which showed that of 269 admitted neurological cases, 137 suffered from neurosyphilis, a condition which occurs as a consequence of the invasion of syphilis into the nervous system and includes symptoms such as altered behaviours, dementia and paralysis.[21] The paper was considered a critical contribution towards understanding a condition that had previously been viewed as rare in tropical regions. Despite these counter-developments, the deculturation thesis – as an explanatory framework for African insanity and a mode of expression for anxieties shaped by the wide-scale social transformation wrought by colonial rule – remained largely dominant within European colonial administrations as well as in the operation of asylums in African colonial territories, until the political context of freedom changed the terms and structures under which mental healthcare provision in Africa could operate.

Colonial asylums: Conditions and patient care

Throughout the first half of the twentieth century, the few colonial asylums established in Africa faced severe, and broadly common, operational constraints – chronically overcrowded and underfunded, with poorly trained and inadequate levels of medical staff. Colonial public health priorities and associated human and financial resources in this period were directed towards other, deemed more pressing, challenges – tropical diseases, such as sleeping sickness and malaria; sexually transmitted diseases, such as syphilis and the apparent population decline in Central and East Africa; occupational diseases, such as silicosis which threatened mining labour in southern Africa. Contemporary accounts, including case notes and the testimonies of health workers, hospital managers, patients and their relatives collected by colonial commissions of enquiry into mental healthcare provision, offer some insights into the conditions at these institutions and the standards of care provided for patients.

The penal origins of many colonial asylums were echoed in their structural edifices and day-to-day operations. Zomba Lunatic Asylum was, in effect, established as a ward of the Central Prison. Yaba Lunatic Asylum and Robben Island Lunatic Asylum were each established adjacent to leper colonies, reflecting their physical separation from neighbouring communities as well as the prevailing social stigma attached to mental illness. Overcrowding was a persistent theme, which forced even the relatively well-resourced mental health asylums of the Cape to re-evaluate the viability of maintaining strict racial divisions of their wards, an issue of concern to other asylums in colonies with significant white settler populations. Woefully poor facilities at Mathari were reported in 1931 to constitute 'a serious menace to the health of the inmates' – this view of patients as 'inmates', exemplified by the common use of physical restraints, as well as the report's general indictment of the asylum as a place of ill-health could certainly be applied to most other colonial mental institutions at the time.[22] Sub-standard diets and the lack of adequate habitation and bedding increased patient susceptibility to diseases such as tuberculosis and pellagra, the latter resulting in symptoms of dementia if left untreated. Furthermore, case notes and colonial reports reveal that infectious diseases such as syphilis, malaria and trypanosomiasis were frequent disease challenges facing asylum patient populations, with little follow-up medical treatment provided.

On the whole, confinement rather than patient care characterized the provisioning of mental health services in most colonial psychiatric facilities, although this should be seen in the context of the marked lack of trained medical personnel throughout this period. Only one full-time psychiatrist was employed in colonial Nigeria up until 1924, and not again until 1949.[23] Even as hypnotic drugs and sedatives were introduced into the colonial asylum setting after the Second World War, these were administered by medical staff with little training in pyscho-pharmacology or psychiatric nursing, and usually without an attending psychiatrist in post. It is little wonder, then, that troubling reports of medical malpractice emerged as the risks associated with emergent psychiatric therapies and drugs increased. In the early 1940s, Ingutsheni hospital staff and management reported that electro-convulsive therapy (ECT) was used indiscriminately on African patients, regardless of whether or not there was a medical rationale for such treatment. Numerous deaths at this institution were attributed to the mis-application of ECT, particularly in cases where patients had underlying health conditions (such as tuberculosis or cardiac disease) that should have precluded its use.[24] Finally, any form of after-care for discharged patients was largely non-existent, which undoubtedly added to the challenge of the social re-integration of individuals for whom long-term confinement in often very distant asylums had severed ordinary community and kin relations.

Intelligence testing

The history of intelligence testing in the first half of the twentieth century, evident most notably in South Africa and Kenya, offers a parallel and intersecting trajectory to the developments mapped above. Advocates of intelligence testing focused on determining the innate mental capacities of Africans and, like ethno-psychiatrists, found in the emergent fields of neuroscience, psychology, evolutionary biology and the social sciences useful explanatory and discursive frameworks. These attempts to create a comparative racial profile of mental aptitude also referenced similar efforts in the United States to determine the intelligence of African Americans in the post-Reconstruction period.

Intelligence testing in South Africa can be traced back as early as 1916, when African, Indian and white schoolchildren in Natal were assessed through adapted versions of the Binet scale.[25] In Kenya, intelligence testing became part of a broader debate on the relative 'educability' of the African mind, a subject of crucial importance to deculturationist explanations for mental disorders.[26] By the interwar period, a vigorous debate had developed within South African and British colonial, medical and social scientific circles, on the validity of intelligence tests and, more controversially, surveys of average cranial capacity as measures of African (and that of other racially categorized groups) mental capacity. Vocal detractors, including the prominent social anthropologist Bronisław

Malinowski, attacked the crude eugenicist underpinnings of some of this research as well as contesting the accuracy and applicability of their findings. If intelligence tests consistently showed African mental aptitude was significantly lower than other groups, critics argued this was only because social and environmental conditions (such as education levels, nutrition and disease) predisposed Africans to under-perform, or because the tests themselves were not sufficiently culturally or linguistically calibrated.

The economic imperative to rank African mental aptitudes and create metrics to reliably predict educational outcomes (for students and trainees) and labour performance (for mineworkers, for example) meant that state-sponsored intelligence testing continued in British East Africa and South Africa, even as new research began to address some of the flaws inherent in these tests' design. Although an industrial psychology approach to intelligence testing did produce by mid-century more effective models to separate Africans by aptitude, this was not used to rebuff the essentialist underpinnings of previous studies on African intelligence, but to enhance opportunities for cost cutting efficiencies in colonial and segregationist regimes.

Post-colonial dynamics: Transcultural psychiatry and mental healthcare

The West Indian psychiatrist Frantz Fanon's clinical experience in Algerian and Tunisian mental hospitals, and his exposure to ethno-psychiatry as propagated by the Algiers School, was formative to his intellectual diagnosis of the 'madness' of colonialism. In *The Wretched of the Earth* (1961), Fanon famously argued that colonialism itself *caused* mental illness, through its creation of a hyper-sensitive and injured psyche which turns inwards onto the self with violence. In an extraordinary final chapter, Fanon presents several cases of mental disorder he encountered in his clinical psychiatric work in Algeria and Tunisia, written as a direct challenge to what he viewed as the crudely determinist and culturally essentializing work of ethno-psychiatrists like Porot and Carothers. These cases can be read as an alternative typology of mental illness, for Fanon one inescapably framed and created by the colonial condition:

> The truth is that colonialism in its essence was already taking on the aspect of a fertile purveyor for psychiatric hospitals ... Because it is a systematic negation of the other person and a furious determination to deny the other person all attributes of humanity, colonialism forces the people it dominates to ask themselves the question constantly: 'In reality, who am I?' The defensive attitudes created by this violent bringing together of the colonized man and the colonial system form themselves into a structure which then reveals the colonized personality. This 'sensitivity' is easily understood if we simply study and are alive to the number and depth of the injuries inflicted upon a native during a single day spent amidst the colonial regime.[27]

For Fanon, the necessary antidote to this psychic suffering was a change in the colonial social order – meaning, fundamentally, freedom. In many ways, Fanon's searing critique of colonialism and its relation to madness was proven by the ways in which the context of political freedom *did* change the institutional operation of psychiatry in African contexts, and allowed for the emergence of potentially more humane and culturally inclusive mental health interventions. However, these developments did not go uncontested, both within the realm of an Africanized psychiatry and through local expressions of, and responses to, mental illness.

Transcultural psychiatry in Africa

The immediate post-independence era of the 1960s and 1970s heralded the demise of ethno-psychiatry and the embrace of a different approach – transcultural psychiatry – which attempted to address, rather than assume, the cultural divides between African and Western healing systems, and to interrogate their interconnectedness in new and interesting ways. Many of the pioneering developments in transcultural psychiatry can be traced to two major centres: the Fann School, based at the University of Dakar and led by its first Chair of Psychiatry Henri Collomb; and the work of Thomas Adeoye Lambo, who from 1954 headed Aro Mental Hospital in Nigeria and became chair of the Department of Psychiatry at the University of Ibadan before serving as Deputy Director-General of WHO from 1973 to 1988.[28] Both championed, in different ways, the *dialogue* between African healing practices and allopathic medicine, rather than the incessant *monologue* of ethno-psychiatric theory and practice.[29] Both also recognized the importance of changing the spatial dynamics of the therapeutic setting, which had become so dehumanizing in the carceral context of the colonial asylum. Fann's hospital courtyard was physically transformed to include 'traditional' houses and space for a 'village council' to meet, and patients were asked to be accompanied by kin during their hospital stay rather than isolated from them.[30] This type of village setting was also advocated by Lambo in Nigeria. Lambo recruited families living near Aro to house mental patients, who would then be able to access psychiatric treatment on an out-patient basis. Traditional healers from across Nigeria were recruited and based at Aro, dispensing treatment but also acting as conduits of information between asylum medical staff and patients. The village system at Aro, however, did not preclude the use of conventional psychiatric therapies available at the time – such as ECT, insulin coma therapy and psychotropic medication – and occupational therapy was also encouraged.

Historical Source: T. Adeoye Lambo, 'The Role of Cultural Factors in Paranoid Psychosis among the Yoruba Tribe', *Journal of Mental Science* (1955)

It is on this great problem of the relationship between mental and cultural processes that the author attempts to shed some light, drawing on the vast clinical and anthropological materials available in Yoruba culture most of which, however, are quite unknown to British psychiatrists. It is also hoped that this may serve to clear the ground of certain prejudiced observations which have been very detrimental to the problem of the brain-mind relationship and to straight thinking about it ....

Paranoid psychosis has been selected for the programme of this research because, according to my clinical experience among the Yoruba tribe, it presents the most florid clinical picture and, particularly it reflects most adequately the psychic stresses which are inherent in the tribal culture. The conclusions are, therefore, supported by practical experience and by an intimate acquaintance with the subject in its clinical and anthropological aspects. Yoruba was the only language used throughout this study ....

I have in this work attempted to show the influence of cultural factors insofar as they determine the peculiar *form* and *content* of this mental disorder. These cultural forces, which are also observed to enter into the aetiology and psychopathology of this mental illness as it occurs in the Yoruba tribe of Nigeria, do not give rise to a true occurrence of a 'peculiar native psychosis' inexplicable by common psychodynamic formulations ... On the basis of deeper psychological determinants, this investigation has shown that the aphorism, 'the nature of men is identical; what divides them is their custom', is a valid statement even at the level of psychotic regression ....

[T]his work has established a firm relationship between the elements of cultural forces and those of mental processes by demonstrating that among the non-literate ('bush') Yoruba tribe the *form* and *content* of paranoid schizophrenia is culturally determined; while the picture of the paranoid schizophrenia occurring in the literate (Westernized) section of the tribe is, in large measure, identical with that found in Europeans.

Source Analysis: This early articulation of T. Adeoye Lambo's transcultural psychiatric approach was published soon after he had become Superintendent of Aro Mental Hospital. The paper was based on clinical research initially undertaken towards his medical degree at the University of Birmingham, which was then followed by a psychiatric specialism at the Maudsley Hospital in London. Like Fanon, in this work Lambo directly addresses, and refutes, the 'prejudiced' and reductionist 'brain-mind' linkages put forth by contemporary ethno-psychiatrists like Carothers (who had published his lengthy study on Mathari in the very same journal). Lambo utilizes his 'intimate acquaintance' with Yoruba culture and language as a distinctive methodological approach, yielding an analysis which combines elements of auto-ethnography with detailed clinical case histories.

This study illustrates a central tenet in transcultural framings of mental illness – that mental disorders, such as schizophrenia, could be universally experienced, even if their specific 'form' and 'content' were 'culturally determined'. Lambo argues that for the non-literate 'tribal' grouping of Yoruba patients, their particular clinical manifestations of paranoid schizophrenia would have been unfamiliar to and thus undiagnosed within prevailing 'psychodynamic formulations'. Mental 'abnormality' for this group could only be detected through, first, obtaining a finely-grained understanding of Yoruba cosmology, social practices and relations, from which deviations could be measured. Although Lambo's study firmly rejects the cultural reification of African mental illness implied by the idea of a 'peculiar native psychosis', it does not abandon problematic oppositional typologies – rural versus urban, literate versus non-literate, 'bush' versus Westernized – which would become a key focus of critiques of transcultural psychiatric approaches in later decades.

Anthropologists aided the development of transcultural psychiatry by advocating for, and legitimizing, the utilization of local knowledge in therapeutic practices. Studies such as Margaret Field's pioneering research on witchcraft and depression in the Gold Coast widened psychiatry's hitherto limited field of vision to consider the incidence of, and responses to, mental illness among rural communities and women. The establishment in 1965 of the scientific journal *Psychopathologie Africaine* opened a channel through which researchers associated with the Fann School could publish, and this represented a distinct academic platform through which a different framing of mental illness in Africa could be disseminated. Furthermore, the 'Africanization' of psychiatric care meshed with changing priorities in the global health agenda, as discussed in Chapter 3, in particular WHO's turn in the late 1970s towards primary healthcare and a 'horizontal' approach to health interventions. The incorporation of local forms of knowledge and indigenous therapies was encouraged in the provision of mental healthcare as in other health contexts.

However, the long shadow cast by deculturation theorists and ethno-psychiatry could still be perceived. The problem of cultural difference and cultural assimilation remained a conundrum within psychiatric circles. Should cultural difference be legitimated, even celebrated, and put at the centre of mental well-being efforts? Should domains of knowledge considered more appropriate to religion or the 'spirit' be divorced from medical interventions? Critics of the Fann School came from within its own ranks, some arguing that incorporating traditional healers into psychiatric institutions amounted to an inappropriate embrace of religion within the 'hallowed halls' of biomedicine and science. More importantly, a cohort of recently trained African psychiatrists, psychoanalysts and psychologists who had embraced post-independence opportunities for medical education viewed these potential fissures from their own positions as a newfound professional class of medics. It is instructive that the most stinging critique of the Fann method in the 1970s came not from French researchers but from Senegalese psychiatrists, who argued that the incorporation of traditional healing into psychiatric care undermined, rather than supported, their authority as clinicians and experts in their own fields. By the 1980s, transcultural psychiatry as embodied in the Aro village concept and the Fann School had declined considerably in importance as a clinical mode of mental healthcare in Africa.

In recent decades, advocates of transcultural psychiatry have argued for a continued dialogue between biomedical and 'traditional' approaches to addressing mental illness, even as the rigid distinctions between these two spheres have come into question. The HIV/AIDS pandemic has exposed the continued fragility and lack of capacity of mental health institutions to cope with the mental trauma associated with the disease and its social and demographic toll. Transcultural psychiatry has also struggled to explain, and effectively address, persistent psycho-social stigmatization within African communities of HIV+ individuals (see Chapter 4). The field has come under attack for failing to adequately integrate anthropological and historical research that has long acknowledged the persistence and complexity of Africans' pluralistic responses to illness as well as their specific and contingent experiences of mental healthcare in the colonial context. Nevertheless, notions of 'collaborative' and 'person-generated' mental healthcare which emerged out of the practice of transcultural psychiatry have found new meaning and impetus within the recently inaugurated 'global mental health' framework, now allied to development priorities, international health agencies and actors as well as the growing sense of urgency worldwide of a shared mental health crisis.[31] Furthermore, recent scientific research has affirmed the role of co-morbidities between infectious disease and mental illness. Mental disorders are now considered important risk factors in contracting tuberculosis and sexually transmitted disease and, conversely, HIV/AIDS and malaria are linked to heightened risks of developing mental morbidities. This has particular resonance for our understanding of present-day and historical patterns of mental illness in Africa.

Local idioms of mental illness in the postcolony

The history of psychiatry and its many incarnations in the African context does not capture the full spectrum of mental healthcare systems, ideologies and practices currently at work. In South Africa, for example, the importance of dream interpretation as a therapeutic as well as diagnostic measure is not only evident in 'traditionalist' rural areas of the country but also actively part of a diverse repertoire of urban African healthcare choices, as I have observed recently in the use of diviners among Xhosa-speaking communities to discern culpability for, and to cope with the psycho-social trauma of, motor vehicle fatalities.[32] Furthermore, evoking Callaway's nineteenth-century account of the Zulu diviner initiate, the notion of being 'called' to a healing vocation through a prolonged experience of illness and psychic distress is a broadly recognizable trajectory in many contemporary southern African therapeutic contexts. Similarly, among Sudanese Muslims, spirit possession is seen as both a symptom of the malaise afflicting the sufferer and an integral part of harnessing a cure. *Zar* healing groups, generally constituted of women and led by a female *shaikha*, undergo spirit possession during pacification rituals to seek appeasement with the offending spirit rather than its expulsion.[33]

The expression and vitality in the twenty-first century of these local idioms attest, on the one hand, to the resilience of older frameworks which absorbed and responded to the challenges posed by mental illness in African societies and, on the other, to the limited reach of colonial and biomedical psychiatric interventions on the continent. This is not to suggest, however, that these dynamics exist in isolation apart from a medicalized sphere, or are merely reproductions of pre-colonial forms. Indeed, recent research into anxiety, stress and suicide in southern Africa has shown that local idioms for these more recently 'discovered' conditions are drawn from the same complex of twenty-first-century psychic stressors – including societal expectations and competition, globalization and inequality, ill-health and unexpected death – which help explain contemporary manifestations of spirit possession and witchcraft.[34] Acknowledging this continuing dialogue across multiple and over-lapping registers of knowing and speaking about mental illness in the African postcolony is a step forward to addressing the silences of the past.

Conclusion

'Locked Up and Forgotten', a documentary produced in 2011 by the American news network CNN, exposed a litany of abuses – including forced seclusion and over-sedation – in the patient care provided at Mathari Mental Hospital, still Kenya's only psychiatric facility and where an ambitious J.C. Carothers had conducted his research on African 'mental derangement' six decades previously. Although it would be erroneous to attribute the failings of mental healthcare provision in Africa solely to colonial legacies, the vestiges of the carceral origins of colonial psychiatric institutions are worryingly evident. The chronic under-resourcing of these same institutions is another persistent theme.

However, as this chapter has shown, the history of mental illness in Africa can only be partially captured by a focus on the asylum setting. Ethno-psychiatry's problematic 'psychodynamic formulations' of African mental disorder had a political and intellectual impact far wider than can be suggested by the colonial lunatic asylum's limited institutional imprint in the first half of the twentieth century. The subsequent emergence and development of transcultural psychiatry, as both an explanatory framework and a mode of health intervention, were emblematic of wider challenges to the decolonization of knowledge and the Africanization of medicine. Although it vigorously contested the racialized assumptions inherent in primitivist and ethno-psychiatric theories of African mental disorder, transcultural psychiatry could not free itself completely from essentializing other aspects of African culture. Ultimately, while the history of ideas of 'African madness' offers an intriguing window into the changing politics of knowledge on and in Africa, critical gaps remain. This chapter has suggested that discerning through the missionary and anthropological archive the historical traces of Africans' *experience* of mental illness, and a genealogy of idioms of that experience, may provide a critical complementary route to understanding the complex and changing spectrum of mental illness, and of mental healthcare approaches, in African societies.

Further reading

Akyeampong, Emmanuel Kwaku, Allan Hill and Arthur Kleinman, eds. *The Culture of Mental Illness and Psychiatric Practice in Africa*. Bloomington: Indiana University Press, 2014.

Anderson, Warwick, Deborah Jenson and Richard Keller, eds. *Unconscious Dominions: Psychoanalysis, Colonial Trauma, and Global Sovereignties*. Durham: Duke University Press, 2011.

Behrend, Heike and Ute Luig, eds. *Spirit Possession: Modernity and Power in Africa*. Oxford: James Currey, 1999.

Bell, Leland. *Mental and Social Disorder in Sub-Saharan Africa: The Case of Sierra Leone, 1787–1990*. New York: Greenwood, 1991.

Bemme, Dörte and Laurence J Kirmayer. 'Global Mental Health: Interdisciplinary Challenges for a Field in Motion'. *Transcultural Psychiatry* 57, no. 1 (2020): 3–18.

Berthelier, Robert. *L'Homme Maghrébin das La Litérature Psychiatrique*. Paris: L'Harmattan, 1994.

Bullard, Alice. 'The Critical Impact of Frantz Fanon and Henri Collomb: Race, Gender, and Personality Testing of North and West Africans'. *Journal of the History of the Behavioral Sciences* 41, no. 3 (2005): 225–48.

Bullard, Alice. 'Imperial Networks and Postcolonial Independence: The Transition from Colonial to Transcultural Psychiatry'. In *Psychiatry and Empire*, edited by Sloan Mahone and Megan Vaughan, 197–219. London: Palgrave Macmillan, 2007.

Callaway, Henry. *The Religious System of the Amazulu*. Natal: J.A. Blair, 1870.

Carothers, John. *The African Mind in Health and Disease: A Study in Ethnopsychiatry*. Geneva: WHO, 1953.

Carothers, John. *The Psychology of Mau Mau*. Nairobi: Printed by the Govt. Printer, 1954.

Comaroff, Jean and John Comaroff. 'The Madman and the Migrant: Work and Labor in the Historical Consciousness of a South African People'. *American Ethnologist* 14, no. 2 (1987): 191–209.

Deacon, Harriet. *Insanity, Institutions and Society: The Case of the Robben Island Lunatic Asylum, 1846–1910*. Cambridge: Cambridge University Press, 2003.

Dubow, Saul. 'Mental Testing and the Understanding of Race in 20th-Century South Africa'. In *Science, Medicine and Cultural Imperialism*, edited by Teresa Meade and Mark Walker. London: Macmillan, 1991.

Fanon, Frantz. *Black Skin, White Masks*, translated by Charles Lam Markmann. First published 1952. New York: Grove Press, 1967.

Fanon, Frantz. *The Wretched of the Earth*, translated by Constance Farrington. First published 1961. London: Penguin Classics, 2001.

Field, Margaret. *Search for Security: An Ethno-Psychiatric Study of Rural Ghana*. London: Faber and Faber, 1960.

Forsythe, Bill and Joseph Melling, eds. *Insanity, Institutions and Society, 1800–1914*. London: Routledge, 1999.

Gilman, Sander. *Difference and Pathology: Stereotypes of Sexuality, Race, and Madness*. Ithaca; London: Cornell University Press, 1985.

Heaton, Matthew. *Black Skin, White Coats: Nigerian Psychiatrists, Decolonization, and the Globalization of Psychiatry*. Athens: Ohio University Press, 2013.

Heaton, Matthew. 'The Politics and Practice of Thomas Adeoye Lambo: Towards a Post-Colonial History of Transcultural Psychiatry'. *History of Psychiatry* 29, no. 3 (2018): 315–30.

Iliffe, John. *East African Doctors: A History of the Modern Profession*. Cambridge: Cambridge University Press, 1998.

Jackson, Lynette. *Surfacing Up: Psychiatry and Social Order in Colonial Zimbabwe, 1908–1968*. Ithaca: Cornell University Press, 2005.

Jones, Tiffany. 'Averting White Male (Ab)normality: Psychiatric Representations and Treatment of "Homosexuality" in 1960s South Africa'. *Journal of Southern African Studies* 34, no. 2 (2008): 397–410.

Junod, Henri. *The Life of a South African Tribe Vol.2 Mental Life.* London: Macmillan, 1927.

Keller, Richard. 'Madness and Colonization: Psychiatry in the British and French Empires, 1800–1962'. *Journal of Social History* 35, no. 2 (2001): 295–326.

Keller, Richard. *Colonial Madness: Psychiatry in French North Africa.* Chicago: Chicago University Press, 2007.

Kleinman, Arthur. *Patients and Healers in the Context of Culture: An Exploration of the Borderland between Anthropology, Medicine, and Psychiatry.* Berkeley: University of California Press, 1980.

Lambo, Thomas Adeoye. 'Changing Patterns of Mental Health Needs in Africa'. *Contemporary Review* 222, no. 1286 (1973): 146–54.

Leighton, A. H., T. A. Lambo, C. C. Hughes, D. C. Leighton, J. M. Murphy and D. B. Macklin. 'Psychiatric Disorder among the Yoruba'. *Transcultural Psychiatric Research Review and Newsletter* 1, no. 1 (1964): 47–51.

Livingston, Julie. 'Suicide, Risk, and Investment in the Heart of the African Miracle'. *Cultural Anthropology* 24, no. 4 (2009): 652–80.

Louw, Johann and Sally Swartz. 'An English Asylum in Africa: Space and Order in Valkenberg Asylum'. *History of Psychology* 4, no. 1 (2001): 3–23.

MacKenzie, John, ed. *Imperialism and the Natural World.* Manchester: Manchester University Press, 1990.

Mahone, Sloan. 'The Psychology of Rebellion: Colonial Medical Responses to Dissent in British East Africa'. *The Journal of African History* 47, no. 2 (2006): 241–58.

Mahone, Sloan and Megan Vaughan, eds. *Psychiatry and Empire.* London: Palgrave Macmillan, 2007.

McCulloch, Jock. *Colonial Psychiatry and 'the African Mind'.* Cambridge: Cambridge University Press, 1995.

Ngubane, Harriet. *Body and Mind in Zulu Medicine.* London: Academic Press, 1977.

Parle, Julie. *States of Mind: Searching for Mental Health in Natal and Zululand, 1868–1918.* Scottsville: University of KwaZulu-Natal Press, 2007.

Sadowsky, Jonathan. *Imperial Bedlam: Institutions of Madness in Colonial Southwest Nigeria.* Berkeley: University of California Press, 1999.

Sadowsky, Jonathan. 'The Social World and the Reality of Mental Illness: Lessons from Colonial Psychiatry'. *Harvard Review of Psychiatry* 11, no. 4 (2003): 210–14.

Summers, Martin. '"Suitable Care of the African When Afflicted with Insanity": Race, Madness, and Social Order in Comparative Perspective'. *Bulletin of the History of Medicine* 84, no. 1 (2010): 58–91.

Swartz, Leslie. *Culture and Mental Health: A Southern African View.* London: Oxford University Press, 1998.

Swartz, Sally. 'Colonial Lunatic Asylum Archives: Challenges to Historiography'. *Kronos*, no. 34 (2008): 285–302.

Swartz, Sally. 'The Regulation of British Colonial Lunatic Asylums and the Origins of Colonial Psychiatry, 1860–1864'. *History of Psychology* 13, no. 2 (2010): 160–77.

Vaughan, Megan. 'Idioms of Madness: Zomba Lunatic Asylum, Nyasaland, in the Colonial Period'. *Journal of Southern African Studies* 9, no. 2 (1983): 218–38.

Vaughan, Megan. *Curing Their Ills: Colonial Power and African Illness.* Cambridge: Polity, 1991.

Vaughan, Megan. 'Suicide in Late Colonial Africa: The Evidence of Inquests from Nyasaland'. *The American Historical Review* 115, no. 2 (2010): 385–404.

Vaughan, Megan. 'The Discovery of Suicide in Eastern and Southern Africa'. *African Studies* 71, no. 2 (2012): 234–50.

CHAPTER 6
TROPICAL DISEASE REDUX: MALARIA AND SLEEPING SICKNESS

Introduction

In 2019, the World Health Organization (WHO) announced the commencement of the Malaria Vaccine Implementation Programme (MVIP). A significant breakthrough in global health efforts to control malaria, MVIP launched in three African countries – Malawi, Kenya and Ghana – where malaria vaccines are now given as part of routine child immunization programmes, until 2022. At the centre of MVIP is the vaccine RTS,S, considered the first vaccine ever developed to clinically show reduction of malaria in young children. The vaccine's efficacy against *Plasmodium falciparum*, the predominant malaria-causing parasite in Africa and also the deadliest globally, has been particularly hailed.

In many respects MVIP represents the culmination of a fruitful and highly focused period of cross-sector partnership and fundraising from the late 1990s to the present. The pharmaceutical company that developed the vaccine, GlaxoSmithKline (GSK), has been supported since 2001 by the Bill and Melinda Gates Foundation to continue research into malaria vaccine development. The Gates Foundation also supported the Phase 3 clinical trials of the vaccine in seven countries, concluded in 2014. Whilst WHO is coordinating MVIP and is responsible for technical assistance and evaluating implementation, the non-governmental organization PATH is helping with project management. Furthermore, it is funded by the Gavi Vaccine Alliance, Unitaid and the Global Fund to Fight AIDS, Tuberculosis and Malaria. GSK has promised 10 million free doses as part of its commitment to the initiative.

Although the MVIP represents a singular scientific achievement bolstered by a multi-sector, private-public partnership funding model and coordinated support from global health institutions, WHO was quick to caution against any notions that this vaccine represented the 'magic bullet' or cure-all for the disease. The vaccine itself is not completely effective – Phase 3 trials showed the vaccine prevented malaria in 29–39 per cent of cases.[1] Notwithstanding the vaccine's importance, WHO strongly urged countries to continue with existing malaria-control protocols based on WHO's own recommendations, including the use of insecticidal bed nets and artemisinin-based combination drug therapies (called ACTs).

WHO's sense of caution is understandable. The overall impact of this scientific development, in particular on childhood morbidity and mortality due to malaria, is yet to be determined. Moreover, the sheer scale of the prevalence of malaria in Africa tempers any predictions of immediate, or comprehensive, success. In 2018 alone, malaria affected 213 million Africans and was responsible for 380,000 deaths on the continent –WHO noted this figure is in fact a dramatic reduction from the 530,000 deaths reported in 2010. WHO's World Malaria Report revealed that six African countries account for more than half of the 228 million worldwide cases of malaria: in descending order, Nigeria (25 per cent of total cases), Democratic Republic of Congo (12 per cent), Uganda (5 per cent), and Niger, Mozambique and Cote d'Ivoire (each at 4 per cent).[2] Furthermore, the long history of failures of internationally coordinated malaria eradication efforts in Africa has been well publicized and documented. Malaria has proven a formidable, flexible and tenacious foe.

Malaria: The basics

Scientists believe malaria has been present in some form on the African continent for several thousand years. Malaria is endemic to Africa, and that endemicity is present in two broad patterns – 1) occurring seasonally and in populations that have less developed immunity; and 2) occurring at stable levels of transmission throughout the year within populations that have developed some levels of resistance, although this low-level immunity is not conferred onto babies and young children. Malaria is caused by the interaction of three elements: the *Plasmodium* protozoan, the female *Anopheles* mosquito, and humans. Each is essential to the development and transmission of malaria. The protozoan first enters the anopheline mosquito through a mosquito bite from an infected human host. The protozoan undergoes asexual reproduction inside the mosquito's gut and, when developed, moves to the mosquito's salivary glands, which enable the mosquito to transmit *Plasmodium* into humans when bitten.

Malaria is not the same worldwide. Different types of malaria are marked by different *Plasmodium* species, and different species of anopheline mosquitoes can act as vectors or hosts of malaria. The key to understanding the immense human toll of malaria on the African continent is in the coming together of a particular parasite with a specific anopheline mosquito. The most virulent and potentially fatal form of malaria is caused by *Plasmodium falciparum*, which is also the most common and endemic strain to Africa. It is uniquely destructive in the aggressive way it invades and destroys red blood cells in the human host, as compared to *Plasmodium vivax* which is predominant in the southeast Asia region and the Americas. Also, the *Anopheles gambiae*, which is a species native to Africa, is by far the most efficient mosquito transmitter of the parasite which causes malaria. *Anopheles gambiae* almost exclusively feeds on humans, and do not require a large density of mosquitoes in order to maintain malaria transmission levels. This species is also particularly susceptible to *Plasmodium* infection. It is the combination of virulent protozoan with efficient human-feeding mosquito which makes the African form of malaria particularly deadly, and its transmission cycle very difficult to break.

Scientists indicate these evolutionary developments took thousands of years to develop. It is also the case that humans have evolved genetic responses as adaptations to these millennia-long conditions of malaria endemicity. One such genetic adaptation is known as 'Duffy's antigen' and is in fact the absence of a specific antigen which prevents *Plasmodium vivax* from entering human red blood cells. This antigenic property is present in a large majority of West and Central African population groups, and can provide nearly complete protection against the less virulent form of malaria. The other genetic adaptation is related to sickle cell anaemia, and is present in significant percentages of Central African populations as well as diasporic African populations descended from such groups. If an individual inherits a single sickle cell allele, some protection is conferred against *Plasmodium falciparum*, reducing the risk of death from malaria caused by this pathogen.

The current recommended treatment for *Plasmodium falciparum* is combination drug therapy including artemisinin, which is a naturally occurring compound first described in ancient Chinese medical treatises. A new vaccine – RTS,S – which has demonstrated significant levels of prevention against *P. falciparum* has been rolled out on an initial three-year basis to Malawi, Kenya and Ghana, as part of their routine child immunization programmes.

This chapter examines the history of two classic 'tropical' infectious diseases – malaria and sleeping sickness (or trypanosomiasis, as it is known in scientific circles) – from the pre-colonial period to the present day. They are significant to the history of health and illness in Africa in several critical ways. First, **the numbers** attest to the undeniable significance of these two diseases over the long durée of African history. Malaria prevalence remains an infectious disease of enormous proportions, whose cumulative toll in terms of both African mortality and morbidity has yet to be fully acknowledged. Although sleeping sickness is now classed as a 'Neglected Tropical Disease' (NTD) by WHO, and the present incidence of the disease appears relatively low, a century ago it was considered by European powers the single greatest health challenge in Africa. The considerable machinery of the colonial health service and international tropical medical science was mobilized to understand and control this disease. Sleeping sickness epidemics in Central and East Africa at the turn to the twentieth century decimated entire areas in a short span of time, with recurring outbreaks through the interwar period. A well-cited figure is that by 1920 an estimated 500,000 died in a major epidemic centred around the Congo River basin, and between 250,000 and 300,000 in the Lake Victoria Basin.[3] As well as its potentially fatal consequences, sleeping sickness can cause infertility and miscarriage, increasing its capacity to render a 'demographic shock' to a given population. It is generally acknowledged by historians that sleeping sickness epidemics contributed significantly to what was likely a population decline or lull in East-Central Africa in the 1920s and 1930s.

Second, the history of these two diseases in Africa is critical to our understanding of how a particular category of vector-borne infectious disease – **tropical disease** – posed particular challenges to African patients, health practitioners, and local and international

Sleeping sickness: The basics

Sleeping sickness is caused by the *Trypanosome* parasite. Two species of *Trypanosome* cause two variants of Human African Trypanosomiasis (HAT), one referred to as '*gambiense*', which presents in more chronic form (and accounts for the vast majority, 98 per cent, of current cases of sleeping sickness) and the other as '*rhodesiense*', characterized by more acute infection. Uganda is the sole country in which both forms of HAT are currently present. The animal form of trypanosomiasis which affects cattle is referred to by its Bantu name, *nagana*. Tstese flies of the *Glossina* genus are hosts and vectors for the parasite, which is acquired through biting an infected human or animal. Domesticated and wild animals are important reservoirs for trypanosomiasis, particularly in the *rhodesiense* form. Because of this, HAT is considered a 'zoonosis', meaning an infectious disease which involves (normally vertebrate) animals in transmission of the disease to humans. Tsetse-infested vegetation – commonly called 'tsetse-bush' – has also been acknowledged by WHO as a contributing factor to HAT transmission.

Early symptoms of HAT include joint pain, fever and headaches. In the latter, more serious stage, the parasite crosses the blood-brain barrier and affects the workings of the central nervous system. Humans affected by trypanosomiasis in this latter stage demonstrate disrupted sleeping patterns, producing the classic symptoms that gave trypanosomiasis its more colloquial name. If left untreated, sleeping sickness is commonly fatal. Sleeping sickness can cause infertility and amenorrhea in infected women. Pregnant women with HAT can suffer miscarriages, and may give birth to congenitally infected children, risking retarded physical and intellectual development.

Despite the harsh consequences of HAT infection, drug development has not seen marked innovation, and many of the same drugs developed in the first half of the 20th century continue to be utilized to this day. The type of drug therapy pursued is related to the stage of the disease present in the patient. Early stage HAT can be treated with Pentamidine for the *gambiense* form, and the drug Suramin for the *rhodesiense* form. Once the parasite crosses the blood-brain barrier, however, the risk associated with drug interventions rises considerably, with potentially fatal consequences for certain drugs such as Melarsoprol. There is at present no vaccine available to offer protection against HAT.

health systems and infrastructures. As discussed in Chapter 2, the moniker 'tropical disease' was somewhat artificially constructed in the early twentieth century. Malaria, for example, was not wholly confined to the tropics and had been historically endemic in temperate regions, including parts of Europe and Eurasia. However, as Randall Packard and James Webb have shown in their respective global histories of malaria, the unique epidemiological challenges posed by malarial transmission in Africa and the success of eradication efforts elsewhere in the world meant that malaria increasingly became, over the course of the twentieth century, a disease predominant in tropical regions, and one closely associated with Africa – a trajectory discerned in the overwhelming proportion (93 per cent in 2018) of African cases in the total global malaria caseload.[4] Furthermore, recent efforts to classify Human African Trypanosomiasis as a Neglected Tropical Disease reflect global health organizations' re-appropriation of this historic moniker, as a way to direct donor funding and public attention back to a 'forgotten' disease.

The complex interaction of an array of actors including the parasite, the insect vector, humans, and – in the case of sleeping sickness – animal reservoirs and tsetse bush historically stymied scientific attempts to observe and understand both the process of disease transmission and the ecological and environmental conditions which help facilitate its spread. For malaria, the resilience and adaptability of both the parasite and insect vectors meant that chemical and pharmacological interventions offered an often very temporary reprieve. Moreover, as the scientific understanding of so-called **zoonotic diseases** developed in the twentieth century, integrating vertebrate animal reservoirs into the epidemiology of sleeping sickness made both surveillance and control strategies even more challenging. Overall for both diseases, the full arsenal of the developing medico-scientific disciplines from the late nineteenth century onwards – bacteriology, entomology, zoology, parasitology, epidemiology, immunology, pharmacology and chemistry, to name but a few – has helped to provide specific insights into the pathways of transmission of these two diseases. However, in many ways the limitations of these fields have been cruelly exposed by diseases that have stayed a step ahead of successive scientific advances in vector control and chemotherapeutic approaches, accounting in part for the resilience of indigenous pharmacopeia such as quinine and artemisinin in malaria therapeutics. In light of this, the development of a vaccine for malaria can be seen as a fundamental shift. The **history of tropical medicine** and allied scientific fields can be discerned, then, through the trajectories of these two diseases.

Third, the story of international responses to malaria and trypanosomiasis has been emblematic of the successes and failures of **international and global health approaches** in the African context. The necessity of inter-territorial communication and collaboration amongst colonial powers in the face of the cross-border challenges presented by malaria and sleeping sickness, combined with the growing mandate of the post-First World War League of Nations Health Organization (LNHO), spurred some of the first attempts at a coordinated internationalist approach to disease. As will be seen, the features which came to be closely associated with the workings of colonial tropical medicine – scientific expeditions, field research and sanitary campaigns – were experienced by Africans as, at best, obscure vertical interventions which bore an indirect relation to health outcomes and, at worst, exploitative and extractive practices at a bodily and social level. Even as independence from colonial rule freed African health infrastructures from European control, the problems inherent in this internationalist approach to disease in Africa tended to be replicated in some form in the post-colonial context. Far from learning the lessons of history, disease eradication efforts in the latter half of the twentieth century were for the most part lessons in failure, with poorly conceived and implemented programmes that often neglected the integration of African health infrastructures and the training of African medical personnel, and favoured narrowly defined targets at the expense of a broader, multi-pronged approach. The role of philanthropic funding in the twentieth century, and its intersection with international health agendas and strategies, is integral. In many respects, the history of these two diseases has exposed the weaknesses of successive global health frameworks.

Fourth, alongside the development of the field of tropical medicine was a growing recognition of the **ecological and environmental determinants** of disease. There is certainly a long history of an 'ecological critique' of biomedical and scientific knowledge, and an ecological perspective on malaria and sleeping sickness could be discerned in the early twentieth century operating in tension with growing scientific understanding of the aetiology of these parasitic, vector-borne diseases. Whilst it could be argued that the birth of tropical medicine designated an analytical focus at the level of microscopic pathogens, scientists, missionaries and colonial officials to varying degrees also realized that wider environmental conditions as well as human patterns of settlement, animal management and land use could significantly shape the habitats which harboured insect and animal disease reservoirs, as well as determine the nature and frequency of human contact with these vectors. Indeed, as this chapter will show, this ecological orientation was partly cultivated through observation of local African practices that emphasized controlled environmental management as a tool to suppress infectious disease transmission. Many of the key debates in the historiography of malaria and sleeping sickness in Africa exist at this juncture between micro- and macro-level processes. Ecological approaches to both malaria and sleeping sickness, alongside other wide-angle perspectives that considered larger systemic factors (such as poverty, famine, violence and migration) to explain disease incidence and transmission, waxed and waned in prominence throughout their recorded histories. This parallel history of an ecological critique also helps us to understand how and why disease prevention and treatment developed along particular pathways and not others.

Finally, a dual focus on both malaria and sleeping sickness in this chapter serves as an acknowledgement of the **intertwined histories** of malaria and sleeping sickness over the *longue durée* in Africa. It is now understood that in the millennia-long evolution of both of these endemic diseases on the continent, the predations of infected tsetse flies created an 'epidemiological barrier' that militated against African attempts to domesticate livestock, the absence of which in equatorial regions encouraged the anthropophilic (human-seeking) tendency of the *Anopheles gambiae* (the efficient carrier of the virulent *P. falciparum* strain of malaria).[5] Put more simply, the presence of endemic trypanosomiasis shaped the particular pathway malarial transmission took in tropical Africa. Also, scientists and health professionals have begun to acknowledge the role of co-morbidities in sleeping sickness and malaria – for example, trypanosomiasis infection can exacerbate the clinical severity of malaria – and this further attests to the importance of examining the historic inter-relation between these two diseases.

Conceptualizing tropical disease in African history

Tracing the history of malaria and sleeping sickness in Africa is complicated by several factors. The **lack of baseline data** for these endemic diseases means we have little comparative or longitudinal understanding of changing patterns of disease prevalence and associated mortality in Africa. For example, although local accounts from the late nineteenth and early twentieth centuries tend to coalesce around the depiction of sleeping sickness epidemics as 'new' and exceptional in their intensity and severity (especially in terms of mortality rates), this cannot be confirmed by any sustained comparison with pre-colonial accounts, which are few and tend to relate to specific locales.

The difficulty of assessing the historical evidence on malaria and sleeping sickness that exists from European sources in the eighteenth and nineteenth centuries, both qualitative and quantitative, is complicated by commonly held **misperceptions of the aetiology** of these diseases and **misperceptions about African immunity** to them. Until the early twentieth century when the full aetiology of both diseases was established and became more widely known, Europeans believed that Africans were innately immune from the 'fevers' that had afflicted European visitors and settlers in much of tropical Africa (as discussed in Chapter 1). The embeddedness of this notion of 'native immunity' meant that malaria morbidity among African populations was probably significantly under-reported in colonial health surveys, particularly data from the nineteenth century. Even more glaring a gap was the lack of data collected on child mortality from malaria, which continued to be a statistical blind spot until well into the twentieth century. It is likely that in areas where malaria endemicity was stable, child mortality from malaria was high, because children under five could not develop the protective immunity acquired by repeat infection – these deaths largely escaped European observations and data-gathering efforts.

African resistance to complying with colonial and later international health surveillance and control measures is also important to consider. In particular during the colonial period, when scientific expeditions were instigated by colonial powers alarmed by reported high mortality from sleeping sickness in their territories, African families were known to have actively hidden ill patients for fear they would be forcibly relocated. Furthermore, diagnostic measures utilized in the early twentieth century could be highly invasive and painful, such as the lumbar puncture (which was utilized to positively confirm cases of sleeping sickness), and further increased the reluctance of ill patients to put themselves forward for testing. As will be seen in this chapter, these patterns of African resistance to, and scepticism of, large-scale trans-national or trans-territorial surveillance and control measures were to an extent replicated in the post-colonial period.

Historians also have difficulty assessing textual records because of **problems of diagnosis** related to both diseases. What were described as 'fevers' in eighteenth- and nineteenth-century accounts, for example, could have been any number of diseases, such as typhoid, although the particular cyclical nature of malarial fevers helped differentiate it from others to contemporary observers and have also helped historians retrospectively identify malaria incidence. In a similar vein, with regards to sleeping sickness up until the interwar period, debate persisted on whether sleeping sickness and trypanosomiasis were distinct or the same disease. When the scientist David Bruce in 1903 observed trypanosome parasites at the microscopic level in the blood of patients showing symptoms of sleeping sickness, his contemporaries expressed scepticism that this amounted to conclusive evidence the two were connected. Furthermore, scientists did not fully understand the relationship between the animal form of trypanosomiasis – known as *nagana*, which afflicted livestock – and sleeping sickness in humans. It was not until the interwar period that the distinction between trypanosomiasis and sleeping sickness was effectively erased, and the role of the trypanosome parasite in causing sleeping sickness in both animal and human forms was firmly established.

The historical sources we have to reconstruct the history of malaria and sleeping sickness in Africa are decidedly uneven, characterized by marked gaps and silences alongside an abundance of archival material clustered around periods when the pre-occupation (and anxieties) of European colonial governments and international health organizations was at its highest with regards to the demographic and health impacts of these two diseases. There are also important differences between how malaria and sleeping sickness were described in the historical record. As stated earlier, with regards to malaria in Africa in the pre-colonial and early colonial periods, European concerns lay chiefly with *European* morbidity and mortality rather than on African casualties, as illustrated in the discussion in Chapter 1 of the imagination of Africa as the 'white man's grave'. Indeed, any sustained collecting of data on African incidence of malaria did not begin until the 1930s. The written archive for malaria in Africa up to this point, then, largely consists of **statistical data on European mortality** alongside episodic entries in **journals** and **travel narratives** which tend to describe European encounters with malaria, rather than any description of African experience or management of the disease.

In contrast, sleeping sickness was differently perceived in the pre-colonial and early colonial periods, and this has left a different sort of material trace in the written record. Sleeping sickness was not considered a 'European' disease of the tropics in the way malaria was. It was termed 'African lethargy' for a reason, for its pronounced symptoms of prolonged drowsiness that were visible manifestations of this disease on African bodies. The Arab historian Ibn Khaldun reported that King Diata II, the Sultan of the kingdom of Mali, died of the 'lethargy' (likely *gambiense* trypanosomiasis) in 1373, further noting this was a 'disease that frequently befalls the inhabitants'.[6] In the memoir of his time stationed as a physician in Sierra Leone in the last decade of the eighteenth century, Thomas Winterbottom recorded slave traders' particular attentiveness to any swelling on the back of captured slaves' necks as a way to screen out cases of lethargy amongst slaves destined for the Americas – this telltale marker of sleeping sickness, in fact a swelling of the cervical lymph glands, came to be known as 'Winterbottom's sign'.[7] The animal variant of trypanosomiasis was a concern particularly for southern and East African populations where cattle constituted a key form of capital in the moral and political economy of the region, and this concern was registered by missionary and other European observers as early as the mid-nineteenth century, alongside local awareness of other livestock-related diseases such as rinderpest and lung sickness. Interestingly, it is the centrality of cattle in the social, spiritual and economic lives of Africans which encouraged the development of local responses of containment and control. These techniques, which largely involved manipulating the natural environment in which tsetse flies gathered, were mentioned in **missionary accounts** and are amongst some of the only recorded evidence of indigenous control of trypanosomiasis in the pre-colonial period.

In the colonial period, the voluminous **scientific literature** on sleeping sickness in Africa came off the backs of a sustained and focused period of research in the early twentieth century, largely through scientific expeditions as well as strategically positioned 'centres' of research into the disease, its human and animal reservoirs and insect vectors. These investigations produced colonial **expedition maps** of Africa which schematically illustrated disease prevalence and, for sleeping sickness, **maps of tsetse distribution** or tsetse fly 'belts' (an indicator of tsetse infestation and their habitat). Historical scholars of colonial map-making and of African cartography have cautioned against a wholesale acceptance of colonial maps of Africa as factual representations, and as will be seen later in this chapter, scientific maps of infectious disease distribution were far from accurate or complete.

Pre-colonial African approaches to disease control

As stated earlier, any historical reckoning of pre-twentieth-century patterns of incidence for sleeping sickness and malaria is obscured by European pre-occupations with their own morbidity and mortality from infectious disease as well as a lack of knowledge regarding disease transmission and its prevalence among African populations. With respect to uncovering how *Africans* approached and understood malaria and sleeping sickness in this earlier period, the historical record is uneven and sparse. As can be seen in Richard Burton's *The Lake Regions of Central Africa* (1860), African experiences of and responses to infectious disease tended to be markedly absent in eighteenth- and nineteenth-century European travellers' accounts, focusing instead on European anxieties and frames of reference (see box). Somewhat exceptionally, Mungo Park, whose ill-fated journeying through the Niger basin at the end of the eighteenth century is described in Chapter 1, recorded his unreserved praise for a particular technique used by the Mandingo to relieve the suffering of a malarial patient – a vapour 'bath' utilizing the branches of the *Nauclea orientalis* bush, producing excessive perspiration which 'wonderfully relieves the sufferer'.[8] Whilst Park does not dwell in his account on the extent to which the Mandingo themselves were afflicted with fevers, the success of this particular remedy in terms of relieving symptoms suggests that the Mandingo were well acquainted with the disease and its effects. Anecdotal evidence provided by missionaries in the nineteenth and early twentieth centuries as well as oral accounts later collected by colonial scientists indicate that sleeping sickness was not only endemic in certain regions of pre-colonial Africa, but that African communities had already developed a repertoire of responses. For example, elderly chiefs were cited as key informants in missionary accounts of disease prevalence in the Congo - they recalled its existence when they were boys and attributed the more recent rise in sleeping sickness in the waning years of the nineteenth century to the after-effects of conflict and population displacement. An important local strategy to suppress sleeping sickness was the management of tsetse bush. In southern and East Africa, this was done through the controlled burning of savannah scrub. This accomplished two things – first, to clear bush that provided a favourable breeding environment for tsetse flies; and second, to create land more suitable for agricultural farming and livestock rearing, which indirectly helped to control trypanosomiasis levels in both humans and animals. The 'recovery' of these indigenous techniques was later advocated, first, by select colonial scientists and, second, by scholars and commentators seeking a broader, more ecologically balanced approach to understanding infectious disease transmission and control.

Historical Source: Richard Burton, *The Lake Regions of Central Africa* (1860)

The 'mkunguru' begins with coldness in the toes and finger-tips; a frigid shiver seems to creep up the legs, followed by pains in the shoulders, severe frontal headache, hot eyes, and a prostration and irritability of mind and body. This preliminary lasts for one to three hours, when nausea ushers in the hot stage: the head burns, the action of the heart becomes violent, thirst rages, and a painful weight presses upon the eyeballs: it is often accompanied by a violent cough and irritation. Strange visions, as in delirium, appear to the patient, and the excitement of the brain is proved by unusual loquacity. When the fit passes off with copious perspiration, the head is often affected, the ears buzz, and the limbs are weak. If the patient attempts to rise suddenly, he feels a dizziness, produced apparently by a gush of bile along the liver duct: want of appetite, sleeplessness and despondence, and a low fever, evidenced by hot pulses, throbbing temples, and feet painfully swollen, with eruptions of various kinds, and ulcerated mouth, usher in the cure. This fever yields easily to mild remedies, but is capable of lasting three weeks ….

In this foul jungle our men also suffered severely from the tzetze. This fly, the torment of Cape Travelers, was limited, by Dr Livingstone, to the regions south of the Zambezi River. A specimen brought home by me and submitted to Mr. Adam White, of the British Museum, was pronounced by him to be a true *Glossina morsitans*, and Mr. Peterick has fixed its limits about eight degrees north of the equator. On the line followed by the expedition, the tzetze was found extending from Usagara westward as far as the central lakes; its usual habitat is the jungle-strip which incloses [*sic*] each patch of cultivated ground, and in the latter it is rarely seen. It has more persistency of purpose even than the Egyptian fly, and when beaten off it will return half a dozen times to the charge; it can not be killed except by a smart blow, and its long sharp proboscis draws blood even through a canvas hammock. It is not feared by the naked traveler; the sting is as painful as that of an English horse-fly, and leaves a lasting trace, but this hard-skinned people expect no evil consequences from it. In the vicinity of Kilwa it was heard of under the name of 'kipanga,' the 'little sword.' It is difficult to conceive the purpose for which this plague was placed in a land so eminently fitted for breeding cattle and for agriculture, which without animals can not be greatly extended, except as an exercise for human ingenuity to remove. Possibly at some future day, when the country becomes valuable, the tzetze may be exterminated by the introduction of some insectivorous bird, which will be the greatest benefactor that Central Africa ever knew.

Source Analysis: Richard Burton was an explorer and amateur anthropologist, linguist and botanist who travelled through south Asia, East and West Africa, and the Middle East. He was a prolific writer, publishing forty-three volumes on his travels and explorations. In this book on his travels, which began in Zanzibar and took him to the lake regions of present-day Tanzania, Burton provides a lively account of the symptoms associated with mkunguru, *which was the local term for malaria, and of his expedition's encounter with the 'tzetze' fly. Unlike the account of the Mandingo approach to 'fevers' detailed by Scottish surgeon-turned-explorer Mungo Park, Burton's description yields very little information on how the peoples of the lake regions treated or understood* mkunguru, *and instead focuses on how the disease afflicted the unfortunate 'patient'.*

Burton's description of the tsetse fly characterized it as a pestilence of biblical proportions ('this plague'), and emphasized the fly's resilience and aggressive nature ('little sword'). The link between the tsetse fly and sleeping sickness was not confirmed at this time, although Burton intimates that 'breeding cattle and agriculture' were hindered by tsetse belts. This may have indicated his awareness of local linkages between the presence of tsetse flies and the viability of pastoral agriculture, or it may have simply reflected his connection to the Scottish missionary David Livingstone, who had suggested the link between tsetse flies and nagana *(the animal form of sleeping sickness) in his own memoirs published in 1857 – nearly four decades before the microbiologist David Bruce isolated the trypanosome that caused* nagana. *Neither Burton nor Livingstone considered the tsetse fly a risk to human health.*

Burton also provides precise information on the location and reach of the tsetse fly belt his expedition encountered. This precision contrasts with the emotive language that colours his account of 'this foul jungle', a phrase which expresses European fears of Africa as a 'white man's grave' and also suggests the persistence of earlier notions of disease causation – in this case, miasma. Interestingly, Burton's view that the 'extermination' of tsetse would be a gift to the region was taken up directly over a century later by the ecologist John Ford, who argued Burton's legacy could be seen in the ill-advised, colonial scientific pre-occupation with tsetse elimination, rather than more holistic and balanced methods of disease control.

The study of African veterinary science, a field only beginning to be integrated into the history of health and illness in Africa, has shown how livestock management practices could be a window onto local aetiologies of disease and methods of disease control. Local veterinary pharmacopeia particularly with respect to livestock health was well developed, and a variety of established southern African plant-based remedies were recorded in 1915 by Kropf in his Xhosa-English dictionary. For example, knobwood (in Xhosa, *umnungumabele*) was used to treat livestock that suffered from tsetse bites, and the existence of this local remedy in the vernacular may well have pointed to long-standing indigenous knowledge on the subject.[9] Practices of transhumance – the movement of livestock to ensure the regeneration of grazing areas – are integral to this management. It is thought that in pre-colonial East Africa, communities such as the Maasai understood that tsetse flies were harmful and that wild animals could be reservoirs that could potentially pass on infectious disease to livestock. They understood that livestock needed to graze away from tsetse belts, as well as away from other insects (such as ticks) believed to harbour disease potentially harmful to livestock, and they managed their crops as well as the surrounding bushland to keep a manageable distance away from tsetse flies. Oral histories of the Zulu collected by the naturalist and tsetse scientist Charles Swynnerton pointed to an earlier strategy – which Swynnerton named 'Umzile's Principle', after the Zulu leader who advocated this approach – of tsetse suppression through the controlled annual burning of grass fires that cleared native habitat of tsetse flies and ticks.[10] Similarly, the noted ecologist and trypanosomiasis scholar John Ford suggested Zulu pastoralists took advantage of their knowledge of tsetse belts and the flexibility of customary land tenure practices to move their cattle herds away from potentially infectious and active tsetse flies, from the high 'veld' during the wet summer months and onto the low veld for the dry and cold winter months.[11] This was, for Ford and for scholars such as Helge Kjekshus and James Giblin, part of a suite of pre-colonial indigenous techniques – including controlled burning around human settlements and intensive agricultural cultivation – which emphasized disease *suppression* and the *co-existence* of the parasite with human and animal populations, rather than outright eradication. This fine balance of ecological controls over trypanosomiasis was ultimately upset in the colonial period by environmental and demographic shocks – such as epidemics of rinderpest that decimated trypano-resistant cattle populations in the late nineteenth century, land dispossession, famine and changing cultivation methods, all patterns linked in some way to increased settlement, conquest and rule by European powers.

It is important to note that much of what may have been considered 'pre-colonial' local understandings and practices tended not to be derived from contemporaneous accounts, but rather from memories or retrospective extrapolations back from a later period. It is difficult to definitively assert, for example, when exactly controlled bush-burning was adopted by the Zulu or transhumance by the Maasai, even though these were assumed by colonial and later observers to be long-standing practices that pre-dated European penetration into these regions. The narrative of decline, then, in analyses of local approaches to disease control has yet to be precisely situated within the larger history of transition to colonial rule.

From colonial medicine to international health: Trans-border responses to tropical disease in Africa

The history of sleeping sickness and malaria in the long twentieth century to the present has emphasized that vector-borne infectious disease knows no border.[12] Arguably, the trans-border threat posed by tropical disease was the main driver for the formation of modern international health frameworks, conventions, and the subsequently established permanent organizations such as the League of Nations Health Organization and the World Health Organization, to coordinate responses to these threats. However, when looking at a longer history of malaria and sleeping sickness in the African context, it is evident that the need for inter-territorial cooperation amongst European colonial powers was recognized much earlier. The roots of both the problems and possibilities of 'international health' as a concept and as a set of structures, priorities and mechanisms, as well as its uncertain and uneven relation to African health, can be seen in the colonial period.

Scientific expeditions, research stations and inter-colonial tropical medicine – 1890s to 1930s

Tropical disease presented particular and severe challenges to European colonial powers in terms of consolidating control and administrative management of their African territories. Malaria posed a persistent health risk to European officials, merchants and missionaries throughout the turn to the twentieth century, and threatened nascent efforts at establishing functioning and profitable colonial and settler economies. Major sleeping sickness epidemics in East and Central Africa between 1890 and 1910 – concentrated in Uganda, Tanganyika (now Tanzania), Kenya and the Congo, although Nigeria was also affected – coincided with the onset of colonial rule. With respect to what appeared to be alarmingly high mortality levels due to sleeping sickness, the fear of loss of potential manpower animated some of the concern with the mounting human toll of this disease, particularly in areas such as the Congo where extractive labour regimes were established to harvest rubber and mine copper. However, some of the pre-occupation with infectious disease was not wholly determined by anxieties related to the economic 'cost' of European and African mortality and morbidity. Scientific innovation was another and different consequence of colonial involvement in the region – as the historian Helen Tilley has shown, Africa came to be viewed as a 'living laboratory'.[13] There was a growing consensus amongst colonial powers that the newly inaugurated field of tropical medicine would provide the requisite expertise and manpower through which locally based fieldwork allied to scientific methodologies could yield transformative knowledge in this area.

The scientific expedition in colonial Africa served as the archetype of a particular colonial mode of trans-border health intervention, and vestiges of this specific form can be found in mid-century efforts at disease eradication and more recent initiatives in the twenty-first century to 'roll back' malaria and eradicate sleeping sickness. These expeditions were usually commissioned and financed by metropolitan powers, working through powerful research institutes which had emerged in the early twentieth century such as the London School of Tropical Medicine, the Koch Institute and the Liverpool School of Tropical Medicine, which sent trained scientific men to work in specific, local African contexts. Expeditions provided a mutually beneficial arrangement for scientists and colonial authorities – scientists were able to gather precious data through fieldwork, mobile laboratory research, and surveillance of human and animal populations, while colonial governments drew directly from expert recommendations to develop their sanitary and health policies.

The Liverpool School sent no less than seven anti-malaria expeditions to British West Africa between 1899 and 1902, under the supervision of Ronald Ross. In line with Ross' emphasis on vector eradication as the most effective route to control malarial transmission, these expeditions tended to take the shape of 'mosquito brigades' which advocated techniques such as the drainage and destruction of mosquito breeding grounds, as well as the application of larvicides. These recommendations were applied in widely varying degrees, to Ross' consternation, by the colonial administrations of Sierra Leone, Lagos, Southern Nigeria and the Gold Coast (now Ghana). Even in its nascent years, tropical medicine was not a uniform field, and the contentious issue of whether anti-malarial campaigns would be better served by vector elimination or parasite control approaches (through mass quininization, for example, as the German scientist Robert Koch advocated) divided scientists and colonial officials alike.

The (British) Royal Society funded a Sleeping Sickness Commission in 1902 to the Lake Victoria region, which bordered Uganda, British East Africa (now Kenya) and German East Africa (Tanzania), another area of high reported mortality. The Commission established a laboratory at Entebbe in Uganda, which became the base of important local research on testse flies as well as human research involving active cases of sleeping sickness. In 1903, at the behest of King Leopold II of Belgium, the Liverpool School sent a team to investigate a sleeping sickness outbreak in the Congo Free State (see map and box):

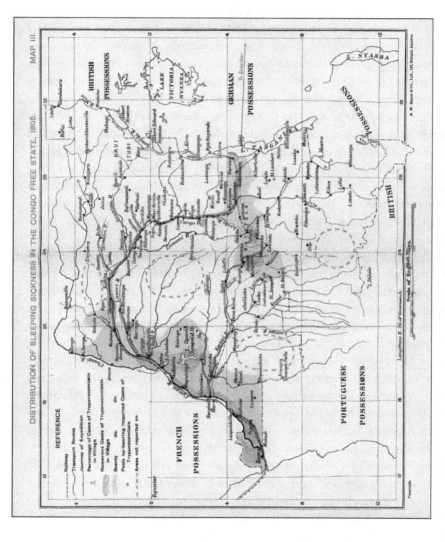

Figure 6.1 Map of distribution of sleeping sickness in the Congo Free State, 1905, in J.L. Todd, 'The Distribution, Spread and Prophylaxis of "Sleeping Sickness" in the Congo Free State: From the Expedition to the Congo of the Liverpool School of Tropical Medicine', *Transactions of the Epidemiological Society of London*, 25 (1906).

Historical Source: Map of distribution of sleeping sickness in the Congo Free State, 1905

Source Analysis: This map was produced to illustrate the findings of the 1903 scientific expedition to the Congo, led by the Liverpool School of Tropical Medicine. Colonial maps such as this demarcated areas of sleeping sickness incidence, confirmed through various surveillance methods, such as physical examinations of suspected active cases of sleeping sickness as well as written surveys sent to colonial administrators and medical officers. The red shading indicates a high concentration of sleeping sickness cases clustered around the lower Congo River, including Leopoldville and Boma, as well as a secondary area in the centre of the territory bisected by two smaller rivers. The 'journey of the expedition' is represented through a dashed line, showing the circular route the team took through the Congo and its dependence on the river system as the main transport route. Key areas which were 'not reported on' by the expedition are indicated by cross-hatch marks – on closer inspection, four such circular areas are marked on this map. Distribution maps of sleeping sickness, as well as maps which illustrated tsetse infestation (or 'tsetse belts') and malarial distribution, served as visual representations of the research findings of particular scientific expeditions. These were widely circulated through international publications on infectious disease, like Transactions of the Epidemiological Society of London, *and through official colonial channels.*

Historians of colonial cartography have critiqued the notion of maps as 'truthful' and authoritative representations, and have argued for their deconstruction through a consideration of the processes behind their creation. This is no less applicable to scientific maps of infectious disease distribution in colonial Africa. As Maryinez Lyons has shown, this particular map inaccurately depicted the northern Uele district – one of the areas indicated on the map by cross-hatch marks – as being 'free' of sleeping sickness. The underestimation of the extent and spread of sleeping sickness derived in part from the failure of expedition scientists to undertake tests in the area, even though it was known to have been an area of sleeping sickness incidence. Furthermore, many Africans actively evaded expedition surveillance measures to avoid painful and invasive diagnostic examinations, including the lumbar puncture – considered at the time the best technique to achieve a definitive sleeping sickness diagnosis, involving the deep insertion of a needle into the spinal canal to extract cerebro-spinal fluid, which was then examined under a microscope to detect the trypanosoma parasite. Africans may have also understood the potential harmful social consequences of a positive diagnosis (such as re-location), and acted accordingly.

Thus, while it may be tempting to treat these maps as valuable historical 'snapshots' of infectious disease incidence, like for other source types a critical perspective is required in their analysis. James Giblin has argued that historians of the colonial period may inadvertently perpetuate false narratives of the spread (or containment) of sleeping sickness if distribution maps such as these are not adequately cross-examined against other contemporary sources, such as missionary and colonial administrative accounts.

Scientific expeditions in the early decades of tropical medical research provided an important site of innovation situated in the specific environs of African territories. Vital milestones in understanding the complex aetiology of tropical diseases – such as David Bruce's observations in 1903 of the connection between sleeping sickness and the trypanosome parasite – were achieved through the clinical, diagnostic and microscopic work of these expeditions. Expeditions also operated as roving field sites to test out the efficacy of various disease control measures, as was the case with anti-malarial expeditions in the early twentieth century. An important feature of these expeditions was that they operated through an inter-territorial and inter-colonial frame, partly necessitated by the trans-border spread of infectious diseases. For example, the close collaboration between German and British scientists and colonial officers to apprehend the scope and human impact of the sleeping sickness epidemic in the Lake Victoria region in the first decade of the twentieth century led to a type of 'inter-colonial intimacy', as Mari Webel has shown, via overlapping scientific and colonial administrative networks. This intimacy also extended to the analysis of the human body. The search for what the scientist and bacteriologist Robert Koch had himself termed *Krankenmaterial* – literally, 'sick [person's] substance' – animated expeditionary scientists and informed the bodily technologies they utilized to extract blood, lymph and cerebrospinal fluid from Africans with suspected sleeping sickness.[14]

In many respects, these expeditions laid the groundwork for subsequent coordinated international health interventions, such as the League of Nations International Commission on Sleeping Sickness (1925–7), and for the more permanent research stations that were established in colonial African territories in the interwar period – such as Amani Agricultural Research Station (established 1919 in Tanganyika, later becoming the East African Malaria Unit in 1949) and the Permanent Mission to Fight against Sleeping Sickness in Cameroon at Ayos (1926) – which further embedded scientific knowledge production in an African field context. Funded by imperial powers and also supported by the newly formed LNHO and private philanthropic bodies such as the Rockefeller Foundation, research centres enabled longitudinal data in local vicinities to be collected, resulting in more finely detailed analyses of change over time in disease incidence as well as insect populations and climactic and environmental conditions. Indeed, research centres utilized their settings within specific African landscapes and geographies to their advantage, conducting studies that reflected a more 'wide-angle' ecological approach as compared to the more narrow focus on microscopic pathogens and insect vectors which had characterized earlier roving scientific expeditions. Of particular note is the work of scientist and naturalist Charles Swynnerton, who became head of the newly formed Tsetse Research Department in Tanganyika in 1927. From his position at this well-staffed, metropolitan-funded centre, Swynnerton conducted numerous influential field studies in the 1920s and 1930s which examined factors involved in trypanosomiasis transmission as diverse as livestock and game management, tsetse ecology, human land use and settlement patterns. Importantly, he sought the involvement of African interlocutors in his large-scale studies, for example, utilizing elderly oral informants to assemble a historical portrait of changing environmental conditions, tsetse habitat and distribution. His interaction with African informants encouraged an orientation towards, and a sustained appreciation of, indigenous methods of disease control, in particular techniques which limited the expansion of tsetse habitat such as the controlled burning of tsetse bush as well as *citemene* cultivation practices observed in southern African societies.[15] A young John Ford entered trypanosomiasis research in the late 1930s, and to some extent Ford's appreciation of local ecological approaches can be traced back to his insertion in the research milieu created by Swynnerton and other field-based scientists.

The training of local naturalists, field assistants and laboratory technicians was also integral to the successful operation of these research institutes, and some Africans such as Swedi bin Abdallah were able to coordinate and lead their own scientific studies, although their intellectual labour was seldom recognized.[16] Alongside medical auxiliaries (see Chapter 2), they comprised the 'first generation' of African intermediaries involved in the production and interpretation of medical and scientific knowledge. It should be no surprise that the first African Native Medical Corps and the greatest concentration at mid-century of trained medical doctors were drawn from the same regions that had been the focus of an earlier generation of tropical disease expeditions and institutes.

Arguably, the 'new epidemiology' that emerged in the interwar period represented a transformative turn in understanding infectious disease transmission as well as theorizing successful disease control strategies.[17] The wide-angle lens afforded by this more ecological approach enabled the complex interactions of animal, pathogen, human and plant species to be more fully integrated into what had been a narrowly defined, and pathogen-focused, field of tropical medicine. However, it is important to acknowledge the limitations of the scientific knowledge produced through research centres and earlier expeditions, particularly in terms of meaningful impacts on African health outcomes. As discussed in Chapter 2, colonial sanitary and health interventions designed to contain malaria and sleeping sickness tended to be unevenly based on emerging scientific knowledge on tropical disease in the early twentieth century. Although expeditions and research institutes produced specific recommendations on infectious disease control based on detailed fieldwork and surveillance of active human cases and insect distribution, this guidance was taken up in widely varying ways by colonial governments and health authorities.

Furthermore, it is difficult to assess African perceptions and experiences of these processes of knowledge production at work. The search for *Krankenmaterial* in the case of sleeping sickness expeditions – through drawing blood, lumbar puncture and cervical lymph gland aspiration – was done with little consideration of bodily comfort or therapeutic care for those Africans with visible symptoms of sleeping sickness. The historical record does not reveal much of African experience of these procedures, although expeditionary scientists' noted frustration regarding African resistance to or evasion of these diagnostic methods can provide an indirect approximation. Also, as the historian Luise White has shown, official documentary sources point to the circulation of 'vampire' rumours in the 1930s in African areas of Northern Rhodesia (now Zambia), where aggressive trypanosomiasis surveillance and control measures were implemented – including the use of local 'fly boys' to capture and inspect tsetse flies, and to act as 'fly pickets' on paths to remove tsetse from the bodies of passing travellers. African 'vampires', known as *banyama*, were characterized in these rumours to be in the employ of colonial or medical authorities, encharged with the task of waylaying unsuspecting victims and extracting their blood or other bodily fluids for the nefarious purposes of their colonial masters.[18] These rumours suggested the parallel circulation of vernacular understandings of trypanosomiasis transmission as well as offered an explicit moral commentary on the extractive bodily practices embedded in tropical medicine, and the role of African intermediaries in these processes.

Finally, the ecological impacts of colonial social and economic polices arguably had a greater impact on tropical disease transmission than the ameliorative sanitary and health interventions that were adopted to suppress it. Large-scale irrigation works and other major environmental engineering projects designed to scale up agricultural production in French West Africa and in British-held Sudan created new mosquito breeding sites and disturbed the balance of human and vector habitats in these areas, and arguably led to increased rates of malarial infection. In interwar South Africa, a combination of expansion of white settlements, damming projects, the forced relocation of Africans to 'native' reserves and the increased mobility of labourers on railways connecting previously malaria-free regions in southern Africa to hyperendemic areas where intensive agricultural production was taking place created a 'perfect storm' of conditions where periodic severe malaria epidemics occurred in the 1920s and 1930s, extending to neighbouring territories.[19] The regional migration of agricultural labourers contributed to major malaria epidemics in the Congo, Kenya and Madagascar in this period as well.

Mid-century transformations: International health and eradication agendas

When the Japanese took control of the island of Java in 1942, upwards of 90 per cent of the world's supply of quinine was immediately disrupted. The Allied Powers soon realized they urgently needed to produce an effective synthetic anti-malarial and enlisted the help of companies and institutions such as Dow Chemical, Parke Davis and Company, the National Institute of Health, Johns Hopkins, and Harvard University. In the early 1940s, over 15,000 anti-malarial compounds were synthesized and screened in a coordinated effort. In 1942 the synthesis of the drug mepacrine (or atabrine) represented the first major breakthrough for Allied scientists, produced by recovering the manufacturing process earlier developed by German scientists. In 1945 a French-American collaboration led to the successful production of chloroquine, also originally synthesized by German scientists (in 1934), which proved a revolutionary prophylaxis and therapeutic drug. Another key development was the manufacture of Dichlorodiphenyltrichloroethane – more commonly known as DDT. It had been originally synthesized in 1874, but its insecticidal properties were not understood until 1939. By 1944, American chemical companies were producing hundreds of thousands of pounds of crystalline DDT. Its value as an anti-malarial weapon was soon grasped – when sprayed on indoor surfaces, DDT could kill mosquitoes and effectively interrupt the chain of malaria transmission, and its residual insecticidal properties were potent enough that repeat applications could be spaced out for potentially several months or even a year at a time. It was also relatively cheap to manufacture, did not corrode metals and appeared not to have toxic side effects for humans; the deleterious consequences of long-term exposure to DDT in human and animal tissue were not fully investigated until decades later.

These wartime technological advances, combined with the re-invigoration of an internationalist health agenda spurred by the establishment of World Health Organization in 1948, enabled a rapid scaling-up of ambitions to eradicate malaria in parts of Europe, the Americas and Asia. The place of Africa within this newly vested malaria eradication landscape was highly contested. In 1950, the first major international conference on malaria in Africa was held in Kampala (the capital of Uganda), bringing to the fore a core debate between expert malariologists over the risks involved in pursuing an eradication approach. This debate mirrored to an extent earlier conflicting views, seen in early twentieth-century sanitary campaigns in colonial Africa as well as in the development of an anti-malaria agenda within the LNHO, over whether vector control (through mosquito elimination strategies) or parasite control (through widespread quininization) was the most effective and prudent strategy. Those in Kampala cautioning against eradication argued that such efforts would interfere with, and potentially compromise, the acquired immunity of Africans in holoendemic areas (areas with stable levels of malarial transmission throughout the year), an immunity which relied on continuous infection and a degree of childhood exposure to malaria. Eradicationists, on the other hand, stressed that the discoveries of DDT and chloroquine had profoundly altered the odds of comprehensively defeating malaria worldwide, and that the global health community had a moral obligation to use these tools to finally tackle an infectious disease with profound health impacts in Africa.[20] The eradicationist school won out, temporarily, and for a short period international eradication programmes were enacted in several tropical African contexts.

It is worthwhile examining in more detail the rise and fall of mid-century eradication efforts in Africa, some of which began as wartime interventions and lasted through the 1950s. The importance of Accra in the Gold Coast as an Allied waystation and airbase during the Second World War meant considerable investment was made by Allied Powers in health and sanitation for the military, and this included a coordinated anti-malaria campaign. The Inter-Allied Malaria and Control Group was set up in 1942 to act as a coordinating body of British and American medical and scientific experts to conduct and monitor the efficacy of a range of anti-malarial measures – including the expensive construction of drainage works, sanitary segregation of military quarters from nearby settlements, quinine and mepacrine distribution for the military, indoor residual spraying (IRS) of villages and pesticidal spraying of mosquito-breeding areas. The drive of the Allied Powers to pursue scientific breakthroughs at any cost could be seen in their use of migrant labourers as human 'bait' who were required to stay each night unprotected in enclosed shed 'traps', as part of an experiment to monitor local mosquito biting and flying habits.[21] After American forces left Accra, however, investment in vector control methods declined precipitously and the British returned to pre-war techniques of quinine prophylaxis, alongside occasional DDT spraying. By the 1960s, with the development of DDT resistance in the mosquito population, malaria became firmly re-established in Accra.

Liberia's experience of malaria control interventions from the immediate post-war period to the mid-1960s is a second case in point.[22] Malaria control became another chapter in Liberia's entangled history with the United States during the Second World War, when Liberia's Firestone Tire and Rubber Company became crucial to Allied war efforts, after the Japanese cut off the world's supply of rubber in seizing control of Malaya. As part of the deepening of US-Liberian relations, the United States committed to public sanitation and health interventions in Liberia, and began a multi-pronged approach to malaria eradication in the mid-1940s including drainage operations, insecticidal larvicide and IRS using DDT-based insecticides, as well as supplying medical personnel to oversee the programme. Although some gains were achieved in the initial post-Second World War period, particularly in the capital Monrovia in terms of decreased hospital malarial admissions, those gains were quickly eroded as sanitation measures became too expensive to maintain and local resistance to residual spraying of homes and storage structures in rural areas resulted in a patchwork of insecticidal coverage. Furthermore, a persistent lack of understanding of the architecture of local housing beset American and then WHO-led interventions in Liberia – for example, the efficacy of IRS was greatly diminished in cases where DDT was applied to walls made up of overly absorptive clay material, or in timber-framed houses where mosquitoes could escape through ill-fitting gaps in the roofs. Cross-border labour migration into Liberia from hyperendemic (seasonally affected) malarial areas further complicated eradication efforts, by bringing into the region a cohort with no acquired immunity to malaria. By the early 1960s, malarial transmission patterns in Liberia in both urban and rural areas had been firmly and devastatingly re-established.

There were minor but notable 'successes' in this period. For example, as the historian Amina Issa has shown, colonial Zanzibar drew on a history of successive decades of widespread and locally available quinine (dating back to Robert Koch's championing of mass quininization in Tanganyika in 1904) allied to increasingly aggressive and technologically sophisticated efforts at drainage and the elimination of household mosquito-breeding grounds through larvicidal and insecticidal applications. This resulted in the near eradication of malaria in the city and immediate surrounds by the early 1960s.[23] Arguably, Zanzibari experience of this multi-pronged approach, which involved public awareness campaigning to encourage both quinine usage and the destruction of domestic mosquito-breeding areas, helped lay the civic and infrastructural groundwork for its effective participation in later anti-malarial interventions. In southern Cameroon, a pilot WHO-led project achieved some success in halting malarial transmission in the late 1950s. In the same period, residual DDT spraying in Swaziland resulted in the elimination of anopheline mosquito populations and led to extremely low levels of malaria transmission for successive years. In this case, however, 'eradication' was not consolidated, and endemic malaria soon returned due to the poor maintenance of irrigation canals and the influx of migrant workers from malarial areas. Swaziland remains an area of malaria endemicity vulnerable to periodic epidemics after

Historical Source: 'The Malaria Programme in the African Region', Dr M.A.C. Dowling, Senior Regional Malaria Advisor, WHO Africa Region, 1 November 1960

The interruption of transmission in holoendemic conditions demands a very high degree of efficiency, with an organization capable of ensuring total coverage with insecticide, and capable also of carrying out and interpreting a continuous evaluation of the programme. The subsequent stage, that of systematic elimination by case detection measures of the parasite residue and of any remaining foci of transmission, cannot be brought to a successful conclusion by the type of organization which suffices for malaria control. The data supplied to the 1959 meeting in Brazzaville made it clear that the majority of current projects had not been adequately planned and that no real attempt had been made to convert them into the pattern of eradication. The concept was still one of control without adequate emphasis on perfection of detail. In the absence of geographical reconnaissance of the project area, the spraying programme was incapable of achieving total coverage. The staffing was inadequate at all levels, particularly at the level of field supervisor responsible for the control of spraying techniques and coverage. The projects were often directed by part-time officers and were given very little autonomy within the government framework. The financing was usually too limited, so that the activities and staffing within the project area were dependent on current financial state, rather than on the direct requirements of eradication. This was attributable largely to inadequate planning, and to the local failure to appreciate the needs of a programme which has eradication as its objective. In addition, in spite of WHO advice to the contrary, the projects were often too small, so that the wide-ranging population movements, so characteristic of African communities, tended to nullify the efforts at interrupting transmission … In many parts of tropical Africa, villages and hamlets are only reached after days of tramping through swamp and jungle. Only a supervisory staff with a true sense of devotion to their work can carry out such difficult duties in an efficient manner, and without total coverage the programme must fail. The second essential category is the staff of laboratory technicians, on whom depends the whole evaluation of progress.

Source Analysis: This report by a senior WHO official illustrates the organizational precision and attention to detail that WHO believed were required in the turn from malaria 'control' measures to malaria 'eradication'. Dowling dismisses the efforts of the pilot projects in the Africa Region up to then – in Uganda, Cameroon, Senegal, Liberia and Nigeria – as 'inadequately planned' and without the necessary emphasis on 'perfection of detail'. He is critical of the planning and infrastructural capacities of African states – by the time of this report, only Uganda remained under colonial rule – and questions the scaling of the projects, which did not sufficiently take into account the characteristic geographic mobility of African populations.

This primary source is useful in revealing the high stakes involved in WHO's eradicationist approach – attention to detail in every aspect of planning, logistics, financing, technical and surveillance was the key to success. Without 'total coverage' and a 'true sense of devotion', then eradication in Africa could never be achieved. This passage is emblematic of WHO's vertical approach to global malaria eradication at this time, particularly in its emphasis on top-down management – seen in the importance placed on the quality of the field supervisor, as well as the autonomy of the project officers vis-a-vis state governments. The participation of African communities as health actors within this vertical framework is conspicuously absent. This document gives an indication of the pessimism of WHO officials at the prospects of any sort of eradicationist agenda succeeding in Africa, given the region's infrastructural, operational and financial constraints. It also provides one window into understanding why tropical Africa was never fully incorporated into WHO's Malaria Eradication Programme, which formally ended in 1969.

major environmental or climactic fluctuations.[24] For the most part, the experiences of Swaziland, Accra and Liberia encapsulated how short-lived were any major gains made in malaria control, and illustrated the immense logistical, technical and epidemiological challenges facing international malaria eradication efforts in Africa at mid-century. Worrying reports, already in circulation in the late 1950s, of the development of insect resistance to DDT further tempered the prospects of outright eradication, at least for this part of the world. By the time WHO globally implemented its Malaria Eradication Programme (MEP, 1955–69), the association of 'eradication' with malaria control efforts in tropical Africa had been largely decoupled.

Importantly, the failures of malaria control strategies already evident at mid-century did not apply to sleeping sickness. In the same period when halting gains were turning to reversals with regards to reductions in malaria infections, a more systematic and effective control over trypanosomiasis transmission was achieved. This was in part because of the shift to widespread spraying of tsetse habitat with DDT, particularly in East Africa where regular tsetse brigades were launched. Also, the development in 1949 of the drug Melarsoprol, still in use today to treat late stage sleeping sickness, aided in the significant reduction of mortality rates. Finally, the principles of Eugène Jamot, the French physician who became head of the Permanent Mission to Fight against Sleeping Sickness in Cameroon, were widely adopted in this period in British, Portuguese and Belgian colonial territories. Developed in the interwar period, *La Jamotique* targeted the trypanosomal reservoir in humans rather than the tsetse vector, and called for the use of mobile teams of doctors and medical auxiliaries who could reach remote populations, quickly diagnose active cases and administer drug treatments.[25] The widespread application of *La Jamotique* resulted in significant declines in sleeping sickness prevalence, particularly in Cameroon, Ghana, Nigeria, Congo and Angola.

WHO reported that by the late 1960s, new *gambiense* cases of sleeping sickness had fallen to extraordinarily low levels – below 0.01 per cent.[26]

Post-eradication agendas and realities – 1970s to the present day

WHO's Malaria Eradication Programme, which formally ended in 1969, achieved total eradication in eighteen countries, including the United States, parts of southern and eastern Europe, Singapore and several islands in the Caribbean and Pacific. Mauritius, the island nation which became independent of British control in 1968, was the only African state to have achieved this distinction.[27] From 1978, malaria control was folded into the Primary Health Care framework formulated by WHO, emphasizing surveillance measures and technical guidance. By this time, international health authorities acknowledged that particularly with respect to *falciparum* malaria in sub-Saharan Africa, eradication had spectacularly failed. Furthermore, it was clear by the 1970s that both the malarial parasite and anopheline mosquitoes had rapidly evolved resistance, in part due to the uneven application of chemotherapies and insecticides as part of eradication efforts. *P. falciparum*'s demonstrated resistance to the once-miracle drug chloroquine was a particular blow to malaria prevention and control measures, although chloroquine may have had a suppressive effect on malarial mortality figures in Africa well into the 1980s. The lack of research into developing new chemotherapeutics meant that the same drugs were utilized to treat Africans with malaria, with diminishing returns.

The re-introduction of sleeping sickness experienced in tropical Africa in the 1970s and 1980s can be linked in part to violent conflict in certain regions. As was seen in the period of transition to colonial rule in the late nineteenth century, conflict created vulnerable and mobile refugee populations and upset fragile eco-systems and land-use patterns, producing ecological conditions ripe for heightened disease transmission. These same consequences were felt nearly a century later, with the additional impacts that warfare had on state-run health services and ongoing disease control interventions. A mundane but illuminating example is the experience of Uganda, whose National Tsetse Control Department lost all of its vehicles during the civil warfare from the late 1970s to mid-1980s. Without any vehicles, control and surveillance measures were significantly hampered.[28] The related collapse of cotton production in Uganda resulted in the re-growth of tsetse habitat in abandoned agricultural areas, resulting in the re-infestation of tsetse and a dramatic rise in sleeping sickness cases. The linkage of violent conflict with increased infectious disease burdens was to be repeated in later decades. In Burundi, civil war forced an interruption to domestic malaria control measures and combined with heavy rains to increase insect vector populations and result in an explosive epidemic of malaria in the early years of the twenty-first century. For the Democratic Republic of the Congo, protracted civil and trans-national conflict since the 1990s has decimated local health services, affected access to anti-malarial drugs and forcibly relocated Congolese off cultivated land, all of which have contributed to a resurgence of malaria.[29] According to WHO, since 2009 70 per cent of global sleeping sickness cases have been reported in the country.[30] More recently, the conflict in South Sudan has created its own particular difficulties with respect to trypanosomiasis control measures.[31]

An important shift in the global health approach towards malaria was ushered in by the Roll Back Malaria (RBM) campaign which was launched in 1998. RBM's strategy centred on the widespread distribution of low-cost Insecticide Treated Nets (ITNs), increased access to a new combination drug treatment utilizing artemisinin, enhanced surveillance measures including the early detection of malaria in children, and an emphasis on behavioural change which targeted pregnant women and encouraged them to use ITNs rigorously as well as report early symptoms of malaria. The RBM initiative came in the context of a profoundly changing funding landscape for global health initiatives. The Bill and Melinda Gates Foundation (launched in 1999) brought its immense financial resources as well as its global profile to bear on malariology and vaccine research, and established the Malaria Vaccine Initiative (MVI) which has been so pivotal to the development of the RTS,S vaccine now being delivered to Malawi, Kenya and Ghana. In 2007, the Gates Foundation boldly declared malaria 'eradication' again a goal worth publicly striving for. Malaria received a further boost from the formation in 2002 of the Global Fund to Fight AIDS, Tuberculosis and Malaria, which helped to pool billions of dollars from governments, agencies, civil society and the private sector to fund prevention and treatment initiatives for these three diseases. Other high-profile public-private partnerships such as Malaria No More, co-founded in 2006 by Wall Street tycoons Ray Chambers and Peter Chernin, helped to raise public awareness and funding towards the purchase of bed nets.

Roll Back Malaria was not uniformly effective, not least because it replicated some of the same weaknesses evident in earlier malaria eradication initiatives of the mid-twentieth century. Despite the emphasis stated at its founding of the need to recognize and support local health infrastructures, as a whole RBM did not result in the strengthening of health systems or services in affected countries. Furthermore, the lack of integration of local authorities in the design and implementation of RBM meant that strategies could not be adapted to local conditions and constraints, which had knock-on negative effects on malaria control measures. Lack of funding for more advanced forms of chemotherapy meant that outdated drugs such as chloroquine continued to be used or provided to patients in improper dosages, both resulting in decreased efficacy. Also, the emphasis of RBM on effecting behavioural change was met with resistance. In some areas, pregnant women were not fully compliant with surveillance or treatment measures, and did not follow prescribed drug regimes. In addition, although insecticide-impregnated bed nets were widely distributed, its use within households could not be regulated – for example, it is not clear that children and infants were prioritized within households with limited numbers of bed nets. The costs related to maintaining bed nets through re-impregnating them with insecticide could not be borne by some households, again decreasing their efficacy.

In 2012, Human African Trypanosomiasis was designated a Neglected Tropical Disease, one of ten which were declared at a gathering in London of WHO officials, the World Bank, government representatives, pharmaceutical companies and the Gates

Foundation. The NTD designation was meant to highlight the significant discrepancies in international health funding for and visibility of certain infectious vector-borne diseases, particularly in light of the global health funding spotlight on malaria. Whilst the designation of HAT as one of the NTDs has helped to focus some international health efforts and funding towards prevention and treatment measures, it is clear, as with RBM, that the lessons from the failures of past interventions have not been fully learned. Although WHO has espoused a 'One World' approach to health that ostensibly advocated a coordinated global health partnership, a key partner and indeed the main partner – African states – have not been fully integrated into these efforts. Similarly, the evidence indicates that the governments of countries with a significant threat from sleeping sickness re-emergence, such as Uganda (which is the only country where both the *gambiense* and *rhodesiense* form of HAT are endemic), tended to be bypassed by both global health agencies and non-governmental organizations that mobilize surveillance and control measures. So, although the rhetoric of 'crisis' and 'eradication' has helped to bring prominent international players into sleeping sickness-stricken areas, these have not translated into sustainable measures which support African health infrastructures to continue preventative and treatment work once these agencies (and their associated personnel, equipment and medication) leave their posts.[32] Ultimately, it appears that the vertical approach espoused by disease eradication programmes of the past has not been entirely abandoned, at least in the context of HAT in Africa.

Conclusion

This chapter's depiction of the interlocking histories of sleeping sickness and malaria in Africa has revealed the persistent challenges both presented in terms of African health. Malaria's complex aetiology, combining a virulent and highly adaptable parasite with the unique efficiency of the insect vector, presented often insurmountable challenges to an array of African and international health agents and institutions. Although there is reason to hope that the recent malaria vaccine developed will finally 'turn the tables' on malaria, its history suggests that it can remain one step ahead of the biomedical and chemical arsenal arrayed against it. Like malaria, the intricate web of vectors and reservoirs associated with sleeping sickness transmission presented an epidemiological puzzle that was not unlocked well into the twentieth century. The zoonotic aspect of the disease, as well as the importance of the testse bush as a favourable environment for the tsetse fly vector, further complicated efforts to understand it. That remains the case into the twenty-first century, even though it is hoped that as a named Neglected Tropical Disease HAT will now attract attention from the wider public, and more specifically the global health funding complex, which may help direct funds towards the research and development of preventative and curative agents.

This history has also illustrated that an internationalist approach was both a desirable and indeed a necessary feature of tropical disease interventions. The scale and nature of the epidemiology of both sleeping sickness and malaria, in particular their sensitivity to population movements, have meant that trans-border coordination was requisite to surveillance and control. Where those mechanisms have lapsed, in cases of violent conflict or weakening health infrastructures, then conditions could quickly decline, allowing diseases to re-emerge. For malaria, partial eradication was never a winning strategy as it compromised acquired immunity in holoendemic populations and bred the very conditions which fostered the development of insecticidal and chemotherapeutic resistance. Yet, it appears that international health authorities were, for a short period, willing to risk this dangerous outcome to pursue the alluring goal of complete eradication.

Although vector control measures such as cattle spraying (for sleeping sickness) and insecticide-impregnated bed nets (for malaria) have become 'standard issue' in global health interventions in Africa and have been adopted within domestic health service provision, African adherence to these measures is far from universal, with wide variation. Furthermore, unless funded generously, African health infrastructures may not prioritize the use of the most advanced insecticides or larvicides, which may contribute to the development of chemical-resistant insect vectors. The effectiveness of the latest synthetic and combination drug therapies to mitigate against infectious disease is contingent upon widespread and full compliance by patients, and in the twentieth century the ability of the *Plasmodium* parasite to quickly evolve drug resistance has been an important determinant in the historic failure of many treatment and control programmes. As the early history of scientific expeditions and the quest for *Krankenmaterial* has vividly illustrated, the willingness of Africans to be 'captured' by scientific surveillance and diagnostic mechanisms cannot be presumed and must be cultivated.

Finally, the history of these two diseases has revealed that ecological approaches which consider the interaction of disease with wider social and environmental forces have enduring relevance. European missionaries and colonial scientists came to associate indigenous African methods of disease control with this more balanced, ecologically attuned orientation, and this depiction was later integrated into a narrative of 'decline' that explained why and how diseases such as sleeping sickness were experienced in epidemic form during the colonial period. This 'wide-angle' perspective on disease causation has also served as a useful riposte to the narrow, vertical approaches which characterized the long history of campaigns against malaria and sleeping sickness in Africa. From the mosquito brigades of the early twentieth century to the malaria eradication programmes of mid-century, to the more recent efforts of Roll Back Malaria, the Malaria Vaccine Implementation Programme and Neglected Tropical Disease frameworks, the overriding emphasis has been on pathogens and vectors at the expense of a focus on African patients, their decision-making and health infrastructures. An approach attentive to the long history of the human ecology of sleeping sickness and malaria can help us critically analyse the successes and failures of these interventions, as well as provide a persistent alternative subtext of how 'African health' could have been differently imagined.

Further reading

Anderson, Warwick. 'Immunities of Empire: Race, Disease, and the New Tropical Medicine, 1900–1920'. *Bulletin of the History of Medicine* 70, no. 1 (1996): 94–118.

Arnold, David, ed. *Warm Climates and Western Medicine: The Emergence of Tropical Medicine, 1500–1900*. Amsterdam: Rodopi, 1996.

Beinart, William and JoAnn McGregor, eds. *Social History & African Environments*. Oxford: James Currey, 2003.

Beinart, William and Karen Brown. *African Local Knowledge & Livestock Health: Traditional, Environmental & Biomedical Approaches in South Africa*. Oxford: James Currey, 2013.

Bengy Puyvallée, Antoine de and Sonja Kittelsen. '"Disease Knows No Borders": Pandemics and the Politics of Global Health Security'. In *Pandemics, Publics, and Politics*, edited by Kristian Bjørkdahl and Benedictine Carlsen, 59–73. Singapore: Palgrave Pivot, 2018.

Curtin, Philip D. 'Medical Knowledge and Urban Planning in Tropical Africa'. *The American Historical Review* 90, no. 3 (1985): 594–613.

Dumett, Raymond. 'The Campaign against Malaria and the Expansion of Scientific Medical and Sanitary Services in British West Africa, 1898–1910'. *African Historical Studies* 1, no. 2 (1968): 153–97.

Ford, John. *Role of the Trypanosomiases in African Ecology*. Oxford: Clarendon Press, 1971.

Giblin, James. 'Trypanosomiasis Control in African History: An Evaded Issue?' *The Journal of African History* 31, no. 1 (March 1990): 59–80.

Harrison, Gordon. *Mosquitoes, Malaria, and Man: A History of the Hostilities since 1880*. New York: Dutton, 1978.

Headrick, Daniel R. 'Sleeping Sickness Epidemics and Colonial Responses in East and Central Africa, 1900–1940'. *PLOS Neglected Tropical Diseases* 8, no. 4 (2014): e2772. https://doi.org/10.1371/journal.pntd.0002772

Hoppe, Kirk Arden. 'Lords of the Fly: Colonial Visions and Revisions of African Sleeping-Sickness Environments on Ugandan Lake Victoria, 1906–61'. *Africa: Journal of the International African Institute* 67, no. 1 (1997): 86–105.

Iliffe, John. *A Modern History of Tanganyika*. Cambridge: Cambridge University Press, 1979.

Issa, Amina. 'Malaria and Public Health Measures in Colonial Urban Zanzibar, 1900–1956'. *Hygiea Internationalis* 10, no. 2 (2011): 35–51.

Kjekshus, Helge. *Ecology, Control and Economic Development in East African History: The Case of Tanganyika, 1850–1950*. London: Heinemann, 1977.

Lyons, Maryinez. *The Colonial Disease: A Social History of Sleeping Sickness in Northern Zaire, 1900–1940*. Cambridge: Cambridge University Press, 2002.

MacKenzie, John M. 'Experts and Amateurs: Tsetse, Nagana and Sleeping Sickness in East and Central Africa'. In *Imperialism and the Natural World*, edited by John M. MacKenzie. Manchester: Manchester University Press, 1990.

Mbopi-Keou, Francois-Xavier, Laurent Bélec, Jean-Marie Milleliri and Chong-Gee Teo. 'The Legacies of Eugène Jamot and La Jamotique'. *PLoS Neglected Tropical Diseases* 8, no. 4 (2014): e2635. https://doi.org/10.1371/journal.pntd.0002635

McGregor, Joanne and Terence Ranger. 'Displacement and Disease: Epidemics and Ideas about Malaria in Matabeleland, Zimbabwe, 1945–1996'. *Past & Present*, no. 167 (2000): 203–37.

McKelvey, John. *Man against Tsetse: Struggle for Africa*. Ithaca: Cornell University Press, 1973.

Musere, Jonathan. *African Sleeping Sickness: Political Ecology, Colonialism and Control in Uganda*. Lewiston: Edwin Mellen Press, 1990.

Najera, J. A. 'Malaria and the Work of WHO'. *Bulletin of the World Health Organization* 67, no. 3 (1989): 229–43.

Neill, Deborah Joy. *Networks in Tropical Medicine: Internationalism, Colonialism, and the Rise of a Medical Specialty, 1890–1930*. Stanford: Stanford University Press, 2012.

Packard, Randall M. *The Making of a Tropical Disease: A Short History of Malaria*. Baltimore: Johns Hopkins University Press, 2007.

Packard, Randall M. "'Roll Back Malaria, Roll in Development"? Reassessing the Economic Burden of Malaria'. *Population and Development Review* 35, no. 1 (2009): 53–87.

Palmer, Jennifer J., Ann H. Kelly, Elizeous I. Surur, Francesco Checchi and Caroline Jones. 'Changing Landscapes, Changing Practice: Negotiating Access to Sleeping Sickness Services in a Post-Conflict Society'. *Social Science & Medicine*, 1982, 120 (November 2014): 396–404.

Park, Mungo. *Travels of Mungo Park*, edited by Ronald Miller. First published 1799. London: J M Dent & Sons Ltd, 1954.

Patterson, K. David. *Health in Colonial Ghana: Disease, Medicine, and Socio-Economic Change, 1900–1955*. Waltham: Crossroads Press, 1981.

Perry, Alex. *Lifeblood: How to Change the World, One Dead Mosquito at a Time*. London: C. Hurst & Co., 2011.

Roberts, Jonathan. 'Korle and the Mosquito: Histories and Memories of the Anti-Malaria Campaign in Accra, 1942–5'. *The Journal of African History* 51, no. 3 (2010): 343–65.

Smith, James, Emma Michelle Taylor and Pete Kingsley. 'One World-One Health and Neglected Zoonotic Disease: Elimination, Emergence and Emergency in Uganda'. *Social Science & Medicine* 129 (2015): 12–19.

Snow, Robert W., Jean-Francois Trape and Kevin Marsh. 'The Past, Present and Future of Childhood Malaria Mortality in Africa'. *Trends in Parasitology* 17, no. 12 (2001): 593–7.

Snow, Robert W., Punam Amratia, Caroline W. Kabaria, Abdisalan M. Noor and Kevin Marsh. 'The Changing Limits and Incidence of Malaria in Africa: 1939–2009'. *Advances in Parasitology* 78 (2012): 169–262.

Tilley, Helen. *Africa as a Living Laboratory: Empire, Development, and the Problem of Scientific Knowledge, 1870–1950*. Chicago: University of Chicago Press, 2011.

Vail, Leroy. 'Ecology and History: The Example of Eastern Zambia'. *Journal of Southern African Studies* 3, no. 2 (1977): 129–55.

Webb, James L.A. *Humanity's Burden: A Global History of Malaria*. Cambridge: University Press, 2009.

Webel, Mari K. 'Trypanosomiasis, Tropical Medicine, and the Practices of Inter-Colonial Research at Lake Victoria, 1902–07'. *History and Technology* 35, no. 3 (2019): 266–92.

White, Luise. 'Tsetse Visions: Narratives of Blood and Bugs in Colonial Northern Rhodesia, 1931–9'. *The Journal of African History* 36, no. 2 (1995): 219–45.

Worboys, Michael. 'The Comparative History of Sleeping Sickness in East and Central Africa, 1900–1914'. *History of Science* 32, no. 1 (1 March 1994): 89–102.

Worboys, Michael. 'Germs, Malaria and the Invention of Mansonian Tropical Medicine: From "Diseases in the Tropics" to "Tropical Diseases"'. In *Warm Climates and Western Medicine: The Emergence of Tropical Medicine, 1500–1900*, edited by David Arnold. Amsterdam: Rodopi, 1996.

Woster, Donald. *Nature's Economy: A History of Ecological Ideas*. Cambridge: Cambridge University Press, 1994.

CHAPTER 7
OCCUPATIONAL LUNG DISEASE AND ECONOMIC EXPLOITATION IN SOUTH AFRICA

Introduction

In March 2003, Cape plc, the South African subsidiary of the British company Cape Asbestos, agreed to a once-off compensation settlement of £7.5 million for 7,500 claimants suffering from asbestos-related illnesses. This represented an outcome that was 'welcomed' by claimants and community groups such as Concerned People Against Asbestos and Action for Southern Africa (ACTSA), which had helped galvanize support in South Africa and in Britain, where much of the legal action surrounding the case took place. There were some important 'firsts' in the legal journey towards this settlement. The impending trial, which was negated by the out-of-court settlement, was itself possible only because the British High Court determined that Cape plc could be tried in the UK rather than in South Africa. In July 2000, five Law Lords had decided unanimously in favour of five former Cape plc workers suffering from asbestos-related illnesses, on the grounds that the plaintiffs were likely not to receive justice if tried in South Africa due to the lack of appropriate legal aid. This was the first time that an overseas subsidiary of a British parent company could be brought to court in Britain.[1]

Few, if any, saw the final 2003 settlement as a clear victory for the claimants and their families. The settlement did not allow for future claims by un-registered claimants. Furthermore, as noted by Ngoaka Ramathlodi, the then-Premier of Limpompo province (where many of the claimants resided), 'Once the money is divided amongst the claimants, it will amount to next to nothing.' Aditi Sharma of ACTSA decried Cape plc's evasion of legal responsibility as well as its lack of commitment to dispose of toxic asbestos dumps left behind, even as the monetary settlement signalled Cape plc's partial acknowledgement of the plight of its former workers:

> The Truth and Reconciliation Commission identified the mining industry as central to apartheid's continuation. Multinational companies like Cape [plc] should be ashamed that they still deny their responsibility to make reparations to devastated communities. While this settlement is welcome, children in the Northern Cape and Limpopo have no alternative but to continue to play in asbestos dust in years to come.'[2]

The lustre on the settlement fades further in the context that the company had two years earlier agreed a settlement for a far greater sum of money (£21 million), but had failed to pay out the promised funds to the claimants – the company blamed financial restructuring and failure to secure loans from British banks to cover the settlement. In the two years that the company dragged its heels, more than 200 of the original claimants passed away.

What does this sobering tale reveal? On the one hand, the development of a more globalized judicial-legislative framework that could implicate South African subsidiaries of powerful multi nationals has provided new hope for compensation for the many thousands of South Africans suffering from compensable forms of occupational disease. The activism of non-governmental organizations who sought to rally a local as well as a global audience to the cause of these claimants further shows how older activist networks have found a new and powerful stage through which the legacies and inequities of global capital and apartheid economic engineering could be addressed. Yet, the tempering of any sense of triumph in the reactions of the 'victors' clearly reveals that communities and their advocates feel that the war is far from won, particularly when powerful companies can utilize a host of legal and financial mechanisms to avoid or delay compensation, including what could only be viewed as a callous waiting game for claimants with life-shortening illnesses to simply die. The final aspect of this story is that it is not new. In many ways, this account sits in the long shadow cast by the workings, for more than a century, of global capital on the lives and bodies of southern Africans, a painful legacy sharpened by the recognized ties between the mining industry and the apartheid state (1948–94). The more recent Marikana massacre in 2012 at Lonmin Mines, which began as a mineworkers' strike to address poor working conditions and ended with a violent response by police with thirty-four miners dead, has further shown that the associated ills of the mining industry cannot be relegated to the 'past' as one of the forgotten evils of apartheid.

This chapter focuses on occupational disease, particularly the history of lung disease contracted through labouring on the gold, diamond and asbestos mines of South Africa – this includes non-communicable lung diseases such as asbestosis and silicosis, as well as the infectious disease tuberculosis. Although the geographical focus is South Africa and its mining industries, this history has much broader implications – South African mines were a significant magnet drawing African workers from southern and Central Africa, including Mozambique, Lesotho, Malawi and Swaziland. The particular system of labour migration that the mining industry helped generate was one of the most powerful dynamics that shaped southern African history, through its sheer numbers as well as its manifold social, economic and health consequences. As has been noted at numerous points in this book, mobility is an enabler of disease, and the migrant labour system was one of the most significant conduits of disease (and diseased bodies) in the region.

The scale of occupational disease, its devastating health consequences and its link with the systematic economic exploitation of the African population merit further research and a central place in any book that concerns itself with the history of African health. In 2006 it was estimated there were almost half a million ex-mineworkers in southern

Africa suffering from work-related lung disease, with compensation due amounting to ZAR 2.8 billion.[3] However, apart from a handful of fairly recent disease-specific studies – most notably by Randall Packard (on tuberculosis), Elaine Katz (on silicosis) and Jock McCulloch (on asbestosis) – occupational lung disease is hidden from the medical history of Africa. The primary reason for its relative hiddenness in history is the paucity of morbidity and mortality statistics. The absence of data is particularly striking from the late nineteenth century until the interwar period, although even mid-twentieth-century statistics are questionable. These gaps are largely due to the lack of adequate screening measures for most of this earlier period and the persistent policy of the 'repatriation' of ill black labourers to their rural natal 'homes', as will be discussed later in this chapter. Thus, urban and specifically mine-related incidence of disease was probably vastly under-reported. Historians, then, need to rely on data from hospital records and reports from state and local medical officers and health inspectors, mining industry records, and legislative and judiciary sources. Although the relevant mining ministry (first established as the Department of Mining in 1891 and evolved in both title and portfolio, becoming the Department of Minerals and Energy in 1997 in the new democratic government) in South Africa left a sizeable archival trail in the form of annual reports and 'Inspector's Reports', these were problematic in their own right. For example, with respect to asbestos, Inspector Reports from the crucial period 1960–80 went 'missing', which further undermined efforts to historically reconstruct asbestos-related health impacts in this period.[4]

Another reason for this hiddenness is the particular orientation of the study of occupational disease within the wider field of African medical history. Analyses of occupational disease tend to be centrally concerned with the interaction between workers' health, the state and industry, and have primarily utilized 'political economy' approaches to examine this nexus. Whilst illuminating, a materialist or class-based approach has not proven as popular amongst historians in recent decades as other interdisciplinary approaches that have more centrally emphasized symbolism, discourse and subjectivity, exemplified in the historiography of mental illness and STDs (see Chapters 4 and 5). However, these discursive and interdisciplinary approaches have proved less amenable to the study of 'mundane' yet pervasive killers such as occupational disease.[5] Occupational disease remains a significant and under-represented public health challenge in sub-Saharan Africa in the twenty-first century, and this chapter is reflective of recent efforts to provide a historical corrective to this narrative.

Finally, this chapter's efforts to examine as a collective the histories of tuberculosis, silicosis and asbestosis acknowledge the historical and bodily entwinement of these diseases. Mineworkers often suffer the debilitating effects of tuberculosis and silicosis in combination, and they are mutually reinforcing diseases. Silicosis significantly facilitates the onset and development of tuberculosis in the infected person's lungs. Indeed, the affliction commonly known in the late nineteenth century as 'miners' pthisis' gradually became understood as a secondary stage lung disease that moves from an initial 'uncomplicated' silicosis to include an active tuberculosis element – a 1938 international conference on silicosis confirmed that a majority of fatal pthisis cases had active tuberculosis in their lungs.⁶ Moreover, the history of compensatory claims against mining companies illustrates that these diseases are linked. Particularly with respect to asbestosis and silicosis, gold mining houses and asbestos companies have kept abreast of legal developments on compensable lung disease as a whole across the mining sector, and legal advocates as well as claimants stress the commonality of experience (and of exploitation) wrought by lung disease across disease types.

The peculiar history of industrialization in southern Africa

It is necessary to understand the peculiarities of industrialization in southern Africa in order to contextualize the particular disease trajectories that emerged from the late nineteenth century onwards. The discoveries of diamonds in Kimberley (in 1867) and of gold in the Witwatersrand (in 1886) were the initial sparks which ignited processes of industrialization and urbanization, and drew in labour from surrounding regions both within and outside of South Africa to these fast-growing conurbations. In the two and a half decades following the discovery of gold, the population of the greater Witwatersrand area ballooned to half a million and the city of Johannesburg had become a thriving metropolis of 240,000.⁷

Historians of southern Africa have argued that it was the rapidity and intensity of the industrialization that followed these initial mineral discoveries which marked it apart from the industrializing patterns in other regions of the continent. A unique confluence of factors drove the twin transformative forces of industrialization and urbanization. By the late nineteenth century, the British colonial regime had violently subdued local African resistance throughout its colonial territories and forced an orientation towards cash-based economies and administrations through measures such as the imposition of hut taxes. This combined with the pronounced generational and gendered moral-political order within southern African societies, and facilitated the 'push' of young male Africans into the urban proletarianized workforce and the compelling of their monetary remittances back towards rural economies. Declining African control over land and other means of agrarian production, symbolized most pointedly by the Natives Land Act of 1913 in South Africa, which formalized the gross alienation of land from Africans in favour of white settlers, made it more difficult for an African peasantry to maintain livelihoods for their families and further propelled the forces of proletarianization. Africans became, in increasing numbers, waged labourers on white-owned farmlands or part of the wave of wage-seekers flocking to urban areas. Certainly, the injection of ready-made international capital through powerful mining houses such as De Beers and Anglo American contributed to the scale and intensity of industrialization in southern Africa, as did the relative lack of pre-colonial local forms of urbanisms that had existed, for example in West Africa, which could act as a counter-balance to these more recent and Western forms of urban intensification.

Furthermore, as came to be evident soon after the initial euphoria of the discovery of gold in the Witwatersrand, the relatively poor quality of the gold and the high technical sophistication necessary to extract the ore and process it meant that profit margins were, and continue to be, notoriously slim. The seam of gold in the Rand required deep drilling and the use of explosives, both extremely hazardous. Low-grade ore required a further expensive chemical processing to extract the gold that could be sold on the market. The fixed and relatively high cost of converting this low-grade gold ore mined under expensive and hazardous conditions has meant that the focus of mining houses, and the government-supported mining industry as a whole, historically has been on suppressing the cost of the main variable they had power over – the price of labour. This would have significant health consequences for African mineworkers.

The solution to the 'problem' of the price of labour in the nascent mining sector was, in effect, systematizing a form of labour migration. The migrant labour system emerged in the late nineteenth century to ensure a steady and cyclical flow of cheap labour to the mines and surrounding urban areas, although in its full flowering by mid-twentieth century the migrant labour system became the main conduit of labour to other major metropoles in South Africa such as the port cities of Cape Town, Port Elizabeth and Durban. Central to the functioning of the system in the mining context was the use of short-term contracts by mining houses to employ African labourers. These temporary contracts were designed to be coupled with an enforced period of a few months back 'home' at the contract's end in the labourer's natal area of origin. In theory these contracts were renewable, although mineworkers seldom if ever returned to the same employer. This was an opportune arrangement for mining houses, who did not have to provide more than the most rudimentary residential accommodation for their male labourers. These contracts also represented a convenient cost-saving device for the South African state and for fledgling municipalities, who would then not be compelled to devote significant funds towards the creation and maintenance of a viable urban infrastructure, including schools and hospitals, if African families remained decidedly rural-based.

Importantly, the health myth that underpinned these temporary contracts was that African labourers would use the time 'off' to recoup their strength through the fresh air and sustenance provided by rural-dwelling family members. Furthermore, sending mineworkers back 'home' periodically was believed to be a form of disease prevention, in that any of the ill-effects of working in hazardous conditions could be counteracted by a lengthy period distant from the source of those conditions. Both these myths – of the inherent healthiness of green and 'untouched' rural societies, as well as the supposed regenerative benefits of time spent away from the mines – would be exposed as falsehoods in decades to come. In reality, the social and economic forces unleashed by the imposition of the migrant labour system helped to shape the declining agricultural productivity and increased poverty of the rural areas. Instead of the idealized image of workers recuperating back to full health in rural havens, sick and convalescent miners were sent back to die in impoverished rural communities, where the communicable diseases labourers brought with them, such as tuberculosis, found captive and vulnerable populations.

The social, material and physical consequences of the migrant labour system on southern African societies were profound. The migrant labour system expanded

Historical Source: *Sefala* song by Lethetsa Malimatle, in David B. Coplan, *In the Time of Cannibals: The World Music of South Africa's Basotho Migrants* (1994)

I left home at night
When the cocks were crowing;
Further, crowing the first cocks,
The second crew while on the way,
The third ones as I was passing the Phuthiatsana [River]
I entered Maseru, in town yonder
When the sun touched the mountains,
B.A. Maseru at Mejametalana.
Me, at seven in the morning I was hired,
Then at eight cows were milked.
At nine schools were in [session]
At ten I was taken to the doctor:
It was 'Mokose,' my companions.
He put a metal [stethoscope] on the chest here,
I breathed twice he was satisfied:
'alright! Child of Malimatle,
There is nothing my brother,
Go and drive them at the mines yonder.'
Masimphane is a man, he works

Source Analysis: Sefala *songs are poems of comradeship shared amongst the Basotho people of southern Africa. They are a creative and oral form of popular memory. In this* sefala, *part of a collection of songs compiled by the anthropologist David Coplan, the narrator reflects on his steps towards becoming a 'hired' labourer on the mines. The narrator utilizes numerical and temporal frameworks in a striking yet highly controlled fashion. Each sequential step of the journey to Maseru is punctuated by an event. Once in town, each hour is marked by a similar cadence – 'at seven in the morning I was hired, then at eight cows were milked'. In the course of a day, through these seemingly mundane steps, the narrator sees himself undertake a radical transformation – from a 'Child of Malimatle' to a miner who 'works'.*

Historical sources such as these are invaluable in capturing the lived experience of migrancy and minework. They also help recover details relevant to the occupational health history of minework in southern Africa. For example, this sefala *describes the rudimentary medical examination the would-be miner underwent to be approved for minework, as well as the simple diagnostic technology employed (the stethoscope). These basic medical procedures were indicative of the under-resourcing of health services in the mining industry, and led to failures in adequately diagnosing lung diseases as they progressed in mineworkers' bodies as they moved back and forth between mining areas and their rural 'homes'.*

manyfold the geographical corridors through which disease travelled. In urban areas, it enabled the mixing of large populations from across southern Africa – Mozambique was a particularly vital source of mining labour, and 'foreign' workers comprised over half of the Rand's labour force from the late nineteenth century until 1910 – which brought with it the mixing of different disease environments.[8] And the movement of sick migrants back to their 'home' areas enabled diseases like tuberculosis (and later HIV) to take root in 'virgin' rural populations, although we should acknowledge the migrant labour system never fulfilled its idealized incarnation as a fully circular process and migrants and their households instead re-orientated or 'stretched' themselves in complex ways across both rural and urban poles.[9] Furthermore, the deepening of malnutrition as a result of the declining agricultural productivity of the rural areas across the twentieth century and the influx of nutritionally poor foodstuffs available in a monetized food economy increased the vulnerability to disease of rural populations and of the migrants they produced.[10]

Miners' health in southern African history

> Mountain-Mashai, it fell on people [miners]
> It's there a hundred men died.
> It's me who survived, a cannibal of a man.
> I alone survived among that tribe [of corpses].
> I was pulling corpses from under rocks.
> People's children have rotted; they smell.
> They already swarm with maggots –.
> No, but these mine affairs, you can leave them.
> A *sefala* song by Majara Majara (Ngoana Rakhali)[11]

Minework and conditions in, on and around the mines

The narrow confines of the mine-shaft were marked by extreme hazards. The threat of death or injury from dynamite explosions, failure of machinery or the collapse of mine-shafts were routine risks associated with deep-level minework. Little longitudinal recorded data exist on injury and death through mining accidents. However, it is evident that on the Rand at the turn to the twentieth century, mining companies began to make provisions for cemeteries on mine property to inter those who died while working on the mines. As shown by Tshidiso Maloka, Basotho miners in the early decades of the twentieth century evolved unique moral and ritual responses to the mortal dangers posed by this hazardous environment. As dead miners were sent to mine morgues and subject to medical autopsies, rumours circulated that whites would use African body parts for their own harmful 'medicines'. Autopsies themselves were viewed as cannibalistic intrusions into mortal bodies – indeed, the seSotho word for an operating theatre is *madimong*, which translates to 'the place of the cannibals'.[12] As Majara's *sefala* song, above, attests, these consumptive processes could also transform labourers themselves – from a miner into a soulless vestige of himself, 'a cannibal of a man' who survives mine collapses but is forced to pull the bodies of his fellow miners out.

Apart from the spectre of accidental death, minework itself could pre-dispose labourers to disease. Dynamite blasting, machine drilling and the shovelling of dry ore, all conducted in humid, high-temperature environments with little if any ventilation, significantly increased the risks of fine silica dust entering into minerworkers' lungs – this was already widely known by the first quarter century of gold-mining on the Rand.[13] In 1910 the introduction of axial drills, which used water to cut down on dust generated by drill work, meant that mine-shafts became an even damper environment. It is questionable whether axial drills were efficacious in getting rid of the finest dust particles, which were the most hazardous if inhaled. However, what is without doubt is that the introduction of water-fed drills increased the risk of tuberculosis transmission, by multiplying exponentially air-borne droplets which could serve to transmit tuberculous bacteria.[14] Miners emerging from these damp conditions would be exposed to the cold temperatures, which could easily reach below freezing in winter, and become more susceptible to influenza, which had the added consequence of activating dormant tuberculosis.

As well as being exposed on a daily basis to the close, dusty, damp and dark quarters of the mine-shaft, mineworkers on the Rand were housed in single-sex dormitory-style hostels which tended to be divided amongst ethnic lines, although many labourers also resided in the numerous informal settlements which sprang up in the shadow of the mine dumps on the Rand, like the fictional 'Malay Camp' colourfully depicted in Peter Abraham's popular novel, *Mine Boy* (1946). Along with miners' barracks at the diamond mines of Kimberley, Rand mining compounds were characterized by their confined, crowded and poorly ventilated spaces as well as the lack of adequate sanitation, all of which facilitated the transfer of communicable diseases. South African miners' living quarters were markedly different from the family-style housing that was offered to Copperbelt miners in both the Congo and northern Rhodesia (now Zambia) in the late colonial period in the hopes of encouraging the reproduction of the labour force (see Chapter 2).[15]

Poor living and working conditions were ideal for the transmission of not only tuberculosis and influenza, but also (particularly in mining's early decades) hookworm and typhoid. Scurvy was also prevalent in the early years of mining because of the poor nutrition afforded to miners, and scurvy reduces resistance to tuberculosis, as does poor levels of vitamin A. In the early years of the mining industry, the financing for food tended to be left to miners and not supplied by mining companies, which meant that workers on limited budgets would protect their meagre earnings by purchasing cheaper and less nutritious foodstuffs – foregoing protein and fresh fruit and vegetables for carbohydrate-heavy and nutritionally deficient meals. Some attempts at dietary reforms were introduced after 1906, when a recommended minimum diet to be supplied by mining houses was introduced by the Native Affairs Department. However, even this diet was severely lacking in protein and fats, and relied primarily on a disproportionate

Figure 7.1 Photograph by David Goldblatt, *Water has been intersected at the shaft bottom: The team drills deep cover holes into which cement grout will be pumped to staunch the flow. President Steyn No.4 Shaft. Welkom, Orange Free State, 1969/1970.* Courtesy of the David Goldblatt Legacy Trust and Goodman Gallery. Copyright: The David Goldblatt Legacy Trust.

Figure 7.2 Photograph by David Goldblatt, *Masotho shaftsinking Machine Man, President Steyn No. 4, Welkom,* 1969. Courtesy of the David Goldblatt Legacy Trust and Goodman Gallery. Copyright: The David Goldblatt Legacy Trust.

Historical Source: Photographs by David Goldblatt. *Water has been intersected at the shaft bottom: The team drills deep cover holes into which cement grout will be pumped to staunch the flow. President Steyn No.4 Shaft, Welkom, Orange Free State (1969/70); Masotho shaftsinking Machine Man, President Steyn No. 4, Welkom (1969).*

Source Analysis: David Goldblatt (1930–2018) was an internationally renowned South African documentary photographer. He is particularly noted for his striking series of photographs detailing a vibrant and emotionally rich urban African existence during the mid-twentieth century, a period when apartheid's racialized structures regimented and suppressed African lives and livelihoods. The city of Welkom was established in 1948, several years after a seam of gold (part of the same gold reef system as in the Rand) was discovered running deep beneath this area, hastening the creation of new mining ventures.

Through the blurred outlines of the miners, Goldblatt evokes the wet working environment of shaftsinking as well as the dynamic movement of the mineworkers assembled. This photograph also gives a sense of the rudimentary protection offered to mineworkers in this period – the mineworkers wear very minimal protective equipment and there is little evidence of safety features in place, for example to protect against falls at height. In the portrait of the maSotho 'shaftsinker', the dust generated by underground drilling is clearly evident in the fine coating left on his work clothes and helmet.

These visual sources comprise an 'alternative archive' for African medical history, more specifically histories of occupational risk and disease. It was the particular combination of exposure to extremely damp and dusty working conditions that made mines ready incubators of a host of respiratory diseases. These photographs also portray a striking human element that is not readily available in the textual archive. For example, the steady gaze and calm demeanour of the shaftsinker are made more poignant when set against oral histories of Basotho mineworkers of the same time. As Jeff Guy and Motlatsi Thabane's study has shown, oral sources suggest Basotho regarded themselves as particularly suited (physically and mentally) for the arduous and hazardous task of shaftsinking, and indeed took pride in being the first to descend into the mine's depths.

quantity of 'mealie meal', a maize-based foodstuff. Historians have begun to examine this larger shift among southern African societies towards maize-dependence in the twentieth century, and its links to nutritional deficiencies and associated diseases, such as pellagra.[16] Changes in diet, though, did not have an appreciable effect on the timing of their meals. By in large throughout this period and into the mid-twentieth century, miners continued to eat their main meals after emerging from the mine-shaft, and thus performed the entirety of their heavy labour on largely empty stomachs.[17]

Tuberculosis – the archetypical disease of labour migration

The characterization of tuberculosis as a product of industrialization was by the late nineteenth century well established in the history of Europe. It is generally accepted by historians that tuberculosis was an imported disease brought by European immigrants and was not endemic in the southern African region. Tuberculosis spread rapidly amongst 'unseasoned' southern African populations in the late nineteenth century. Many of the Cornish miners who made up the majority of the white minework force in the early decades of the South African mining industry came with tuberculosis, and its mutually reinforcing nature with silicosis meant that tuberculosis infections became 'reactivated' and then spread to black miners who were working under conditions of high physical stress with little access to appropriate nutrition or housing. From 1902 to 1907, it was recorded that 18 per cent of mortality amongst African mineworkers could be attributed to tuberculosis.[18]

Tuberculosis: The basics

Tuberculosis is a disease caused by the inhalation of *Mycobacterium tuberculosis*. It is normally spread by prolonged close contact with someone who has 'active' tuberculosis. The World Health Organization estimates that up to a quarter of the global population has 'latent' tuberculosis, which is not infective to others but may develop from its latent form into active tuberculosis over time. In an immuno-compromised individual, or in situations of personal stress and malnutrition, the 'primary complex' or latent tuberculosis can become destabilized and lead to active tuberculosis and acute infection. Symptoms of active tuberculosis include coughing, chest pains, fever and weight loss. If left untreated, tuberculosis can lead to disability and death.

The diagnosis of tuberculosis in many lower and middle income countries is done through the conventional laboratory-based method of analyzing sputum (phlegm) through a microscope. However, this method cannot detect all cases and can not identify whether the tuberculosis is of a drug-resistant strain. WHO has recommended the use of advanced diagnostic procedures which detect tuberculosis on a molecular level as well as identify whether the strain is drug-resistant.

Tuberculosis can be treated through antibiotics. Although the main form of tuberculosis is curable, drug adherence is a challenge, as infected patients normally need to take multiple medications regularly over the course of six months to be fully cured. Drug resistance is increasingly a concern world-wide, and multi-drug-resistant tuberculosis (MDR-TB) and extensively drug-resistant tuberculosis (XDR-TB) have been identified as health security threats. Medication is available to treat and cure MDR-TB – however, these 'second-line' drugs are expensive, have toxic side effects and may require a much longer course of treatment (up to two years). There is currently no cure for XDR-TB.

Africans were uniquely pathologized, as scientific understanding of the complex aetiology of tuberculosis was fused with Darwinist notions of 'natural selection' in segregationist South Africa in the 1920s and 1930s, as Randall Packard has shown. This 'virgin soil' theory, which was prevalent in medical circles at the time, framed Africans as uniquely susceptible to tuberculosis compared to Europeans, by virtue of Europeans' longer historic exposure to the disease.[19] Africans, the theory went, thus could gain resistance only through hereditary traits, which as a convenient consequence for mining authorities and municipalities meant that improvements in housing, nutrition and sanitation measures for African communities would likely have little appreciable effect on tuberculosis infection rates.

Tuberculosis incidence as well as mortality rates were acknowledged to have increased dramatically in urban areas in the interwar and post-Second World War periods. It also spread to rural areas of southern Africa in significant numbers – by the early 1950s tuberculosis was established, and in some areas of the Transkei and Orange Free State its prevalence in local populations over five years old was recorded at over 2 per cent.[20] The growth in tuberculosis prevalence in rural areas was due to concurrent factors including overcrowding, growing malnutrition, environmental degradation and declining agricultural production, all of which led to the general impoverishment of rural communities, and policies which tended to remove rural people's abilities to build up food supplies as a bulwark against food scarcity or famine. In the Eastern Cape, where cattle was held not only as a social and sacred commodity but also as an important supply of milk for the local population, milk consumption declined rapidly because of the imposition of native creameries which encouraged Africans to send away rather than consume milk. This combined with an increased consumption of nutrient-poor products and refined sugars, which had been introduced to southern African societies in the nineteenth century.[21]

Silicosis: From 'white death' to 'black death'

Historically, particularly in the early decades of mining activity in South Africa, exposure to hazardous mining conditions and occupational disease was not confined to African labourers. Europeans, particularly working-class immigrants from Europe, such as the well-known influx of Cornish miners from England, were vulnerable to ill-health as well. In South Africa, silicosis was highly publicized and appeared to be an affliction borne by white miners at a far greater rate than black miners. Its particular racialized characteristics and its high mortality rate were enshrined in the moniker given to silicosis at the time – the 'white death'.[22] The mortality rate for silicosis was higher than that experienced in the same time span by the British Army during the South African War (1899–1902). A white mineworker in this period had a life span, on average, twenty-eighty years shorter than that of the general white male population.[23] The idea of 'native immunity', so prominent in debates across colonial Africa over malaria transmission (see Chapter 6), was a salient theme in contemporary discussions of the white death in South Africa, as it appeared that Africans were somehow less vulnerable to the disease. It is now understood that the

Silicosis: The basics

Silicosis is a lung disease caused by long-term exposure to silica dust. It occurs in three forms: acute silicosis, which results in a cough, shortness of breath, fatigue and weight loss, and can appear from within weeks to years after exposure to silica; chronic silicosis, which results in lung swelling and difficulty breathing, and can appear 10 to 30 years after exposure; and accelerated silicosis, which occurs within 10 years of exposure. Silica inhalation creates an inflammatory reaction in the lungs, which over time can cause progressive scarring of lung tissue and makes it difficult to breathe. In extreme cases, progressive massive fibrosis may result, characterized by stiffened dense masses within the lungs, and can be fatal.

Silicosis is diagnosed by a chest X-ray or CT-scan, as well as through lung biopsy and scoping procedures. There is no cure for silicosis. Treatments such as oxygen support and steroid inhalers are focused on the alleviation of symptoms. Lung transplants may be a potential intervention for those with acute silicosis – however, there are considerable risks and prohibitive expenses associated with organ transplant procedures.

apparent 'immunity' of Africans masked a large incidence of silicosis amongst African miners which was not recorded in either industry or health authority statistics, because ill miners were either sent back or voluntarily left for 'home' and died in their rural areas of origin without a verified diagnosis of silicosis. One estimate is that between 1902 and 1930, about 108,000 black miners in South Africa died of injury and disease on the mines, although this figure does not count mortality from repatriated miners or differentiate between diseases.[24]

White miners were able to utilize their political clout and unionized to vocally advocate for their own interests, including better living and working conditions. Powerful and crippling strikes in 1907 and 1913–14 brought instability to the mining industry and prompted a vigorous response by the state and mining magnates. The South African state passed a series of laws in the 1910s which provided a firm legal framework for compensation for miners' phthisis, and included regular medical examinations, the provision of healthcare on site and paid annual leave.[25] However, these concessions were not applied to the many thousands more black mineworkers on the same premises. By the 1920s, white workers' living conditions and pay had improved, and the improvement of their health outcomes soon followed in measurable ways.

Thus, there is a shift in the understanding of silicosis in the South African historical context, from 'white death' to 'black death'. In small part, the shift is underpinned by the marked reduction in mortality amongst white miners by the 1920s and 1930s. However, silicosis itself did not progress from affecting one racial population to another, but marked *both* white and black mineworkers' bodies in time, its severity dependent on exposure to unsafe dust levels in the mine-shaft and access to adequate healthcare and medical inspections, and not on any inherent native immunity to the disease. Mining companies' repatriation policy, which sent morbidly ill miners to die far away from the compounds, led to a profound undercounting of incidence of silicosis amongst black mineworkers and reinforced the false view of native immunity to the disease.

Asbestosis mining – individual and community exposure

In South Africa, mines began producing asbestos in 1893, although full production was not attained until the First World War. Asbestos was in high demand by the end of the nineteenth century – it was an extremely versatile product with characteristics (able to withstand high temperatures, light-weight and strong) which made it the material of choice for a range of industrial and construction uses. In South Africa, asbestos 'mills' had much of its operations at ground-level and were predominantly geared towards sorting and bagging asbestos fibres, which could be divided many times over into progressively thinner and longer strands. At their peak, South African mills produced 97 per cent of the global supply of blue asbestos. In contrast to the gold and diamond mining industries, which historically employed male labour, asbestos mills employed women as well as men, and also juveniles (under the age of sixteen) which in one asbestos mine

Asbestosis and mesothelioma: The basics

Asbestosis is a chronic respiratory disorder and results from exposure to tiny asbestos fibres which lodge in the lung's alveoli (the tiny air sacs that facilitate oxygen and carbon dioxide exchange) and produce scarring. Over time, the scarring builds up, making it increasingly difficult for the lungs to expand and contract.

Asbestosis and mesothelioma have a long latency period, and it can take from ten to forty years post-exposure for the diseases to develop. Although the underlying cause of asbestosis and mesothelioma is the same – asbestos exposure – and having asbestosis greatly increases one's risk for mesothelioma, they are different in key respects. Unlike asbestosis, mesothelioma is a cancer and develops when asbestos fibres affect the lungs' lining (rather than the alveoli). The symptoms of mesothelioma are more severe than asbestosis, and prognosis for mesothelioma is fatal, with life expectancy usually less than a year from diagnosis.

Diagnosis for both diseases involves an imaging scan, normally an X-ray or CT-scan of the lungs, alongside a detailed occupational history to determine the extent of possible asbestos exposure. With mesothelioma, an additional biopsy and blood test are taken to confirm the presence of cancerous cells. There is no cure for asbestosis – it is an irreversible condition. Treatments are focused on slowing down the disease's progression and relieving symptoms – shortness of breath, chest pain and coughing – with treatments ranging from inhalers and supplemental oxygen to pulmonary medication.

in South Africa in 1940 amounted to a quarter of the workforce.[26] Young hands were considered able to separate the fine fibres more easily and efficiently. The employment of juveniles in combination with women, who brought the children under their care with them, meant that exposure to harmful levels of asbestos fibres was not limited by gender or age. Surface-level mills also meant that the wider environmental fallout from asbestos production affected entire communities, which became enveloped in a characteristic blue haze caused by asbestos fibres.

As early as 1928, medical research in South Africa had established that lung disease was present amongst asbestos labourers – twenty-three out of hundred asbestos mill workers had lung disease in one study, nearly a quarter of the study's population. At mid-century, asbestos mining moved from surface level to deep-shaft mining, but the diverse demographic composition of the asbestos labour force continued. Women and children continued to play an important role in asbestos sorting, and continued to be exposed to hazardous levels of asbestos fibres. The growing awareness of the harmfulness of asbestos as a material led to a declining global demand for asbestos from the 1970s. However, asbestos mining in South Africa endured well into the late twentieth century.

Thinking through the 'gaps' in the history of occupational disease

The human toll of occupational lung disease radiated outwards to the 'home' communities of miners, becoming a health crisis in newly affected and infected rural societies. How can we account for its wide scope and its continuance into the twenty-first century? Occupational lung disease in South Africa, perhaps more so than other disease types, suffered from a specific confluence of factors which undermined any effective response to these diseases. A better understanding of these 'gaps' can reveal how occupational lung disease became such a significant hazard for black miners over the course of the twentieth century.

Gaps in knowledge

All three of the diseases that are the focus of this chapter – silicosis, asbestosis and tuberculosis – are complex diseases whose aetiology and inter-relationship with other diseases are not fully understood in the twenty-first century. Cures do not yet exist for silicosis or asbestosis, and treatment is merely geared towards easing the symptoms of sufferers. With respect to silicosis, historically the knowledge of the link between levels of dust inhaled and the period of exposure to the development of silicosis has been incomplete as well as imprecise. Also, in the early decades of the twentieth century, when much of the pioneering research on this disease was being done in South Africa and elsewhere, the widespread premise of native immunity meant that the incidence of silicosis amongst black mineworkers went largely undetected and valuable data was not collected. The co-incidence of silicosis and tuberculosis amongst African miners in the early decades of the twentieth century was similarly obscured through highly racialized perceptions that silicosis was a 'white' disease and that, in contrast, Africans were more prone to be tuberculosis 'carriers'. The understanding that silicosis and tuberculosis were mutually reinforcing diseases would not become accepted understanding until the latter half of the twentieth century. By 1930 the first study on asbestosis commissioned by the South African Institute of Medical Research (SAIMR) had been published, and the British asbestos industry knew in basic terms how asbestosis occurred and how to begin to prevent it in the workplace. However, it took nearly twenty years, until 1948, to definitively illustrate the connection between asbestos exposure and the diseases asbestosis and lung cancer.[27]

To acknowledge these gaps in medical knowledge is vital because it allows us to understand why some of the resultant interventions in the realm of health and safety were not effective or were extremely slow in development. For example, the focus on dust produced in asbestos mills came at the expense of attention paid to fibres, in particular the finer fibres (or fibrils) that are the most hazardous to humans. The 'konimeter' instruments used by the Department of Mines for much of the mid-twentieth century were not calibrated to detect these fibrils.[28] Furthermore, scientific research has confirmed that spending time away from the source of silica or asbestos-inhalation does not translate into less susceptibility to disease – silica dust and asbestos fibres which build up over time in one's system cannot simply be flushed out or even reduced with less exposure. This meant that time spent at 'home' by migrant African labourers when their contracts ended made no measurable impact in terms of reducing their vulnerability to occupational lung disease, as mine companies would have wanted to believe. Finally, the lack of understanding of how the tubercle bacillus could be transmitted meant that there was little appreciation of the potentially harmful knock-on effects of introducing water-based measures to reduce exposure to silica dust – as mentioned earlier, the introduction of axial water-based drilling from 1910 helped to create the wet working conditions in the mine-shaft where tuberculosis could easily spread.

Moreover, the temporary contracts that were prevalent amongst black mineworkers prevented medical histories from being accumulated over time. Some Anglo American mines, until as late as 1979, did not keep accounts of their mineworkers' previous employment histories, and did not retain medical records of former employees.[29] New documentation and 'new' medical files, which focused on a mineworker's present medical condition rather than their previous medical history, were generated for each contract. This lack of longitudinal health data on an individual mineworker would have negative consequences for diagnosing, tracking and treating diseases that could develop over the course of the working lifetime of any patient. The slow, years-long progress of lung diseases such as silicosis, and the difficulties involved in diagnosing early stages of these diseases, made the need for such longitudinal data even more pressing.

Gaps between knowledge and legislation

The second 'gap' which is vital to explore is the gap between developing scientific knowledge on occupational lung disease and legislation enacted based on that understanding. As discussed in Chapter 2, colonial administrations in African territories implemented public health policies which were based on incomplete knowledge of medical and scientific advances at the time, or were even at odds with accepted scientific understanding. In other words, there was an *uneven* integration of medical knowledge into colonial practice. Similarly, the South African state was slow to concretize expanding medical knowledge of occupational lung diseases, and the environmental and work conditions that enabled their rapid transmission, into definable legislation. This may in part be due to the inability of medical officers, mines inspectors and scientific researchers to influence the passage of protective legislation and compel the mining industry to act. The South African Institute of Medical Research, founded in 1912, is a case in point. Although SAIMR conducted research on various lung diseases, its independence and the influence of its reports were severely constrained by its close association to the mine industry – it was funded by mine revenue and was staffed by personnel who also worked with the Chamber of Mines and the Department of Mines. A damning report produced by a SAIMR researcher in 1926 on silicosis on the Rand, and its relation to different types of dust, was not acted on.[30]

Also, as discussed earlier in this chapter, improvements in living conditions and pay which helped to address white miners' health in broad terms were only enshrined in legislation after crippling strikes which both demonstrated and consolidated the political power of the white mineworkers constituency. The Mines Act of 1911 was illustrative of the essentially reactive nature of the state in responding to workers' demands for better pay and working conditions, privileging white miners and separating them from the non-white proletarianized, rather than an example of the state attempting to incorporate prevailing scientific understandings of silicosis and tuberculosis into regulatory form.

With respect to the asbestos industry, the South African state consistently claimed that the Mines Act of 1911 did not apply to asbestos fields since they were not underground mines. This was despite conclusive knowledge of its potential hazards since the 1930s. This legislative evasion also meant that women and boys under sixteen, whose employment by gold and diamond mining companies was outlawed by the Mines Act, did not apply to asbestos mills. The asbestos industry was effectively able to escape health regulation until the mid-twentieth century. It was only in 1954 that blue asbestos mines were proclaimed registered mines under the Silicosis Act of 1946, which had mandated medical exams of mineworkers prior to their employment and subsequent regular checks. Following on from this, asbestosis was finally included in the Pneumoconiosis Bureau's list of certifiable diseases, which led to some closures of the worst asbestos mills and new access to mobile X-rays.[31]

Gaps between legislation and implementation

The history of occupational lung disease in South Africa reveals that even when legislation existed, effective implementation of new policies was never guaranteed. For example, the Miners' Phthisis Act of 1912 was instrumental in providing for the health and compensation of exposed white miners. In discussions about how to implement the Act, it was decided that compulsory exams of Native labourers could not be accomplished due to the high expense involved. Those regulations which would have extended medical surveillance to African mineworkers were not published. Furthermore, Africans' rights under the Act were not published in Native languages because that was thought to encourage African labourers to put claims in for compensation.[32] Throughout the twentieth century, until the late 1980s with the growth of a more radical unionism amongst non-white mineworkers, black miners were rarely informed as to their rights of possible compensation for occupational lung disease.

Even if legislation existed, few mines were targeted for unhealthy practices or conditions, and the scale of occupational disease at any given mine was unknown. Few black miners were examined by X-ray before the mid-twentieth century, even though X-rays as a medical technology were available and had been used since the early decades of the century on white miners. Without this technology, a stethoscope-based examination would not be sufficient to reliably diagnose early-stage silicosis and tuberculosis. And, as discussed earlier, mining companies' medical records of their labour force were woefully incomplete and lacked longitudinal consideration of individual medical histories.

It is important to note that African miners absented themselves from some of the medical surveillance mechanisms instituted in mining contexts. African miners were reluctant to be diagnosed for the simple reason that they did not want to lose their jobs. This means they may have concealed symptoms – in the case of silicosis, this could have amounted to years of evasion – until the symptoms became too pronounced to ignore. Compensation was pegged to wages, so black miners would have received far less compensation for the same disease than white miners, and this was the case for much of the twentieth century. The racialized history of compensation makes for grim reading. For example, in terms of silicosis-related compensation, in 1912 white mine workers with first-degree silicosis received £96 compensation, compared to a sliding scale of from £1 to £30 for the same stage silicosis for black mineworkers; for second-degree silicosis, white miners received £400 and black miners received from £30 to £50. In 1978, for first-degree silicosis white mineworkers received ZAR 12,000, compared to ZAR 1,000 for black mineworkers; for second-stage silicosis, white miners were paid ZAR 18,000, a fifteenfold increase from the ZAR 1,200 for black miners. For tuberculosis, white mine labourers were compensated ZAR 5,000 in 1978 versus ZAR 600 for black mineworkers, a factor of more than eight.[33] Unfortunately, although the reluctance to submit to medical examinations is understandable given the paucity of compensation available and the overwhelming need for employment, delayed diagnoses of occupational lung disease often meant higher mortality rates for these diseases. Medical interventions, where they existed, were often applied too little and too late for many black miners.

Winds of change? Post-apartheid dynamics

In the latter decades of the twentieth century, on the tide of growing black militancy and worker militancy in the 1980s, the National Union of Mineworkers (NUM) was established in 1983, with Cyril Ramaphosa as its first secretary-general. The formation of this union and its prominent position as part of a wider Congress Alliance-led activism against apartheid signalled that mineworkers had coalesced into a political force. The formal ending of apartheid and the first democratic elections in 1994 marked a potentially significant shift in the history of this exploitative industry and its collusion with a century of pronounced coercive racial capitalism. The same year, compensation for occupational lung disease was equalized across racial categories and was no longer based on wages earned. The Leon Commission, established in 1995, is another example of the newly inaugurated democratic government seeking to reflect on and change the worst excesses of the mining industry. This is buttressed by more recent research by social scientists and clinicians who are seeking to fill in the gaps in knowledge through concerted empirical research, particularly in 'sending communities' such as rural areas where the extent of lung disease in residents is so poorly known.

Despite these gains and despite the fact that the former miner and secretary-general of NUM Cyril Ramaphosa is currently the president of South Africa, the post-apartheid period has not witnessed a comprehensive transformation in the livelihoods and health prospects of black mineworkers. The reliance of the state on the coffers of the mining industry has meant that a tight regulation of this industry remains undesirable. Furthermore, as the Cape plc case which began this chapter illustrates, the truly multinational structure of mining houses has meant that the destruction of apartheid did not lead to the erasure of the bodily exploitation of workers in South Africa, but merely shifted their geographical locus. Rather than the apartheid state, activists are targeting these multinational companies to provide for greater compensation for victims of occupational lung disease. The difficulty and expense of these pursuits can be seen in the limited success of their efforts.

These dark legacies have been brought into renewed focus in South Africa's time of AIDS. South Africa has the highest national HIV+ population in the world – in 2018 at 7.7 million, or 13 per cent of its total population – with a cumulative death toll from 1990 to 2014 estimated to be a staggering 4.4 million (see Chapter 4 for a detailed discussion). HIV and tuberculosis are co-morbid infections, in that one increases the speed of the other's development in the body. The World Health Organization estimates that HIV+ individuals are nineteen times more likely to develop active tuberculosis, because they are immuno-compromised. Moreover, the most common cause of AIDS-related death is tuberculosis. Similarly, the multiple morbidities of silicosis, tuberculosis and HIV/AIDS are becoming understood – for example, 'silicotics' (individuals diagnosed with silicosis) who are also HIV+ have been found to have demonstrably higher tuberculosis infection rates.[34] These complex synergies between respiratory disease and HIV/AIDS mean that any narrow approach to treatment for occupational lung disease is likely to have a negligible effect – the mining company Anglo America's announcement in 2002 that it would provide antiretrovirals to all of its employees who tested positive for HIV should thus be seen in this light.[35]

Conclusion

More recent events such as the violent crackdown in 2012 by state police of protests by Lonmin mineworkers have thrown these historical dynamics into sharp relief. Critics of the Marikana massacre, as the event has now become known, have called it an example of the persistent violence (continuing from the apartheid period) of the police and the state, and how this violence is again exacted disproportionately on the bodies of the African underclass. It is also a testament to the continuing frustrations of black mineworkers, who continue to work under intolerable conditions and low pay. The mining industry and its exploitative practices, as well as the social and health consequences of those employed within it, continue to be highly politicized flash-points in contemporary South Africa. The HIV/AIDS epidemic has only exacerbated these fault lines. The prognosis for decisive transformation in the health outcomes of mineworkers is poor.

Further reading

Abrahams, Peter. *Mine Boy*. London: D.Crisp, 1946.

Baker, Julie J. 'The Silent Crisis': Black Labour, Disease, and the Economics and Politics of Health in the South African Gold Mines, 1902–1930. Québec: Micromedia, 1990.

Beinart, William. *Twentieth-Century South Africa*. Oxford: Oxford University Press, 1994.

Bonner, Philip. 'African Urbanisation on the Rand between the 1930s and 1960s: Its Social Character and Political Consequences'. *Journal of Southern African Studies* 21, no. 1 (1995), 115–29.

Bozzoli, Belinda, ed. *Town and Countryside in the Transvaal: Capitalist Penetration and Popular Response*. Johannesburg: Ravan Press, 1983.

Burke, Gillian and Peter Richardson. 'The Profits of Death: A Comparative Study of Miners' Phthisis in Cornwall and the Transvaal, 1876–1918'. *Journal of Southern African Studies* 4, no. 2 (1978): 147–71.

Coovadia, Hoosen, Rachel Jewkes, Peter Barron, David Sanders and Diane McIntyre. 'The Health and Health System of South Africa: Historical Roots of Current Public Health Challenges'. *Lancet (London, England)* 374, no. 9692 (2009): 817–34.

Coplan, David. *In the Time of Cannibals: Word Music of South Africa's Basotho Migrants*. Chicago: University of Chicago Press, 1994.

Crais, Clifton. *Poverty, War, and Violence in South Africa*. Cambridge: Cambridge University Press, 2011.

Crush, Jonathan, Alan Jeeves and David Yudelman. *South Africa's Labour Empire: A History of Black Migrancy to the Gold Mines*. Cape Town: David Philip, 1991.

Ehrlich, Rodney. 'A Century of Miners' Compensation in South Africa'. *American Journal of Industrial Medicine* 55, no. 6 (2012): 560–9.

Elder, Glen. *Hostels, Sexuality and the Apartheid Legacy: Malevolent Geographies*. Athens, OH: Ohio University Press, 2003.

Ferguson, James. 'Mobile Workers, Modernist Narratives: A Critique of the Historiography of Transition on the Zambian Copperbelt [Part One]'. *Journal of Southern African Studies* 16, no. 3 (1990a): 385–412.

Ferguson, James. 'Mobile Workers, Modernist Narratives: A Critique of the Historiography of Transition on the Zambian Copperbelt [Part Two]'. *Journal of Southern African Studies* 16, no. 4 (1990b): 603–21.

Flynn, Laurie. *Studded with Diamonds and Paved with Gold: Miners, Mining Companies and Human Rights in Southern Africa*. London: Bloomsbury, 1992.

Giliomee, Hermann and Bernard Mbenga. *New History of South Africa*. Cape Town: Tafelberg, 2007.

Guy, Jeff and Motlatsi Thabane. 'Technology, Ethnicity and Ideology: Basotho Miners and Shaft-Sinking on the South African Gold Mines'. *Journal of Southern African Studies* 14, no. 2 (1988): 257–78.

Katz, Elaine. 'Silicosis of the Witwatersrand Gold Mines: Incidence and Prevalence; Compensation; 1902–1978'. *South African Labour Bulletin March* 4, no. 9 (1978): 66–84.

Katz, Elaine. *The White Death: Silicosis on the Witwatersrand Gold Mines 1886–1910*. Johannesburg: Witwatersrand University Press, 1994.

Kynoch, Gary. '"Your Petitioners Are in Mortal Terror": The Violent World of Chinese Mineworkers in South Africa, 1904–1910'. *Journal of Southern African Studies* 31, no. 3 (2005): 531–46.

Legassick, Martin. 'South Africa: Capital Accumulation and Violence'. *Economy and Society* 3, no. 3 (1974): 253–91.

Maloka, Eddy. *Basotho and the Mines: A Social History of Labour Migrancy in Lesotho and South Africa, c.1890–1940*. Dakar: Codesria, 2004.

Maloka, Tshidiso. 'Basotho and the Experience of Death, Dying and Mourning in the South African Mine Compounds, 1890–1940'. *Cahiers d'Etudes africaines* 38, no. 1 (1998): 17–40.

Marks, Shula. 'The Silent Scourge? Silicosis, Respiratory Disease and Gold-Mining in South Africa'. *Journal of Ethnic and Migration Studies* 32, no. 4 (2006): 569–89.

Marks, Shula and Neil Andersson. 'Epidemics and Social Control in Twentieth-Century South Africa'. *The Society for the Social History of Medicine Bulletin* 34 (1984): 32–4.

McCulloch, Jock. *Asbestos Blues: Labour, Capital, Physicians & the State in South Africa*. South Africa edition. Oxford: James Currey, 2002.

McCulloch, Jock. 'Counting the Cost: Gold Mining and Occupational Disease in Contemporary South Africa'. *African Affairs* 108, no. 431 (2009): 221–40.

Moodie, Dunbar. *Going for Gold: Men, Mines and Migration*. Berkeley: University of California Press, 1994.

Morris, Rosalind C. 'The Miner's Ear'. *Transition*, no. 98 (2008): 96–115.

Murray, Colin. *Families Divided: The Impact of Migrant Labour in Lesotho*. Cambridge: Cambridge University Press, 1981.

Packard, Randall M. *White Plague, Black Labor: Tuberculosis and the Political Economy of Health and Disease in South Africa*. Berkeley: University of California Press, 1989.

Parpart, Jane. 'The Household and the Mine Shaft: Gender and Class Struggles on the Zambian Copperbelt, 1926–64'. *Journal of Southern African Studies* 13, no. 1 (1986), 36–56.

Ramphele, Mamphela. *A Bed Called Home: Life in the Migrant Labour Hostels of Cape Town*. Cape Town: D. Philip, 1993.

Schapera, Isaac. *Migrant Labour and Tribal Life: A Study of Conditions in the Bechuanaland Protectorate*. London: Oxford University Press, 1947.

Skinner, Rob. *Modern South Africa in World History: Beyond Imperialism*. London: Bloomsbury Academic, 2017.

Van Onselen, Charles. *Chibaro: African Mine Labour in Southern Rhodesia, 1900–1933*. London: Pluto Press, 1976.

Van Onselen, Charles. *Studies in the Social and Economic History of the Witwatersrand, 1886–1914 – Vol.1 – New Babylon*. London: Longman, 1982.

Walker, Cherryl. 'Gender and the Development of the Migrant Labour System c.1850–1930: An Overview'. In *Women and Gender in Southern Africa to 1945*, edited by Cherryl Walker. Cape Town: James Currey, 1990.

Webster, David. 'The Political Economy of Food Production and Nutrition in Southern Africa in Historical Perspective'. *The Journal of Modern African Studies* 24, no. 3 (1986): 447–63.

Williams, Brian, Catherine Campbell, Nokuzola Mqoqi and Immo Kleinschmidt. 'Occupational Health, Occupational Illness: Tuberculosis, Silicosis and HIV on the South African Mines'. In *Occupational Lung Disease: An International Perspective*, edited by Daniel E. Banks and John E. Parker. London: Chapman & Hall Medical, 1998.

Wylie, Diana. *Starving on a Full Stomach: Hunger and the Triumph of Cultural Racism in Modern South Africa*. Charlottesville: University Press of Virginia, 2001.

NOTES

Introduction

1 Albert R. Cook, *Uganda Memories, 1897–1940* (Kampala: Uganda Society, 1945).

2 Shula Marks, 'What Is Colonial about Colonial Medicine? And What Has Happened to Imperialism and Health?' *Social History of Medicine* 10, no. 2 (August 1997): 205–19.

3 Alfred W. Crosby, *The Columbian Exchange: Biological and Cultural Consequences of 1492* (Westport, CT: Greenwood Press, 1972); Philip Curtin, 'Epidemiology and the Slave Trade', *Political Science Quarterly* 83, no. 2 (1968): 190–216; Philip Curtin, 'Disease Exchange across the Tropical Atlantic', *History and Philosophy of the Life Sciences* 15, no. 3 (1993): 329–56.

4 Maynard Swanson, 'The Sanitation Syndrome: Bubonic Plague and Urban Native Policy in the Cape Colony, 1900–1909', *The Journal of African History* 18, no. 3 (1977): 387–410.

5 Steven Feierman and John M. Janzen, eds., *The Social Basis of Health and Healing in Africa* (Berkeley: University of California Press, 1992).

6 John Iliffe, *Africans: The History of a Continent* (Cambridge: Cambridge University Press, 1995), p. 1.

7 Michel Foucault, 'Technologies of the Self', in *Technologies of the Self: A Seminar with Michel Foucault*, ed. Luther H. Martin, Huck Gutman and Patrick H. Hutton (Amherst: University of Massachusetts Press, 1988).

8 Nancy Rose Hunt, *Suturing New Medical Histories of Africa* (Zürich: Lit, 2012).

Chapter 1

1 Mungo Park, *Travels in the Interior Districts of Africa: Performed in the Years 1795, 1796 & 1797* (Gullane: FrontList Books, 1799).

2 Philip Curtin, '"The White Man's Grave:" Image and Reality, 1780–1850', *Journal of British Studies* 1, no. 1 (1961): 94–110.

3 Marion Wallace and John Kinahan, *A History of Namibia: From Earliest Times to 1990* (London: Hurst, 2010).

4 John M. Janzen, 'Ideologies and Institutions in Precolonial Western Equatorial African Therapeutics', in *The Social Basis of Health and Healing in Africa*, ed. Steven Feierman and John M. Janzen (Berkeley: University of California Press, 1992).

5 William Beinart and Karen Brown, *African Local Knowledge & Livestock Health: Traditional, Environmental & Biomedical Approaches in South Africa* (Oxford: James Currey, 2013).

6 Eric Silla, *'People Are Not the Same': Leprosy and Identity in Twentieth-Century Mali* (Portsmouth: Heinemann, 1998).

7 Wallace and Kinahan, *A History of Namibia*.

8 Abu Al-Bakri, *Kitab Al-Masalik Wa al-Mamalik, The Book of Routes and Realms*, first published 1068 (Beirut: Dar Sader, 1990).

9   Ibn Baṭṭūṭa, *The Travels of Ibn Battuta, A.D. 1325-1354* (London: Oriental Translations Fund, 1829).

10 Silla, *'People Are Not the Same'*.

11 João dos Santos, *Ethiopia Oriental*, first published 1609 (Lisboa: Escriptorio da Empreza, 1891).

12 Helen Tilley, *Africa as a Living Laboratory: Empire, Development, and the Problem of Scientific Knowledge, 1870-1950* (Chicago: University of Chicago Press, 2011).

13 James Webb, 'The Historical Epidemiology of Global Disease Challenges', *The Lancet* 385, no. 9965 (2015): 322-3.

14 Alfred W. Crosby, *Ecological Imperialism: The Biological Expansion of Europe, 900-1900* (Cambridge: Cambridge University Press, 1986).

15 David Arnold, 'The Indian Ocean as a Disease Zone, 1500-1950.' *South Asia: Journal of South Asian Studies* 14, no. 2 (1991): 1-21.

16 Park, *Travels*.

17 Philip D. Curtin, 'Epidemiology and the Slave Trade', *Political Science Quarterly* 83, no. 2 (1968): 190-216.

18 Randall M. Packard, *The Making of a Tropical Disease: A Short History of Malaria* (Baltimore: Johns Hopkins University Press, 2007).

19 Helen Bradford, 'Herbs, Knives and Plastic: 150 Years of Abortion in South Africa', in *Science, Medicine and Cultural Imperialism*, ed. Teresa Meade and Mark Walker (London: Macmillan, 1991).

20 Janzen, 'Ideologies and Institutions', 205.

21 John M. Janzen, *Lemba, 1650-1930: A Drum of Affliction in Africa and the New World* (New York: Garland Pub., 1981).

22 Jeff Peires, *The Dead Will Arise: Nongqawuse and the Great Xhosa Cattle-Killing Movement of 1856-7* (Johannesburg: Jonathan Ball, 2003).

23 Nehemia Levtzion and Randall Lee Pouwels, eds., *The History of Islam in Africa* (Athens: Ohio University Press, 2000).

24 Ismail H. Abdalla, 'Diffusion of Islamic Medicine into Hausaland', in *The Social Basis of Health and Healing in Africa*, ed. Steven Feierman and John M. Janzen (Berkeley: University of California Press, 1992).

25 John Parker, 'The Cultural Politics of Death & Burial in Early Colonial Accra', in *Africa's Urban Past*, ed. David Anderson and Richard Rathbone (Portsmouth: Heinemann, 1999).

26 Janzen, 'Ideologies and Institutions', 210.

27 Robin Law, 'Religion, Trade and Politics on the "Slave Coast": Roman Catholic Missions in Allada and Whydah in the Seventeenth Century', *Journal of Religion in Africa* 21, no. 1 (1991): 42-77.

28 Philip D. Curtin, *Death by Migration: Europe's Encounter with the Tropical World in the Nineteenth Century.* (Cambridge: Cambridge University Press, 1989).

29 Philip D. Curtin, 'The End of the "White Man's Grave"? Nineteenth-Century Mortality in West Africa', *The Journal of Interdisciplinary History* 21, no. 1 (1990): 63-88.

30 Paul E. Lovejoy, *Transformations in Slavery: A History of Slavery in Africa* (Cambridge: Cambridge University Press, 1983).

31 Slave Voyages – Trans-Atlantic Slave Trade Estimates, https://www.slavevoyages.org/assessment/estimates, accessed 30 June 2020.

32   Patrick Manning, *Slavery and African Life: Occidental, Oriental and African Slave Trades* (Cambridge: Cambridge University Press, 1990).

33   Patrick Manning, 'African Population, 1650–2000: Comparisons and Implications of New Estimates', In *Africa's Development in Historical Perspective*, eds. Emmanuel Akyeampong, Robert H. Bates, Nathan Nunn and James Robinson (Cambridge: Cambridge University Press, 2014): 131–50.

34   Barbara Bush, *Slave Women in Caribbean Society 1650–1832* (Kingston: Heinemann, 1990).

35   Janzen, 'Ideologies and Institutions'.

36   Megan Vaughan, 'Slavery, Smallpox, and Revolution: 1792 in Ile de France (Mauritius)', *Social History of Medicine: The Journal of the Society for the Social History of Medicine* 13, no. 3 (2000): 411–28.

37   David Eltis, 'Nutritional Trends in Africa and the Americas: Heights of Africans, 1819–1839', *The Journal of Interdisciplinary History* 12, no. 3 (1982): 453–75.

38   Kenneth Morgan, 'Slave Women and Reproduction in Jamaica, c.1776–1834', *History* 91, no. 302 (2006): 236.

39   Todd L. Savitt, *Medicine and Slavery: The Diseases and Health Care of Blacks in Antebellum Virginia* (Urbana: University of Illinois Press, 1978).

40   John Campbell, 'Work, Pregnancy, and Infant Mortality among Southern Slaves', *The Journal of Interdisciplinary History* 14, no. 4 (1984): 793–812.

41   Paul Gilroy, *The Black Atlantic: Modernity and Double Consciousness* (Cambridge: Harvard University Press, 1993).

Chapter 2

1   Megan Vaughan, *Curing Their Ills: Colonial Power and African Illness* (Cambridge: Polity, 1991).

2   Megan Vaughan, 'Healing and Curing: Issues in the Social History and Anthropology of Medicine in Africa', *Social History of Medicine: The Journal of the Society for the Social History of Medicine* 7, no. 2 (August 1994): 283–95.

3   Philip Curtin, 'Medical Knowledge and Urban Planning in Tropical Africa', *The American Historical Review* 90, no. 3 (1985): 594–613; Dumett, 'The Campaign against Malaria'.

4   Patrick Manson, *Tropical Diseases: A Manual of the Diseases of Warm Climates*, 7th edition (London: Cassell & Company, 1921).

5   Myron Echenberg, *Black Death, White Medicine: Bubonic Plague and the Politics of Public Health in Colonial Senegal, 1914–1945* (Portsmouth: Heinemann, 2002); Liora Bigon, *French Colonial Dakar: The Morphogenesis of an African Regional Capital* (Manchester: Manchester University Press, 2016).

6   Maynard Swanson, 'The Sanitation Syndrome: Bubonic Plague and Urban Native Policy in the Cape Colony, 1900–1909', *The Journal of African History* 18, no. 3 (1977): 387–410.

7   Raymond Dumett, 'The Campaign against Malaria and the Expansion of Scientific Medical and Sanitary Services in British West Africa, 1898–1910', *African Historical Studies* 1, no. 2 (1968): 153–97.

8   Guillaume Lachenal, 'A Genealogy of Treatment as Prevention (TasP): Prevention, Therapy, and the Tensions of Public Health in African History', in *Global Health in Africa: Historical Perspectives on Disease Control*, ed. Tamara Giles-Vernick and James Webb (Athens: Ohio University Press, 2013).

9   Philip Curtin's Medical Knowledge.

10 Warwick Anderson, 'Immunities of Empire: Race, Disease, and the New Tropical Medicine, 1900–1920', *Bulletin of the History of Medicine* 70, no. 1 (1996): 94–118.

11 Dumett, 'The Campaign against Malaria'.

12 Maryinez Lyons, *The Colonial Disease: A Social History of Sleeping Sickness in Northern Zaire, 1900–1940* (Cambridge: Cambridge University Press, 2002).

13 Elizabeth B. van Heyningen, 'The Social Evil in the Cape Colony 1868–1902: Prostitution and the Contagious Diseases Acts', *Journal of Southern African Studies* 10, no. 2 (1984): 170–97.

14 Karen Jochelson, *The Colour of Disease: Syphilis and Racism in South Africa, 1880–1950* (London: Palgrave Macmillan, 2001).

15 Paul Landau, 'Explaining Surgical Evangelism in Colonial Southern Africa: Teeth, Pain and Faith', *The Journal of African History* 37, no. 2 (1996): 261–81.

16 Markku Hokkanen, 'The Government Medical Service and British Missions in Colonial Malawi, c.1891–1940 Crucial Collaboration, Hidden Conflicts', in *Beyond the State: The Colonial Medical Service in British Africa*, ed. Anna Greenwood (Manchester: Manchester University Press, 2016).

17 Ibid.

18 John Manton, 'Making Modernity with Medicine: Mission, State and Community in Leprosy Control, Ogoja, Nigeria, 1945–50', in *The Development of Modern Medicine in Non-Western Countries*, ed. Hormoz Ebrahimnejad (London: Routledge, 2008); Eric Silla, *'People Are Not the Same': Leprosy and Identity in Twentieth-Century Mali* (Portsmouth: Heinemann, 1998); Michael Jennings, 'Cooperation and Competition: Missions, the Colonial State and Constructing a Health System in Colonial Tanganyika', in *Beyond the State: The Colonial Medical Service in British Africa*, ed. Anna Greenwood (Manchester: Manchester University Press, 2016).

19 Vaughan, Curing Their Ills.

20 Ibid.; Landau, 'Explaining Surgical Evangelism'.

21 Jennings, 'Cooperation and competition'.

22 Peter Warwick, *Black People and the South African War 1899–1902* (Cambridge: Cambridge University Press, 2004).

23 Joe Harris Lunn, 'War Losses (Africa)', in *1914–1918-Online. International Encyclopedia of the First World War*, ed. Ute Daniel, Peter Gatrell, Oliver Janz, Heather Jones, Jennifer Keene, Alan Kramer and Bill Nasson (Berlin: Freie Universität Berlin, 2014), https://encyclopedia.1914-1918-online.net/pdf/1914-1918-Online-war_losses_africa-2015-06-22.pdf, accessed 18 June 2020.

24 John Iliffe, *East African Doctors: A History of the Modern Profession* (Cambridge: Cambridge University Press, 1998).

25 Howard Philips, 'Influenza Pandemic (Africa)', in *1914–1918-Online. International*, https://encyclopedia.1914-1918-online.net/article/influenza_pandemic_africa, accessed 20 June 2020.

26 James Ellison, '"A Fierce Hunger": Tracing Impacts of the 1918–19 Influenza Epidemic in Southwest Tanzania', in *The Spanish Influenza Pandemic of 1918–19: New Perspectives*, ed. Howard Phillips and David Killingray (London: Routledge, 2003).

27 Nancy Rose Hunt's, Le Bebe en Brousse.

28 Norman Howard-Jones, 'Origins of International Health Work', *The British Medical Journal* 1, no. 4661 (1950): 1032–7.

Notes

29 Helen Tilley, *Africa as a Living Laboratory: Empire, Development, and the Problem of Scientific Knowledge, 1870-1950* (Chicago: University of Chicago Press, 2011); Megan Vaughan, 'A Research Enclave in 1940s Nigeria: The Rockefeller Foundation Yellow Fever Research Institute at Yaba, Lagos, 1943-49', *Bulletin of the History of Medicine* 92, no. 1 (2018): 172-205; Paul Wenzel Geissler, ed., *Para-States and Medical Science: Making African Global Health* (Durham: Duke University Press, 2015).

30 Jochelson, *The Colour of Disease.*

31 Deanne van Tol, 'Mothers, Babies, and the Colonial State: The Introduction of Maternal and Infant Welfare Services in Nigeria, 1925-1945', *Spontaneous Generations: A Journal for the History and Philosophy of Science* 1, no. 1 (2007): 110-31.

32 Lynn Thomas, *Politics of the Womb: Women, Reproduction, and the State in Kenya* (Kampala: Fountain, 2005).

33 Nancy Rose Hunt, '"Le Bebe En Brousse": European Women, African Birth Spacing and Colonial Intervention in Breast Feeding in the Belgian Congo', *The International Journal of African Historical Studies* 21, no. 3 (1988): 401-32.

34 Dumett, 'The Campaign against Malaria'.

35 Iliffe, *East African Doctors.*

36 Tilley, *Africa as a Living Laboratory.*

37 Walima T. Kalusa, 'Language, Medical Auxiliaries, and the Re-Interpretation of Missionary Medicine in Colonial Mwinilunga, Zambia, 1922-51', *Journal of Eastern African Studies* 1, no. 1 (2007): 57-78.

38 Constitution of the World Health Organization, https://apps.who.int/gb/bd/PDF/bd47/EN/constitution-en.pdf, accessed 20 June 2020.

39 Brock Chisholm, 'The World Health Organization', *The British Medical Journal* 1, no. 4661 (1950): 1021-7.

40 Echenberg, *Black Death, White Medicine.*

41 Nancy Rose Hunt, *A Nervous State: Violence, Remedies, and Reverie in Colonial Congo* (Durham: Duke University Press, 2016).

42 Jochelson, *The Colour of Disease.*

43 Helen Bradford, 'Herbs, Knives and Plastic: 150 Years of Abortion in South Africa', in *Science, Medicine and Cultural Imperialism*, ed. Teresa Meade and Mark Walker (London: Macmillan, 1991).

44 Karen Flint, *Healing Traditions: African Medicine, Cultural Exchange, and Competition in South Africa, 1820-1948* (Athens: Ohio University Press, 2008).

45 Amina Issa, 'Malaria and Public Health Measures in Colonial Urban Zanzibar, 1900-1956', *Hygiea Internationalis* 10, no. 2 (2011): 35-51.

46 Terence Ranger, 'Godly Medicine: The Ambiguities of Medical Mission in Southeast Tanzania, 1900-1945', *Social Science & Medicine. Part B: Medical Anthropology*, Special Issue: Causality and Classification in African Medicine and Health, 15, no. 3 (1981): 261-77.

47 Florence Bernault, 'Body, Power and Sacrifice in Equatorial Africa', *Journal of African History* 47 (2006): 207-39.

48 John M. Janzen, 'Therapy Management: Concept, Reality, Process', *Medical Anthropology Quarterly* 1, no. 1 (1987): 68-84; Ranger, 'Godly Medicine'.

49 Jochelson, *The Colour of Disease.*

50   Joel Cabrita, *The People's Zion: Southern Africa, the United States, and a Transatlantic Faith-Healing Movement* (Cambridge, MA: Harvard University Press, 2018).

51   Dumett, 'The Campaign against Malaria'.

52   A. H. M. Kirk-Greene, 'The Thin White Line: The Size of the British Colonial Service in Africa', *African Affairs* 79, no. 314 (1980): 25–44.

Chapter 3

1   Matthew Heaton, 'The Politics and Practice of Thomas Adeoye Lambo: Towards a Post-Colonial History of Transcultural Psychiatry', *History of Psychiatry* 29, no. 3 (2018), 315–16.

2   Achille Mbembe, 'The Power of the Archive and Its Limits', in *Refiguring the Archive*, ed. Carolyn Hamilton et al. (Dordrecht: Springer Netherlands, 2002); Luise White, 'Hodgepodge Historiography: Documents, Itineraries, and the Absence of Archives', *History in Africa* 42 (2015): 309–18.

3   John Iliffe, *East African Doctors: A History of the Modern Profession* (Cambridge: Cambridge University Press, 1998).

4   Noémi Tousignant, 'Pharmacy, Money and Public Health in Dakar', *Africa* 83, no. 4 (2013): 561–81.

5   Anne Digby and Howard Philips, *At the Heart of Healing: Groote Schuur Hospital, 1938–2008* (Auckland Park: Jacana, 2008), 103–4.

6   Paul Wenzel Geissler with Ann H. Kelly, Peter Mangesho and Rene Gerrets, eds. 'Amani', in *Traces of the Future: An Archaeology of Medical Science in Africa*, ed. Paul W. Geissler et al. (Bristol: Intellect, 2016), 115.

7   Susan Reynolds Whyte, 'Pharmaceuticals as Folk Medicine: Transformations in the Social Relations of Health Care in Uganda', *Culture, Medicine and Psychiatry* 16, no. 2 (1992): 163–86.

8   William Schneider, 'The Long History of Smallpox Eradication: Lessons for Global Health in Africa', in *Global Health in Africa: Historical Perspectives on Disease Control*, ed. Tamara Giles-Vernick and James Webb (Athens: Ohio University Press, 2013).

9   John Manton and Martin Gorsky, 'Health Planning in 1960s Africa: International Health Organisations and the Post-Colonial State', *Medical History* 62, no. 4 (2018): 425–48.

10   Sung Lee, 'WHO and the Developing World: The Contest for Ideology', in *Western Medicine as Contested Knowledge*, ed. Andrew Cunningham and Bridie Andrews (New York: Manchester University Press, 1997).

11   Ann H. Kelly, 'Remembering a Soviet Method', in *Traces of the Future: An Archaeology of Medical Science in Africa*, ed. Paul W. Geissler et al. (Bristol: Intellect, 2016).

12   Ruth Prince, 'Russia', in *Traces of the Future: An Archaeology of Medical Science in Africa*, ed. Paul W. Geissler et al. (Bristol: Intellect, 2016).

13   Randall M. Packard, *The Making of a Tropical Disease: A Short History of Malaria* (Baltimore: Johns Hopkins University Press, 2007).

14   Dennis Michael Warren with Patrick A. Twumasi, 'The Professionalisation of Indigenous Medicine: A Comparative Study of Ghana and Zambia' in *The Professionalisation of African Medicine*, ed. Murray Last and G.L. Chavunduka (Manchester: Manchester University Press, 1988): 121, 125.

15   Isaac Sindiga, Chacha Nyaigotti Chacha and Mary Peter Kanunah, *Traditional Medicine in Africa* (Nairobi: East African Educational Publishers, 1995): 103–6.

16 Jack K. Githae, 'Ethnomedical Practice in Kenya: The Case of the Karati Rural Service Centre' In *Traditional Medicine in Africa*, ed. Isaac Sindiga, Chacha Nyaigotti-Chacha, Mary Peter Kanunah (Nairobi: East African Educational Publishers, 1995): 55–63.

17 John Iliffe, *The African AIDS Epidemic: A History* (Oxford: James Currey, 2006).

18 UNAIDS AIDSinfo, https://aidsinfo.unaids.org/, accessed 16 July 2020.

19 Ruth Prince and Paul Wenzel Geissler, 'Global Health Amnesia', in *Traces of the Future: An Archaeology of Medical Science in Africa*, ed. Paul W. Geissler et al. (Bristol: Intellect, 2016).

20 Guillaume Lachenal, '"Scramble for Cameroon": Atypical Viruses and Scientific Zeal in Cameroon (1985–2000), in *The HIV/AIDS Epidemic in Sub-Saharan Africa in Historical Perspective*, ed. Philippe Denis, and Charles Becker. Online edition. Published by Academia-Bruylant and Karthala, 2006, 187–205.

21 Carla Tsampiras, 'From "Dark Country" to "Dark Continent": AIDS, "Race," and Medical Research in the *South African Medical Journal*, 1980–1995', *Journal of Southern African Studies* 41, no. 4 (2015): 773–96.

22 Steven Robins, '"Long Live Zackie, Long Live": AIDS Activism, Science and Citizenship after Apartheid', *Journal of Southern African Studies* 30, no. 3 (2004): 651–72.

23 Jonas Svensson, '"Muslims Have Instructions" Modernity and Islamic Religious Education in Kisumu, Kenya', in *Aids and Religious Practice in Africa*, ed. Felicitas Becker and Paul W. Geissler (Leiden: Brill, 2009), 189–219.

24 Isak Niehaus, *AIDS in the Shadow of Biomedicine* (London: Zed Books, 2018).

25 Heike Behrend, 'The Rise of Occult Powers, AIDS and the Roman Catholic Church in Western Uganda', *Journal of Religion in Africa* 37, no. 1 (2007): 41–58.

26 Frederick Klaits, *Death in a Church of Life: Moral Passion during Botswana's Time of AIDS* (Berkeley: University of California Press, 2010).

27 Paul Gifford, *African Christianity: Its Public Role* (Bloomington: Indiana University Press, 1998).

28 Deborah Potts and Shula Marks, 'Fertility in Southern Africa: The Quiet Revolution', *Journal of Southern African Studies* 27, no. 2 (2001): 189–205.

29 Patrick Manning, 'African Population, 1650–2000: Comparisons and Implications of New Estimates', in *Africa's Development in Historical Perspective*, ed. Emmanuel Akyeampong et al. (Cambridge: Cambridge University Press, 2014), 131–50.

30 Potts and Marks, 'Fertility in Southern Africa'.

31 Rebecca Hodes, 'The Medical History of Abortion in South Africa, c.1970–2000', *Journal of Southern African Studies* 39, no. 3 (2013): 527–42.

32 Mira Grieser et al., 'Reproductive Decision Making and the HIV/AIDS Epidemic in Zimbabwe', *Journal of Southern African Studies* 27, no. 2 (2001): 225–43.

33 Rebecca Hodes, 'The Culture of Illegal Abortion in South Africa', *Journal of Southern African Studies* 42, no. 1 (2016): 79–93.

34 Susan Reynolds Whyte et al., 'The Visibility of Non-Communicable Diseases in Northern Uganda', *African Health Sciences* 15, no. 1 (2015): 82–9.

35 Julie Livingstone, *Improvising Medicine: An African Oncology Ward in an Emerging Cancer Epidemic* (Durham: Duke University Press, 2012).

36 Megan Vaughan, 'Conceptualising Metabolic Disorder in Southern Africa: Biology, History and Global Health', *BioSocieties* 14, no. 1 (2019): 123–42.

37 Emily Mendenhall, *Syndemic Suffering: Social Distress, Depression, and Diabetes among Mexican Immigrant Women* (California: Left Coast Press, 2012).

38 Myron Echenberg, "'Snake in the Belly" Africa's Unhappy Experience with Cholera during the Seventh Pandemic, 1971 to the Present', in *Global Health in Africa: Historical Perspectives on Disease Control*, ed. Tamara Giles-Vernick and James Webb (Athens: Ohio University Press, 2013).

39 Samuel Cohn and Ruth Kutalek, 'Historical Parallels, Ebola Virus Disease and Cholera: Understanding Community Distrust and Social Violence with Epidemics', *PLoS Currents* Outbreaks 8 (26 January 2016). Edition 1. 10.1371/currents.outbreaks. aa1f2b60e8d43939b43fbd93e1a63a94

Chapter 4

1   See www.gold.ac.uk/deathinafrica for further information on the project.

2   Visit www.unaidsinfo.unaids.

3   Guillaume Lachenal, "'Scramble for Cameroon": Atypical Viruses and Scientific Zeal in Cameroon (1985–2000)', in *The HIV/AIDS Epidemic in Sub-Saharan Africa in Historical Perspective*, ed. Philippe Denis and Charles Becker. (Louvaine la-Neuve and Paris: Online edition published by Academia-Bruylant and Karthala, 2006), 187–205, https://www.dphu. org/uploads/attachements/books/books_1448_0.pdf

4   Carla Tsampiras, 'From "Dark Country" to "Dark Continent": AIDS, "Race," and Medical Research in the *South African Medical Journal*, 1980–1995', *Journal of Southern African Studies* 41, no. 4 (2015): 773–96.

5   John Iliffe, *The African AIDS Epidemic: A History* (Oxford: James Currey, 2006), 3–9.

6   Tamara Giles-Vernick, Ch. Didier Gondola, Guillaume Lachenal and William H. Schneider, 'JAH Forum: Social History, Biology, and the Emergence of HIV in Colonial Africa', *Journal of African History* 54 (2013): 11–30.

7   A. Nicolosi et al., 'The Efficiency of Male-to-Female and Female-to-Male Sexual Transmission of the Human Immunodeficiency Virus: A Study of 730 Stable Couples. Italian Study Group on HIV Heterosexual Transmission', *Epidemiology* 5, no. 6 (1994): 570–5.

8   Carolyn Baylies and Janet M. Bujra, eds., *AIDS, Sexuality and Gender in Africa: Collective Strategies and Struggles in Tanzania and Zambia* (London: Routledge, 2000).

9   Kyle D. Kauffman, 'Why Is South Africa the HIV Capital of the World? An Institutional Analysis of the Spread of a Virus', in *AIDS and South Africa: The Social Expression of a Pandemic*, ed. Kyle D. Kauffman and David L. Lindauer (London: Palgrave, 2004), 17–30.

10 Steven Robins, 'From "Rights" to "Ritual": AIDS Activism in South Africa', *American Anthropologist* 108, no. 2 (2006): 312–23; Vinh-Kim Nguyen, *The Republic of Therapy: Triage and Sovereignty in West Africa's Time of AIDS* (Durham, NC: Duke University Press, 2010).

11 The Keiskamma Trust, http://www.keiskamma.org/the-keiskamma-guernica/, accessed 5 July 2020.

12 Jonathan Morgan, Kyle Thomas and the Bambanani Woman's Group. *Long Life: Positive HIV stories* (Cape Town: Double Storey, 2003).

13 Howard Philips, 'Influenza Pandemic (Africa)', in *1914–1918-Online. International Encyclopedia of the First World War*, ed. Ute Daniel, Peter Gatrell, Oliver Janz, Heather Jones, Jennifer Keene, Alan Kramer, and Bill Nasson (Berlin: Freie Universität Berlin, 2014), https://encyclopedia.1914-1918-online.net/article/influenza_pandemic_africa, accessed 26 May 2020.

14 'Syphilis Fact Sheet', Centre for Disease Control and Prevention, https://www.cdc.gov/std/syphilis/stdfact-syphilis-detailed.htm, accessed 5 July 2020.

15 Megan Vaughan, 'Syphilis in Colonial East and Central Africa: The Social Construction of an Epidemic', in *Epidemics and Ideas: Essays on the Historical Perception of Pestilence*, ed. Terence Ranger and Slack (Cambridge: Cambridge University Press, 1992), 269–302.

16 Ibid., 269–70, 280.

17 Karen Jochelson, *The Colour of Disease: Syphilis and Racism in South Africa, 1880–1950* (Basingstoke: Palgrave Macmillan, 2001), 94.

18 Charles Becker and Rene Collignon, 'A History of Sexually Transmitted Diseases and AIDS in Senegal: Difficulties in Accounting for Social Logics in Health Policy', in *Histories of Sexually Transmitted Diseases and HIV/AIDS in Sub-Saharan Africa*, ed. Philip Setel, Milton James Lewis and Maryinez Lyons (Westport: Greenwood Press, 1999), 72.

19 Vaughan, 'Syphilis in Colonial East and Central Africa'; Megan Vaughan, *Curing Their Ills: Colonial Power and African Illness* (Cambridge: Polity, 1991), 129–54.

20 Ludwig Alberti, *The Kaffirs of the South Coast of Africa*, reprinted as *Ludwig Alberti's Account of the Tribal Life & Customs of the Xhosa in 1807* (Cape Town: A.A. Balkema, 1968), 52–3.

21 Isaac Schapera, *Married Life in an African Tribe* (London: Faber & Faber, 1940).

22 Vaughan, *Curing Their Ills*.

23 Vaughan, 'Syphilis in Colonial East and Central Africa', 294–7.

24 Myron Echenberg, 'Historical Perspectives on HIV/AIDS: Lessons from South Africa and Senegal', in *The HIV/AIDS Epidemic in Sub-Saharan Africa in a Historical Perspective*, ed. Philippe Denis and Charles Becker (Online edition published by Academia-Bruylant and Karthala, 2006), 89–96; Becker and Collignon, 'A History of Sexually Transmitted Diseases and AIDS in Senegal'.

25 Bryan T. Callahan and Virginia Bond, 'The Social, Cultural and Epidemiological History of Sexually Transmitted Disease in Zambia', in *Histories of Sexually Transmitted Diseases and HIV/AIDS in Sub-Saharan Africa*, ed. Philip Setel, Milton James Lewis, and Maryinez Lyons (Westport: Greenwood Press, 1999), 171–6.

26 Rebekah Lee, *African Women and Apartheid: Migration and Settlement in Urban South Africa* (London: I.B. Tauris, 2009).

27 Karen Jochelson, *The Colour of Disease: Syphilis and Racism in South Africa, 1880–1950* (Basingstoke: Palgrave Macmillan, 2001), 20.

28 Ibid., 108.

29 Maryinez Lyons, 'Sexually Transmitted Diseases in the History of Uganda', *GenitourinMed* 70 (1994): 139.

30 https://aidsinfo.unaids.org, accessed 28 May 2020.

31 James Putzel, 'A History of State Action: The Politics of AIDS in Uganda and Senegal', in *The HIV/AIDS Epidemic in Sub-Saharan Africa in a Historical Perspective*, ed. Philippe Denis and Charles Becker (Louvaine la-Neuve and Paris: Online edition published by Academia-Bruylant and Karthala, 2006), 171–84, https://www.dphu.org/uploads/attachements/books/books_1448_0.pdf

32 https://aidsinfo.unaids.org, accessed 28 May 2020.

33 John Caldwell, Pat Caldwell and Pat Quiggin, 'The Social Context of AIDS in Sub-Saharan Africa', *Population and Development Review* 15, no. 2 (1989): 185–234; John Caldwell and Pat Caldwell, 'The Nature and Limits of the Sub-Saharan African AIDS Epidemic: Evidence from Geographic and Other Patterns', *Population and Development Review* 19, no. 4 (1993): 817–48.

34 Fraser G. Mcneill, '"Condoms Cause Aids": Poison, Prevention and Denial in Venda, South Africa', *African Affairs* 108, no. 432 (2009): 353–70.

35 Echenberg, 'Historical Perspectives on HIV/AIDS'.

Chapter 5

1 Megan Vaughan, 'The Discovery of Suicide in Eastern and Southern Africa', *African Studies* 71, no. 2 (August 2012): 234–50.

2 John Carothers, *The African Mind in Health and Disease: A Study in Ethnopsychiatry* (Geneva: WHO, 1953); Jock McCulloch, *Colonial Psychiatry and 'the African Mind'* (Cambridge: Cambridge University Press, 1995).

3 Megan Vaughan, 'Idioms of Madness: Zomba Lunatic Asylum, Nyasaland, in the Colonial Period', *Journal of Southern African Studies* 9, no. 2 (1983): 226.

4 Martin Summers, '"Suitable Care of the African when Afflicted with Insanity": Race, Madness, and Social Order in Comparative Perspective', *Bulletin of the History of Medicine* 84, no. 1 (2010): 69.

5 Frantz Fanon, *Black Skin, White Masks*, trans. Charles Lam Markmann, first published 1952 (New York: Grove Press, 1967).

6 Megan Vaughan, *Curing Their Ills: Colonial Power and African Illness* (Cambridge: Polity, 1991), 101–2, 118.

7 Megan Vaughan, 'Suicide in Late Colonial Africa: The Evidence of Inquests from Nyasaland', *The American Historical Review* 115, no. 2 (April 2010): 385–404.

8 Alice Bullard, 'Imperial Networks and Postcolonial Independence: The Transition from Colonial to Transcultural Psychiatry', in *Psychiatry and Empire*, ed. Sloan Mahone and Megan Vaughan (London: Palgrave Macmillan, 2007), 197–219.

9 Henri Junod, *The Life of a South African Tribe Vol.2 Mental Life* (London: Macmillan, 1927): 466–7.

10 Julie Parle, 'Witchcraft or Madness? The Amandiki of Zululand, 1894–1914', *Journal of Southern African Studies* 29, no. 1 (2003): 105–32.

11 Harriet Deacon, *Insanity, Institutions and Society: The Case of the Robben Island Lunatic Asylum, 1846–1910* (Cambridge: Cambridge University Press, 2003).

12 Leland V. Bell, *Mental and Social Disorder in Sub-Saharan Africa: The Case of Sierra Leone, 1787-1990* (Westport, CT: Greenwood Press, 1991)

13 Richard Keller, 'Madness and Colonization: Psychiatry in the British and French Empires, 1800–1962', *Journal of Social History* 35, no. 2 (2001): 314.

14 Summers, 'Suitable Care of the African', 72.

15 Vaughan, *Curing Their Ills*, 108–14.

16 Ibid., 100–1.

17 Keller, 'Madness and Colonization', 315.

18 Summers, 'Suitable Care of the African', 68.

19 Ibid., 90.

20 John Carothers, 'Frontal Lobe Function and the African', *Journal of Mental Science* 97, no. 406 (1951): 12–48.

21 John Iliffe, *East African Doctors: A History of the Modern Profession* (Cambridge: Cambridge University Press, 1998), 87.

22 Jock McCulloch, *Colonial Psychiatry and 'the African Mind'* (Cambridge: Cambridge University Press, 1995), 37.

23 Jonathan Sadowsky, *Imperial Bedlam: Institutions of Madness in Colonial Southwest Nigeria* (Berkeley: University of California Press, 1999), 30.

24 McCulloch, *Colonial Psychiatry*, 38–40.

25 Saul Dubow, 'Mental Testing and the Understanding of Race in 20th-Century South Africa', in *Science, Medicine and Cultural Imperialism*, ed. Teresa Meade and Mark Walker (London: Macmillan, 1991), 152.

26 Sloan Mahone, 'East African Psychiatry and the Practical Problems of Empire', in *Psychiatry and Empire*, ed. Sloan Mahone and Megan Vaughan (London: Palgrave Macmillan, 2007), 41–66.

27 Frantz Fanon, *The Wretched of the Earth*, trans. Constance Farrington, first published 1961 (London: Penguin Classics, 2001), 200–1.

28 Matthew Heaton, 'The Politics and Practice of Thomas Adeoye Lambo: Towards a Post-Colonial History of Transcultural Psychiatry', *History of Psychiatry* 29, no. 3 (2018): 315–16.

29 Keller, 'Madness and Colonization'; Robert Berthelier, *L'Homme Maghrébin das La Litérature Psychiatrique* (Paris: L'Harmattan, 1994).

30 Bullard, 'Imperial Networks and Postcolonial Independence', 203.

31 Dörte Bemme and Laurence Kirmayer, 'Global Mental Health: Interdisciplinary Challenges for a Field in Motion', *Transcultural Psychiatry* 57, no. 1 (February 2020): 3–18.

32 Rebekah Lee, 'Death in Slow Motion: Funerals, Ritual Practice and Road Danger in South Africa', *African Studies* 71, no. 2 (2012): 195–211.

33 Pamela Konstantinides, 'Women Heal Women: Spirit Possession and Sexual Segregation in a Muslim Society', *Social Science & Medicine* 21, no. 6 (1985): 685–92.

34 Vaughan, 'The Discovery of Suicide in Eastern and Southern Africa'; Julie Livingston, 'Suicide, Risk, and Investment in the Heart of the African Miracle', *Cultural Anthropology* 24, no. 4 (2009): 652–80; Hayley MacGregor, 'The Grant Is What I Eat: The Politics of Social Security and Disability in the Post-Apartheid South African State', *Journal of Biosocial Science* 38, no. 1 (2006): 43–55.

Chapter 6

1 WHO, 'Malaria: Q&A on the Malaria Vaccine Implementation Programme (MVIP)', March 2020, https://www.who.int/malaria/media/malaria-vaccine-implementation-qa/en/, accessed 25 June 2020.

2 WHO – World Malaria Report, 2019, https://www.who.int/publications/i/item/world-malaria-report-2019, accessed 14 June 2020.

3 WHO – The History of Sleeping Sickness, https://www.who.int/trypanosomiasis_african/country/history/en/index5.html, accessed 26 June 2020.

4 WHO – World Malaria Report, 2019, https://www.who.int/publications/i/item/world-malaria-report-2019, accessed 14 June 2020.

5 James Webb, *Humanity's Burden: A Global History of Malaria* (Cambridge: University Press, 2009): 38–9.

6   Ibn Khaldun, *The Muqaddimah: An Introduction to History*, first published *c.* 1377 (London: RKP, 1978).

7   Thomas Winterbottom, *An Account of the Native Africans in the Neighbourhood of Sierra Leone: To Which Is Added, an Account of the Present State of Medicine among Them* (London: C. Whittingham, 1803).

8   Mungo Park, *Travels of Mungo Park*, ed. Ronald Miller, first published 1799 (London: J M Dent & Sons Ltd, 1954).

9   William Beinart and Karen Brown, *African Local Knowledge & Livestock Health: Traditional, Environmental & Biomedical Approaches in South Africa* (Oxford: James Currey, 2013).

10 Helen Tilley, *Africa as a Living Laboratory: Empire, Development, and the Problem of Scientific Knowledge, 1870–1950* (Chicago: University of Chicago Press, 2011).

11 John Ford, *Role of the Trypanosomiases in African Ecology* (Oxford: Clarendon Press, 1971).

12 Antoine de Bengy Puyvallée and Sonja Kittelsen, '"Disease Knows No Borders": Pandemics and the Politics of Global Health Security', *Pandemics, Publics, and Politics* (2018): 59–73.

13 Tilley, *Africa as a Living Laboratory*.

14 Mari K. Webel, 'Trypanosomiasis, Tropical Medicine, and the Practices of Inter-Colonial Research at Lake Victoria, 1902–07', *History and Technology* 35, no. 3 (2019): 266–92.

15 Luise White, 'Tsetse Visions: Narratives of Blood and Bugs in Colonial Northern Rhodesia, 1931–9', *The Journal of African History* 36, no. 2 (1995): 219–45.

16 Tilley, *Africa as a Living Laboratory*.

17 Ibid.

18 White, 'Tsetse Visions'.

19 Randall M. Packard, *The Making of a Tropical Disease: A Short History of Malaria* (Baltimore: Johns Hopkins University Press, 2007).

20 Packard, *The Making of a Tropical Disease*; Webb, *Humanity's Burden*.

21 Jonathan Roberts, 'Korle and the Mosquito: Histories and Memories of the Anti-Malaria Campaign in Accra, 1942–5', *The Journal of African History* 51, no. 3 (2010): 343–65.

22 James Webb, 'The First Large-Scale Use of Synthetic Insecticide for Malaria Control in Tropical Africa: Lessons from Liberia, 1945–1962', *Journal of the History of Medicine and Allied Sciences* 66 (2011): 347–76.

23 Amina Issa, 'Malaria and Public Health Measures in Colonial Urban Zanzibar, 1900–1956', *Hygiea Internationalis* 10, no. 2 (2011): 35–51.

24 Packard, *The Making of a Tropical Disease*.

25 Francois-Xavier Mbopi-Keou et al., 'The Legacies of Eugène Jamot and La Jamotique', *PLoS Neglected Tropical Diseases* 8, no. 4 (2014).

26 WHO – Human African Trypanosomiasis, https://www.who.int/trypanosomiasis_african/country/history/en/index7.html, accessed 24 June 2020.

27 C. Gramiccia and P. F. Beales, 'The Recent History of Malaria Control and Eradication', in *Malaria: Principles and Practice of Malariology*, ed. Walther Wernsdorfer and Ian McGregor (Edinburgh: Churchill Livingstone, 1988), 1390.

28 Jonathan Musere, *African Sleeping Sickness: Political Ecology, Colonialism and Control in Uganda* (Lewiston: Edwin Mellen Press, 1990).

29 Packard, *The Making of a Tropical Disease*.

Notes

30   WHO – Trypanosomiasis, Human African (Sleeping Sickness) Fact Sheet, https://www.who.int/news-room/fact-sheets/detail/trypanosomiasis-human-african-_sleeping-sickness_, accessed 7 April 2020.

31   Jennifer Palmer et al., 'Changing Landscapes, Changing Practice: Negotiating Access to Sleeping Sickness Services in a Post-Conflict Society', *Social Science & Medicine* 120 (2014): 396–404.

32   James Smith, Emma Michelle Taylor and Pete Kingsley, 'One World-One Health and Neglected Zoonotic Disease: Elimination, Emergence and Emergency in Uganda', *Social Science & Medicine* 129 (2015): 12–19.

Chapter 7

1   Jock McCulloch, 'Beating the Odds: The Quest for Justice by South African Asbestos Mining Communities', *Review of African Political Economy* 32, no. 103 (2005): 63–77.

2   'Cape Caves in on South African Asbestos Case', Press Release, 13 March 2003, https://brandonhamber.blogspot.com/2003/03/british-company-cape-plc-has-today.html, accessed 18 May 2020.

3   Shula Marks, 'The Silent Scourge? Silicosis, Respiratory Disease and Gold-Mining in South Africa', *Journal of Ethnic and Migration Studies* 32, no. 4 (1 May 2006): 569–89.

4   Jock McCulloch, *Asbestos Blues: Labour, Capital, Physicians & the State in South Africa* (Oxford: James Currey, 2002).

5   Marks, 'The Silent Scourge?'

6   Gillian Burke and Peter Richardson, 'The Profits of Death: A Comparative Study of Miners' Phthisis in Cornwall and the Transvaal, 1876–1918', *Journal of Southern African Studies* 4, no. 2 (1978): 147–71.

7   William Beinart, *Twentieth-Century South Africa* (Oxford: Oxford University Press, 1994), p. 28.

8   Ibid., p. 32.

9   James Ferguson, 'Mobile Workers, Modernist Narratives: A Critique of the Historiography of Transition on the Zambian Copperbelt [Part One]', *Journal of Southern African Studies* 16, no. 3 (1990): 385–412; James Ferguson, 'Mobile Workers, Modernist Narratives: A Critique of the Historiography of Transition on the Zambian Copperbelt [Part Two]', *Journal of Southern African Studies* 16, no. 4 (1990): 603–21; Rebekah Lee, *African Women and Apartheid: Migration and Settlement in South Africa* (London: I.B. Tauris, 2009).

10   Diana Wylie, *Starving on a Full Stomach: Hunger and the Triumph of Cultural Racism in Modern South Africa* (Charlottesville: University Press of Virginia, 2001).

11   David Coplan, *In the Time of Cannibals: Word Music of South Africa's Basotho Migrants* (Chicago: University of Chicago Press, 1994).

12   Tshidiso Maloka, 'Basotho and the Experience of Death, Dying and Mourning in the South African Mine Compounds, 1890–1940'. *Cahiers d'Etudes africaines* 38, no. 1 (1998): 17–40.

13   Burke and Richardson, 'The Profits of Death'.

14   Randall M. Packard, 'Industrialization, Rural Poverty and Tuberculosis in South Africa, 1850–1950', in *The Social Basis of Health and Healing in Africa*, ed. Steven Feierman and John M. Janzen (Berkeley: University of California Press, 1992).

15   Jane Parpart, 'The Household and the Mine Shaft: Gender and Class Struggles on the Zambian Copperbelt, 1926–64', *Journal of Southern African Studies* 13, no. 1 (1986): 36–56.

16 David Webster, 'The Political Economy of Food Production and Nutrition in Southern Africa in Historical Perspective', *The Journal of Modern African Studies* 24, no. 3 (1986): 447–63.

17 Randall M. Packard, *White Plague, Black Labor: Tuberculosis and the Political Economy of Health and Disease in South Africa* (Berkeley: University of California Press, 1989).

18 Elaine Katz, 'Silicosis of the Witwatersrand Gold Mines: Incidence and Prevalence; Compensation; 1902–1978', *South African Labour Bulletin March* 4, no. 9 (1978): 66–84.

19 Packard, *White Plague, Black Labor,* pp. 196–7, 203.

20 Ibid., pp. 212–13.

21 Paul Landau, 'Explaining Surgical Evangelism in Colonial Southern Africa: Teeth, Pain and Faith', *The Journal of African History* 37, no. 2 (1996): 261–81.

22 Elaine Katz, *The White Death: Silicosis on the Witwatersrand Gold Mines 1886–1910* (Johannesburg: Witwatersrand University Press, 1994).

23 Ibid, pp. 2–5; Julie Baker, *'The Silent Crisis': Black Labour, Disease, and the Economics and Politics of Health in the South African Gold Mines, 1902–1930* (Québec: Micromedia, 1990).

24 Baker, *'The Silent Crisis'.*

25 Marks, 'The Silent Scourge?', p. 574.

26 Jock McCulloch, 'Surviving Blue Asbestos: Mining and Occupational Disease in South Africa and Australia', *Transformation: Critical Perspectives on Southern Africa* 65, no. 1 (2008): 68–93.

27 McCulloch, *Asbestos Blues.*

28 Jock McCulloch, 'Counting the Cost: Gold Mining and Occupational Disease in Contemporary South Africa', *African Affairs* 108, no. 431 (2009): 221–40.

29 Marks, 'The Silent Scourge?', p. 577.

30 McCulloch, *Asbestos Blues*; McCulloch, 'Counting the Cost'.

31 McCulloch, *Asbestos Blues.*

32 Baker, *'The Silent Crisis'.*

33 Katz, *Silicosis on the Witwatersrand*

34 E. L. Corbett, G. J. Churchyard, T. C. Clayton, B. G. Williams, D. Mulder, R. J. Hayes and K. M. De Cock, 'HIV Infection and Silicosis: The Impact of Two Potent Risk Factors on the Incidence of Mycobacterial Disease in South African Miners', *AIDS (London, England)* 14, no. 17 (2000): 2759–68.

35 Marks, 'The Silent Scourge?'

INDEX

A

ABC approach (Abstain, Be faithful, Condomize) 10, 143–5

abortion 108–9

Abraham, Peter 216

Achmat, Zachie 102

Action for Southern Africa (ACTSA) 209

African Assistant Medical Officers 72

'African madness' 4, 11, 153–4, 164, 176

African Native Medical Corps (ANMC) 71, 196

Africanization, of health services 86–7, 91–3, 115, 174, 176

Afrikaners 66, 147

Al Bakri 21

Alberti, Ludwig 140

albinism 75

Algiers School of ethno-psychiatry 163, 165, 168, 171

Allada 32

allopathic medicine. *See also* biomedicine
African resistance to 9–10, 76–81
in Africanized health systems 86–7, 97–9
hegemonic narrative of 3
HIV/AIDS 103, 164
indigenization of 93
medical auxiliaries, role of 72
in mental health 172

Alma Ata Conference (1978) 93, 95

Amani Hill Research Station 69, 92, 96, 195

American South 38–40, 76, 163, 170

Anderson, Warwick 5

antenatal health 70

anthropological studies, as historical sources 3, 5, 51, 74–5, 89, 155

antiviral (ARV) drugs 100–1, 103, 110, 122, 124–5, 129–30, 132–3

apartheid 91, 102, 106–7, 142, 209–10, 219, 228–9

Apostolic Church 103

archaeology 19–20, 155

Arnold, David 5, 26

Aro Mental Hospital 85, 172–3, 175

art-based therapeutic interventions 133

artemisinin-based combination drug therapies (ACTs) 179

asbestosis 210–12, 223–6

Ashforth, Adam 104–5

asylums. *See also* mental illness

colonial 10, 161–5, 176
conditions and patient care 169–70
records as historical sources 151, 154–5

B

Bailey, Carolyn 128

Bantu people 20, 30–1, 163, 165, 182

Basotho people 11, 29, 139–40, 214–15, 219

Beinart, William 6

Bell, Leland 154

Berlin, Conference of (1884–5) 47

Bill and Melinda Gates Foundation 100–1, 124, 179, 203

bin Abdallah, Swedi 72, 196

Binet scale 170

biomedicine. *See also* allopathic medicine
African response to 77, 81, 87
colonial 6
indigenization of 72, 93, 98–9
in mental health 174
rise of 50–1

Birmingham, University of 173

Black Death 69

Blida psychiatric hospital 161–2

body maps 6, 130–3

Bono 101

Brown, Karen 6

Bruce, David 53, 186, 189, 195

bubonic plague 5, 27, 56–60, 64, 74, 78, 112

Buganda people 136

Bujra, Janet 128

Burton, Richard 27, 187–90

Bush, George W. 101

C

Caldwell, John and Pat 146

Callaway, Henry 156–61, 175

cancer 109–10, 122, 223, 225

cannibalism, mining industry as 11, 214–16

Cape plc 209, 228

Cape Town 57–8, 63, 66, 97, 108, 160, 213

Cape Town, University of 97

Carothers, J.C. 154, 165–8, 171, 173, 176

cattle
diseases 57, 75, 187
economic, social and spiritual life, role in 156–7, 187, 221

CPSIA information can be obtained
at www.ICGtesting.com
Printed in the USA
LVHW051035250722
724322LV00004B/33